ALSO BY BELINDA JACK

Negritude and Literary Criticism:
The History and Theory of "Negro-African" Literature in French

Francophone Literatures:
An Introductory Survey

GEORGE SAND

GEORGE SAND

A Woman's Life Writ Large

☙

BELINDA JACK

Alfred A. Knopf
New York
2000

THIS IS A BORZOI BOOK
PUBLISHED BY ALFRED A. KNOPF

www.aaknopf.com

Originally published, in slightly different form, in Great Britain by
Chatto & Windus, London, in 1999.

Library of Congress Cataloging-in-Publication Data
Jack, Belinda Elizabeth.
George Sand : a woman's life writ large / Belinda Jack.
p.   cm.
ISBN 0-679-45501-9
1. Sand, George, 1804–1876.   2. Women novelists, French—19th century—Biography.
3. Novelists, French—19th century—Biography.   I. Title.
PQ2412.J33   2000
843'.8—dc21
[B] 99-40857
CIP

Manufactured in the United States of America
First American Edition

*For my dear mother who—in the absence
of grandmothers, aunts, sisters, and
daughters—has managed to be all of these*

Contents

Contents

An insert of illustrations follows page 144.

Illustrations

Aurore Dupin, drawing by René Deschartres.

Louis-Claude Dupin de Francueil, pastel, artist unknown, mid–eighteenth century.

Aurore de Saxe, Aurore's grandmother, natural child of the Maréchal de Saxe, wife of Maurice Dupin, anonymous pastel, mid–eighteenth century.

Maurice de Saxe, pastel by Maurice Quentin de La Tour, Salon of 1747 or 1748.

Le Château de George Sand, seen from the gardens.

George Sand's Nohant.

Le Château de George Sand, dining room.

Aurore Dupin and Hippolyte Chatiron.

Maurice Dupin, oil on canvas, artist unknown, c. 1800.

Sophie-Victoire Dupin, *née* Delaborde, charcoal drawing by George Sand.

George Sand, lithograph after Alcide Lorenz.

George Sand and Ledru-Rollin, anonymous engraving.

El Mallorquín, anonymous engraving.

"The priest's visit to George Sand, her children and Chopin, at Valldemosa, 1839," drawing by George Sand.

The Charterhouse of Valldemosa, drawing by Joseph-Bonaventure Laurens.

Alexandre Manceau, drawing by Grandsire.

George Sand, drawing by Manceau.

The house at Gargilesse, painting by Jules Véron, c. 1860.

Frédéric Chopin, oil by Eugène Delacroix, 1838.

Gustave Flaubert, painting by Eugène Giraud.

Lina Sand (*née* Calamatta), by Nadar.

Maurice Sand, by Nadar.

Solange Clésinger (*née* Dudevant), by Nadar.

Jean-Baptiste Clésinger, photograph by Nadar.

Solange Sand, by Mercier.

Casimir Dudevant, anonymous drawing.

Maurice Sand dressed as an Officer of the National Guard, drawing by George Sand.

Aurélien de Sèze, anonymous engraving.

Marie Dorval, lithograph by Léon Nöel, c. 1835.

Pietro Pagello age twenty-eight, engraving after a portrait by Bevilacqua.

Louis-Chrysostome Michel (Michel de Bourges), anonymous lithograph.

Alfred de Musset, self-portrait.

Stéphane Ajasson de Grandsagne, lithograph by Déveria.

Jules Sandeau, pencil by George Sand, 20 March 1831.

View of part of the new road to Cauterets, engraving by J. Jacottet.

"Gondola: Remembrance of Venice," ink sketch by George Sand.

Proclamation of the Republic of 1870, anonymous engraving.

George Sand, by Nadar, 1866.

The invitation to George Sand's funeral.

Acknowledgements

I am deeply grateful to Allan Doig, Jane Jack, Carol Janeway (my editor at Knopf), and Irene Skolnick (my literary agent), all of whom read my manuscript in something close to its final form and gave invaluable advice and much-needed support. I remain responsible for any errors that may remain in the text, and for those idiosyncrasies of approach and style which I have stubbornly decided to retain.

Friends and colleagues who read parts of the book, and those who have listened to my endless ramblings and indulgently engaged with them, are too numerous to name: their contribution is warmly appreciated. I have been touched by those confessions, generously delivered up in discussion, which have broadened my insight into women's lives.

I have been nourished by Georges Lubin's scholarship, and was greatly encouraged by Jean Bruneau's early enthusiasm for my biography. I would also like to thank my husband and sons, Allan, John, Jamie, and Nicholas, for their kindness, and for always believing that the mounds of paper would one day metamorphose into a book; my brother Colin for technical help; and my father for a bibliophile's support.

My research has been generously supported by the British Academy, the Faculty of Medieval and Modern Languages, Oxford, and Christ Church, Oxford. I am grateful to a large number of curators and librarians at: the Bodleian and Taylor Institute Libraries, Oxford; the British Library, London; the Bibliothèque Nationale, the Bibliothèque Historique de la Ville de Paris, the Musée Carnavalet, and the Musée de la Vie Romantique, Paris; the Bibliothèque Spoelberch de Lovenjoul, Chantilly; the Musée George Sand, La Châtre; the Maison George Sand, Nohant; and the Maison George Sand, Gargilesse.

Prologue: A Note on Biography

This life of George Sand sets out to chart the course of an extraordinarily full life. But my interest is in both her "outer" visible life and her inner life—of feelings and fantasies, ideas and beliefs. Because she was a writer and so prolific, there is ample evidence of that hidden life, although its treatment remains problematic and always open to speculative error. I think it is a risk worth taking.

Establishing many of my "facts" has been straightforward. Her own vast two-volume autobiography, *The Story of My Life,* and the twenty-five volumes of her *Correspondance* have been meticulously edited by the great French scholar Georges Lubin. He is a tremendously engaging presence even in his footnotes, occasionally expressing his own delight in her, or his gently scolding disappointment—where he has found her out. Thanks to his years of devotion, we know about almost every day of her adult life. We know with virtual certainty where she was, and with whom, and we know mostly what she was doing—except perhaps when in bed, although some of her letters are refreshingly frank about that too. I have been guided too by earlier biographies, which often point to that same rich material, an accretion of pithy quotation. My reservations about aspects of earlier biographies have also helped to shape and strengthen my own intuitions and convictions.

I have had to select—savagely—from a vast body of reliable documentation. Otherwise this book would be no more than the first of numerous volumes. But in any case I do not believe that there is any such thing as a comprehensive biography: life isn't like that. And in Sand's case such a tome, or tomes, would be a monstrous work of reference—and virtually unreadable.

Nor am I at all convinced by the related notion of wholly "objective" biography. You cannot lay material before a reader without first selecting it, unless there is very little to go on indeed. And you have to order it: lives are not altogether linear; there are, at the very least, simultaneities of experience. The selection of material and the way it is shaped are necessarily informed by the biographer's knowledge and, I believe, instincts and intuitions about who the subject actually was. There is something of a paradox here. I would argue that the so-called scientific approach is to a degree spurious, because of the way the facts are chosen and presented; that process is to some extent informed by interpretation, but it remains largely invisible. The reader thinks that these are simply "the facts," but there is an element of deceit.

On the other hand, the openly interpretive biography, in presenting a viewpoint, exposes a line, an argument. If the relevant facts supporting this are carefully presented, even where contradiction and confusion arise, then the reader remains in a position to agree or disagree with the view of the biography. So what follows is, necessarily, a highly condensed story of her life, and a portrait of who I think George Sand really was.

Belinda Jack
Christ Church, Oxford
June 1999

GEORGE SAND

Introduction

"Excessive work, like excessive pleasure, brings perfect death."[1]

↝There is something wonderfully excessive about George Sand's life and writing. I was astonished and delighted when I first discovered her in my teens. She seemed a fantastically vampish yet androgynous figure, and her sexuality struck me as peculiarly intriguing. I found portraits of her: drawings, engravings, and paintings. She is beautiful only in some, but her eyes are always beguiling, disproportionately large, almost black, and invariably mysterious. The photographs of her in later life are full of character: there is remarkable strength in her face, but also the suggestion that she has suffered. Then there are cartoons, quite as vicious as today's cartoons of media figures caught up in scandal.

I wondered particularly about the hidden life of George Sand, who was born Aurore Dupin in 1804 and died in 1876. She is France's most famous nineteenth-century woman writer, but she is best known as the famous lover of the celebrated Chopin, and variously described not in relation to her writing but rather as a frigid, bisexual, nymphomaniac, or "Good Lady of Nohant." Were there not, the indignant primitive feminist in me asked, contradictions and prejudices to be explored and explained? And what inner compulsion explained her quite extraordinary productivity? How had she maintained her prolific writing while enjoying such an active, highly colourful, and daring private life? In short, the origin of this biography was my discovery, twenty years ago, of a possible role model, at once intriguing, inspiring, and subversive.

The woman I found out more about then is not the woman I know now. But the familiar caricature I had first encountered is not altogether fanciful: exaggeration lends itself naturally to parody and comic representation. And there *is* something exaggerated about almost every aspect of her life. Her long love affair with Chopin was only one of a large number of affairs with well-known figures of her times, mostly writers, mostly some years younger than Sand. Indeed most of the notable artistic figures of her day became her friends, often despite themselves, visiting her at her glorious country estate at Nohant, in Berry, or in Paris. Most were surprised by the unassuming, positively shy woman who received them. A small but representative selection from the veritable roll call of famous nineteenth-century men who were her friends includes musicians, Franz Liszt most notably, French writers including Flaubert, Balzac, Baudelaire, Sainte-Beuve, Alfred de Vigny, Chateaubriand, and Zola, and writers from numerous other countries, Heinrich Heine, Henry James, Browning (and his wife), Dostoevsky, and Turgenev, as well as painters, Eugène Delacroix being the best known. The engraver Alexandre Damien Manceau, the last of her great loves, was unique in giving her both love and friendship: a combination no earlier lover had offered.

One of her most intense, abandoned, and desperate love affairs was, however, with a woman, Marie Dorval, one of the most famous and beautiful actresses of the Parisian stage. They met in January 1833, when Sand was in her late twenties and Dorval in her mid-thirties. Sand had seen her act, and experienced an uncanny sense of recognizing her own suppressed emotions in all of Dorval's movements, expressions, and tones of voice. It was as though her soul had materialized and appeared on the stage before her. The two women were opposites, and each was strongly drawn to the other. Sand wrote to Dorval. The love affair that followed aroused outrage and jealousy and, needless to say, excited widespread and malicious gossip.

Sand's dress also drew attention: this was not altogether her intention. She cross-dressed, sometimes for practical reasons, sometimes for fun, and sometimes to see the world, and be treated, differently. She also had a penchant for exotic costumes. Smoking was a pleasure that she indulged in public at a time when for women the practice was wholly unacceptable. She smoked cigars, for which she is famous, but also cigarettes, which she rolled with deft expertise, and she delighted in her beloved hookah. She became thoroughly tobacco-dependent: numerous letters testify to her fear of running out of stock.

Professionally, Sand participated in a wide range of activities: journalistic, political, theatrical, and literary. Her involvement goes beyond that of other nineteenth-century women: she not only wrote for the press but was the only woman on the staff of the *Figaro*. After the Revolution of 1848 she acted as minister for propaganda.

Her literary production is vast. Honoré de Balzac was deemed phenomenally productive: Sand was mocked for her output. There was an implication that such a stream of works was unfeminine in its proportions. She wrote a huge number of novels and plays, a massive two-volume autobiography, stories, essays, and articles. And her letter writing was quite as prolific as that of other writers of the time: her published correspondence comprises twenty-five volumes. She was a skilled draughtswoman and painter: her work, on permanent display in the Musée de la Vie Romantique in Paris, is highly accomplished. Her domestic life was also full: she educated her children, and was later deeply involved in the lives of her grandchildren. She showed real concern for the lot of her servants and neighbours, and she was a keen and knowledgeable gardener. She felt none of the contempt for home life so often displayed by successful women. She felt soothed by needlework, and adored jam-making. Even in this she displayed her characteristic tendency to overdo, producing ludicrous quantities. The length of her life too is something of an affront: despite her excesses, she outlived almost all of her contemporaries, stretching into her eighth decade and continuing to bathe regularly in the River Indre, strictly against the advice of her doctors.

It is a life "writ large," but the pun of my title both points to the scale and fullness of her life and allows for a blending-together of her life and her writing. She wrote a great deal from personal experience, but more unusually she tested out, in her fiction, possibilities for life which she then had the courage to live out, *after the writing event*. Life gives rise to stories, but writing can also shape life. There is no doubt that her affairs fed her writing, but equally and more unusually, the chains of events that she also invented in her fiction were sometimes tested out in life. She explored feelings and ideas that motivated experience.

It was the writer-explorer in Sand that drew so many people to her. She was loved for her courage, her determination, her refusal of hypocrisy and compromise, her desire for equality of all kinds, her acts of kindness.

As a writer she was enormously popular because of her ability to fashion, out of the muddle of her experience, writing that was passionate, full of conviction, and full of compassion for people. She was highly successful commercially because of the compelling texture of her work, but also because her writing is brimming over with the same pithy, often shocking subject matter that was part of her life. Sex, sexuality, incest, and cross-class relationships are some of the recurrent themes of her fiction, sometimes clearly visible, sometimes tantalizingly half-submerged, as they are in the life.

Only when I began to read George Sand's novels did I become uneasy with my image of her as a somewhat monstrous public figure, one which suggested a self-seeking, unreflecting, and egotistical inner self. What I encountered reading her was a quite different presence. Her voice can be intimate, unpretentious, gentle, sympathetic, and disarmingly honest. Reading George Sand's novels, you hear her tone: anguish, suffering and hope, frustration and yearning, despair and courage, tenderness are all written in. There is remarkably little anger, and great compassion. On the other hand, her insight into people, combined with a recognition of the injustices and hypocrisy of society, suggests a capacity to manipulate others with subtle skill. And her astute awareness of the way in which women collude in their own unhappiness, because of a lack of courage to take control, reveals a deep frustration with women whose solution is to assume the role of victim. She considered marriage a primitive institution and looked forward to a time when another kind of arrangement would allow for the coming into the world of children without forever shackling the freedom of their parents. She believed in the essential equality of women and men, despite their differences. These did not imply a spiritual or intellectual feminine inferiority. Vanity alone, she believed, explained men's adherence to an unjust social order.

The more I found out about Sand and the more I read of her writing, the more I began to wonder about the effects of her deep unhappiness as a child. To what extent had the vigorous contempt for compromise which she developed in her late teens compelled her to take risks and to keep going, however seemingly impossible life became? Would slowing down, even stopping, have forced her to live in the presence of a gnawing and intolerable pain? Great pain had been inflicted on her as a small child, and it gradually became an ache, sometimes acute, sometimes closer to numbness. Had she sought to cure this inner legacy of suffering by loving, and being loved? As a child she had longed to be tucked up close to her mother, and the need for physical closeness never went away. She never gave up her search.

From the moment of her birth, on 1 July 1804, she was muddled up in complex and antagonistic family passions. She was born Amantine-Aurore-Lucile Dupin. She was always known simply as "Aurore," the third Aurore in her family.

Marie-Aurore de Saxe, the second "Aurore" (later Mme Dupin de Francueil), Sand's grandmother on her father's side, became Châtelaine of Nohant. She was the granddaughter of the King of Poland. His wife was the first "Aurore," de Königsmarck. Mme Dupin's son, Captain Maurice François Dupin, married Antoinette Sophie-Victoire Delaborde, a former prostitute, and their (only just) legitimate daughter was baptized in Paris the day after her birth. Sand's parents had married by civil ceremony less than four weeks earlier. There is no known illegitimacy on the maternal side, but there is a long history of bastardy on the grand paternal side.

Sand's grandfather had been the proprietor of a billiards hall and had sold birds, canaries, and goldfinches on the streets. His daughter, Sophie-Victoire, had grown up in poverty, making a little money herself by the only and obvious means possible, as a common prostitute. Knowing what Mme Dupin's reaction to his lowly love would be, Maurice kept the marriage secret until after the baby's birth.

Sand's parents' families could hardly have been more different. Her background was one that would allow her to develop precocious insights into the complexities of class and the respective lots of men and women in society. As a small child she moved freely among very different social groups, some humble, some grand. This was a freedom she lost, but which with enormous determination she regained, in order fully to explore, and later communicate in her writings, her fluid and changing vision of what life was about, and, more importantly, how life might be made better—for women, and men.

I have often been disconcerted, while writing this life, by a sense that Sand had not one but many lives. Sand herself came to believe in the notion of the self as multiple and constantly changing. At the end of her life she had formulated a typically modern notion of the self as fundamentally unstable: "It seems to me that we change from day to day and that after some years we are a new being."

These were ideas that she discussed at length with Gustave Flaubert, the giant of the nineteenth-century French novel and famous misanthropic recluse. Sand constantly looked for ideas in which she could believe.

Flaubert advertised his cynicism with panache. He had confessed to Sand that he had, while a young man, decided to run away from life. Sand was shocked by the terrors of human existence when a small child, but she decided to confront life with all the energy and determination that she could summon.

It is telling that a man like Flaubert should have become both an intimate companion and an admirer of her life. His suspicion of sentimentality is legendary, but he confessed after her death to the equally broken-hearted giant of the nineteenth-century Russian novel, Ivan Turgenev: "At her funeral I cried like an ass."[2]

I

Auguries

"Life is a novel that each of us carries within us."[1]

⁓There is a strange unreality about the details of Aurore's birth, at least the way it is told in the autobiography, *Histoire de ma vie*. What is more, there are two somewhat incredible accounts, and they are not altogether consistent.[2] In both, Aurore's dashing hussar of a father is back in Paris, on leave.

In the first, they are at home, at number 15 Rue Meslay (now number 46). Sophie-Victoire's sister, Lucie-Marie Delaborde (Aurore's aunt from Chaillot), is celebrating her engagement to Amand-Jean-Louis Maréchal, a former officer. The expectant father, Maurice, is playing the violin. He was an accomplished musician and he loved to perform. There is dancing, and Sophie-Victoire, his glowing wife, is joining in despite having reached the term of her pregnancy. She is wearing a beautiful pink dress. The implication is—obvious to an almost comic degree—that she is in full bloom. Sophie-Victoire, followed by her sister, withdraws to an adjoining room during the opening bars of the dance. She is feeling the stronger stirrings of the first movement of labour. Lucie reappears—even before the final bars of the dance have been played: "Come, come, Maurice . . . you have a daughter." The scene—celebration of a family engagement—has been topped by cause for further celebration. The atmosphere is one of gaiety and abundant love. The newborn is immediately in the presence of an

9

extended and harmonious family, and adoring parents, who are also adoring of each other. The whole scene could equally be a theatrical denouement, the closing scene of a comedy. But it is a beginning, and one bound up in history, as the mature Aurore—George Sand—points out: "It was 1804, the last year of the Republic, the first year of Empire."

Two members of her immediate family felt moved to prophesy and interpreted the significance of the festive circumstances of the birth. Aurore's Aunt Lucie not only announced the birth but provided the assembled company with a no doubt predictable augury: "Born in the midst of pink and music, she will be happy." But different social classes make very different prophecies. Taking the baby in his arms, her father responded: "She will be called Aurore, like her grandmother, who is not here to bless her, but who will one day." The humble Aunt Lucie's superstition, her sense of hope, impotent hope, contrasts with the aristocrat's realism, associated not simply with hope but with a sense of his influence, his control, his power over his world.

The autobiographical story has been carefully crafted, and its beginning, an ideal birth—her mother's labour was apparently remarkably short and the delivery easy—hints at tragedy to come. We read of the dancing, but we prepare to come down with a bump. We are told the supposed time and date of the birth: at one o'clock in the afternoon, on the fifth of July 1804.[3] But like all autobiographical births, it is told by a narrator who has not yet been born. The story has been based on others' recollections— filled out, and no doubt altered, by the autobiographer's imagination. But the question of truth, in terms of the detail, is in many ways unimportant. We know that the date of birth given is wrong: she was born on 1 July. In the second volume of her autobiography, she gives the correct date. But this time her mother is at a "ball" and it is the baby that is wrapped in pink. Her aunt's prophecy is repeated but the autobiographer gives a gloss this time: "Auguries are only justified when they foretell disaster."[4]

The first account is a delightful story, a fairy tale, but it verges on parody. Sleeping Beauty was, after all, called Aurore too. The telling of the tale also suggests the exaggeration of melodrama and the formal characteristics of the dramatic romantic tradition (a genre to which Sand was to make a substantial contribution). There is sentimental extravagance, coincidence, and even music, each a necessary ingredient of romantic drama.

But Sand goes on to turn what might have been the final, happy scene into a dramatic beginning, her own beginning and one which coincides with a new beginning in France's political history. The tension necessary for the story to come—that of her first years—depends on conflict. This is bound up with class, already introduced in the stark contrast between two very different auguries, both bound up in the historical moment. However romanticized, the essential drama—that of class difference—is true.

Maurice Dupin had married Sophie-Victoire Delaborde in secret, and against his mother's wishes. He had married below his station. The conflict is not the stuff of romantic drama but a tragedy rooted in the antagonisms of rival social, cultural, and economic groups. Sand's life is the playing out of a class drama, which in turn was to become very much part of her writing. In many of her novels and plays, marriage between two people belonging to very different classes stands as a powerful symbol of a wider social reconciliation.

The real protagonist in Sand's birth story was neither her mother nor her father, casting themselves respectively as heroine and hero representative of the two rival families, but their daughter. For some years, however, Aurore had no say in the scenario, in the script. Hers was a very minor part. Her father was to be the challenged hero, required to surmount the obstacles and bring about family reconciliation: acceptance, by his aristocratic mother, of his lowly wife. This would in turn confirm Aurore's sense of legitimacy within her paternal grandmother's aristocratic family. But the continuing success of the story, as Sand tells it, depends not only on the hero's energy and skill but also on his continuing presence in the drama of Aurore's early years. His sudden death in 1808—when Aurore was only five—will require an understudy, a new and very young heroine—Aurore herself. For some years she could do no more than read someone else's part. Like all children caught up in family conflict, she became sometimes a pawn, sometimes a go-between in the lives of the adults around her.

There is heavy irony in Sand's mock naïvety when she scolds her biographers, especially her foreign biographers, for their marked bias in favour of her father's glorious lineage to the virtual exclusion of her mother's:

> They have all bestowed on me (those who ought to have known better) an illustrious origin while ignoring a very visible stain on my blazon. One is not only the offspring of one's father, one is also a little, I believe, that of one's mother. It seems to me that the latter is even more the case, and that we are attached to the entrails of the one who gave birth to us in the

most immediate, powerful, and sacred way. Hence, if my father was the great-grandson of Augustus II, King of Poland, and if on that side I am myself the illegitimate, but nevertheless very real, next of kin to Charles X and Louis XVIII, it is no less true that my bloodlines are tied to the people in a way as intimate and direct; and what is more there is no bastardy on this side.[5]

Aurore's mother had been born in 1773, and baptized Antoinette Sophie-Victoire Delaborde. Her origins were working class: her father, Antoine Delaborde, had run a billiards hall and later sold birds on the Quai de la Mégisserie. According to police records in the Archives Nationales de Paris, his daughter, aged sixteen, was living by 1789 with a certain Claude-Denis Vantin Saint-Charles, by whom she had what is presumed to be her first child. Ten years later she had a second child, Caroline, Aurore's half-sister by another father. A year later she accompanied General Collin to Italy, where Aurore's father, Maurice Dupin, met her for the first time.[6] She was pretty, with fine features and a slim figure. She knew how to dress. Maurice was also finely built, handsome, with a moustache that accentuated his aquiline nose. His hair was dark, as were his eyes. They were large, and almost black, the same strikingly attractive eyes which his daughter was to inherit.

Maurice Dupin had been born, in 1778, into the stable relationship and stable economic and social milieu of Marie-Aurore and Louis-Claude Dupin de Francueil (shortened to Dupin after the Revolution), and was brought up in considerable aristocratic style. Marie-Aurore (Sand's grandmother) was the illegitimate daughter of Maurice de Saxe, himself the illegitimate son of King Augustus II of Poland and his mistress Aurore de Königsmarck. Maurice de Saxe's niece, Marie de Saxe, married the eldest son of Louis XV. Thus Sand herself was a second cousin, although through an illegitimate line, to Louis XVI, Louis XVIII, and Charles X.

Sand's grandparents had belonged to a pre-Revolutionary intellectual and artistic world which she, a socialist, nevertheless in some ways regretted. She was nostalgic, above all, for stability: "Of course it was agreeable and seductive, this philosophy of wealth, independence, tolerance and affability; but you needed an income of five or six thousand pounds to support it, and I don't quite see how the poor and oppressed could benefit from it."[7] Her father had benefited, however. When Dupin de Francueil died, on

6 June 1786, he left his widow and son an annual revenue of 75,000 francs. They were poorer than they had been, but they were scarcely "ruined," as Maurice's mother declared.

The eight-year-old Maurice and his mother abandoned the impressive château overlooking the Indre near Châteauroux and returned to Paris, to the family residence in the Rue Roi-de-Sicile, near the Bastille. They were joined by twenty-six-year-old François Deschartres (1761–1828), a tonsured cleric who was to be Maurice's tutor.[8]

Maurice's life and his mother's were very much bound up in the violence of the age, in political and social upheaval. For those whose loyalties were undivided, the Revolution was a force to be either supported or resisted. For Maurice's mother the matter was more complicated. In terms of her marriage, wealth, and education, she was a member of the aristocracy. But her illegitimacy had been the cause of humiliation and offence. The court had not been generous towards her and she had been led to despise the regal coterie. She and her husband were well educated, and they had kept up with the philosophical and social ideas of their times. They had been profoundly influenced by the thinking of Voltaire and Rousseau. She felt that she had suffered moral injustice and that it was a function of a corrupt system. On the fourteenth of July 1789 the Bastille was stormed. Sand described her grandmother's response: "She added her shouts of joy to those of the victors, among whom, with her support, were a number of her domestic servants."[9] But Sand's grandmother was dismayed and frightened as factions inevitably emerged among the revolutionaries, and as the unpredictability and horrors of the Terror were unleashed.

She could have emigrated, like so many others. Instead she moved, as a temporary measure, to stay a step ahead of the authorities, to the Rue de Bondy. Maurice and Deschartres went with her. She tried to find a rural retreat, at a safe distance from Paris. Then, on the twenty-third of August 1793, she bought an unpretentious manor house at Nohant in the Vallée Noire, southeast of Paris. But on 3 December, as they were about to leave, the authorities discovered the money and valuables which she had hidden in the wall. She was imprisoned in the Couvent des Augustines Anglaises, the very convent which was to be the educational establishment to which she would later entrust her rebellious future granddaughter, George Sand.

Maurice was left in the care of Deschartres and they quickly destroyed papers relating to the financial support which Mme Dupin had sent to the Count d'Artois, later Charles X, who had emigrated. Numerous pleas for release from the Couvent des Augustines were refused. Maurice, along with other "ex-nobles," was exiled from Paris. The ever-loyal Deschartres went with him. On 27 July 1794 Sand's grandmother was let out of prison. When she arrived at Nohant she had, according to Sand, "never been so rich as now that she was poor." It was only relative poverty, and she knew how lucky she was.

Maurice resumed his formal education under the tutelage of the extraordinary Deschartres, albeit protected from his rages, to a large extent, by his mother. Deschartres, a paradoxical figure, was summed up by Sand: "He had all the great spiritual qualities, married to an impossible character; and he was self-satisfied to a maniacal degree." He boasted "omnicompetence" and was intellectually pretentious. But he was well informed in a wide range of areas, sometimes even scholarly in his knowledge. Sand described him as the "tyrant, saviour and friend" of three generations of Dupins.[10] He was enormously dogmatic, but this was obvious to the point of rendering it surmountable for his pupils. Like all truly influential teachers, those who affect *lives* rather than ensure the acquisition of a formal, more limited education, he was eccentric. He also displayed a terrifying force of character. Maurice was artistic and played the violin well, and composed. He also enjoyed rhetoric, modern languages, drawing, and literature. He was less interested in subjects which required a different kind of discipline, in particular mathematics, Greek, and Latin. Deschartres's educational method was little suited to him. Sand's father was, she declared, "all instinct, a large sensibility, vigour, courage and confidence."[11]

Two dominant passions emerged in Maurice's life: a love and facility for music, with a particular passion for opera, and a growing interest in the army. Maurice travelled long distances to be stirred by opera. And he would travel abroad as a military man.

Maurice was propelled towards his chosen goal by the prospect of general conscription under the Directory of 1798. Introduced to M. de La Tour d'Auvergne, a celebrated military man, he was asked, "Would the grandson of the Maréchal de Saxe be afraid of participating in a military campaign?" He reported his response to his mother: "I replied: 'Certainly not,' looking him straight in the eye." He was fixed up in the Tenth Infantry Regiment.[12]

Maurice fought in Germany, Switzerland, and Italy. It was in Milan that he met Sophie-Victoire. He was struck by her gentleness, her timidity, her sensibility, and no doubt by her beauty. Maurice had had other mistresses. He was already the father of Hippolyte Chatiron, who had been given the surname of his mother, Catherine, a servant girl at Nohant. She was sent away, although provided for financially, and Hippolyte, Sand's half-brother, was brought up at Nohant by Maurice's mother, the boy's paternal grandmother (and Sand's).

Maurice's letters home to his mother while away on campaigns refer to other conquests, but it was Sophie-Victoire whom he would eventually marry. This certainly had not been his initial intention. It may be that the presence of General Collin, Sophie-Victoire's former protector, in Orléans, the very town where he had settled Sophie-Victoire, pushed him into marrying her.[13] His actual letters, as opposed to those rewritten, fictionalized epistles which Sand published in her autobiography, make it clear that he had not expected to marry her and was well aware that any such project would not have found favour with his mother. Mme Dupin wanted him to marry a woman of equal social standing: she was afraid of seeing the family revert to the pattern from which she had been saved. But Maurice was headstrong and had been used to having things his own way. Sand summed up her father's upbringing in a way that would contrast with her bleak descriptions of her mother's: "He was brought up, in all matters, wrapped in cotton-wool."[14] Their daughter's childhood would be a strange mixture of the two.

The day after Aurore's birth she was christened in the Church of Saint-Nicolas-des-Champs and named Amandine-Aurore-Lucile. Curiously, in the Town Hall where her birth had also to be registered, her first name is given as Amandine.[15] But in any case it was her father's will that she be known as Aurore: it was one of the names in his family, and it conferred belonging. For a good many years this was her name. Maurice attended his daughter's christening. Some months later, on 21 December, despite his imprudent choice of wife, he was made captain of the First Hussars and decorated with the Légion d'Honneur. His military contribution had been recognized.[16]

He left Paris soon after to play his part in the Napoleonic campaigns. But before leaving his family to take to the stage of history, he orchestrated a recognition scene to win his grandmother round to his new family.[17]

Aurore was a strong baby. Maurice's occasional references to her in his letters to his mother are subtle in their brevity and apparent offhandedness. They can be read as part of an unhurried but determined plot to convert his mother. There is a possessiveness in his choice of pronoun which may have been equally calculating; typically he writes, that autumn: "*My* Aurore is doing remarkably well" (my emphasis). Maurice bided his time, waiting for an opportunity that would allow for a more daring move to reconcile his grander mother to his lowly wife, and to his daughter. His chance came with an unannounced visit to Paris by Mme Dupin. Her intention was to explore the possibilities of having her son's marriage annulled. The mature Sand doubted whether she would actually have carried this out, and in any case it is highly unlikely that this would have been possible in post-Revolutionary France: this kind of string-pulling had become more difficult. But Aurore's grandmother was concerned to know more about her son's position, and anxious to discover more about his wife.

Sand tells the story. Hearing that his mother was in Paris, Maurice acted swiftly and decisively. He lifted Aurore into his arms, left the flat, descended the stairs, went out onto the pavement, and hailed the first available cab. He may have quickly devised his plan in the carriage, with little Aurore on his knee, as they travelled through the busy streets of Paris. Or he and his wife may have considered all manner of possible schemes before lighting on this.

Arriving at the house where his mother was staying, he charmed the concierge with characteristic ease. She was no doubt moved by those aspects of the story that Maurice chose to tell her in order to encourage a convincing performance. With great delight she took the baby, and set about realizing his plan with the guile some might suppose innate in Parisian women of her profession. She quickly found a pretext to speak to Mme Dupin, and her words were chosen to arouse her contemporary's potential for jealousy and to stir any hidden or suppressed heartache: "Just look at my pretty little granddaughter. Her nanny has left her with me for the day and I just can't bring myself to put her down." It was a polished performance and she responded to Mme Dupin's politely admiring remarks by offering her the baby, an apparently generous gesture. As Mme Dupin took the child, she looked into her unusually dark brown eyes. The moment of recognition occurred. Mme Dupin spoke with untypical spontaneity: "Liar. This child does not resemble you in the slightest."

This time it was the little Aurore's turn to respond on cue. Disconcerted by the harshness of Mme Dupin's tone of voice, by the instinctive awareness of a conflict in which she found herself at the centre, she started to cry. The concierge continued to interpret the sketchy scenario she had been given by the baby's father: "Come, my little one," she said, lifting the baby from Mme Dupin's lap. And to Mme Dupin: "I can see she isn't happy with you." From then on neither the concierge nor the baby was required to animate the script. "No, give her back. Poor little thing. It isn't her fault," the grandmother declared. The concierge quickly explained that she had gone along with the whole charade in the expectation that the naïve participant, Mme Dupin, would be pleased by the denouement. Having reassured the concierge that she understood that her involvement had been well intentioned, Mme Dupin established that it had been her son who had brought the baby to the house, and asked that he be summoned.

Aurore was left for a few moments in the care of her grandmother, as she would be in a very much more permanent way only a few years later. Pressing Aurore tightly to her, and while trying to make her laugh, Mme Dupin wept. To her, the baby was, it seems, tangible proof that her son loved another woman more than herself. This was something she found difficult to accept. She was saddened that he had married against her wishes, and secretly. She was afraid for his future, one that would no doubt be damaged, in terms of his career, by his wholly incautious choice of wife. Above all, however, she must have been moved by a knowledge of the difficulties in life which her granddaughter would face. Mme Dupin had been born illegitimate. But she had lived in a period of comparative social stability. She had been determined. With the support of aristocratic and influential friends she had achieved the dignified status she had desired. She had no doubt been lucky. Aurore, although just legitimate, would live a life still more difficult than her own. Holding the baby in her arms, what she felt was that emotion fundamental to classical tragedy: pity. And no doubt she experienced a degree of self-pity too. She slipped a ring from her finger, a ring set with a large ruby, and pressed it into the palm of Aurore's hand, to be given to the baby's mother. It was a generous gesture of reconciliation, of acceptance: of the infant, and of her mother. But Aurore's role was, as it would be so many times in her childhood, that of passive participant in the complex and passionate emotional lives of those of her deeply divided family. The manipulative strategies of her grandmother and mother, in particular, were to be played out, for years, in relation to Aurore.

But that day, when Maurice bounced in to greet his mother, now holding little Aurore on her knee, he must have been well pleased by the spectacle of the final scene he had skilfully directed from offstage. It was some weeks before his mother would receive her daughter-in-law, but when Mme Dupin became aware that her antagonism to the marriage would further exacerbate the difficulties of her son's position, she agreed to meet. Sand claims that her parents then married in church, their initial marriage having been a civil one. She also adds that her grandmother was there to bless their union. No record of such a ceremony, nor any other corroborating evidence, has ever been found.[18]

But it seems likely that superficially and temporarily at least, the family was reconciled. But this was not to last, even on the surface. Further twists and turns in the plot precede the tragic climax of Aurore's first years of fragile belonging.

II

A Man of Action and a Passionate Woman

"What will remain eternal is the sense
of beauty in a good heart."

Early on Aurore saw little of her father. She remembered him as a glamorous figure who occasionally appeared, changing everything. The otherwise claustrophobic and reclusive life that Sophie-Victoire and her daughter normally led would be gloriously transformed by his dashing presence. His arrival would mark the beginning of a brief spell of contented domesticity and sociability, and bring to a temporary end a life of constant struggle and loneliness. When Sophie-Victoire was at her husband's side, her emotional and psychological instability seemed less severe. Both were associated in part with the relentlessness of impoverished day-to-day living with two small children. Aurore felt an otherwise unknown sense of security in her father's presence: home became a happy haven when he was around. Later she would write, "I inherited from my parents that secret wildness which makes the world difficult to bear, and the home essential."[1]

Her parents' domestic life was fairly unconventional, because of the nature of their marriage: it had brought with it economic and social constraints. But the principal reason for their poverty, Sand later realized, was the extent of the expenses incurred by her father as an officer. Maurice was attentive to Sophie-Victoire and indulged Aurore: he was reassuring and entertaining. Sophie-Victoire's strong sense of inferiority was soothed, her confidence and sense of well-being increased. Aurore's mother was proud of her husband, and Aurore was proud of her father: "Even in his uniform he felt no shame carrying me in his arms through the streets."[2] By association, mother and child were transformed into worthier beings, and quite ordinary things around them became unusual and delightful, right down to the table napkins which he could fold, origami-like, into comic puppet figures, now a rabbit, now a monk.[3] In this he displayed a magic touch: he transformed inanimate mundane objects into real beings. Her astonishing father somehow transported her from a dull real place into a marvellous fantasy.

Maurice had a strong sense of the world as the stage on which life was acted out. He was conscious of Aurore's birth having coincided with a momentous historical moment, a new beginning. Born in the first year of Empire, she arrived only weeks before Napoleon's coronation. From Paris, Maurice supplied his mother in Nohant with an eyewitness account:

> I saw one, two, three, four, five regiments: hussars, cuirassiers, dragoons, carabineers and Mamelukes; one, two, three, four, five, six, seven, eight, nine, ten, eleven, twelve, thirteen, fourteen carriages full of courtiers, drawn by six horses each; a carriage with ten windows full of princesses; the Lord Chancellor's carriage and finally the Emperor's, eight cream-coloured horses, beautiful beasts, caparisoned and decked with pompons as high as the first storey of the houses. . . .
>
> Inside Notre-Dame, the throne set up near the door, at the back, a fairly hefty triumphal arch— the Greek style looked wholly out of place within the Gothic of the church. . . . The Pope put some oil on the forehead and hands of the Emperor and Empress; then Bonaparte rose, went to take the crown from the altar, placed it on his head with his own hands and pronounced in a loud voice the oath to uphold the rights of the people and maintain their liberty. He walked back to the throne and the *Te Deum* was sung. As the procession returned there were magnificent illuminations, dances, fireworks, etc., etc.[4]

His vivid description peters out, like the pyrotechnics. His concluding remarks are reflections: "It was all very beautiful, very impressive, the play well directed, the main parts well acted. Goodbye to the Republic. Neither you nor I will miss it for what it was but for what it should have been, for what it used to be in my childhood dreams. . . ."[5] Aurore's mother had been on the stage, and there remained a good deal of the actress in her. Aurore's father was also conscious of playing his part in the heroic theatre of history.

But Maurice's dramatic appearances in Paris, during periods of leave, inevitably throw those longer times of absence into bleak relief. In those days, weeks, and months, Aurore lived mostly with her unstable mother.

For the most part the apartment in the Rue Grande-Batalière was home, and Aurore and her mother rarely went out. Her mother was a strange woman, and she became stranger still. In her autobiography, Sand gives her mother all three Christian names "because during the agitated course of her life, she used them successively. . . . In her childhood Antoinette was probably preferred; Antoinette was then queen. During the victories of Empire, Victoire was naturally favoured. And after her marriage, my father always called her Sophie."[6] Her sense of identity was as fluid as the times through which she lived, and as shifting and changing as her names and financial circumstances. She had been forced to play a variety of parts and had a natural talent for dissembling. She had mastered it to the point of scarcely knowing who she really was.

Sand described Sophie-Victoire years later, in 1843, to Charles Poncy, the proletarian poet, no doubt in order to establish a more convincing sense of solidarity with him:

> My mother did not belong to the hard-working conscientious class. . . . She belonged to that degraded, vagabond race, the bohemians of the world. She was a dancer, no, less than a dancer, an extra in one of the humblest theatres in Paris, and rich men removed her from this degradation only to subject her to worse. My father met her when she was already thirty and living amid who-knows-what debaucheries. But he had a kind heart. He saw that this beautiful creature could still love, and he married her against the wishes, under the curse even, of his family.[7]

But the gentle and timid woman who had smitten her father's heart was not the woman Aurore came to know. Her feelings were often violent, and she had a wildness about her. She was motivated above all by instinct. Capable of enormous guile, she could be skilfully manipulative, sometimes almost unknowingly. She was full of natural wit, but it could be cruelly cutting. She was childish, childlike, and she could be tremendous fun. Her behaviour was often spontaneous and contradictory. Violent curses would suddenly be replaced by equally violent self-reproach and she would scold others for having allowed her to say such terrible things. She was lively, teasing, and hostile to social constraints. In practical matters she showed great competence and application. On the whole she cared reasonably well, in the circumstances, for Aurore and Caroline, and did what she could to ensure them an education. But she was inconsistent, and what might have been seen as youthful spontaneity became, later on, pushed by successive tragedies, something closer to serious mental instability. She had undoubtedly suffered. But she had always displayed more unreflecting passion than compassion. As she aged, what had been seen by her family as her "exaggerations" came to be seen as madness. Describing her mother towards the end of her life, Sand repeatedly uses the word "derangement." But there is little doubt that even as a young woman she was far from stable, and depended heavily on others.

As a child Aurore was swept up in her mother's unrestrained and unrestraining joie de vivre, but at the same time she felt that she could not altogether depend on her mother.

This absence of stability in her mother made her in some ways irresponsible, and prevented Aurore from feeling properly and unconditionally loved. It was a failing that Sand could explain, but never forgave, and also the origin of the deep, gnawing ache which Sand later used as a metaphor for human existence: "Life is a great wound that nothing heals."[8] Throughout her own life the pain never really went away.

Yet in many ways Sophie-Victoire was good company for Aurore. She had a colourful imagination and Aurore was spellbound by her stories. In her soft beguiling voice she sang lullabies and songs which soothed and enchanted Aurore. Her mother's voice was "the freshest and gentlest imaginable." She sang:

> *Let us go to the barn*
> *To see the white hen*

Who will lay a fine silver egg
For this dear little child.[9]

Aurore believed in the promise of the glistening egg each time she heard the song and the love in her mother's voice. The promise, of course, never came true, but for years she cherished the magical sense of hope that the song inspired.

Her first moment of utter despair remained equally vivid. She had never, knowingly, seen a wood, nor as far as she could remember had she ever seen laurel trees, but she remembered the overwhelming sense of despair that she felt when she first heard the lines of another song:

We will never go to the woods again
For the laurels have been felled.[10]

The immediacy of the emotion that swamped her was never lost. And the beauty of the woods, seen in her mind's eye, remained more beautiful than any she subsequently saw.

Her mother also taught her to recite La Fontaine's fables. They filled her with terror, and she failed to grasp their moral message. Perrault's tales, which her mother also read to her, were infinitely more enjoyable— and edifying in their own way. Aurore was enchanted by them, and by the versions her mother invented. They made her believe in the impossible and so, Sand would later argue, encouraged a kind of early faith. The beauty of these stories, at once abstract and intangible, like the pure emotion of music, taught her what she considered to be the most vital moral lesson. The recognition of beauty was, she believed, the fundamental prerequisite for a reasoned Christian faith: "We make a child more mad than good if we try to encourage a conception of the realities of the universe, when an understanding of its beauty is enough."[11]

Aurore was also taught to recite her prayers. These, Sand later wrote, might as well have been in Latin for all she understood them. "Give us today our daily bread" was all that the child, living in poverty, under-stood.[12] Aurore learnt to read without any great difficulty, but she was not an altogether exemplary pupil. From time to time she resisted rote learning, displaying "an innocent but stubborn tendency." On one occasion, not wanting her alphabet lesson, "I replied to my mother: 'I know how to say *A,* but I don't know how to say *B.*' It seems that my resistance lasted a long time; I named all the letters except the second, and when I was asked why I left this one out, I replied, unperturbed, 'It's that I don't know *B*.' "[13] Was this childish, capricious stubbornness quite without significance, in terms of the woman she would later be? Or should it be read as a precocious sign of resistance to the unquestioning assimilation of "knowledge"? The account reveals that even as a small child she could behave unpredictably, encouraged by some intuited but otherwise unformed notion of principle, perhaps. It is also clear that she was reluctant to renounce aberrant behaviour regardless of the adult's encouragement, even order, to do so. As so often in Sand's own account of the child that she was, she skilfully writes into her narrative an ambiguity that allows apparent self-criticism to reveal a belligerent and delightful childish individualism. This subversive side would continue to develop apace.

For all the songs and storytelling, Sophie-Victoire's life was dull and lonely. She missed her husband, and was only too aware that there would always be other women like herself, keen to attach themselves to the handsome French officers away from home. The poverty and tedium of her life in Paris contrasted with the glamour and excitement of life as part of a regimental entourage abroad. She had little to lose by leaving Paris and joining her husband when Aurore was two or three. Sand claims that her mother travelled to Italy to be with Maurice, but if the dates she gives are correct, Maurice was not then stationed there. Either Sand has made some mistake, or her object was not that supposed by Sand.[14] Sophie-Victoire had a taste for adventure, and she left Paris—and her daughters.

Aurore and Caroline were cared for by their Aunt Lucie, with her daughter Clotilde. Aurore adored her cousin and always remained utterly devoted to her. Sophie-Victoire was away for two or three months, but life in and around Chaillot, then a village outside Paris, now part of the city, was happy and carefree. On Sundays, the girls would be taken to Paris, carried in large baskets on either side of a donkey along with the cabbages and carrots to be sold at Les Halles, the largest of the Parisian markets.

The house and garden at Chaillot were modest. But for Aurore it was paradise. Sand remembered it well, claiming later in life that the clarity and precision of her memory of the house and garden were such that she could draw a precise plan of them. "The garden was a long rectangle, quite small in reality, but it seemed immense to me despite the fact that I ran right round it two hundred times a day. It was regularly laid out as was the custom then; there were flowers and vegetables; no view whatsoever, because it was entirely surrounded by walls. . . ." Here Aurore saw her first butterflies, and "cobwebs, white and shimmering in the autumn sun; my sister was there that day; it was she who earnestly explained that the Blessed Virgin herself had spun these threads on her ivory distaff. I dared not break them, and made myself very small to pass under them. . . ."[15]

At Chaillot she first came close to the Emperor: "We heard the clopping of the hooves and the shuffle of the crowd. We could not see over the wall, but it formed quite an image in my imagination, and we too, filled with sympathetic fervour, cried with all our might, 'Long live the Emperor!' " Chaillot was an Eden, and a place of delight and well-being, of "warmth and gaiety," of hope.[16] But just as the gaiety of life during her father's brief visits served also to highlight the ordinariness of life without him, so the glories of Chaillot threw life in the Paris apartment into shadow.

The garden at Chaillot "was the only garden I had ever been in."[17] She was never taken to the Tuileries Gardens in Paris, those delightful formal gardens enjoyed then as now by Parisians who have no garden of their own. She and her mother would not have been sufficiently well dressed. Although it was a public space, only the better-off walked out there.

Back in Paris, after her mother's return, the tedium of day-to-day life was occasionally broken by visits to another quite magical place: the theatre. "We left our sad retreat only to go to the theatre, for which my mother had a great liking, as already I had too."[18] Sophie-Victoire was passionate about the stage, and Aurore, only three years old, accompanied her mother into that other reality.

The stimulus of movement between the city and the country (essential to the pastoral tradition to which she would later contribute), of song, stories, and theatre, nourished Aurore's imaginative life. Given her isolation and unhappiness with life in the Parisian apartment, it is not altogether surprising that she started telling tales. This peculiar facility, even compulsion, for inventing stories emerged very early.

Her mother, while busy with chores, would create a makeshift playpen out of a number of chairs to keep her small daughter safe. Aurore would sit in the middle of them, contentedly holding forth. Of the stories which she told, George Sand wrote in her autobiography (unaware or unconcerned as to just how much her detractors would make of the description): "I can't remember anything of these . . . compositions, but my mother told me a good deal about them. She declared that they were terribly tedious because of their length and the extent of my digressions. . . . It seems that my tales were a kind of pastiche of everything that haunted my little brain. . . . I have today the same irrepressible abandon for storytelling." Her mother described these stories as her "novels."[19]

Life in the apartment was not wholly devoid of drama. Caroline, Aurore's half-sister, who was sometimes boarded out, came and went, as did, more regularly, the enigmatic Louis Mammès Pierret (1783?–1844).[20]

Sand claims that Pierret was devoted and loyal to her mother, if tyrannical and dictatorial for both their sakes. Maurice had apparently encouraged his protection of Sophie-Victoire and Aurore. Before leaving the family to return to war he would say, "Pierret, I commend to you my wife and children, and if I do not return, remember it is for your whole life."[21] Pierret's involvement with Aurore as a baby was unconventional but he was not to be influenced by the dictates of public opinion. He was a man of conviction and, Sand is at pains to convince her reader, essentially kind. He had willingly accepted the surrogate roles of protector and father to Sophie-Victoire and her baby daughter. He is often completely overlooked, or mentioned only very briefly by Sand's biographers, but he played an influential, if to some degree mysterious, role in Aurore's first years, and continued to play an important part in her mother's life right up to her death.[22]

Sand told Pierret's story in the autobiography apparently to pay homage to him. While her father is clearly cast as the tragic hero of the drama of her first years, Pierret, on the other hand, is introduced as the unsung hero. Pierret, the autobiographer claims, has failed to be appreciated.[23] But as in so much of Sand's autobiographical writings, it is not just contradictions of fact that provoke a sense of unease in the reader, but shifts in perspective and tone. In addition, the reader cannot help wondering whether she deliberately protests too much when she strenuously asserts the innocence of Pierret's intimate involvement in the lives of a grass widow and temporarily abandoned daughter. Combined with the stark contradictions which quickly emerge in Sand's account, does the reader not detect a touch of irony in her exaggerated defence of Pierret? How, for example, does the reader reconcile her somewhat trite assertion, "He bestowed on me the tenderness of a father and the care of a mother," with her statement, but a few lines later, "He assumed a paternal right which would have been nothing short of tyranny if it had ever been possible for him to carry out his threats"?

According to Sand, Pierret witnessed her birth. Her father, it will be remembered, was meanwhile playing the fiddle. His intimate involvement continued: it was Pierret who weaned her from her mother's milk. Exhausted and incapable of ignoring the baby's crying, her mother was beginning to suffer from extreme insomnia. "On his own authority," Pierret took the crib and removed it to his own lodgings, where he kept the baby for two or three weeks, scarcely sleeping himself on account of his anxieties, encouraging Aurore to drink sweetened milk and keeping her clean and comfortable. During the day the infant was returned to her mother while he went to work at the Treasury, and then on to the White Horse, his drinking hole, before returning to Sophie-Victoire to pick up the baby. If Sophie-Victoire showed any signs of doubting this course of action, or of anxiety, he would lose his temper, going red in the face and accusing the mother of imbecile weakness. "He didn't," Sand remarks, "choose his epithets." The White Horse was, in effect, his home for thirty years, and its clientele his family. He was somewhat indiscriminate when it came to beverages, liking both wine and beer, and enjoyed a pipe and a game of billiards or dominoes. It is difficult to imagine that an evening in the White Horse prepared him for the allegedly sleepless nights and hours of patient nursing demanded by a baby suddenly withdrawn from her mother's breast. Sand, however, avoids all explicit judgement, and rather would have us believe that he was almost saintly: "I do not believe that there ever existed a man more pure, more loyal, more devoted, more generous, more just." There is a good deal of hyperbole in Sand's description of Pierret. And the exaggeration flirts with irony—particularly when contradictory elements are introduced: "He was, however, highly strung, and consequently irascible and touchy." "He was the ugliest of men. . . ."

Those occasional outings to the theatre were less frequent than domestic dramas. Sophie-Victoire and Pierret staged momentous battles. There were rows, heated disputes, and melodramatic reconciliations. But bad feeling tended not to linger long in the air. Confrontation reached a climax, and reconciliation followed. Sometimes Pierret would leave, adamantly claiming that he would never return. But in the evening he would appear, having quite forgotten the threats he had made in the morning. Normal life would resume. The curtain would have fallen on that row; that show was over. This was to contrast, a few years later, with the lingering oppressiveness of Aurore's life at Nohant with her grandmother. There the past, weighty with history and tradition, made its heavy presence felt, and forgiveness was only ever partial. Flotsam and jetsam from the past obscured the present, and clouded the prospect of the future.

Sand protests in her autobiography against those who claimed that her mother's domestic habits were slovenly, just as she protests against those who suspected that her mother's relationship with Pierret was something other than one of platonic friendship. It may well be that on both scores she protests too much. Sand wanted to present her mother in a way that explained her shortcomings, even if she never wholeheartedly forgave her. But what emerges from her account is, she claims, "a complete picture," a portrait of a "terrible child destroying itself."[24] Elsewhere Sand explored the "rage, the chaos, the forgetfulness of self, in the terrible fact of poverty."[25] Here, although this was not her intention, she surely was describing her mother. She also wrote of the unformed life stories of the poor: "I know their story, because they had a story; indeed, every man has a story, the tale of his life in which he could interest us all, if only he had understood it himself."[26] Aurore's mother neither conceived of herself as an independent being, nor had she ever considered the course of her own life.

From the Rue Meslay, Sand's birthplace, the family had moved at some point to 22 Rue de la Grande-Batalière (now number 13).[27] Her first memory was of an event that happened there. She describes a violent and painful moment of coming to consciousness:

> A maid dropped me against the fire-surround. I was
> cut on the forehead and terrified. This shock shook
> me into awareness of life, and I clearly saw, I still see,
> the pink marble of the fire-surround, and the blood
> running down it, and the distraught look of the maid.
> I also remember the doctor's visit, the leeches applied
> behind my ear, my mother's anxiety, and the dismissal
> of the maid for drunkenness.[28]

Her "coming to awareness" was apparently wholly self-conscious: she was aware of herself as bound up in a microcosm of society. The event is experienced both subjectively and objectively. She remembered her own fear, but equally the maid's "distraught look" and her mother's "anxiety." The whole experience was remembered as a sequence of events which not only affected her but also affected the lives of all the people close to her. Being dropped by a maid, the event which initiates the story, has significant consequences, including the dismissal of the young woman. What is remembered is in part no more than a moment of acute sensory experience, one of physical pain and fear. But what is recalled is not simply the detached moment of acute sensory and emotional experience, it is the makings of a short story: had the maid been drinking? What would become of her? Would she be saved from destitution by a handsome prince?

We may well suspect that the act of recollecting has filled out Sand's first memory, like so many others. Later she became convinced that each individual is bound up in the lives of others. It is a recurrent subject within her autobiography, often implied in the many fragments of story which make up the work, as in the story of her bloody fall, sometimes unmentioned but nevertheless implicit. But she did learn, as a very small child, to transform her own experience into stories of a kind, and to "rewrite" the stories she had heard. What she created were extraordinary pastiches which drew on everything she had absorbed, even dreamt. Sand describes these primitive narratives in her autobiography: "They were always in the form of a fairy story, with a good fairy, a noble prince, and a beautiful princess. There were few wicked characters, and no great misfortunes. . . . My aunt also remembers my stories. . . . She remembers saying to me more than once, 'Well, Aurore, has your prince still not found a way out of the forest? Will your princess ever be done with putting on her gown and golden crown?' 'Let her be,' my mother would say, 'I can't get on with my work until she embarks on her novels. . . .' "[29]

Aurore could absent herself from the mundane experiences of everyday life, from the grimness of life in Paris. But she was also all too easily capable of seeing the degree to which real life fell short of the lives she could imagine for herself. Imagination, for the helpless child powerless to change circumstances, or to make things happen or not happen, cuts both ways: it makes escape possible but also throws reality into relief and stimulates a rational comparison between things as they are and things as they might be.

When the mature Sand describes her childhood she tells of events, but we are not always wholly convinced of their truth. Yet at the same time, she conveys a sense of the texture and idiosyncratic nature of her experience of those perhaps misremembered happenings. And here she is convincing. She knows, for example, that she spent time with her maternal aunt's family in Chaillot: she remembers the real place vividly, while at the same time remembering the fantastic place into which the house and garden at Chaillot were transformed by her childish imagination. While recalling this double place—real and imagined—she also remembers an acute sense, a childish feeling, of not knowing where she really was. The experiences existed in parallel.

In the autobiography she describes the child's exciting but unnerving sense of the vagaries of place, of geography. She also conveys the child's peculiar grasp of time. She evokes with extraordinary lucidity the memory of struggling to conceive of time projected into the future, and her asking when the dead would wake. Sand's memory of actual events is often shadowy and inaccurate. But her recollections of the nature and individuality of childish consciousness are focused and vivid. Here she glimpses—as do her readers—what was to transform a childish imaginative life that bordered, in its chaos, on a kind of madness, into an imaginative life controlled and ordered by a writer's skills. We see how early on she struggled to turn life into something like stories. Through the dark glass of the adult's memory, she explored, in her autobiography, why it might have been that Aurore Dupin became the woman she was.

Her deep fascination with childhood is visible in much of the writing. What interested her most was the child's mental life, and she likened childish consciousness, in its solipsistic moments when the mind turns in on itself, to "a kind of calm ecstasy, one in which images—marvellous, terrible, laughing—follow in rapid succession."[30] Although given to occasional and spectacular tantrums, Aurore was usually, at least in the company of adults, peculiarly composed for a small child. Her often staring, large, and deep brown eyes were the most striking feature of a face which often remained unanimated for long periods. The outward sign of the inner experience was an uncanny glazed expression which her family described as her "idiot look."[31]

By the age of three and a half, Aurore had developed a lively imagination, enriched by considerable experience. What lay ahead was an adventure of a quite different order. Her mother was once again contemplating a journey and this time she would take Aurore with her. Maurice had been home some months earlier and Sophie-Victoire had fallen pregnant. She decided to travel from Paris, through war-torn Spain, to Madrid—an extremely dangerous venture on which to embark. But knowing that her husband was about to be granted a period of leave in the Spanish capital, Sophie-Victoire made up her mind. She may have been prompted by "a tinge of jealousy." In any event, once she had thought of going, "she allowed herself to be seduced by the idea."[32]

As Sophie-Victoire prepared to leave Paris in 1808, Aurore attended to last-minute matters. Like her mother, she felt no regret for the people they were leaving behind. But she regretted leaving her dolls. To her they were still real. The loyal Pierret reassured her that he would feed them and care for them in her absence.[33] Sand later recognized the importance of idols, and idolatry, and the child's need to believe in the reality of the symbolic.

But children reach an age when they break their dolls. In so doing "they protest against a lie."[34] It cannot be wholly coincidental that Sand explored these difficult questions in a section of her autobiography which precedes her description of the journey to Spain, and the stay in Madrid. Before preparing to leave Paris, Aurore still inhabited that privileged child-hood world. But while carefully seeing to her dolls, before saying goodbye to them, she became aware that she had entered a new, unstable state of consciousness: she knew that she was only pretending to believe in them. She had reached a uniquely impressionable and vulnerable stage, one of choice: an anxious point of transition between a state of belief and one of nonbelief, which she would later describe as "a truly singular state where a growing sense of reason, on the one hand, and a need for illusion, on the other, battle it out."[35] The military image that Sand uses is metaphorical. Aurore and her mother, on the other hand, were about to embark on a jour-ney that would take them across real battlegrounds, into a real war.

III

Adventure Real and Imagined

"We are living through an age when violent events
have shaken us all and left every family bereaved."

~Aurore and her mother left Paris in April 1808, bound for Madrid. The
journey would take the little Aurore from her parents' modest, if not dingy,
apartment in Paris to a residence more sumptuous than those of her wildest
imaginings. But this was only the outward passage and their stay in Madrid
would be temporary, one of some two months. The return journey would
land Aurore at her grandmother's beautiful country estate. The round trip
may have taken her from poverty to luxury, and then to a more permanent
position of relative wealth. But it is a tragic story—and one that marked
Aurore for life.

Aurore's father was General Murat's aide-de-camp. Murat (and Maurice) had been dispatched to Spain following a revolt against the Spanish
queen's favourite, Manuel de Godoy, an unpopular prime minister. The
Napoleonic armies, under Murat, had initially been welcomed in Spain as
liberators, but this attitude would soon change. However, it was in
Godoy's former residence, the Palace of Peace, that Maurice was to spend
his leave, soon to be joined by his pregnant wife and daughter. Here his son
and heir would be born.

When Sophie-Victoire left the French capital she was seven or eight
months pregnant. She and her three-year-old daughter travelled by coach
in the spare seats offered by the wife of a quartermaster, also on her way to

Spain. A twelve-year-old groom went with them. It was a foolhardy journey on which to embark, but Sophie-Victoire may have felt that not
uncommon urge, experienced in late pregnancy, to be with the father of the
child she was about to bring into the world. And the glamour and excitement of life amid the military entourage, which she knew well, offered
pleasures and excitement which had been sadly lacking in Paris. She loved
travel and adventure, and marvelled at the sensory delights as they reached
the south and moved through the gentle foothills, then magnificent mountains, of the Pyrenees.

Sand claims that her mother was motivated by feeling, rather than
rational reflection, and that she was incapable of ordering her experiences.
This explained her mother's persistent habit of deliberately trying to
impress certain memories on her daughter. A "strange and passionate
woman," Sand would write, she "could never follow any train of recollections" and "tried to fight this trait in me. . . . She was always saying, 'You
must remember what you see here,' and each time she urged me to, I did."
Apparently quite unconcerned as to what lay ahead in Spain, Sophie-
Victoire was caught up in the present moment. "When she saw the morning glories she said, 'Smell them, they have a honey scent; and don't forget
them!' This is the first recollection of smell I can remember; and by one of
those chains of memory and sensation . . . I never smell wild morning glories without seeing that same spot in the Spanish mountains."[1]

Like Marcel Proust's famous chains of remembrance, Sand's descriptions of her mother's desire to stimulate her daughter's sensibility are also
reminiscent of Jean-Jacques Rousseau. Sand's grandmother had met him,
and remained convinced by his theories despite her own incapacity to
respond spontaneously, unlike Sophie-Victoire. According to Rousseau,
the happy, integrated child develops only if there is a free and harmonious
flow into the individual consciousness of the sights and sounds of the natural world. It was this relationship with the world around her that Sand's
mother instinctively encouraged in Aurore, not because of her reading
(unlike her grandmother) but because it was her way. "From my tenderest
infancy my mother instinctively guided me towards beauty. . . . Whenever
a beautiful cloud appeared, or a striking effect of light, or clear running
water, she would say, 'Look—there's something beautiful!' and at once
these objects revealed their gloriousness to me."[2]

Sophie-Victoire possessed a "magic key" which opened Aurore's sen-
sibilities. And there was plenty to see as they travelled on—mother and
daughter talked with great animation. But their interaction was clearly

peculiar, and Mme Fontanier, the quartermaster's wife, is said to have remarked, "How queer you are with your daughter."[3] Given what lay ahead, Sophie-Victoire's delight in her immediate surroundings was more typical of a child than a heavily pregnant woman with responsibility for a small daughter.

Once they were over the border, Sophie-Victoire's mood changed dramatically and so did her behaviour. She became less aware of the landscape and more concerned about the people who inhabited it. She felt threatened and expressed her anxieties with the same spontaneity that characterized her response to the earlier delights. In the Spanish mountains she became convinced that the carriage was surrounded by brigands. The "brigands" turned out to be a family of bears. "Her lively imagination constantly presented her with the idea of fearful dangers."[4] Nor, more tellingly, did she seek to hide or disguise her anxieties, or to protect Aurore from the frightening scenarios suggested to her by her overactive imagination.

On the floor of one of the inns in which they stayed, Sophie-Victoire had noticed fresh and extensive trails of blood. She persuaded the disconcerted but incredulous Mme Fontanier that they should follow the blood trail because it would lead to the bodies of travellers murdered by the proprietor of the inn. Sophie-Victoire was convinced—and convincing. Aurore, exhausted and disoriented by days of travel, was included in the terrifying torchlit search. What she witnessed, in the flickering, shadowy light, was the gory sight of a mountain of slaughtered pigs.[5] She was horrified to the point of disbelief.

What is most bizarre in all this is that her mother made no effort to distance Aurore from what she herself was quite convinced they would find: human corpses. It is little wonder that it was during this period that, perhaps precociously, Aurore desperately struggled to separate the real from the imagined, actual experience from fantasy. Fear, Aurore had recognized, can be a remarkable imaginative stimulus.

Another deeply memorable event on the journey was Aurore's first sighting of a real "queen." This was not alarming in the least, but it was quite as disturbing, and still more formative in terms of her imaginative life. The Spanish Infanta, Maria Luisa, daughter of Charles IV, was fleeing Spain to take refuge in Bayonne, under the protection of Napoleon. Aurore and her mother were waiting at an inn while the horses were changed when a large carriage suddenly swept into the courtyard and the local villagers called out excitedly, "The Queen, the Queen!" The innkeeper tried to keep the crowd at a distance, but a chambermaid lifted Aurore up so that she could look in through the carriage window as the far from impressive vehicle drew up. What she saw fell a long way short of those extravagant princesses and queens of her fairy-tale world. The reality of her imagined fairy-tale people, like that of her dolls back in Paris, was instantly threatened, if not destroyed: "The poor queen that I beheld was dressed in a little white dress that was very tight, as was the fashion of the day. It had turned yellow from the dust. Her daughter, who looked about eight or ten, was dressed the same way, and they both seemed to be very dark-skinned and rather ugly."[6]

On arrival in Madrid, Sophie-Victoire became calmer: "Seeing my father, she forgot her terrors and her suffering."[7] But Aurore was rarely with her mother, who was either required to be seen out with her husband or was resting in anticipation of the imminent birth. Aurore was left in the care of a servant who disappeared as soon as the child's parents were out of the way. Her father's manservant Weber, a German who knew scarcely any French, was also sometimes charged with her care. He would take her out to one of the impressive squares of Madrid. But they had no common language. Most of the time, and with no playmate, she escaped into her familiar but changing fantasy world. She now felt compelled to explore, to question, to measure the world of her imagination against the apparently real world of the extraordinary so-called Palace of the Prince of Peace.

The family stayed in a huge apartment, hung with damask and silk, on one of the upper floors. The beds, the chairs, the sofas were all painted in gold-leaf—Aurore thought it was made of solid gold like the furniture in her fairy stories. Huge, fearsome portraits stared down from high on the walls. Their eyes followed her movements. But she soon adjusted to the place.[8] Here the royal children, who had had to leave with little warning, had abandoned their glorious toys. They had also abandoned a pet rabbit—the animate creature interested her most. He became her silent, and thus, she assumed, satisfied, audience. She told him her endless, rambling stories.

During one of these solitary periods, she first saw herself in a full-length mirror. Was this other self real? Or did this mere reflection confirm her own reality? She confronted for the first time the separateness of her own being, her individual self.

Aurore was all but unaware that a real war was raging all around, vividly depicted in Goya's famous wartime sketches. Left alone for long periods in this bizarre temporary home, she delighted in her freedom. The apartment was vast and she had the run of the place. The "psyche" (cheval glass) was the real source of fascination. She stood before it and experimented with theatrical poses. And she involved another player, her only companion:

> Then I would take my white rabbit, and I would try to force him do the same thing: or I played at sacrificing him to the gods. I wrapped myself in my mantilla to play priestess, following all my own movements. Or we would dance a bolero . . . for the Spanish dances had enchanted me, and I aped their poses and graces with a child's facility for imitating what they see. And so I quite forgot that the figure dancing in the mirror was my own, and was astonished when it stopped when I stopped.[9]

The specular other self, seen in the mirror, was soon confused with another double, this time heard rather than seen. When the quiet around her became unnerving, she experimented with her voice: "One day this silence frightened me and . . . I called out." She heard

> a voice just like my own. . . . This voice reassured me: I was not alone; but curious to know who was playing at copying me, I went into the apartment, expecting to find someone there. . . . I was quite alone in the place, as usual. I went back out onto the terrace and called my mother; the voice repeated the word very softly. . . . Then I arrived at an extraordinary explanation: I was double and somewhere nearby was another me whom I could not see, but who could always see me, because it always responded to me.[10]

She decided that this must have always been the case, it was simply that she had never noticed before. Moving from the self out, she concluded that everyone must have a reflection, a double, another self. She longed to meet her own. One day, while experimenting with this other self, her mother arrived:

> I asked her where the person was who repeated all my words, and she told me "It's your echo." . . . Happily

she did not explain what an echo was. . . . For days I was free to continue to toss words to the wind. The voice in the air astonished me no longer, but it charmed me still; I was content to be able to give it a name, and to cry out to it, "Good morning, Echo!"[11]

The presence of doubles became part of the hazy sense of life as theatre that had occasionally been a fragment of life in Paris. Aurore saw herself in the mirror and began to explore possibilities for self-transformation. She had also embarked on her first dialogue with herself, when calling out to her Echo. Sand's mature sense of a multiple and shifting identity no doubt has its origin in her playful self-inventions in Madrid. But she was equally drawn into other people's fantasies.

She cross-dressed for the first time—on her mother's insistence. Aurore's costume was calculated to flatter General Murat and it worked: the miniature aide-de-camp was presented to Murat's visitors, drawing her parents closer into his circle. Most guests assumed the little figure was a boy. Sophie-Victoire had made a complete and carefully tailored outfit: Aurore was instantly transformed into an endearing mascot.[12] Aurore carried it off with éclat, but the fur, the trailing sabre, and the red Moroccan-leather boots made it an uncomfortable get-up, and far too hot. Aurore was relieved to change back into the luxurious black silk dress, tailored in a full Spanish style: it allowed her greater freedom and it exaggerated her graceful gestures and movements. For the time being she preferred the feminine costume to the masculine disguise.

Meanwhile the drama of history was rapidly moving on. The French were soon to be forced to retreat from Spain, and Maurice wrote excitedly to his mother in Nohant. They would soon be setting off for home. In a matter of weeks his family would be reunited in the safe house and grounds of Nohant in the peaceful Berry countryside. And he would be returning with the newly born heir of Nohant, Louis. Aurore heard her mother's screams of pain. Maurice wrote triumphantly to his mother:

> After long agonies, Sophie has given birth this morning to a bouncing boy who squawks like a parrot. Both mother and child are in excellent health. Before the month is out the Prince will leave for France, and the Emperor's doctor, who attended to Sophie, says she and the baby will be fit to travel in twelve days.

Aurore is in the pink of health. I will bundle them all
into a four-wheeler I have found, and we will be off to
Nohant, where I expect to arrive on 20 July and to
stay as long as we can. The very thought, my dear
Mother, fills me with joy. I am living in the certain
hope of our reunion, thinking of the delights of
home, without duties, anxieties or onerous distractions! How I have longed for that complete
happiness![13]

But his letter home was not altogether frank—and far too optimistic. And
what might otherwise have been the happy interlude Maurice projected in
his letter was transformed into a period of anxiety and terror. Far from
being "in excellent health," Louis had been born, they feared, blind.
Sophie-Victoire even suspected the Spanish surgeon of having deliberately
pressed his thumbs into the baby's eye sockets. She was desperate to leave
Spain, and the Spanish, far behind. And Maurice hoped that the omniscient
Deschartres would somehow be able to restore the baby's sight.

The journey north was still more dramatic and dangerous than the
journey south. Aurore, her baby brother, and Sophie-Victoire travelled by
carriage. Maurice rode Leopardo, the "indomitable" charger that even he
feared to a degree and that Sophie-Victoire had implored him not to ride.
They travelled with the retreating French armies. Mostly they slept in the
carriage as they journeyed through the devastated landscape. Houses and
whole villages burned around them. One night they managed to find a
room in an inn. The boom of cannons signalled that a battle was raging not
far off. Sophie-Victoire lifted her daughter to the window so that she could
witness the sight. She even informed her daughter that her father might be
there, amid the fighting.

For part of the journey their carriage was requisitioned and they had
to hitch a ride on a baggage cart travelling north. The heat was stifling and
Aurore remembered the terrible thirst that afflicted them for hours on end.
There was scarcely any food to be had. At one point a kindly soldier shared
his soup with them: it was made of candle ends heated into a strange broth.
As they approached the frontier their carriage was returned to them.
Sophie-Victoire took it into her head that they should travel from the coast
of northern Spain to Bordeaux by sea. The sloop ran aground and Maurice, true to character, made a brave, not to say foolhardy, rescue. He saved
his family, his horse, his sabre, and the carriage. Or so Sand tells the story.[14]

Arrival at Nohant must have been welcome indeed. After the journeying, the instabilities of life in Madrid, and the fears for little Louis's health, the Vallée Noire must, even to the young Aurore, have meant something of what it would later come to mean:

> A region where the shock of social change loses its force, in the calm of habits and in the gentleness of relations . . . the Vallée Noire is a kind of oasis, where, through good times and bad, change comes without great jolts; and this since time immemorial.[15]

Here was a place outside history—but when Mme Dupin appeared she immediately struck Aurore as a personification of the past.

Aurore had no memory of that first encounter with her grandmother in Paris when she had been handed to her by the anonymous concierge. She saw her, as for the first time, as she was lifted down from the carriage.[16] What she remembered of her first impressions was her grandmother's old-fashioned appearance, her dated clothes and peculiar hairstyle, her dignified self-control, her air of calm composure. Her "mannered" behaviour contrasted sharply with Sophie-Victoire's "natural" ways. She also remembered her own sense of self-disgust, in her grandmother's presence. Aurore, like her mother and the baby, had contracted scabies, but Mme Dupin insisted that while Sophie-Victoire attended to the baby, she would look after Aurore. She took the little girl in her arms—but Sophie-Victoire protested that she might be infectious—and carried her to her own fine four-poster bed. Sand vividly recalled her fear that her diseased body would soil the fine linen, would somehow infect her grandmother's superior world. How much did the mature Sand confuse her memory of her feelings about scabies with a more deep-seated feeling that, as the fruit of her mother's womb, she, like her mother, was stained? Her grandmother would, after all, soon inform Aurore that her mother was a "fallen woman." The scabies could and would be cured. But Aurore would always remain, in her own eyes and those of her grandmother, her mother's daughter. For many years this was Aurore's decision, an act of choice, a heroic gesture of loyalty. There was a degree of contrariness and stubbornness about it too, and it was a choice which greatly complicated her relationship with her grandmother. Aurore would soon be handed over to the guardianship of the austere Marie-Aurore Dupin.

A good deal of history is bound up in the story of Aurore's "two rival mothers": her natural mother and her adoptive mother, her grandmother, Marie-Aurore. There is more common ground than one might first suppose. Marie-Aurore's mother, Aurore's great-grandmother, was Marie Rainteau. She was just seventeen when she met Marie-Aurore's father, Aurore's great-grandfather Maurice de Saxe. Marie, like Sand's mother, was an actress only of sorts, and she quickly became Maurice de Saxe's official mistress. Sand's grandmother, Marie-Aurore, and her younger sister, Geneviève, were protected by him. Sand's grandmother's baptismal certificate, dated 19 October 1748, reads "Marie-Aurore, daughter of Jean Baptiste de La Rivière, bourgeois of Paris, and of Marie Rainteau, his wife." Jean Baptiste was an invention, and as Sand explained, "The story is a curious illustration of the mores of the time."[17]

Marie-Aurore's first years were spent in the *demi-monde* of her mother and aunt, "a corrupt world," as Sand described it, one of pretence and hypocrisy. Sand's mother's world, on the other hand, would simply be described as "miserable." Sand despised, as had Marie-Aurore, the double standards and arrogant self-confidence of the world into which her great-grandmother had been born. It was a luxurious ambience, boasting all the outward signs of aristocratic life. The women, despite their very ordinary backgrounds, enjoyed a "prestige which gave them a kind of self-respect." They represented the "flower" of a certain eighteenth-century cynicism. They symbolized the "elegance amid chaos" of their age, and gave immorality "a kind of *grandeur.*" This was a social world into which gentlemen pressed to gain entry.

Sand's grandmother's father, Maurice de Saxe, died when Marie-Aurore was only two. His inheritor was not, of course, his mistress, but his nephew, the Comte de Frise, who granted Marie-Aurore an annual income, supplemented by support from the dauphine, Maurice's niece. When Marie-Aurore was taken from her mother by one of the dauphine's ladies-in-waiting, her mother had expected nothing other than this. Sand's grandmother was sent first to the Convent of Saint-Cloud, then to the Convent of Saint-Cyr, from which she emerged, recognized by the magistrates of the Parliament of Paris as the "natural child of Maurice, Comte de Saxe, General of the Camps and Armies of France, and of Marie Rainteau."[18] Thus she attracted a suitable husband, the Comte de Horn, aged forty-four. He was not, as Sand claims, or as Sand's grandmother may have led her to believe, an illegitimate son of Louis XV. Sand may have provided a more accurate portrait of her grandmother's first husband, and of the attitudes of the aspirant aristocracy, in *Jeanne*. In the novel a certain Guillaume is described as follows: "Guillaume had not examined his genealog-ical tree very closely; like so many nobles of his time, he was animated by chivalrous ideas, and, adding them, through force of imagination, to those of consanguinity, he truly believed that he felt their unadulterated blood coursing in his veins."[19]

The Count died only months after their marriage. Widowed at eigh-teen, Sand's grandmother was driven, once more, to seek protection. She wrote to Voltaire, whom she believed would have sympathy for her plight. He could only suggest approaching Mme la Duchesse de Choiseul. She finally secured a small income from the Choiseuls and returned to her mother and aunt. She participated in their theatrical performances. Sand describes Marie-Aurore at this point in flattering terms: "She had a superior intelligence, a sound education, had one of the loftiest and most enlight-ened sentiments of her time; and her intelligence was cultivated and devel-oped by the business, conversation and company of her mother. She had, in addition, a magnificent voice and I have never met a better musician."[20]

Among Marie-Aurore's aunt's visitors was M. Dupin de Francueil. He was drawn to her but she cannot have been an easy conquest. Sand wrote of her grandmother, "Her soul was strong, visionary, nourished by a sense of pride and self-respect. She ignored coquettishness, and was too talented to need it, and this system of provocation wounded her sense of, and manner of retaining, dignity. She lived through a free and corrupt age and emerged without a ruffled feather; and, condemned by a strange fate never to know love in marriage, she succeeded in solving the riddle of how to live calmly, avoiding all malevolence, all calumny."[21]

At the age of twenty-seven she withdrew to another convent, that of the Dames du Calvaire. She continued to be visited by Dupin de Francueil, however, and for reasons which remain mysterious, their eventual mar-riage, in 1777, took place at the French Embassy in London. The religious ceremony took place in Paris. Almost exactly a year later, on the thirteenth of June 1778, a son, Maurice, was born—Sand's father. In her auto-biography Sand recounts her grandmother's description of her marriage: "She told me that during the ten years that they lived together, he was, with their son, the dearest affection of her life; and though she never used the word love, a word which I have never heard from her lips *à propos* of him or anyone, she smiled when she heard me say that it seemed to me impossible 'to love' an old man. . . . 'An old man is better able "to love" than a young man,' she said. . . . 'And it is impossible not "to love" when you are "loved" perfectly.' "[22]

In the presence of her grandmother Aurore was instinctively aware of, and gradually came to understand, the complexities and significance of gender, class, and wealth. This was immediately visible in the differences in behaviour of her mother and her grandmother, but equally obvious in the respective lots of her half-brother and half-sister. For Aurore this was the most tangible insight into the relationship between illegitimacy, gender, and class. Social attitudes to it were a source of fascination and confusion to her as a child. Why was she to be brought up in the close company of her illegitimate half-brother on her father's side, Hippolyte Chatiron, but kept away from her illegitimate half-sister, Caroline, on her mother's side? From the moment of their arrival at Nohant her grandmother encouraged intimacy with Hippolyte, while ensuring that she be kept away from Caroline. Aurore missed her half-sister desperately.

Even at the age of five, arriving at Nohant, Aurore had strong feelings about physical intimacy with her grandmother, not wholly explicable in terms of her scabies. She must have recognized almost instantly that there was a difference between her mother's and her grandmother's attitudes to physical closeness.

Sand's grandmother's first marriage may not have been consummated. Her second marriage had been a close friendship with a much older man, and largely chaste. Sophie-Victoire, on the other hand, had loved passionately, wildly. Physical love, the little Aurore was forced to begin to acknowledge, also had a politics of its own. At the same time, she was made conscious, and self-conscious, of her own body, and the questions of health and chastity associated with it. This too was somehow bound up with gender and class.

It is unlikely that Maurice and his family would have stayed long at Nohant; antipathies between mother- and daughter-in-law were too great. But they had planned to stay at least until Louis's health had been restored, and maybe even his sight. But while Aurore's health rapidly improved, Louis continued to deteriorate. Sophie-Victoire scarcely dared touch him as he lay quite still in her lap. Aurore shared her mother's sorrow and lived in the presence of unremitting anxiety. She recognized, precociously, the cruel and terrible miseries thrown up by life.[23]

After long moans on his mother's lap the baby grew colder and colder. He was wrapped in more and more blankets. The fire was furiously fed and stoked. But nothing could be done to warm him. He died on Friday, 8 September 1808. In some sense his death had been peaceful and undramatic, but the days that followed were to be days of high melodrama, because of

Sophie-Victoire's traumatized response. The baby was buried the next day. No doubt Mme Dupin and Deschartres, the rationalists, considered it best to act quickly without too much sentiment or ritual. But Sophie-Victoire needed time to grieve for the baby, to come to terms with his death.[24] She had not yet acknowledged its reality.

The story, as Sand tells it in her autobiography, is an extraordinary one, but it testifies to a very human need. Her father and mother wept together for some time but her mother was unable to sleep and became hysterical. She could not accept the suddenness of the separation. She railed against the "savage" custom of burial. This prompted her husband to reflect that sometimes people are actually buried alive. This occurred not altogether infrequently in the nineteenth century.

Sophie-Victoire lost all self-control. She was convinced that the baby was not dead at all, but in some kind of unconscious state. She insisted that she wanted to see the child again. Initially Maurice protested against what he could only suppose were irrational imaginings. Whether she succeeded in convincing him that the baby might actually still be alive, or whether he decided that his utterly distracted wife could only be brought through her agonies by seeing the baby again, he agreed to dig up the coffin. He carried it in to his wife and they prised off the lid. The baby was quite dead, but Sophie-Victoire took comfort in rubbing the little body with scent, swaddling it in the best linen, and laying it in its cradle so that she could imagine, at least, that the baby was only sleeping. They kept the infant hidden in their room throughout the next day, but by nightfall agreed that Louis should again be buried. Sophie-Victoire filled the space around the body with rose petals. This time he was buried not in the graveyard—a place reserved for the dead—but in the garden—a place enjoyed by the living—under an abundantly yielding pear tree. And for the next eight days husband and wife gardened furiously, transforming the area around the burial spot into an elaborate formal garden. During this brief period, allowing Aurore and Hippolyte to ride in the wheelbarrow between earth-moving trips, pretending that he was about to tip them out, Maurice enjoyed a brief period of tenderness with his wife and family, amid great sorrow.[25]

Terrible though Louis's death had been, Sophie-Victoire still had her husband to depend on. But not for long. Just eight days later, on 16 September, Maurice set out on the wild Leopardo—ignoring his wife's protests—to visit friends. Sophie-Victoire and her mother-in-law were both concerned when, late in the evening, he had still not returned home, so Deschartres set off in the hope of meeting him on his way back. He found him, dead. He was thirty years old. The "indomitable" Leopardo had thrown him. Mme Dupin had lost her grandson only days earlier and had now lost her son. Sophie-Victoire had lost her son and her husband. Aurore had lost her brother and her father. That happy childhood augured by the supposedly ideal birth in the Rue Meslay a little more than five years earlier had ended in a double tragedy.

What the mature Sand remembered of the days following her father's death was its unreality. The scale of suffering around her, she could only assume looking back, was somehow so great that she failed to recognize it. The pain of those around her was more than she could make sense of. It washed over her. She remembered instead the immediate and tangible grimness of being dressed in mourning, like everyone else. She was particularly horrified by the black stockings—they enveloped her legs in death. And she asked, every day when her mother came to dress her in the same terrible legwear, whether her father was still dead that day.[26]

It is small wonder that the mature Sand recognized and insisted on the importance of the dead. They had always mattered a great deal to her, particularly her own dead. They were not, she knew as a small child, forgotten, cut off, beyond or outside life. Their lives were terribly, intimately, bound up with those of the living. While writing her autobiography and struggling to remember her own childhood and the people who had filled it, however briefly, she was made aware of just how early on she had felt her own self to be part of something wider and deeper. In 1848, while in the middle of writing her life story, she wrote to Pierre-Jules Hetzel, one of her many editors: "The dead, we are them, without doubt; there is a mysterious link that explains how our lives are nourished by theirs."[27]

In the autobiography this idea of the interdependence of human life was treated at greater length, but its origin lies in those terrible autumn days of 1808:

> All beings are bound up together, and the human being who portrays his own as isolated, without linking it to those like him, offers naught but an enigma to be unravelled. Solidarity is far more obvious when immediate, like that which links children with parents, friends with friends of the past and present. . . . As for myself (and as for all of you), my thoughts, my beliefs, my dislikes, my instincts, my feelings would

be a mystery to me, which I could only attribute to chance, which has never explained anything in this world, if I could not read in the past, the page that precedes the one on which my individuality is written, in the great universal book.[28]

There is something of the *Tristram Shandy* in Sand's story where the entrance of the subject herself is delayed until some third of the way through. What is less obviously explicable is that among the dead whose lives are explored, it is only her father's glorious and relatively brief career that is treated at any length. Sand saw fit to attempt at least to justify this imbalance:

I will continue the story of my father, since he is, no pun intended, the real author of the story of my life. This father whom I scarcely knew and who has remained in my memory like a shining apparition— this young artist and warrior has remained wholly and completely alive in the flights of my fancy, in the weaknesses of my constitution, in the features of my face. My being is a reflection—no doubt weakened, but fairly complete—of his. . . . My exterior life has differed as much from his as the period in which it had developed; but had I been a boy and had I lived twenty-five years earlier, I know and I feel that I would have acted and felt like my father in all things.[29]

Her grieving "rival mothers" first willed her to become that reflection. From the moment of her father's death they—and Deschartres too to some extent—treated her as a replacement, an understudy. But they each had their own visions of how she should interpret her part.

Aurore's response was defensive: her daydreaming became a physical need. Where earlier she had told herself—or her adopted rabbit—stories in part because she was bored and had no one to play with, now her fantasy world became a life-saving haven. And her desire, or compulsion, imaginatively to escape from the acute pressures of real life became one of the many bones of contention between Aurore's two "rival mothers." Her mother understood—instinctively. She recognized that it was a need. Her grandmother may well have understood too, but she thought it unhealthy all the same. This habit would need to be broken.

For both women Aurore had become the tangible face of a double resurrection. Her upbringing was to matter greatly to both of them. And they had very different ideas.

IV

Two Rival Mothers

"In some respects we make our own life; in others,
we submit to the life that others make for us."

⤳"Women are given a deplorable education. This is men's greatest crime against them. Men have introduced abuses in every quarter, monopolizing the advantages of the most important institutions. . . . They have succeeded in bringing about the enslavement and degradation of women, a condition which they now claim was instituted by God, part of an immutable law."[1] Elsewhere Sand argued: "There is nothing in a woman's life . . . equivalent to that basic schooling . . . which, according to Diderot, emerges suddenly from the young graduate's brain to do battle with his first impressions and initial errors."[2] Yet Aurore developed that questioning attitude to life, and it may have been in part because she received, if only for relatively limited periods, what was essentially a boy's education. This was one of a number of aspects of her childhood and upbringing—the two are virtually synonymous—that encouraged, early on, unconventional ideas about gender as opposed to sex, and about sexuality. Of her own son and daughter's early experiences and formation she would write: "I observed the childhood and the evolution of both. . . . My son was I—that is to say, a woman—much more than my daughter, who was an unsuccessful man."[3]

Aurore had just turned five when the family arrived at Nohant from Spain. During those first years Sophie-Victoire had taken seriously certain aspects of her daughter's education. The first foundations of a religious faith had been laid, and Aurore had been taught the basics of reading and writing. She had also been exposed to stories, poetry, and singing. She had been to the theatre. Above all Sophie-Victoire had given Aurore an early and highly formative introduction to the art of stories and the creation of a world of make-believe, both subject to quite different laws from those of the real world.

But Sophie-Victoire's educational concerns were not altogether those of an ambitious mother keen to see her daughter rise into a higher class. The outward signs—the airs and graces of such belonging—Sophie-Victoire thought ridiculous.[4]

Aurore also learnt to write without any great difficulty, encouraged by the exciting promise of written self-expression:

> I learnt to write towards the age of five. My mother made me trace big pages . . . but as she herself wrote like a spider, I would have wasted a good deal of paper before even learning to write my name if I had not myself had a keen desire to record my thoughts with signs. Weary of copying the alphabet every day and penning downstrokes and upstrokes in staring capitals, I was impatient to write whole sentences, and during my ample free time I practised writing letters to Ursule, Hippolyte, and my mother. But I didn't deliver them, for fear I'd be forbidden on the grounds that this activity would "spoil my hand."[5]

At Nohant, Aurore's mother continued to read to her, "from Berquin, or from *Veillées du château* by Mme de Genlis." Her mother's reading acted as a kind of catalyst for her own imaginings:

> By degrees, I would lose track of what my mother was reading, and her voice would lull me into a kind of slumber . . . pictures crowded before me . . . woods, meadows, streams, towns of a strange and gigantic architecture such as I still see in dreams; and enchanted palaces with gardens the like of which have never been seen, with myriad blue, gold and purple birds which fluttered in the flowers and let me catch

them. . . . There were green roses, black and violet roses, and best of all, blue roses. . . . I saw forests . . . Chinese footbridges, and trees laden with fruit. . . . Indeed the whole fantastic world of my fairy tales became palpable. . . .[6]

Her mother's voice acted as an aural trigger of the imagination, and images equally acted as a powerful stimulus. The backwards and forwards movement between the real and imagined continued: the decorative borders of the wallpaper in her bedroom at Nohant had this effect. The border "represented a trained vine whose leaves parted at intervals to disclose a series of medallions wherein I saw old satyrs and bacchantes laughing, drinking and dancing." Among these animated figures was "the one I saw when I woke . . . a nymph or dancing Flora. She wore pale blue and a crown of roses. . . . She seemed to smile at me and beckon to me, willing me to rise and follow her, to frolic in her company. . . . The real and the imagined appeared before me at once."[7]

For all the gloriousness of her childhood imaginings, there were moments when the difference between the real and imagined blurred in a terrifying way: "One day these apparitions became so real that I was almost afraid, and asked my mother if she did not see them too." Aurore saw "high blue mountains." Her mother's response was to bounce her on her knee to bring her "home."[8] But Aurore's capacity and proclivity for escape into a fantasy world became one of the many sources of disagreement between Sophie-Victoire and Mme Dupin during the days and weeks that followed the deaths of Maurice and Louis:

> For hours I would sit on a stool at her [my grandmother's] feet or at my mother's, silent, glassy-eyed, open-mouthed, with my arms dangling, and sometimes looking like an idiot. "She's often like that," my mother would say. "She's not trying to be difficult; it's her nature. You may be sure that she's always meditating on something. She used to chatter when she daydreamed."[9]

Her grandmother, on the other hand, argued: "It's unhealthy for children to daydream so much. I saw her father enter such trances when he was a child, and eventually he fell into a decline. . . . We must beware, or *our* sorrows *will make* her *die. . . .*"[10] Mme Dupin responded with alarm when she recognized certain similarities between Aurore and her father: "My grandmother became more attached to me each day—not, to be sure, on account of my awkward personality, but because of my striking resemblance to my father. My voice, my face, my habits, my tastes—everything about me reminded her of her son as a boy, to such an extent that sometimes when she watched me play she seemed to succumb to some delusion, and called me 'Maurice' and referred to me as 'my son.' "[11]

Mme Dupin's strange fear of the relationship between imaginative experience and mental instability, even madness—in her son and now granddaughter—only partly explains her desire to break Aurore of her habit. The outward sign of the inner experience—Aurore's unbecoming "idiot look"—concerned her too.

Aurore knew what to hide from her grandmother:

> Ah, the fairies and genii! Where did they live, those omnipotent beings, who with one wave of a wand could lead you into a world of delights? My mother never wanted to say that they didn't exist, and I now know that I am indebted to her. My grandmother would not have beaten around the bush if I'd dared to ask her these questions. Full of Rousseau and Voltaire, she would have demolished the whole enchanted structure of my imagination without regret or pity. But my mother went about things differently. She did not confirm, nor did she deny, anything. Reason came to me in its own good time, and then I knew for myself that my fantasies would never come true; but if the door of hope was no longer wide open . . . it was not yet locked, and I was allowed to linger at it, and to try to find a crack through which to peep.[12]

It is not altogether clear at what age Aurore learnt to read for herself, and reading is, in any case, a whole series of stages. But fairly early Aurore began to make some sense of Mme d'Aulnoy's and Perrault's tales. She also started to read a collection of Greek myths. "The nymphs, the zephyrs, Echo . . . turned my mind towards poetry."[13] Later, Sand reflected on her early passions: "Perhaps it was my upbringing; perhaps the inspiration of what I'd seen and heard; perhaps some innate trait of my own—

whatever the case, I was passionately taken with the novel before I'd fully learnt to read."[14]

The experience of living in the presence of "two rival mothers" further encouraged escape into books and the imagination. Aurore was the "innocent cause of bitterness" between the two women, and believed that it was she who "felt the pain most acutely." "Cruelly torn between two affections . . . I fell victim to each of these vulnerable women in turn."[15] The two women, mother- and daughter-in-law, respected each other's strengths, felt each other's grief, and were violently intolerant of each other's weaknesses. When it came to Aurore, everything about their relationships with her, their feelings, intuitions, and ideas about her upbringing, served to make concrete and visible a relative abstract: their differences in background.

During Aurore's early months at Nohant she enjoyed the freedom of the extensive gardens—and the countryside beyond its high walls. Within the grounds Sophie-Victoire built a formal rockery, complete with miniature grottoes, enthusiastically assisted by Aurore and Hippolyte. Mme Dupin remained unimpressed: it was not to her taste.

Aurore was also allowed to mix freely with the people of Nohant: the servants, the peasants, the children. She ran barefoot, drove the swine, and climbed trees. She learned to understand Berrichon, the regional patois, and listened enchanted to the local stories, told at the hearths of the cottages adjacent to the manor. She could soon communicate in the local dialect.

But however sympathetic—in theory—to Rousseau's convictions about the merits of a "natural," "classless" upbringing, Mme Dupin was increasingly alarmed by both the unkempt appearance and uncontrolled boyish ways of her granddaughter and heir. Mme Dupin was forced to acknowledge that the results of Aurore's first months at Nohant had made her not so much "natural" as positively "wild." For one thing, Aurore had to be cured of her gaping stare.

Mme Dupin needed sage advice, and the arrival of Uncle Beaumont—Aurore's great-uncle—reassured her, and brought a new calm to the troubled atmosphere. Aurore immediately took to her "uncle": "He was the most beautiful old person I have ever met." His clothes were made of velvet, silk, and black satin. He was an abbot, master storyteller—and playwright.[16] One evening he directed a little performance, by the children, of a play he had written. Deschartres played the flageolet. Happiness broke in on the mourning of Nohant.

With Uncle Beaumont in the house, tensions between Mme Dupin and Sophie-Victoire somehow eased, and life assumed greater stability. On Sundays Aurore was taken to church at Saint-Chartier, a couple of kilometres away. They went by mule, picnicking on the way home in the grounds of a ruined medieval château.

But as the year drew to a close it became clear that decisions had to be taken about Aurore's future. Sophie-Victoire disliked the country and worried about Caroline, back in Paris. There was no question of her moving to Nohant. Maurice's death had left Sophie-Victoire with an income of 1,000 francs a year—to be set against his debts. As Uncle Beaumont pointed out, it was not enough to provide her two children with a good education. Aurore listened to the discussions and begged her mother not to "sell" her to her grandmother.[17]

On 29 January 1809 an agreement was signed between Aurore's mother and grandmother: the latter would take charge of her education. As far as her grandmother was concerned, this was only a first step. On the third of February 1809, when Aurore was four, a second agreement was signed: Mme Dupin would grant Sophie-Victoire an allowance. In exchange Mme Dupin would become Aurore's guardian. Her mother would leave Nohant and return to Paris—to Caroline, and Pierret. Aurore and her grandmother would also travel to Paris, a fortnight later, and, initially at least, live nearby so that Aurore could be weaned gradually from her mother.

Mme Dupin saw to it that Aurore had a child her own age to play with: her chambermaid's niece, Ursule. She was brought to Nohant from La Châtre to keep her company. Ursule, a kind-hearted country girl, tried to make her inconsolable playmate see things from her own very different perspective: "How good it is all the same to have a large house, a large garden to stroll in, and carriages and dresses and good things to eat every day. Do you know where it all comes from? . . . You mustn't cry, you know, because with your grandmama you'll always have your golden age. . . . When I go to Mama in La Châtre, she says I'm taking on airs at Nohant playing at being a lady. 'Pooh-pooh,' I say, 'I'm in my golden age. I'm helping myself to riches while I can.' "

But those two weeks at Nohant without her mother were a great misery. "Though I was apart from her only a fortnight, that fortnight is clearer in my memory than the three years which followed."[18] Aurore's grandmother tried to distract her with work. "She gave me my lessons and proved much more indulgent than my mother. Gone were the scoldings, the punishments. . . . By rights this should have been very pleasant for me, for my mother was unbending, and without pity for my laziness and naughtiness. But," Sand the mature writer reflects, "a child's heart is a little world as odd and inconsistent as an adult's. So it was that I found my grandmother's patience more severe and more frightening than my mother's exasperation. Until then I had loved her, and had shown her with my caresses that I trusted her. But from then on—and until long after—I felt cold and reserved towards her."[19] Aurore's mother had occasionally instilled terror in her, but these were no more than "passing moments of pain." The next moment she would be on her mother's lap again. But her grandmother's kisses were no more than "rewards for good conduct." Most difficult to bear was the notion that since her mother's departure she had suddenly "grown up": "This idea . . . quite terrified me. . . . I had to learn all sorts of manners that I thought simply absurd." And there were all sorts of things that were forbidden: "Not to work so that my eyes would retain their sparkle; not to run and play in the sun . . . ; not to walk in heavy clogs for fear of deforming my ankles; to wear gloves, that is, to renounce the dexterity and strength of my hands . . . ; never to tire myself, when everything urged me to use up my energy; to live in short under a bell jar; to be neither tanned, nor chapped, nor faded by time. . . . I was fresh only for a moment."[20] Aurore was taught to drop-curtsy to passers-by, was forbidden to go into the kitchen, and had to refer to her grandmother in the third person, "Does grandmama wish to allow me to go into the garden?"[21] The effect of her grandmother's regime was, according to Sand, "to subdue" rather than "to reform."[22]

Aurore was no longer to feel the intimacy with the world that her mother had encouraged, the sensory experience of being close to, and celebrating, nature. She was no longer to be close to people, to mix with the Berry peasantry and to hear their tales, their ways of explaining the world in the Berrichon dialect. She was to be made to deny her knowledge of this other language, and gradually to forget its wisdom. She was to employ a formal French, simultaneously distancing herself from her grandmother, who was to become only that, "grandmother." Her daydreaming, her "novels," were "unhealthy," and everything was to be done to educate her formally in order to fill her with appropriate "knowledge." The "daydreaming," above all, would have to stop.

Mme Dupin believed that Aurore had a duty to her grandmother, a duty rendered all the more significant by the deaths of Maurice and Louis. The burden she believed to be Aurore's lot was an intolerable one: "To console me," she would say, "you must be perfectly brought up." Her grandmother was, Sand describes, "bent on developing my mind, of which she had a high opinion," but "a child whose nervous system has been too violently shaken is soon still more impetuous again, precisely because it has been curbed all at once."[23]

Mme Dupin, on the other hand, was surprised and delighted by her apparent success, but wanted more than just to ensure that Aurore behave as she thought fit. "She craved not only pious respect but also passionate love." Sand firmly believed that a child needs a youthful mother: "The little being who embarks on life needs another who is still young and full of zeal." Aurore described her experience of her grandmother's "solemn ways" as "like iron in the soul." When asked to play quietly, she felt that she was "being shut in a shoe box." Most tellingly Sand writes, "I was horribly afraid of becoming like her, and when I was with her, and she ordered me not to fidget or shout, I felt she was asking me to be dead."[24]

The tail end of the winter—February to April 1810—was spent in Paris, as promised. Mme Dupin's apartment was in the Rue Neuve-des-Mathurins. The rooms were filled with furniture salvaged from the Revolution. The walls were hung in sky-blue damask. There were rugs everywhere and fires in every grate. Aurore was amazed "by every aspect of this studied luxury." And it is the "studied" that is telling. Sand described her grandmother's tastes as "schooled." Mme Dupin wanted to form her granddaughter's discriminating judgement. She would comment on form, scale, composition, and colour. Aurore found her grandmother's friends equally, if not more, mannered and unnatural, and their ideas and views equally assumed and artificial. Aurore used her mother's term to refer to Mme Dupin's Parisian friends: they were the "old countesses."[25]

On the other hand, everything about Paris, seen through her mother's eyes, simply enchanted her: "The Chinese baths, with their hideous rocaille decorations and their stupid apes . . . the performing dogs . . . the toy shops, the print sellers and the bird sellers—they were the stuff of my delight and my mother, stopping before anything that caught my fancy, took pleasure in whatever I did and doubled my joy by sharing it."[26]

Aurore went out with her mother daily and delighted in her company, and in the city. But Mme Dupin's refusal to acknowledge Caroline, Aurore's half-sister, was a source of misery, and no doubt of incomprehension. After all, Hippolyte was also a half-sibling and back at Nohant they lived like brother and sister. How could Aurore have understood that her mother's illegitimate daughter and her father's illegitimate son belonged to different social classes? Caroline, who was about twelve years old at the time, even tried to make a clandestine visit to see Aurore at her grandmother's apartment. When Mme Dupin realized this, Caroline was summarily dispatched. Aurore heard Caroline weeping: "I heard a stifled, piteous sob, a cry out of the depths of a soul, which pierced my own soul. . . . It was Caroline; she was weeping, and she went away dismayed, crushed, humiliated, wounded in her natural self-esteem and in her innocent love for me." This is, of course, the perspective of the mature Sand; what Aurore responded to was an acute awareness of Caroline's misery: "I burst into tears and rushed to the door, but it was too late, she had gone. My maid was crying too, and she took me in her arms, urging me to hide my grief from my grandmother. . . . I only cried out despairingly for my mother and sister. . . . I was put to bed, and all night I sighed and moaned in my sleep."[27] On waking, she clasped her favourite doll to her, delightedly. The doll was a "little Negress." Suddenly remembering the night before and the agony of her separation from Caroline and her mother, and seeing the doll's wide smiling mouth and white teeth, Aurore was overcome with disgust at it and threw it violently across the room. Smitten by remorse and recognizing the idiocy of her reaction to her favourite doll, she then ran to pick her up and console her with maternal devotion. The episode then came to a climax in prodigious vomiting.[28] The complexities and ideologies of class could not have been understood by Aurore at the time, but they were profoundly *felt* and never forgotten.

Not long after the incident with Caroline and the doll, Aurore developed a high fever, and measles.[29] Worried at Aurore's pallor even after her recovery, Mme Dupin decided it was time to return to the country. Alarmed by Aurore's anguish at the thought of being separated once more, and perhaps permanently, from her mother, Mme Dupin invited Sophie-Victoire back to Nohant. Caroline was dispatched back to her boarding school, there being no question, as far as Mme Dupin was concerned, of her staying even temporarily with the rest of her family.

Back at Nohant, and no doubt increasingly aware of the complexities of her relationship with Aurore, Mme Dupin placed Aurore's education in the hands of Deschartres, who had been Aurore's father's tutor and who was, at the time, Hippolyte's. Deschartres looked like "a cad. . . . To complete the role he should have been illiterate, greedy and craven. But in fact he was learned, sober and madly brave."[30] The education she received was thus very much like that of both her father and her half-brother. Deschartres saw no reason to teach Aurore differently.

But although in many ways Aurore received a boy's education, the question is more than one of curriculum. Soon after arriving at Nohant, Aurore had been presented with a bouquet of flowers by a boy a few years older. The boy was Hippolyte, but it was some years before either he or she was aware that they were half-brother and -sister. Aurore was educated alongside Hippolyte, and from the moment of her arrival at Nohant she noticed his disappointment that she was "only a little girl." She soon demonstrated that she was quite as much "a hearty chap."[31] This made Deschartres's life easier too. He knew where he was with boys. He did, however, spare Aurore the physical violence he regularly meted out to Hippolyte.

Aurore learnt French and Latin, history and maths. These core subjects were supplemented by rather more feminine lessons: her grandmother taught her the elementary principles of music and introduced her to Gluck and Piccinni (whom her grandmother had known years earlier in Paris), and to airs by Leo, Hasse, and Durante: "These were simple, grand ideas, classical, calm forms." Her grandmother's musical tastes, as opposed to her tastes in the tangible, were "pure, severe, serious. . . ."[32]

Hippolyte was a far from model pupil. He was a great prankster and mimic, and Deschartres, if he caught him at one of his tricks, regularly threw things at him and beat him. Aurore admired Hippolyte's rebelliousness, and no doubt took considerable vicarious pleasure in it. His behaviour provided distraction for Aurore when her mother returned once again to Paris in the autumn.

Separation from her mother was a misery which swept over Aurore, then receded, in long-drawn-out movements, for years. Her mother's absence was an ache, and she longed for her. Just as daydreaming was regarded so differently by her grandmother and mother—by her grandmother as losing a grip on reality, while her mother saw it as innocent imaginative escape—so attitudes to physical closeness, to the appropriateness of human love manifest in physical intimacy, were also emblematic of the two older women's differences—and rivalry for Aurore's love.

At the age of seven, when Aurore saw, as she had so many times before at the end of a visit to Nohant, that her mother was packing, she was once again "terror-struck." Despite her imploring, despite her entreaties, her mother would leave the following morning. But they had agreed on a plan. Her mother would go to Orléans and find premises for a millinery shop. "Then I'll get everything ready in Paris, and write to you secretly . . . and come and fetch you. I'll announce my decision to your grandmama, and I won't take no for an answer: I'm your mother, and nobody can take away my rights over you!"[33] This was no more than the script of a romantic drama. But as the words were spoken, for the period of their utterance, they were no doubt meant. But Aurore knew her mother's capacity for fantasy, was aware of the limits of its truth, and of her mother's proneness to change her mind. She wanted something in writing, something akin to the formal commitment which her "rival mothers" had made. She wrote a letter, begged a reply, and left it in her mother's bed-room.

Seeing her mother reading the letter, and weeping, Aurore was aware that her mother's hopes, her brave fantasy, had turned into a "hesitation born of despair"; her mother begged her to forget her. Aurore could not. Her mother, then, would return to fetch her within three months. But Aurore, though only seven years old, had a faith in the written word which she did not have in the spoken. Already in bed that night, wondering what her mother might write, she knew what the outcome would be. She was filled with "doubt and despair"; "I wept so bitterly that my brain ached, and when day broke gloomy and pale, it was the first dawn I had ever seen after a sleepless night." Her mother had written nothing; "she had thought it best not to reply," Sand explained in her autobiography. There is a residual numbness in the bald simplicity of her pronouncement. The unwritten letters were something for which Sand would never forgive her mother. She had experienced the regret of betrayal. "I was beginning to suffer from a pain still deeper and more distressing than absence."

The winter of 1811–12 was again spent in Paris.[34] Aurore saw less of her mother, and of Caroline. She submitted to further aspects of her training. Her grandmother introduced her to a new friend, Pauline de Pont-carré, and the two girls, accompanied by Hippolyte, took dancing lessons. Hippolyte, showing no aptitude and obvious signs of resistance, was soon expelled from the class. Three times a week the two girls received lessons in dancing, painting, and writing.[35] This last involved being encased in an extraordinary machine, devised by the master himself, to ensure correct posture, thus facilitating a fine hand. Sand's manuscripts amply testify to its dismal failure.

As winter drew to a close Aurore returned to Nohant. Her mother followed: "The spring of 1811," she wrote in her autobiography, "was cloudless, and the proof thereof is that that year left me with no distinct memories."[36] But as the months passed, differences between Mme Dupin and Sophie-Victoire surfaced.

As a small child, Aurore had been allowed to sleep with her mother when she returned to Nohant for visits: "I was like a small bird nestling against its mother's breast; I seemed to sleep better there and to dream more beautiful dreams."[37] By the time she was eight or nine, this was forbidden by her grandmother. But Aurore's longing for her mother was too great. When she heard her mother come up to bed she would, she described, "tiptoe barefooted from my room to snuggle deep in my mother's arms. She did not have the heart to send me away, and she was happy too, to fall asleep with my head on her shoulder." On one occasion, however, they were found out. Julie, her grandmother's maid, "her *lieutenant de police*," "informed." From then on Aurore would no longer sleep with her mother. She was to experience, as so often in her childhood, the closeness of death: "I felt myself to be physically and morally bound to my mother by a . . . chain which my grandmother vainly tried to break, but only managed to tighten all the more around my chest to the point of choking me."[38] Looking back, Sand does not analyze her mother's feelings, but of Mme Dupin she wrote, "My grandmother claimed that it was neither healthy nor chaste for a girl of nine to sleep with her mother."[39] Physical love, like so much else, had a politics of its own.

Aurore and her grandmother travelled to Paris once a year and stayed a number of weeks. From December 1813 to January 1814, they were back in the capital. Aurore's mother stayed at Nohant for a brief period most years: that April 1814, she returned to the country. The following year was uneventful, except for the arrival at Nohant, of the officers of the Army of the Loire. When, that year, Napoleon made his extraordinary return from Elba and marched triumphantly on Paris, Aurore rejoiced with her mother. Her grandmother and Deschartres, on the other hand, were staunch Republicans. On 18 June 1815 Napoleon was defeated at Waterloo. Aurore mourned with her mother. She was eleven years old.

Nor did dramas of the historical moment pass Hippolyte by. On 19 March 1816 he signed up with the Third Regiment of the Hussars. By the autumn, Aurore's life had become still more restricted: she came down with a bad attack of whooping cough. She regretted her sex, and became increasingly rebellious. This may explain why, counter to her own beliefs, her grandmother arranged for Aurore to take her first communion, at La Châtre, on 23 March 1817. But the rites of the Church did not exercise the necessary degree of social control over her granddaughter.

Aurore's first years at Nohant had left her acutely aware of the apparently irreconcilable contradictions between the various ideologies to which she had been subjected, but she was, as yet, unable to re-create from them a substantial ideology of her own, in which she could believe, and which could guide and support her. Her worries, which threw her into periodic states of despair, were essentially those of faith and reason. Her mother's Catholic faith was absolute. Her grandmother's gods were Voltaire and Rousseau. More importantly, Mme Dupin fervently believed in Rousseau's contention that "what is magical" is a "lie." Her mother, on the other hand, fervently believed in the validity and need for the recognition of imaginative truth.

At Nohant Aurore read Perrault's tales for herself (in Paris her mother had read them to her). "Oh, what hours I spent with 'The Bluebird,' 'Tom Thumb,' 'The Donkey's Skin,' 'Belle Belle, or The Lucky Knight.' . . . I've never read them since, but I could tell each tale straight through, and I don't think anything in all one's intellectual life can be compared to these first delights of the imagination."[40] Aurore recognized that truth exists in different spheres and operates in different ways.

For some years Aurore was also comforted, and her behaviour no doubt calmed, by her faith in a divine being of her own invention: Corambé. Aurore's mysterious companion first came to her in a dream and is transformed, crucially, into both the eponymous hero of what she describes as the first of her imagined and unwritten, in any obvious sense, "childhood novels" and her private god. Corambé is the origin of what she describes as the beginning of both her "poetic life," her life as a writer, and her "moral life":

> Corambé was not, in truth, simply a character in a
> novel, Corambé was the form which my religious
> ideal had assumed and would long retain. . . . Pure
> and charitable like Jesus, shining and beautiful like
> Gabriel; but he also needed some of the grace of the
> nymphs and the poetry of Orpheus. Thus in form he
> was less austere than the Christian God, in sentiment
> more spiritual than those of Homer. And then I had to
> clothe him in women's clothes on occasion, because
> the person whom I had best loved and had best under-
> stood up until then was a woman, my mother. It was
> thus under the guise of a woman that Corambé often

appeared to me. In short, Corambé was without sex
and was clothed in all sorts of different disguises. . . .
He would become man or woman.[41]

Aurore's androgynous cross-dressing god and fictional hero died—and
simultaneously Aurore died one of her many childhood deaths—the day
the sanctuary which she had built was discovered by another child.
Corambé "no longer inhabited the place." Her ceremonies and worship
became "childish" and she was assailed by doubt; all this, "I had not taken
seriously myself." She destroyed the temple with as much deliberation as
had been devoted to its careful and laborious construction. "At the foot of
the tree I dug a hole and buried the garlands, the shells and all the natural
decorations, under the remains of the altar."[42] Corambé was interred and
left this world to join the other cherished dead in the damp, verdant earth of
Nohant.

For Sand the mature writer, what was significant was the necessary
identification of the origin of the writer's desire or even compulsion to be a
writer, which she identified as the mythical being who came to her first in a
dream and made her a writer. But the story flirts with parody. When Sand
later resurrected Corambé, the full artificiality of her invention is manifest.
We cease to believe in him fully:

> When I reached the age at which one laughs at one's
> own naïvety, I restored Corambé to his proper place,
> that is, I returned him, in my imagination, to my
> dreams; but he always occupies the centre of my
> dreams, and all the fictions that were later inspired by
> him always emanated from this main fiction.[43]

We "see through" Corambé as a complete and constant source of creative
inspiration. But his confused identity, his many disguises, his androgyny,
and the needs he fulfilled prevent us from losing faith in his significance for
Sand. He remains true—imaginatively.

Furthermore, his "death" occurred at a particular and highly significant moment in Aurore's late childhood, around the time of a frightening
interview with her grandmother. Mme Dupin's health had started to deteriorate, so there was a new urgency about attending to her fears for Aurore's
future. Her grandmother summoned her. She wanted to talk, and wanted
Aurore never to forget what she would hear. A reverberating echo of the

command "Remember this . . ." resonates in Sand's account of her child-hood. As she remembers being asked to remember, what is evoked is that terrifying sense of the power of other people's accounts, of other people's stories, of the way their "truth" has been encapsulated in words. Her grandmother had called her to her bedside—she had become bedridden. She feared Aurore's apparently uncritical commitment to her mother and where it might lead in the event of her own death. As Aurore arrived at her side she spoke: "Stay on your knees and listen to me carefully, for you have never heard what I am about to tell you, and you will never again hear it from my lips. Such things are said once in life, because they are never for-gotten; but if one does not know them . . . when they are true . . . one loses one's soul." The young Aurore then listened at the bedside as she was told the story of her grandmother's life, "then that of my father's; then . . . the story of my mother's life." Mme Dupin's intention was to suggest the degree to which Aurore's life was a continuation of theirs, that her life would be forever fused with the dead.

A fearful prominence, in her long account, was given to the story of Aurore's mother's life, which is told last: "My grandmama, exhausted by her long narration, beside herself, her voice choked, her eyes burn-ing . . . My mother, she said, was a fallen woman and a blind child who wished to throw herself into the abyss." There is a confused sense of the brutality of a forced, imagined retrospective abortion, displaced from mother to daughter in Sand's description of her own reaction to her grand-mother's story: "I had a huge internal wound. . . . If my mother was con-temptible, then I, the fruit of her womb, was also." Aurore's response to the violence which her father's mother had done to her own mother, the former prostitute "rescued" by her aristocratic father, was to die one of the many nightmarish deaths, at a moment of impotence, of which she tells in her *Story of My Life:* "I was dying. . . . I tried to interrupt, to get up, to run . . . but I could not. . . ." When she finally escaped she met the maid on the stairs: " 'Well, is it over?' she asked. 'Yes, it's over,' I said. 'Forever and ever and ever.' "[44]

The mature Sand explained that her grandmother "told the story of my mother's life—that is, what she thought she knew of it, or what, at the least, she understood of it. There I daresay she was without pity or insight, for the poor in the course of their lives know something of abandonment, of wretchedness, of calamity, which the rich cannot understand, and which they judge as the blind judge colour. All that she said was factually true, and grounded in circumstances whose very details admitted of no doubt."

What Sand the autobiographer is then at pains to explain are the myriad ways in which true facts can be constructed into subtly different stories—as every reader of biography appreciates. She accepts the "facts" of the story, but not its "whole truth." It is the manner in which her grandmother "revealed this terrible story" that Sand dwells on. What she regrets is that her grandmother overlooked "the *causes* of my mother's wretchedness: her abandonment and misery from the age of fourteen," the manner in which "rich men . . . ruin innocent girls," the "pitiless rigour of social opinion." "That story, so told," Sand writes, "would have seemed much more convincing."[45]

Aurore's interview with her grandmother also coincided—not surprisingly—with Aurore's final and complete metamorphosis into an "enfant terrible." Sand recounts a further interview with her grandmother:

> My child, you do not seem to have common sense. You have inherited an excellent intelligence from your father and your grandparents, but you do all in your power to appear an idiot. You could be attractive, but you take pride in looking unkempt. Your complexion is tanned, your hands are rough, your feet are quite out of shape in those clogs which you insist on wearing. You have no bearing, no grace, no tact. Your mind is becoming as deformed as your body. Sometimes you hardly reply when spoken to, and you assume the air of a bold animal that scorns human contact. Sometimes you chatter like a silly bird. You were once a charming girl . . . you mustn't now turn into a ridiculous young lady. You have lost your composure, your grace, your sense of what is appropriate. You have a good heart but a pitiful head. It is time to change all this. You need proper mentors, and I cannot find them here. So I have decided to place you in a convent, and we are going to Paris.[46]

This may well have been a fair description of the kind of young woman Aurore had become, but to hold Aurore responsible was a bit rich. It had, after all, been her grandmother's carefully calculated intention, early on, to bring Aurore up according to the precepts laid down in Rousseau's *Émile*. Admitting no class prejudice, as in his vision of things, Aurore had mixed freely with the Berrichon peasantry and she had had more companions belonging to that social group than any other. It was hardly surprising that she had assimilated its stories and ways of seeing the world, its expressions, and the perspective inherent in these, as well as aspects of its dress, gestures, and body mannerisms.

For a period Mme Dupin had abandoned the programme, but her attempts to tame Aurore had failed. There had also been periods of neglect when Mme Dupin had had less to do with her granddaughter. Mme Dupin's explanation for Aurore's manner of withdrawing, almost solipsistically, from company was that the child "scorned human contact," but it was also the response of an imaginative child. Aurore's "life-ache" encouraged her to escape into fantasy, to avoid the recognition that she was not truly loved as she yearned to be, unconditionally, and for herself, as she actually was. Her mother had all but abandoned her, and Mme Dupin had often demonstrated that she loved her only as a substitute for her father, and on condition that she *become* a particular kind of young woman. The conditions were not easy to fulfil.

While her criticisms of Aurore's bearing and manner were unreasonable, her decision to send Aurore to a religious institution was a blatant contradiction of everything she had taught. A Deist, she subscribed to a humanist faith which admitted no mystery. Furthermore, she despised the Church and all those institutions and positions subsumed within it. But Mme Dupin had chosen her convent carefully. The nuns were English, Irish, or Scottish, and the girls from the best Catholic families. Mme Dupin must have hoped that Aurore would assimilate the superficial outward deportment of her colleagues while remaining sceptical of the convent's dogma in matters of doctrine. But this was to fail to recognize Aurore's incapacity, and growing contempt, for compromise—and her continuing need to belong, and to be loved for herself.

When Mme Dupin announced her decision to Aurore, all that mattered to the child was that the plan would allow her to see more of her mother. But it was not into her care that she was about to be handed over. She was soon to be well and truly "cloistered."[47]

V

Still Water

"It is as a result of this tendency to separate the mind and the body that convents and places of ill repute have been necessary."

When Mme Dupin and her granddaughter arrived in Paris, in late November 1817, Aurore was thirteen years old. She still longed for her mother—and she hoped that Sophie-Victoire would save her from the fate outlined by her grandmother. Her mother would think the convent unnecessary and ridiculous. She would be moved by her daughter's continuing sense of loyalty to her. She would take her back. Sophie-Victoire was vociferous and railed against Mme Dupin's hypocritical decision: despising religious devotion, the absurd woman had nevertheless decided to commit her granddaughter to nuns. But in the midst of her litany of criticisms— and to Aurore's dismay—she announced that she wholeheartedly supported the decision.[1]

On 12 January 1818 Mme Dupin delivered Aurore to the convent, dressed in the regulation serge uniform, with her possessions packed in a small trunk. Aurore would spend two whole years in the convent. Twice a month the girls were allowed to visit their families, during the day, but Aurore often chose not to. For two unbroken years she slept every night in the convent: "It was truly a prison, but a prison with a large garden and plenty of company."[2]

The Couvent des Augustines Anglaises had been founded a good deal earlier than Sand claims. As its name suggests, it was a haven for English

Catholics.[3] Its architecture survived the storms of 1789 serving as a women's prison. Here both Mme Dupin and Aurore's mother had spent brief periods during the Terror.

When the moment of parting came, and as Mme Dupin made to leave, Aurore remained composed, afraid that any show of emotion would make the scene more difficult for her grandmother to bear, or so the mature Sand supposed looking back. The Mother Superior was more perspicacious, no doubt as a function of her very considerable and particular professional experience of young women. Mme Dupin, somewhat uncharacteristically, wept, assuming that Aurore's composure was a sign that her granddaughter felt no emotion at the moment of their parting. Seeing Aurore's expressionless face, her grandmother cried out: "Oh! How heartless you are, it is without regret that we are parting, I see only too clearly!"[4]

The Mother Superior witnessed the leave-taking and asked Aurore what she had said that had so moved her grandmother. Aurore replied that she had said precisely nothing. She had, it seems, developed considerable self-control. Or it may be that she was living more and more in a deliberately unresponsive way, as a form of self-protection. She existed in a state of emotional numbness, exhausted by the all too vivid melodramas of her early childhood and the invisible but powerful tensions of the subsequent years at Nohant. The Mother Superior's identification of that numbness led her to describe her new charge as "still water."[5] What the pedagogue and spiritual director recognized was that Aurore would go one way or the other, and become either saintly or devilish. Sand experimented, during those convent years, with both personae.

At some point soon after her arrival, a lengthy series of "resolutions" was drawn up by Abbé Prémord, one of the priests who served the convent. Aurore neatly copied out the lengthy document. There are few surprises: "Every day I will rise at a fixed time . . . affording sleep only the time necessary to maintain my health, and never staying in bed out of laziness. . . ."[6] Both as a child and throughout her life Sand needed very little sleep. Abiding by other prescriptions would prove very much more difficult: "I will diligently abstain from all vain daydreaming and aimless thinking," and, worse still, "I will never feed on any imaginative thought which, if the secrets of my heart were known, would make me blush." Equally predictable, although somewhat unnecessary within the convent: "I will always avoid finding myself alone with someone of the opposite sex; I will never allow the slightest familiarity, irrespective of their age or condition." And so on. Such were the abbé's recommendations. But as a member of a community, Aurore quickly came under the influence of the alternative ideologies of its younger members and, needless to say, soon exerted her own peculiar influence over her peers.

Aurore joined the "little class" which was presided over by the over-bearing Mlle D***.[7] "You seem to me to be a highly dissipated person," was her extraordinary assessment on meeting Aurore. At one point her dislike drove her to considerable physical violence which culminated in locking Aurore in a bath cubicle.[8] Passions ran high.

The inmates at the convent, those privileged girls of good families on both sides of the Channel, divided, as though predestined, into three groups: the *devoted*, the *meek*, and the *devils*.[9] It would have been quite out of character for Aurore ever to have belonged to the second, and initially it was towards the third group that she gravitated. During her first year she explains her bad behaviour simply as the outward manifestation of an inner "despair," or rather "sense of hopelessness."[10] But that she was also natu-rally attracted to the spirited members of this last fallen group also seems more than likely.

Mary Gillibrand, a lively Irish girl, quickly became a favourite.[11] She was only eleven years old, two years younger than Aurore, but the Irish girl was bigger and stronger. Sand describes her at length: "Her full voice, her frank, bold expression, her independent and indomitable character explain the surname she was given: *boy;* and though she was of course a woman, who was later fine-looking, she was not, in terms of character, of our sex." The manuscript version of this published text is still more reveal-ing of the mature Sand's desire to distinguish between gender and sex. "In terms of character" was originally "in heart and mind." Sand's description continues: "She was pride and sincerity incarnate, she had in truth a kind nature, her strength was wholly virile, her courage more than virile, she combined a rare intelligence, a complete absence of coquettishness, enor-mous energy, a profound contempt for everything false and feeble in soci-ety." Sand's description comes close to being one of her ideal of womanhood. Boyish as a girl, Mary develops into a beautiful woman retaining characteristics more frequently associated with men.

Aurore soon attracted Mary's attention. The two were obviously kin-dred spirits. Aurore's adventurousness, and still more her capacity imagi-natively to transform both herself and her surroundings for the sake of make-believe, were much stimulated by an environment ripe for romantic, even Gothic, interpretation. Aurore's reading at Nohant suggested the potential for outlandish adventures. She had read Mrs. Radcliffe, she had heard the Berrichon tales. The other girls drew on an impressive stock of Scottish and Irish stories. The inmates may have had little to read—of the sort they wanted—but the convent nurtured a strong and varied oral tradition: these were stories that "made your hair stand on end."[12]

And in Mary and the others she found her first audience—unless the Spanish rabbit counts. They responded to Aurore's creative games. The convent buildings were connected by a complex web of dark corridors. Here and there were doorways that had been mysteriously and inexplicably walled up. Some of the rooms had been abandoned, wholly deserted but for fragments of Gothic carving. The garden was surprisingly extensive and divided into sections, some tucked away and little frequented. Large chestnut trees provided dense shade in summer, and the jasmine and rose were peculiarly perfumed, the scent no doubt trapped by the high walls, covered with ivy which shut out most of the clamour of the city.

Aurore explored the garden on her first day, quick to realize its agricultural potential. Soon she became aware of the scope for adventure in and around the buildings and grounds and before long had became familiar with the plan of the entire convent. Possessed by the notion that—with comic improbability—more than a hundred years earlier a victim had been walled up somewhere within the convent, it was Aurore and Mary's responsibility, assisted by others, to find and free the involuntary anchorite. Aurore and her band roamed the dark maze of sometimes all but abandoned cellars and attics after midnight, when they could be sure that the nuns were sound asleep.[13]

Still more telling than the imaginative games were the parodic fragments that she wrote for her colleagues' amusement. There were mock confessions: "Alas! little Father Villèle, I have frequently smudged the ink, snuffed out the candles with my fingers, given myself indigestion with *beans* [a euphemism for flatulence?], as we said in the world in which I was brought up; I have scandalized the young demoiselles in my class because of my uncleanliness. . . . I slept during the catechism class and snored at mass. . . . I have made, this week, at least fifteen howlers in French and thirty in English; I burnt my shoes on the stove and I have exerted an unfortunate influence on the class. I have sinned, I have sinned, verily have I sinned. . . ."[14]

More peculiar, and scribbled inside the cover of an English exercise book, is this strange text:

This respectable and interesting book belongs to my worthy personage: Dupin, otherwise known as the illustrious Marquis de Sainte-Lucy, Commander-in-Chief of the Convent's French Army, great warrior, able Captain, intrepid soldier crowned with oak and laurel wreaths in combat, defender of the oriflamme.

Anna de Wismes is a little kitten. Isabelle Clifford is *charming*.

Down with the English! Let the English dogs die! Long live France! I don't like Wellington.

Interesting sheep, dear little urchins, I miss you terribly, and yet I am enchanted no longer to be in the bottom form. Good night.

To the English Ladies, 1818[15]

The Mother Superior was right: Aurore was busy experimenting with a primitive iconoclasm, beneath the still surface.

The predictable pattern of a rigid routine, the not unpleasant surroundings, and the company of girls her own age made life in the convent in many ways less demanding than life with her grandmother. She missed Nohant, and dreamt about it as a paradise from which she had been expelled, but while longing to be back there, she recognized that she was not now living with a melancholy which she supposed would return if she went back. When she was told by her grandmother that she would not be going home for the holidays, sadness and regret were tinged with relief. She was not yet ready, it seems, to reconnect with her childhood self and its emotions, with the past, with the dead.

On those rare occasions when she saw her grandmother or her mother, she returned to the convent more unsettled than happy. In their company

> my entire bitter past, my tormented present, my uncertain future, presented themselves to me once again. . . . At nightfall I was taken back to the convent. . . . I left behind me a world of emotions too strong for my age. . . . I would hear Mary's voice calling me impatiently . . . "Oh it is awful coming back, isn't it?" . . . I would say nothing. I could not under-

stand my own bizarre nature: I felt more at ease in the convent than with my family.[16]

At times she went out with family friends, relatives like the Villeneuves, sometimes to Uncle Beaumont's. But the experience was equally unsettling: "I would have to return at the very point when I was beginning to feel at ease."[17]

What she enjoyed were the distractions of playing with girls her own age. She masterminded the quest for the hidden involuntary anchorite. She also started to write more. Although, or because, the exchange of letters by girls was strictly forbidden, letter writing within the convent became very much the rage. These missives, Sand later wrote, were tender and innocent, and looking back, she wondered at the convent's exaggerated attitude to chastity. The girls were not allowed to walk in the gardens in twos, only in groups of three or more. At the time, neither she nor, Sand supposed, the other girls knew the reason for these "bizarre prescriptions."[18] Yet it was a love story that Aurore embarked on when she decided to write something more substantial than the fragments with which she had already experimented, and much more ambitious than the other girls' literary efforts: a novella of some hundred pages. Aurore presumably destroyed the manuscript. Looking back, and depending only on her memory of it, Sand was struck by a number of anomalies. The story told of a hero and heroine who meet in the country one evening, at the feet of a statue of the Madonna. They are strongly drawn one to another and the logic of the narrative suggests a developing love story. One of her convent friends, Sophie, had even suggested that this was the only direction in which the story could reasonably move. But as Aurore wrote, she realized that she was quite unable, through lack of experience, to describe the awakenings of love. Instead the hero and heroine, having survived all manner of no doubt quite unbelievable adventures, retreat, the former into the priesthood, the latter into a convent. What later struck Sand as odd was that she had no more experience of Christian devotion or mystery than of love. Sophie and another convent friend, Anna, proved a critical but important audience. They were willing to be brutally frank and declared the hero, Fitz Gerald, unbelievably boring and the heroine no more compelling. Undiscouraged, Aurore went on to write a second novel. This time it was a pastoral novel. Whether or not Sophie and Anna had the privilege of reading it Sand does not say, but Aurore herself deemed it still less successful than the first—and burnt it.[19]

Sand did not remember the period following the double failure of these novels as a period of sterility or noncreativity. She gave up novel writing but continued her interior epic, Corambé's poem. Fragmentary and necessarily lacking form, this interior monologue nevertheless constituted a continuing transformation of life and feeling into words. Writing, Aurore had decided, would never amuse her compared with "the infinite and reassuring pleasure that I had tasted composing without writing."[20]

But it was not only with the genres of supposedly romantic and pastoral fiction that Aurore experimented in the convent. If her fiction had, inadvertently, come close to self-parody, a satirical letter-journal she wrote for her grandmother was deliberately parodic, and based on daily convent life. Aurore both was familiar with everything about which she wrote and had a particular and mischievous perspective on her material. Mme Dupin was quite as critical an audience as the likes of Sophie and Anna and she thought Aurore's texts a triumph. Aurore's descriptions of the unpleasant and violent Sister D*** were burningly acerbic and very funny. No doubt Mme Dupin also delighted in what she would have seen as her granddaughter's healthy scepticism, even iconoclasm. But that Aurore wrote about convent life in the way she did suggests that she could never be fully part of the community to which Mme Dupin had entrusted her. What Mme Dupin required was that Aurore assimilate various outward signs while remaining a kind of conscientious objector in matters religious.

Letters sent out from the convent were censored—unless they were letters to the girls' families. Letters home, new girls were assured, would not be opened. Aurore trusted the Mother Superior and consigned her letters to the system rather than having her letter-journal delivered to her grandmother through the intermediary of servants, which would have been quite possible. The moment of betrayal was a formative one. For several days after reading the first mocking epistle the Mother Superior continued, having said nothing to Aurore, to open and read her letters to her grandmother. Aurore was then summoned to explain herself. What faith Aurore had in the Mother Superior drained away and was never restored. She would always retain a suspicion of those in positions of power.

Mme Dupin was apprised of the Mother Superior's discovery of the nature of Aurore's correspondence with her grandmother, and arrived at the convent for a meeting. The pragmatic solution was to move Aurore into the "big class," where she would no longer have much contact with the dreadful "Soeur D***," whose severity Aurore had described at length in her letters. But however pleased Aurore was with her promotion, she remained deeply disillusioned. What dismayed her was the recognition of the Mother Superior's "duplicity."[21] Elsewhere in her autobiography, in a somewhat light-hearted example, she nevertheless reveals the depths of her abhorrence of feminine deceit: "I have made an observation which seems to me sad: most women cheat at cards. . . . I wonder if this instinct of duplicity, which may be observed even in girls who do not play for stakes, comes from an inborn need to deceive, or rather from a ruthless, nervous desire to escape the laws of chance. I prefer simply to think that the moral education of women is incomplete." Nor are men exempt, but it is in love, rather than in games of cards or money, that society tolerates their dishonesty.[22] Aurore's early recognition of the Mother Superior's capacity for deception, combined with her grandmother's determination that Aurore not be unjustly punished, revealed to Aurore her grandmother's loyalty to her, and her high and dependable moral standards. When, sometime later, Aurore left the convent to return to Nohant she would gradually come to appreciate how very unusual and impressive her grandmother was.

In the meantime, with promotion into the higher class came a "cell."[23] This was small in every dimension and her bed was wedged under the low rafters of the roof. The decor was shabby, the little rug, the only comfort, was dirty and threadbare. The only fine item in the room was a harp that she had been given by her grandmother and on which she had permission to practise for an hour a day. She played very little but it served as a pretext for spending that stretch of time alone, and undisturbed. Aurore was easily stimulated by company, although she talked relatively little. Until she was allocated the little cell of her own, she had spent hardly any time alone. The relief of being able to withdraw to solitude impressed her forcibly. No doubt it is the first requirement for a writer's life to like, even need, considerable stretches of time alone.

She loved this "room of her own," her first writer's room, passionately. In *The Story of My Life* she writes, remembering the detail vividly:

> Although this poor cell was an oven in summer and literally an icehouse in winter . . . I loved it passionately, and I remember naïvely kissing its walls when I left, so attached to it did I feel. I could not say what world of daydreams seemed to me linked to that little dusty and miserable corner. It was only there that I found myself and that I belonged wholly to myself. During the day I thought of nothing; I watched the

clouds, the branches of the trees, the flight of the swallows. At night I listened to the distant and confused rumours of the great city which drifted in like an exhalation of breath. . . .[24]

What Sand remembered of her time in her little rooftop cell were periods of calm contemplation. Unseen, and quite alone, she listened and watched the rhythms of life around her. The view from her little window was magnificent, the eye drawn out from the gardens of the convent towards the fine blue skyline of the city. Aurore's daily withdrawal from the peculiar complexities and petty excitements of the community became "a precious hour of solitude and reverie."[25] All her life, whatever the excitements of the company staying at Nohant or society elsewhere, Sand always chose to withdraw for a period each day, often under pressure to write for publication, but also no doubt because it was time for the reflection and contemplation that was necessary to her emotional and nervous equilibrium.

Her nicknames in the convent were "Madcap" (in English) and "Calepin," the French for notebook.[26] The first underlines the degree to which in company she behaved with subversive exuberance; the second suggests that this overexcited behaviour was balanced by periods of withdrawal, and writing. When she first arrived at the convent there was more of the former in her. By the time she left, she was far more the latter.

Aurore was much admired by the members of her group who enjoyed her nerve and energy, but that ache whose origin was in some way bound up in her estrangement from her mother did not go away. Her relationship with her grandmother remained in many ways strained. If Aurore was oversensitive to Mme Dupin's criticisms, still she wanted to please her grandmother. But there remained, or Aurore feared that there remained, an essential stumbling block to her grandmother's full and unconditional acceptance of her. As she writes in her autobiography: "She adored me, she lived only for me, but it seemed as though there was something in my simplicity, and in this sad absence of feminine charm, something antipathetic to her that she could not overcome, perhaps a kind of original sin which smelt of the people despite all the care taken."[27]

Sand believed that she had been a late developer. She spoke comparatively late, and felt that her body and mind had somehow failed to grow in parallel: "My physical strength developed quickly; I had the air of a young lady, but my dull mind, which was quite turned in on itself, made me a child, and far from helping me to sleep on in this state of grace, people tried to make a person of me."[28] Mme Dupin, fearing that she herself would not live much longer, was anxious to find Aurore a husband, to establish her in society, so that she would not fall under her mother's influence. Mme Dupin continued to try to instil in her a contempt for her maternal family and their plebeian milieu.

During those convent years, it seemed to Aurore that her mother cared little whether or not she remained a part of her life. Sand sums up her mother's attitude with a succinctness that suggests accuracy: "My mother seemed to have abandoned me to my silent and miserable struggle. She always made fun of high society, caressed me a good deal, admired me like a prodigy, but was scarcely preoccupied by my future. It seemed that she would have accepted for herself a future of which I no longer formed an essential part. I was distressed by this kind of abandonment, after the passion she had excited in me as a child. She no longer took me with her to her house. I saw my sister once or twice every two or three years."[29]

Sand appeals to the inadequacy of her relationship with her mother, or her mother's failings, as an explanation for her first strong feelings of love for another woman, to whom she was drawn by a stronger pull than that of companionship. One of the nuns, Sister Alicia, was the object of her desperate longing. Looking back, Sand claims fully to understand her passion for Alicia: "I needed a wise mother. . . . I needed to cherish someone and to place that someone, in my day-to-day thoughts, above all other beings, to dream of perfection, calm, strength, justice, in that someone; to venerate in fact an object superior to me, and to follow in my heart a strict rule, for something like God or Corambé. This something took on the serious serene features of Sister Alicia. She was my ideal, my saintly love, she was my chosen mother."[30] Sister Alicia, it seems, willingly adopted Aurore, while playfully describing this adoption as a torment to be borne stoically. She was disciplined and observant in all aspects of community life, but also good-humoured and not without a sense of fun. When scolded for bad behaviour one day, Aurore declared that if she were to behave better Alicia would think about her less and pray for her less conscientiously. That would be a loss not worth contemplating. Alicia's response to Aurore was indulgent: she offered friendship and guidance and thus perhaps prevented Aurore's love from becoming too desperate, too passionate. The mutual love that they developed—however different—greatly enriched Aurore's life in the convent. And however limited their physical contact, this was Aurore's first passionate relationship, based on closeness, understanding, and love. Intimacy of this kind was, Sand believed, one of the great gifts offered by a life in community and it threw into relief the bleakness of her relationship with Sister D***. Both were part of the experience of a religious education:

> The details [of my account of my life in the convent] offer certain insights which more than one person of my sex will recognize as sometimes the good, sometimes the bad effects of a religious education. I will report them wholly uncensored and, I hope, with complete sincerity of both mind and heart.[31]

Sand described her love for Alicia as a "gentle love."[32] What she craved was a burning passion. From her seat in the chapel Aurore had a good view of a painting that hung behind the choir stalls, which she attributed to Titian. It depicted Jesus in the Garden of Olives fainting in the angel's arms. The painting, which she claimed not yet to understand, nevertheless made a deep impression on her. Contemplating the mysteries of the image, she felt her first intimations of religious or mystical experience: "There was only one moment in the day when I could just about make out the detail, and that was only in winter when the setting sun cast a ray on the angel's red robe and the bare white arm of Christ. The shimmering of the glass made this fugitive moment quite overwhelming, and at that instant, even though I was not yet devout and thought I never would be, I always felt an indescribable emotion." Of the painting's iconography Sand wrote, "I had come not so much to understand it as to sense its meaning."[33] Her faith, sometimes strong, sometimes so weak as barely to make its presence felt, was to become a matter not of rational or intellectual enquiry but of felt experience in which the aesthetic and the emotional played significant parts. Reading the *Lives of the Saints,* Aurore became fascinated by great lives, especially those lived in terrible suffering, and Christ's agony became a special preoccupation. Again the Titian functioned as a stimulus towards faith: "It was summer, the setting sun no longer lit it up at the hour of prayer, but the object of my contemplation no longer needed to be visible to my eye, but to the mind's eye. . . . I questioned . . . the grandiose and confused images in my brain, sought the meaning of the Agony in the Garden, the secret of Christ's willing acceptance of such terrible suffering. Tears welled in my eyes, and furtively I wiped them away, ashamed that I was moved without knowing why."[34]

However archetypally adolescent aspects of Aurore's religious experience may be, her grandmother's attitudes and teaching prevented her from assuming that this experience could be interpreted as evidence of faith. She had been equally impressed by the religious life of Saint Augustine. "It is," Sand later wrote, "a story that bears the stamp of such sincerity and enthusiasm"; it was particularly revered in the English convent. Having read Saint Augustine's life, she returned again to the Gospels. However, as she writes at length in *The Story of My Life:* "My grandmother had so successfully conspired to make the miracles seem ridiculous to me, had so often repeated Voltaire's quips about the demons cast into the herd of swine, and, in sum, had put me so firmly on my guard against religious conviction, that I resisted out of habit, and remained unmoved when I reread the story of the Agony in the Garden and the Crucifixion."[35]

Yet, lingering in the convent chapel one evening, she experienced a more decisive mystical moment. She had been drawn to the chapel in a quite different mood, intent on mocking, she later wrote, "an old hunchback . . . hastening dwarfish and deformed in the shadows, more like a witch running about during her witching hour than a wise virgin!"[36] Time passed and Aurore forgot the hunchback, who, with others, disappeared. A strong awareness of sensory experience is written into Sand's account of what followed: "The fragrance of honeysuckle and jasmine drifted in on a cool breeze. Lost in the vastness of the night, a star twinkled in the window frame and seemed to watch me attentively. The birds sang. There was a stillness . . . a charm . . . a mystery . . . a gathering of spirit . . . that I never dreamed could be." A little later, and quite alone in the building, unaware of time and space, she felt her "being begin to tremble, and a flickering like a white light passed," seeming to envelop her. And she thought that she heard a voice whispering "*Tolle Legge,*" the words Saint Augustine had heard. But she was alone. Despite the strength and extraordinary nature of the moment, Aurore harboured no illusions. She did not believe that the experience had been miraculous, but rather that it had been a hallucination. Nevertheless, she felt that some kind of faith had taken hold of her "by the heart." What she felt committed to was a liberal and humane Christian faith: "I felt that I loved God, that my mind accepted fully this ideal of justice, tenderness and holiness which I have never doubted since then, but which until then had not touched me."[37]

She had been freed to reconsider the matter of faith as a whole being. Her heart had been deeply moved, her emotions deeply stirred. The evening had been beautiful and her sensory awareness of it acute. Intellectually she accepted certain Christian principles. These matters—aesthetic, sensory, emotional, and intellectual—had struck her at once and visited her whole responsive being. The parts added up to a single experience of being embraced by, and embracing, the love of God.

Aurore's life in the convent was, needless to say, transformed by the experience. She became absurdly pious and subscribed to what she later described as a "puerile and narrow orthodoxy."[38] She went as far as to adopt quite extreme forms of bodily chastisement and lived in a state of apparent spiritual ecstasy. She decided that she had a vocation. But the death of one of the convent sisters, Mother Alippe, quickly shook her out of her state of mystical rapture. Actual physical suffering, and death, suddenly struck her as terrifying. In particular she was deeply disturbed by the behaviour of one of the other sisters, Elisa, and her response to Mother Alippe's death. Elisa had been no closer to Alippe than the others, but became hysterical during the services following the death. Apparently, while Aurore and the other girls had not been aware of Mother Alippe's suffering, Elisa, whose cell was divided from the older sister's by no more than a thin partition, had heard everything: "Throughout the night she [Elisa] had, so to speak, participated in her suffering. She did not miss a single word, a single moan of the dying, and the final death-cry had aroused a vicarious reaction on her sensitive nerves."[39]

Christ's agony, despite its pictorial presence about the convent, had, no doubt, remained something of an abstraction. Now it had become vivid. Elisa had witnessed Alippe's suffering and Aurore had witnessed Elisa's. Aurore became depressed. She began to doubt that she was worthy of a vocation. She was haunted by the idea that "many are called but few are chosen."[40] She was rescued from this slippery slide of self-loathing and self-doubt by her humane Jesuit confessor, Abbé Prémord, who may or may not have been in love with her. He was to become her spiritual adviser and close friend, and he remained loyal and devoted for years to come. Aware that Aurore's self-punishment was quite inappropriate and unhealthy, he required her, by way of atonement for her alleged and multiple sins, to play freely and happily again with her contemporaries.[41] This was no easy penance as she was quite out of the habit of living like the other girls, but gradually she settled back into a more balanced way of life.

She also discovered a talent of which she had hitherto been scarcely aware. Her activities as an actor-manager of the convent theatre inaugurated a role that she was to play throughout her life and which brought her enormous pleasure and satisfaction.

The convent theatre was created from the first-form classroom which gave onto the garden. The spectators, during fine weather, were presumably seated under the shade of the big trees outside, while the actors played in the classroom in front of the large French windows. As news of the impressiveness of Aurore's plays spread in the convent, the Mother Superior announced that she wanted to see a full performance and that the girls would be allowed to stay up late if need be. Aurore's colleagues demanded that she invent a play of at least six acts! Sand remembered the responsibility as an onerous one:

> The Mother Superior had to be made to laugh, the most earnest members of the community had to be made merry; and yet things could not go too far. Some small moment of thoughtlessness might be declared scandalous and the whole theatre closed. How despairing my companions were! If I only bored my audience, the theatre could equally be closed on the grounds that it created too much chaos in the evening's recreation and disruption of study during the day, and the reason would have been legitimate; it is certain that the distractions during the day were making a good few heads dizzy, especially in the first class.[42]

Fortunately, Aurore had an author up her sleeve and a play which she remembered well and felt confident she could successfully bowdlerize for her peculiarly sensitive audience. Molière was, of course, strictly forbidden in the convent. On the other hand, Aurore knew that no one in the audience had actually read, far less seen, a Molière play. This meant that she could be confident that they would be entertained by the novelty. "Never," Sand boastfully writes in her autobiography, "within nuns' living memories, had there been so much hearty laughter." The Molière she had chosen was *Le Malade imaginaire* (*The Hypochondriac*). Aurore was somewhat hypochondriacal herself; or at least there is often a correspondence between her periods of unhappiness and anxiety, and illness. Her peculiar sensitivity, combined with her capacity for depriving herself of sleep during difficult and unhappy periods of her life, did make her ill. In any case, *The Hypochondriac* was one of her favourite plays, and theatre would become a lifelong source of entertainment at once serious and fun, in which Sand would generally participate as both producer-manager and actress, being both herself and someone else, sufficiently outside to appreciate the art and artistry, then inside, caught up in the wonder of make-believe. The relationship between health and happiness would equally remain a lifelong interest. Whatever her psychosomatic or hypochondriacal propensities, she remained fascinated all her life by the possible relationships between the psychological, or psychiatric, and the physical. A few years later she would write what are essentially the basic ideas of psychoanalysis into her fiction as cures for apparently physical ailments.[43]

Aurore's plays became a welcome part of convent life and for a period the whole community was drawn together by the common enterprise of staging them. But all this came to a temporary end when political life outside the convent impinged on the gaiety. In February 1820 the duc de Berry was assassinated.[44] The sisters were moved by the recognition of the precarious position of the monarchy: it was only the birth, the following September, of the Duke's posthumous son that guaranteed the continuance of the Bourbon line. On hearing of the assassination the convent went into mourning, and for days the community went about its business in virtual silence. Gradually spirits lifted.

One of the more immediate effects of the assassination was to allow for the passing of increasingly repressive and discriminatory laws. The left began to flirt with revolutionary movements. No doubt this further confirmed Mme Dupin's thoughts that it would soon be time to take Aurore back to the country.

She arrived in Paris within days of the murder. It seems that Aurore's demeanour was now more to her grandmother's liking, but there was a new bone of contention: Aurore's desire to take the veil. Initially when Mme Dupin heard of this she had assumed that it was no more than a phase that would quickly pass. But when she saw Aurore looking so well and happy but still quietly determined to take her vows, she realized that she had been sorely mistaken. She decided, quickly and resolutely, to remove Aurore from the convent and take her back to Nohant.[45] For Aurore this was a terrible proposal that came at the very moment when she had begun properly to find herself, and to live more purposefully: "This news struck me like a bolt of lightning, in the middle of a period of more perfect happiness than I had ever tasted before. The convent had become my paradise on earth. I was there as neither a boarder nor a nun, but something in between, with complete freedom within an environment that I loved, and which I could not leave even for a day without regret."[46]

Place, and stability of place, mattered to Sand throughout her life. The Couvent des Augustines Anglaises had become a safe haven in which she had gradually learnt to live as a whole person. She had been accepted, was admired by the younger girls and respected more and more by the nuns. Most thought that her intention to take the veil was an appropriate one. Only the humane Jesuit and the dear Alicia remained as yet unconvinced. They knew her best and made her promise not to make any foolhardy promises to God—for the time being. Her grandmother, they knew, intended that she would marry. If, they advised, in two or three years' time she was still unmarried and still intent on pursuing a vocation, then she was to return to them. But only then.[47]

The convent had been Aurore's home for a little more than two years, but she had learnt a great deal about women, about religious community, about faith and doctrine, about piety and pleasure. Her own mixed background combined with her astuteness had given her insights into hierarchical institutional structures, into power and its abuse. She had witnessed the human capacity for blatant hypocrisy and deceit. She had also learnt about love—and commitment. She had lost some of her idealistic vision of the life of religious communities, and none of her idealism in relation to romantic love. A good deal of what she had come to understand would be written into her fiction, with a subtlety that allowed for all the contradictions that she had witnessed, and been part of.

Leaving the convent, she felt heartbroken, but as always she successfully disguised her sorrow. She had had four weeks to prepare for the moment of departure, and when the time came she left as composed—outwardly—as she had been on arrival almost two and a half years earlier. "I had to hide from my grandmother, who would have suffered mortally, the mortal regret I felt at having to separate myself from so numerous and charming objects of my tenderness: my heart was broken."[48] Aurore had matured during her years in the convent and had depended on friends, rather than her family. The love and advice of the sisters, and of Abbé Prémord, had guided her. On leaving, she was concerned not to cause her grandmother suffering, and amid numerous inherent contradictions, she still longed to be found acceptable in her sight. But Mme Dupin's health was deteriorating, and her reason would soon come and go. The months ahead were to test Aurore to the limit.

VI

The Fear of Freedom and the Lure of Suicide

"He who holds his horse back thwarts it . . .
and denies himself one of the most striking sensations . . .
of touching death and escaping."

On 12 April 1820 Aurore left the Couvent des Augustines Anglaises. While preparing to leave Paris, Aurore hoped, as she had so many times before, that her mother would accompany her back to Nohant. When she asked, her mother's response was direct—and cruel: "Certainly not. I shall return to Nohant only when your grandmother is dead."[1] Nor did she want Aurore to stay with her in Paris. For the first time in Aurore's life she acknowledged her fear of her mother's "exaggerations," and recognized her unpredictability as instability. She sensed, but kept hidden, a terrifying "secret dread" of her, that otherwise absent mother for whom she had longed with such constancy.[2] The deep ache that she had always suffered would not be cured, nor even soothed. The balm was her mother, and her mother wanted to remain out of sight, out of reach, at least for the time being.

Her convent years had been "a kind of rest in the middle of the war to which I had been subjected"; the convent had been "neutral territory."[3] Now she was back on the battlefield. And this time a third unknown and unknowable "enemy" had joined her grandmother and mother on the scene of action, under Mme Dupin's orders. How could she equip herself and make ready to do battle against what could, at this stage, be no more than an abstract? "Who then is this husband, this master, this enemy of my wishes and hopes?" Just as Mme Dupin had demanded that Aurore be perfectly brought up so as "to console" her grandmother for Maurice's violent death, it was now Aurore's *duty* to accept a husband before her grandmother's death: "My girl, you *must* marry quickly . . . because I feel that I shall soon depart. . . . Consider, I will end my days appalled and despairing if I leave you without a guide and without support in this life."[4] Emotional blackmail was a forte—which she believed it her right to exercise.

But Aurore was older, and stronger. And her grandmother was weaker. Although she recognized that her formal education had come to an end, she knew that she still had a great deal to learn. Back at Nohant Aurore took charge of her own education. She read widely and voraciously in her grandmother's library.

Abbé Prémord had not abandoned her; instead he continued to nourish a more reasonable faith. "Read the philosophers," he would encourage; "all are powerless against faith."[5] The intellectual and spiritual journey on which he suggested it was her duty to embark was to prove as terrifying, indeed life-threatening, as that dangerous journey to and from Madrid which she had survived as a child.

Mme Dupin was older and much frailer, she had considerable respect for Aurore and became, in many ways, an ideal tutor. Her authoritarian, dogmatic, and judgemental manner changed and she became instead an intelligent sounding board, listening to Aurore's ideas and willing to engage in wide-ranging discussions.

The return to Nohant was a return to spring, to the lure of hope, but also of melancholy.[6] Aurore missed the convent and wrote to her friends there. She also continued her jottings in the little leather-bound notebook. Her letters speak of suffering and tears. The same self-conscious sorrowing is written into the fragments of private reflection, sometimes in English, out of some sense of loyalty to the English nuns at the convent. The influence of the English Romantics is blatant: "*Written at Nohant . . . at the setting of the sun, 1820.* Go fading sun! . . . Evening descends to bring melancholy on the landscape. With thy return, beautiful light, Nature will again find mirth and beauty, but joy will never comfort my soul. . . ."[7]

Mme Dupin was aware of Aurore's loneliness and the depressing effects of living in the presence of her own worsening condition. She continued to fear Aurore's contemplative moods.

Mme de Pontcarré and her daughter Pauline were invited to Nohant and stayed for most of August and September 1820. But the distractions of music, of piano duets, and even of little performances of comic operas failed to lift Aurore's spirits. Nevertheless, she took her duties seriously: on 15 August she and Pauline performed a short play to celebrate Mme Dupin's birthday.

The strong tonic Aurore needed was soon to be prescribed by Hippolyte when he came home for a three-month period of leave. He arrived in September—just as her father had, to the little apartment in Paris years earlier—got up in his glorious hussar's uniform. The atmosphere was, as it had been by Maurice Dupin, quite transformed. Hippolyte's extravagant bravado, his compulsion for risk-taking, his desire to court physical sensation before all else were mesmerizing, and addictive. His arrival was life breaking in. The rhythms of Nohant, the pace, accelerated. Aurore's relatively sedentary existence was replaced by intense physical activity. Thinking was relegated to second place. With Hippolyte came a sense of excitement, of possibilities, of both control—and risk:

> On horseback it is as though you are reborn, you come back to life. It is then that you contemplate, that you see nature, because on foot, always occupied by the thought of not tripping, looking always ahead of yourself, you cannot fix on, focus on, the horizon. . . . It is on horseback, at a pace, that you can better dominate the landscape and that it appears more beautiful. It is at a gallop that thoughts leave their usual courses and are displaced elsewhere, so to speak. . . . If a difficulty, a danger, presents itself to you, it's bad luck for anyone afraid of braving it. He who holds his horse back thwarts it, annoys it, loses balance and denies himself one of the most striking sensations that one can experience, that of seeing, touching death and of escaping.[8]

Under Hippolyte's instruction Aurore broke in her new horse, Colette. The theoretical foundation of Hippolyte's equestrian method was seductive in its simplicity, and reductive in its extremes: "It all comes down to two things: falling off, and not falling. Everything else follows."[9] No doubt there was a good deal of their father in Aurore's half-brother and, of course, in Aurore. The horse that Hippolyte rode alongside Colette, now disciplined and responsive, was the grandson of Leopardo "the indomitable," the horse that had thrown and killed their father. There is something of the superstitious gamble in this. Together, half-brother and half-sister challenged the power of history to repeat itself. Hippolyte was encouraging Aurore to ride roughshod over the unhappiness of the past, to ride away from recent history. She took to wearing a man's cap, partly to keep the hair out of her eyes, so as to allow her to ride faster and to take greater risks. She rode cross-saddle and was exhilarated. The attitude of her two grandchildren was shared by Mme Dupin. When asked how she could bear to see them riding as they did when their father had been killed on horseback, she replied with an anecdote. There was a burgher and a sailor. The burgher asks the sailor why it is that he sails if his ancestors have all perished at sea. The sailor replies with a question: where is it then that the burgher's ancestors have died? How is it then, the sailor replies to the burgher's answer, that the burgher can bring himself to sleep in a bed?[10] Mme Dupin believed, as Sand was later to write, that "the object of life is life." Aurore, who had been reading Shakespeare, compared Hippolyte's approach—somewhat pretentiously—to that of Hamlet; what it amounted to was "To be or not to be."[11]

Summer moved relentlessly towards autumn and then winter. Mme Dupin's death could not be far away. Together Aurore and Hippolyte, and their mounts Colette and Pépé, jumped wide ditches and high hedges, rode across open fields and through dense woods. Aurore experienced a resurrection. For some years she had attended to the spirit and the mind. Now she no longer punished her physical being—but enjoyed it. But as Christmas approached, Hippolyte's period of leave came to an end and Aurore was abandoned once again to the company of her infirm grandmother and Deschartres, who was terrified by the thought of Mme Dupin's death. Hippolyte had, however, brought about a physical and psychological liberation that Aurore recognized; and the complexities and mysteries of incestuous love would later become a recurrent, if often submerged, concern of Sand's fiction.

To some extent the frenetic physical activity she had enjoyed had allowed her to escape herself. She had been reawakened to the exhilarations of physical, sensory, and sensual experience that had been so important to her as a child. But the physical freedom that she experienced simultaneously served to throw into relief the degree to which she felt trapped in intellectual and theological impasses. That winter she turned to books. Throughout that year she maintained, with little respite, the same breathtaking pace in her reading that she had enjoyed in her riding: the *Vie des Saints* and Gerson's *Imitation de Jésus Christ* and *Le Jérusalem délivré* comforted and inspired her, but she also read Chateaubriand, Shakespeare, La Bruyère, Molière; *Hamlet* and Byron's writing were the "crowning works of disenchantment, started by the moralists." She struggled with the classics, with philosophers: Aristotle, Bacon, Bossuet, Condillac, Franklin, even Leibniz, Locke, Mably, Montaigne, Montesquieu, Pascal, reading attentively the passages marked by Mme Dupin; many of these texts were proscribed by the Church but they were in Mme Dupin's library.

Sand does not claim, in her autobiography, to have made much sense of her reading, but she responded to a great deal, sometimes moved, sometimes suspicious, sometimes critical, sometimes outraged; she formed strong views. Montaigne failed to understand, or, worse, despised, women. Leibniz's ideas about the "unities," about a "pre-established order," fascinated her. She read the great poets: Dante, Milton, Pope. Rousseau had a profound effect, which she compared to her response to Mozart, "the highest point in my spiritual quest."[12] The more she read, however, the greater was her sense of intellectual inadequacy. In the company of Deschartres, who was explicit, and Mme Dupin, whose criticisms were generally implicit, she was made aware of the contradictions in her thinking, of her intellectual limitations. She was forced to recognize the truth in Deschartres's "favourite expression," which described with typical bluntness the "crass ignorance" that was the legacy of her convent education.[13] Motivated by a sense of loyalty to the sisters and a feeling of shame (mixed with a characteristic intellectual curiosity), she read a good deal in secret so as to be able to demonstrate knowledge that might be attributed to them. During the winter of 1820–21 she established essentially what was to become the working pattern of most of her adult years. For the first time in her life she assumed responsibility for someone else, caring for her grandmother's well-being as her health continued to decline. She combined, as she would for so much of her life, looking after a dependent or partially dependent person with thinking, reading, and writing.

In the late evening, after everyone had gone to bed, she would read, and write, until the early hours of the morning. At some point that year she discovered snuff and quickly took to it to fight off tiredness and retain mental alertness. She slept for only a few hours and returned from a walk or ride in time to breakfast with her grandmother. Much of the day would be spent at her bedside, reading aloud to her, talking, or simply keeping her company, her grandmother dozing while she drew, or painted, or read.

One of the books from which she read to her grandmother was Chateaubriand's *Génie du Christianisme* (*The Genius of Christianity*), a work whose overarching claims Mme Dupin could not accept. But there were passages, turns of phrase, moments of insight, which she revered. For Aurore, intimations of Chateaubriand's fundamental vision, his integrated philosophy, provoked a crisis. How tempted she was by a Christian vision that emphasized the life-embracing, rather than the life-denying. The ideas he explored were to circulate in her mind, to come and go, enticing her to renounce her dogmatic faith, tempting her to believe in something very different, something that would liberate her. Chateaubriand's ideas, and his manner of expression, haunted her throughout that year— and beyond.

In January 1821 she was reading aloud when her grandmother interrupted her. Aurore closed the book at a page which, she would write, "marked a moment of profound pain in my life." Her grandmother's mind had become confused. Suddenly she accused Aurore of talking of "the dead, of a shroud, of bells, of tombs."[14] Mme Dupin had been dreaming. Regaining her mental equilibrium, she then spoke, quite unexpectedly, about a marriage proposal that she had received on Aurore's behalf. Aurore was frightened by her grandmother's confused state, and appalled by the idea of marriage. Mme Dupin went on to describe a man fifty years old, immensely rich, a general. He had, Mme Dupin no doubt felt it her duty to add, a sabre wound right across his face.

He was unconcerned, Mme Dupin continued, about the matter of a dowry and was willing to marry on only one condition: that Aurore never again see her mother. What had her grandmother decided on her behalf? What had been her response? "I know that if I asked you to sever your relations with your mother I would outrage your heart, and your conscience. Have no fear. Never again will a like matter arise."[15]

Mme Dupin no longer presumed to see Aurore's future in the way she had until this moment. She had come to recognize Aurore's courage, her discipline, and her growing intellectual grasp, her integrity. She was no longer afraid that after her death Sophie-Victoire would dominate Aurore absolutely. To some extent, Mme Dupin overestimated Aurore's independence. That evening Aurore reflected on her grandmother's new confidence in her, which was a form of respect, and bound up with something more like love. By accepting, even admiring, Aurore's sense of loyalty to her mother, and by protecting her from a marriage which would have been a lifelong source of regret, Aurore felt that her grandmother had allowed her "to breathe for the first time." "Finally," Sand would write, "I could reunite and conflate my two rival mothers in the same love. . . . I was afraid of nothing. . . . For the first time I was optimistic."[16]

But the moment of emotional reconciliation was soon followed by an intellectual and spiritual crisis. In February 1821 she was again reading Chateaubriand. Until she had encountered his *Genius of Christianity* it had been Gerson's *Imitation of Jesus Christ* that had been her "guide" and she returned regularly to the copy which had been given to her and inscribed by Sister Alicia. Sand quotes from it, not entirely accurately, in her autobiography: "Abandon yourself, destroy yourself, despise yourself; demolish your reason, confuse your judgement; flee the noise of human speech. Crawl on your belly and make yourself dust beneath the Law of the Divine Mystery; love nothing, study nothing, know nothing, possess nothing, neither in your hand nor your head. Become a dispersed and prostrated abstraction within the Divine Abstraction; despise humanity, destroy nature; make yourself a handful of ash, and you will be happy. To possess everything, you must abandon everything." Looking back, she describes Gerson's work as "at once the most sublime and stupid book, one that can make saints, but will never make a man";[17] or, she might have added, a woman. There is a degree of contrivance about Sand's use of these two books as antithetical works: "On the one hand, the absolute annihilation of intellect and sentiment for the sake of personal salvation; on the other, the development of the mind and heart for the sake of a communal religion."[18] The matter is more complicated, but the contrast serves to dramatize extreme opposing tendencies, and provides an insight into her own sense of the pain of being pulled in two quite different directions. The visions of Gerson and Chateaubriand, she knew then, were fundamentally irreconcilable.

The moment of crisis coincided with another: "At seven o'clock in the morning Deschartres came into my room, and as my eyes opened I saw the sadness in his. 'Your grandmother is lost,' he said. 'She wanted to get up in the night. She suffered an apoplectic and paralytic attack. She fell and was unable to rise. Julie has just found her, on the ground, cold, immobile, and out of her mind. She is now in bed, warmed, and she has gained some animation; but she understands nothing and is incapable of the slightest movement. . . . I have sent for Dr. Decerfz. I am going to bleed her. Come quickly and help me.' "[19]

At the very moment that Aurore was beginning to understand her grandmother's "complicated nature," to accept her faults as "excesses of virtue," "we changed roles. . . . I felt for her a tenderness in my entrails which resembled the solicitudes of a mother."[20] The mutual respect and degree of reciprocal understanding that had been briefly established would have allowed for free and open exploration of so much that Aurore longed to discuss. Above all she needed her grandmother's wisdom in order to fathom "the terrible consequences for real life" which Chateaubriand's vision had made her recognize. His ideas were "terrible" only in the sense that they came into direct conflict with the Christian vision that she had largely assimilated at the convent. They were also wonderfully liberating ideas. But she felt that her decision to renounce one doctrine for another required further thought. In particular these were questions that she wanted to talk through with her sage, if fragile, grandmother: "Alas! The time stolen from the obligations of our common destiny was but brief, when, emerging myself from the shadows of childhood, I could at last benefit from her moral influence and the intellectual profits of my intimacy with her. . . . She knew so much and judged so well, she expressed herself with such elegant simplicity, she possessed such taste and refinement, that her conversation was the best book."[21] But such conversation with her grandmother was to be a thing of the past. Later the same day Mme Dupin began to ramble inarticulately. Was it delirium? Aurore asked. " 'Alas no!' Deschartres replied; 'she has no fever, it is *childhood.*' "[22]

For Aurore the cruel trick of chronology in revolt, taking her grandmother backwards in time, was more difficult to witness than death. For a period later that year Aurore was preoccupied by thoughts of self-destruction. But there were, as always, simultaneities in her experience. The severity of her grandmother's condition brought its freedoms: "I lived a good deal, I thought a good deal, I changed a good deal during those ten months during which my grandmother, in her best moments, only regained a half-existence."[23] Looking back, Sand recognized the crucial importance of these months: "If it had been my destiny to pass immediately from the domination of my grandmother to that of a husband or that of the convent, it is possible that, subjected always to some influence to which I would have been resigned, I would never have been myself. . . . But fate decided that from the age of seventeen there would be a period of respite from exterior influence, and that I would belong entirely to myself for almost a year, to become, for better or worse, that which I would be, more or less, for the rest of my life."[24] Unlike her grandmother, Aurore was neither physically nor mentally paralysed, and she set out to explore, to continue her reading, and to gain experience against which to measure her reading. The "anchorite" existence which she described in letters to her friend from the convent, Émilie de Wismes, accounts for only a part of her life during that full year.

Deschartres was concerned that she be initiated into the running of the estate in preparation for the time when she would become its mistress. She learnt a good deal about the financial complexities of land management. This was to be the origin of her business sense, and much of what she learnt could be translated into the context of commercial writing and publishing a few years later in Paris. Deschartres continued to act as Aurore's tutor, but her growing intellectual grasp prevented him from continuing to teach in quite the dogmatic way that he had when she was a child. She refused more than a couple of lessons in higher mathematics. Instead she obliged Deschartres to become a sounding board against which she could test out her ideas and theories, stimulated by her voracious late-night (if not all-night) reading. Essentially this provided her with a grounding in dialectics, one that was to prove of enormous importance in terms of her intellectual development and her development as a novelist of ideas. Aurore also accompanied Deschartres on his visits to the sick and even assisted at operations which he performed. On the recommendation of a local squire Deschartres encouraged her to wear men's clothes so as to be able to ride more freely.

In May 1821 Aurore's cousin, René de Villeneuve, arrived at Nohant. He had come to witness the drawing up of Mme Dupin's will. For Aurore he provided the distractions of a more youthful and energetic companion. Although young-looking in appearance and energetic, he was middle-aged, extremely well read, interesting, and interested in his remarkable young cousin: "He had always known the wider world, and thought nothing of my *eccentricities*."[25] Together they enjoyed lengthy discussions of Aurore's reading—novels, philosophical treatises, essays—often continuing their conversations into the early hours of the morning. He, like her half-brother, encouraged her riding and was happy to provide instruction in pistol-shooting. He thought nothing of her male attire and saw no reason why a young woman should not be encouraged to be physically brave.[26] He encouraged her to continue to take intellectual and artistic risks too. He supported her wide reading, but still more exciting was his suggestion that she should write her own novel. He believed it to be her vocation.[27] But Aurore felt wholly unsatisfied with the results, as she had been by her attempts in the convent: "It was again a fiction outside me, and which I felt unable to bring to life. I enjoyed myself for a period and gave up when it all metamorphosed into dissertation."[28] What she feared was pedantry, and it was towards this that her writing moved inexorably. She abandoned the novel and pursued instead that "interior poem," Corambé's poem. The worlds of her early writings were either true, but unconvincing, or more convincing, but now worlds in which she did not herself fully believe. The imaginative truths of the world of Corambé were not yet truths that she could translate into fictions that would be both accessible and believable to other readers.

Rumours about the nature of the relationship between Aurore and René had begun to circulate: "In La Châtre, the chance to claim that he was my intended wasn't missed, seeing us ride out on horseback together; and that it was a new impertinence, on my behalf, running about alone with him, *under everyone's noses*." René was unconcerned. Aurore had discovered "that he shared none of the narrow prejudices and mean judgements of provincials."[29] But it was to be her intimacy with a younger man, Stéphane de Grandsagne (1802–1845), that excited tongue-wagging of a different order. Even her mother in Paris asked Aurore to account for her behaviour. Deschartres befriended any scientist in the area and he invited the young medical student, with almost comic naïvety, to tutor Aurore in anatomy and osteology. The skeleton which hung in Aurore's bedroom became a subject of colourful, even black, gossip, and excited debate. There was wide-ranging and imaginative speculation about the nature of their intimate relationship and bizarre private activities.

Aurore's reluctance to live within the boundaries set by public opinion had been increasingly sanctioned by her grandmother since her return from the convent, by Hippolyte, by René de Villeneuve, and by Deschartres. Yet for Aurore the echo of the augury "Woe to those on whom scandal descends!" continued to resound in her ears.[30] Unable to arrive at a satisfactory definition, she enlisted Deschartres's assistance; from a definition of scandal they could move on to the question of the nature of public opinion: "Opinion is a vague notion. There are numerous kinds. . . ."[31] The argument was pushed further and further by Aurore; she concluded: "What society calls scandal is not always scandal, and what society calls opinion is no more than arbitrary convention which changes in

accordance with the time, the place, and the people concerned."
Deschartres's response was a cautious one: "No doubt, no doubt . . . but
the good citizen respects the beliefs of the milieu in which he finds himself.
This milieu is made up of the wise and the foolish, the capable and the stupid." There were then, as far as Aurore could see, two opinions; and
Deschartres was forced to concede. Aurore then continued, "If there are
two, there is no opinion"; to which Deschartres replied, "There's the paradox!"[32] Deschartres capacity for sophistry had been strained to its limits,
but Aurore, who was also being taught some geology and mineralogy, was
beginning to locate the fault lines in Deschartres's intellectual edifice.

But Aurore's mother was quick to make adamant accusations about
Aurore's improper behaviour when information about her relationship
with Stéphane was detailed to her in Paris. The letter that Aurore wrote,
dated 18 November 1821, in response to her mother's outraged missive is a
delight. Wounded pride and indignation have been controlled. She translated her thoughts and feelings into a letter which displays a form, tone,
and restrained polemic, crafted with considerable artfulness:

> I read, with as much attention as respect, the letter that
> you had the goodness to write to me, and I would not
> have allowed myself the slightest objection to your
> reproaches had you not ordered me to respond
> promptly. . . . It is reprehensible of M. Deschartres,
> you say, to have abandoned me to my own devices;
> firstly, I allow myself the liberty of pointing out to
> you that M. Deschartres has no, nor can have any,
> form of authority over me, and that he had no rights,
> as far as I am concerned, other than those of a friendly
> adviser. . . . M. de Grandsagne told you that I had a
> warrior character; to add credibility to such an assur-
> ance, you would have to have believed, my dear
> mother, that M. de Grandsagne knew my character
> deeply, and I do not believe that I have been suffi-
> ciently *intimately attached* to him that he could know
> what are my qualities or my faults. . . . He told you the
> truth when he told you that he gave me lessons in my
> room: where would you want me to receive people
> who come to see me? It seems to me that my grand-

mother, in her suffering or in her sleep, would be very disturbed by such a visit [in her room]. . . . You wished that I would, when walking, take the arm of my chambermaid, or a maid. This is apparently to prevent me from falling, and that I needed a harness when I was a child. . . . But I am seventeen and I know how to walk. . . .[33]

Aurore had been able to answer her mother's accusations in writing and she was fully aware of her mother's inability to argue rationally, and of the limitations of her literacy. She knew that her mother would be unable to continue their exchange at the sophisticated level to which she had now raised it.

Her local confessor, the curé of La Châtre, however, confronted her in person. He had heard the rumours and asked, when she came to confession, whether they were true. Was she falling in love? The gossip was nothing, she told him. She had neither done nor even thought such things. The curé, unadvisedly, chose to push the matter further. Overcome by an "irresistible indignation," Aurore left the confessional. But the exchange continued. Why did he doubt the sincerity of her initial denial? She lost some of her composure. Now it was of "the vivacious stirrings whose origin is pride" that she was accused. "No! Sir," she replied. "You are in the wrong and are the cause of my own [vivacious stirrings], of which, I admit, I am not at this moment disposed to repent." He replied with "dryness and anger."[34] She never saw him again.

That Aurore felt sufficient conviction and confidence to act as she had was no doubt bound up in part with her grandmother's recent "conversion." The sequence of events surrounding Mme Dupin's confession and acceptance of the final sacraments had revealed to Aurore the divergent "opinions" of the Church, represented by various men of the cloth. Aurore had corresponded with Abbé Prémord on the matter of her grandmother's faith. Despite Aurore's sense of duty, she had held back from speaking to her grandmother about her position with regard to the Church.[35] Aurore was anxious not to suggest that her grandmother's death might be imminent. The ideas that Abbé Prémord expressed in his letters to her revealed his liberal, tolerant attitudes. They were gentle insights that were to influence her profoundly. Above all he reassured her that she was right not to be guided by dogma: "Never fear when it is your heart that guides you; the heart can never be wrong." He encouraged her to pray, to hope, and to continue to care for her grandmother with self-denying devotion, seeing that Aurore's "love, her modesty, her humility, the 'discretion' of her faith" would inevitably act as a persuasive influence on her grandmother. "This man," Sand would later write, "was a saint, a true Christian, should I say although, or because, he was a Jesuit?"[36]

The archbishop designate of Arles, M. Leblanc de Beaulieu, Aurore's "bastard uncle" (born of a union between her grandfather Dupin de Francueil and Mme Épinay), took it upon himself to regularize Mme Dupin's position with regard to the Church, during the summer of 1821.[37] She confessed, and received the sacraments, for Aurore's sake. Aurore was distressed by the whole run of events, which had been shot through with flagrant compromise. When the priest expressed his satisfaction that he had "saved" Mme Dupin by persuading her to renounce what would otherwise have been a "final impenitence," Aurore spoke up. Her grandmother, she asserted, did not believe in *infallibility*. With or without this final ritual, her grandmother would have been saved. She was a Deist. He accused Aurore of reading pernicious proscribed texts, including Voltaire, which her grandmother had in fact forbidden her to read until she was thirty.[38] Aurore replied that she was reading the Fathers of the Church and that she had found many contradictory points of view. This he adamantly denied. Had he read the Church Fathers? she asked. His final act of profanation, just before his departure, appalled her. He went into the library and set about mutilating or burning a good many books. Deschartres tried to stop him, but it was Aurore who established calm. "The scene," she would later write, "was intense, and one of the most grotesque."[39]

Aurore continued to nurse her grandmother with unflagging commitment, and she became increasingly exhausted. Her reading— Chateaubriand, and Byron, in particular—served only to lure her towards deeper and deeper despair. She was profoundly affected by the all-pervading melancholy of their writings, the wistful nostalgia, the yearning for an elsewhere. Even Chateaubriand's *Génie du Christianisme,* a powerful defence of the faith, had the effect of troubling rather than reassuring her. The Christianity Chateaubriand conjured was so distant from the rigorous self-denying creed instilled in her at the convent. Chateaubriand's argument that faith enriched the imagination, made sense of emotion, and was the foundation of aesthetic accomplishment in the arts was so close to her intuitive ideas: faith, Chateaubriand claimed, can be measured simply by the beauty of what it has inspired. Was this so different from her mother's unintellectual but deeply held convictions? Yet Chateaubriand's vision came into direct conflict with the dogmas she had seen her way to accepting as a teenager.

That autumn Stéphane returned to Paris. He too had impressed her deeply. But she had been shocked and disappointed by his atheism. They maintained a correspondence nevertheless and he sent her various books that she had requested. But their letters soon became "icy." Stéphane visited her mother in Paris and apparently described Aurore's generally unladylike lifestyle in a way which would be likely to turn her mother against her. Aurore could not know exactly what he had said, nor what had motivated him to talk as he allegedly had.[40] Both young people must have supposed that their friendship, their intimacy, was over.

As winter approached, melancholy turned to sadness, and sadness to anguish. "From abhorrence of life to the desire for death is but a step," she would write, looking back on this strange period of her late youth. "My domestic life was so gloomy, so saddened, my body so irritated by the continual struggle against exhaustion, my brain so wearied by earnest thoughts that were too precocious, as by my reading which was too all-absorbing for my age, that I became afflicted by a serious disease . . . : the lure of suicide."[41]

Like those heroes and heroines of Sand's fiction, it was water that drew her, a way into nothingness. The pull could be so strong, so sudden, so bizarre that she recognized it as a form of madness. The attraction became all-consuming, a "monomania."[42] Walking along a riverbank, she would hear nothing but a continual exchange, a loop, a leapfrogging "yes?" or "no?," "yes?" or "no?" Believing suicide to be a crime, according to her faith, she distanced herself from water, and gradually came to assume that she had been cured. But riding out with Deschartres one day, on their way to visit a patient, she found herself on the banks of the Indre, looking for a safe place to cross. Her mount was Colette, not Pépé, but she was overcome by her own sense of utter impotence, of her inability to deny the attraction of the abyss. She told Deschartres that she would take a long way round and cross by a bridge. Surprised by this uncharacteristic timidity, and conscious that they had little time, he mocked her unexpected show of fear, quite unaware of its sinister origin. She followed him into the water. Hearing the fatal "yes" unopposed, she found herself steering her horse away from the safe shallow course into the fast-flowing water. She was at once overcome by "a delirious joy" and "laughed hysterically."

Had Colette not been the extraordinary horse that it was, she would, she believed, undoubtedly have drowned, but the horse swam bravely towards the steep bank. Deschartres reached down and dragged her from the saddle and Aurore watched as the horse struggled desperately to climb up out of the fast current. Despite its strength and perseverance, the horse finally abandoned its attempt and was washed downstream. Aurore feared for its life. She was about to throw herself back into the water in a stupid attempt to rescue it when Deschartres restrained her. Colette swam to an accessible part of the bank and staggered, exhausted, from the river. Deschartres was outraged by Aurore's behaviour. He accused her of being no more than an "animal," a "brute beast." She had little choice but to confess her self-destructive longings. This, he announced, like so much else, must be a matter of heredity. Her father had also been powerfully tempted.[43] Had Maurice's fatal fall been entirely accidental?

Once again Deschartres and Aurore embarked on a subject of wide-ranging and heated debate, arguing the religious, moral, intellectual, and social questions surrounding the act of suicide. Aurore claimed that martyrs took their own lives and were canonized by the Church. The Church had even canonized saints who had died as a result of self-inflicted mortification of the flesh. Deschartres was willing to argue but was also sensitive to the need to readjust domestic arrangements. Sometimes he took over from Aurore at Mme Dupin's bedside, encouraging Aurore to sleep. And he recommended Greek and Latin classics. "History," Sand would explain, looking back, "takes us far away from ourselves, especially the history of ancient times, and vanished civilizations." Aurore, who continued to refuse to learn Latin, was read to by Deschartres, translating as he read. Virgil became a great love, and the French translations allowed her access to an ordered and beautiful elsewhere. Deschartres's "gods," Horace and Cicero, reassured her, not so much because of their content but because of the attention to precision and clarity that Deschartres demonstrated in his translation. His concern for linguistic nuance was a metaphor for his concern for Aurore.

All that Deschartres and Aurore were doing, that winter, was filling up the hours. Mme Dupin's condition continued to deteriorate. Even Deschartres's sophistry could not deny that her death was only a matter of time. But he nevertheless continued to believe that she could live a long while yet, in her numb state, a state between life and death.[44] But on 22 December 1821 she rallied briefly, for the last time. She called Aurore to her bedside and spoke. "You are losing your best friend," she said. These were her last words. She fell into a deep sleep, from which she never woke. Sand described her death as occurring at daybreak, the bells ringing on Christmas morning. This is a mistake—or a comforting novelistic invention. She died the day after Christmas Day, at four o'clock in the morning.[45] Was it that night that Deschartres came to Aurore?

> During the night, Deschartres came to summon me. He was in a state of exaltation and said to me . . . "Have you courage? Do you not think that we must render the dead a still more tender devotion than one of prayers and tears? Do you not believe that they watch us from above, and are touched by our faithfulness and our regrets? If you do, come with me." . . . The night was clear and cold. The ice, which had formed a crust on the snow, made walking so difficult that in order to cross the courtyard and enter the adjoining cemetery, we slipped and fell a number of times. . . .
>
> We approached the open grave that had been dug to receive my grandmother. Within a little burial vault of rough stones was a coffin, which the new coffin was to join in a few hours' time. . . .

He then invited her to descend into the grave:

> You must climb down and kiss the relic. It will be something you remember all your life. Someday, you will have to write your father's life story. . . . Give him whom you scarcely knew, and who loved you so greatly, a sign of your love and your respect. Where he is now, I tell you, he will see you, and bless you![46]

The story of Aurore doing as Deschartres bids is as extraordinary as anything in her most Gothic fiction. Yet Aurore "felt no repugnance at his idea," and, she continues, "we climbed down into the grave and I followed his example and religiously performed this act of devotion." Deschartres had up until this moment fought all notions of "fusedness" with others, but "my grandmother's death had revived the memory of my father's; he had found himself before this double grave, crushed by the two greatest sorrows of his life, and his burning soul protested, in spite of his cold reason, against the decree of an eternal separation. . . . Before the bones of a cherished being," he was no longer able "to accept the horror of nothingness."[47] It is a story entirely characteristic of French Romanticism, but there is no reason to doubt that it happened, whatever the elaborate manner of its telling.

Deschartres's motivation for involving Aurore had been entirely charitable. He had sought comfort and found it: "When I was alone here, I suddenly wanted to lift the lid, and I beheld a skeleton. The skull had come off. . . . I took it and kissed it. At once I felt an enormous relief, for I had never received his final embrace. Then I had begun to wonder if you had ever received it." He was moved to involve the young Aurore in part at least because of his love for her. He hoped that she would experience that same relief in her own brief descent into the underworld.

The following day, Mme Dupin was lowered into the grave, beside her son, and that night Aurore sat at the side of her grandmother's bed. The shape of her grandmother's body was "carved" in the bedclothes and she kissed the negative, the empty mould. She did not believe that her grandmother would return to her in the night. Descending into her father's tomb had filled her with an absolute despair: she no longer believed in the possibility of communicating directly with the dead. Still, she hoped that in her utterly exhausted state some hallucinatory power might reveal to her, one last time, her grandmother's face "lit by the light of eternal life."[48] But she saw nothing, and fell into a deep sleep. On waking, she had quite forgotten that her grandmother had died. When she remembered, tears, which she had so far been unable to shed, ran down her cheeks and were absorbed by the pillow, which still showed the imprint of her grandmother's head. That was the end: "I left that room, where in the morning the seals were placed and which seemed to me to be profaned by the formalities of material interests."[49]

But it was just such material interests that animated the excitable Sophie-Victoire when she arrived to hear the reading of Mme Dupin's will. Aurore's response to her mother was to belie the confident tone of her recent letter. She still felt loyal to Sophie-Victoire. The letter, like so much else that year, had been a game, a relatively safe testing-out of the definition and importance of "opinion" and "scandal." She had started to explore, but largely it had been a map that she had scoured. Even cartographically she had cast only cursory glances over much forbidden territory. She had known nothing of physical love, nor had she, as yet, sought erotic fulfilment, she writes, convincingly, looking back on the year 1820–21, "those vibrations had not yet been set off within me."[50]

But one incident she described in a letter, probably written in July 1821, to Émilie de Wismes, suggests that the games of love and sexual intrigue were not wholly outside her experience.[51] No doubt she exaggerated the encounter, for the sake of the story.

She was out riding, she informs Émilie, dressed in men's clothes, but, she explains at some length, this is local practice among the "demoiselles." There is, however, a crucial difference, which she admits. While others simply dress in men's clothes, Aurore succeeds in passing herself off as a man. Having ridden in her usual equestrian attire to a neighbouring village (where she was a complete stranger, she adds, no doubt for the sake of credibility), she had been sketching an old château, a romantic edifice with Gothic details. A lady emerged from the building and, impressed by the drawing, asked "Monsieur" if she could buy it. A young lady then approached and, unaccustomed to meeting "elegant" men in the environs, engaged in interested conversation. "Blushing" and "narrowing her eyes," the young lady was, as Aurore describes her to Émilie, "extremely responsive" to the "gallant air" which Aurore had successfully assumed.[52] That Aurore enjoyed the charade is beyond doubt and it was a game that she would continue to play. Safe in her disguise, she was able to experiment, to explore, and to see the world from two very different points of view.

VII

A Reasonable Marriage

"I will lift women up from their abject state,
both in my life and in my writings."

⤳Aurore's loyalty to her mother had been immediately tested when
Sophie-Victoire arrived, in January 1822, to hear the reading of Mme
Dupin's will. She had brought reinforcements: her sister and brother-in-
law. What mattered to Sophie-Victoire was that her maternal rights to her
daughter be in no way threatened. Because Aurore remained a minor, all
Mme Dupin had been able to express was a desire that her granddaughter
be protected by her cousin, René de Villeneuve, who had been present as a
witness at the drafting of the will. Mme Dupin had warned Aurore: "Your
mother is more bizarre than you think. You do not know her at all. She is so
uneducated that she loves her young as the birds love. . . . When they have
wings . . . she flies to another tree, chasing her young away, pecking
them."[1] No doubt Mme Dupin had spoken at greater length and more
explicitly to René about her concerns if Aurore were abandoned to her
mother's care. As the details of the will were read, Sophie-Victoire's invective, directed against the deceased, and the strength and crudeness of her
vitriol shocked Aurore, and wounded her deeply. But Aurore submitted,
apparently calmly, to her mother's authority.

Years earlier, Sophie-Victoire had been proud of her daughter's precocious storytelling. She had been struck by the richness of her primitive
narratives. In the early days at Nohant she had defended Aurore's day-

dreaming and encouraged her fantasies. She had called her early stories her "novels" and had denied, to Mme Dupin, the pernicious effects of allowing a powerful imagination free rein. Now, leaving Nohant in the wake of Mme Dupin's death, she would allow Aurore only one or two books when they packed for the journey to Paris on 18 January 1822. Books, as opposed to stories, represented not imagination and fantasy but learning and knowledge. Sophie-Victoire regarded Aurore's books as the tangible symbol of her assimilation into another group, a group to which Sophie-Victoire had never had access. The ideologies and beliefs of books, Sophie-Victoire may have suspected, were those of a different social class. She ridiculed what she described as Aurore's intellectual pretensions, as she had, more gently, in response to one of Aurore's earliest, somewhat flowery letters. "Your fine phrases certainly make me laugh. I hope you're not going to start trying to talk like that," she had replied.[2]

For Sophie-Victoire the sophisticated was associated with sophistry, pretension, and the artificial, and Aurore could not wholly dismiss her mother's instinctive responses, even if they were motivated by no more than intuition and tinged with bitter resentment. Her mother's Parisian speech, its colour, its candour, had appealed to her as a child, in much the same way as the Berrichon patois she had learnt in early childhood. The wisdom of the Berrichon tales that she had heard at the hearths of the Nohant cottages, *she* had no more than intuited. But her bookish learning had in no way denied the poetic meaning, the imaginative truths, of these country narratives any more than the truths of Perrault's tales and the versions of these which her mother and aunt had invented. Nor had her respect for her mother's absolute, albeit superstitious, faith been significantly diminished by her own growing recognition of the complexities and breadth of Christian doctrine and range of biblical interpretation. Much as she had come to admire the control and logic of her grandmother's speech and her rational faith and more individual understanding of Christian conscience, Aurore was also aware of the power of her grandmother's rhetoric. Aurore's mixed class background and unconventional education and upbringing had, above all, served to make her peculiarly aware that truths could be manipulated by words. Different social groups, different interested parties, found different words to give their version of the truth ascendancy over those of others.

They arrived in Paris on 20 or 21 January. Aurore stayed with her aunt and uncle for a couple of weeks and then moved in with her mother, who was living first at 12 Rue Neuve-des-Mathurins, and then 80 Rue Saint-

Lazare. Her life—and behaviour—were as unstable as ever. Sophie-Victoire had no patience for her daughter's ideas, nor her idiosyncrasies, however well she disguised them. Aurore, on the other hand, though deeply distressed by, and fearful of, her mother's growing "exaggerations," continued to consider these, at least in part, symptoms of the hard life her mother had lived. Social prejudice had exacerbated the tragedies, and Sophie-Victoire's response, however inappropriate, however egotistical, was in part motivated by a resilient pride. Aurore could explain, to some extent, why it was that she had been made into the woman she was. Her pride, even arrogance, was something that Aurore could not but respect. But although Aurore admired her mother's disregard for "opinion," whether Deschartres's or the Villeneuves', and accepted and was moved by her mother's determination to maintain her rights in law to her daughter, she was unable to understand what caused her mother's simultaneous cruelty towards her. She became less and less able to withstand it and came to see that her mother's desire to maintain responsibility for her was motivated, in large part, by financial interest.

In Paris Aurore found herself again in the company of her other family, Pierret, her half-sister Caroline, Aunt Lucie, and Uncles Maréchal and Beaumont. Aunt Lucie and Pierret, who knew Sophie-Victoire as well as anyone, encouraged Aurore not to take her rantings too much to heart. During periods of despondency, Sophie-Victoire would tell Aurore "more things about her life than I wanted to know," but then, suddenly overcome by disgust at her own pathetic attempts at self-justification and overwhelmed by paranoid anxiety, she would turn on Aurore: "I have said too much, I can see, and now you blame me, and despise me, now that you know what you know. I prefer it that way! I would rather tear you from my heart and have nothing to love but your father, not even you!"[3] Aurore could accept that the hatred of her outbursts would soon be confused by self-berating and intense annoyance that the company had "allowed her" to say such terrible things. But the punishments she visited on Aurore required a degree of deliberation which Aurore could not reasonably explain away. These punishments, in addition, came to impinge on her freedom. Sophie-Victoire's complete intolerance of Aurore's compulsive reading was symptomatic. Books represented the concrete evidence of that otherwise immaterial commitment to the world of Nohant: "Suspicious to an extreme, and transported quite pathologically, madly committed to condemn anything she could not understand, she would stir up incredible quarrels about everything. She would come and wrench books from my hands, saying that she had tried to read them, that she had not understood a single jot, and that they must be pernicious." Aurore's love of books was, Sophie-Victoire believed, evidence that she was both "vicious and perverse."[4]

Sophie-Victoire could not tolerate the presence of Aurore's maid—she represented the last human link with Nohant. She was dismissed. Pluchon, Aurore's dog, was also banished forever. Suspecting that Aurore's visits to her old convent were no more than a cover for clandestine meetings with Stéphane de Grandsagne, Sophie-Victoire demanded that she censor her daughter's letters. It is true that at the time Stéphane's lodgings were close by the convent, but there is no actual evidence of meetings. Aurore resented her mother's suspicions, her lack of trust, and she resented her interference, her authority.

Books and writing, which might otherwise have provided Aurore with a release, became, for Sophie-Victoire, the tangible manifestations of Aurore's resistance. Whether calculated or not, Aurore's response to these intimidations was one of apparently calm acceptance. Abused by her mother, Aurore would experience that state which she sometimes describes by means of simile or metaphor, sometimes literally. At the end of the first volume of her autobiography, covering this period of her life, she described her "body and soul, undivided, and dead."[5] But the inner state was never visibly manifest. And it was this absolute and dignified self-control—in turn throwing into relief her mother's mad abandon—that enraged Sophie-Victoire. It was all too reminiscent of Mme Dupin de Francueil, the mother-in-law who had always, and deeply, despised her.

Aurore's attitudes to her mother's past are surely written into *Lélia*, George Sand's third and most perplexing novel.[6] A strange pastiche of realism and symbolism, a long dialogue between the eponymous heroine and her sister, Pulchérie, explores some of the ideas that are central to the novel. Lélia has led a tragic but virtuous life. By scrupulously observing the laws of society and its moral imperatives, she has denied life. Pulchérie, on the other hand, a courtesan, has lived for pleasure and has fully embraced life. Lélia considers her sister "defiled," and when Pulchérie admits the tenets of her own creed to her sister, Lélia "shuddered and involuntarily stepped back." Lélia pities her sister, she is "a poor misguided creature," "lost in the wilderness." But Pulchérie argues with Lélia: "Though I may be degraded, at least I am not ridiculous. To be useless, Lélia, is to be ridiculous; to be ridiculous is worse than to be infamous; to serve no purpose in the world is more despicable than to serve the most debasing one."

Pulchérie speaks as the fallen woman. When she speaks again, she surely speaks, to some extent, for Sophie-Victoire:

> What, then, does God ask of us here on earth? . . . To live, surely? And what does society demand of us? Not to steal. Society is so constructed that many people have no other way of making a living but by a trade which the social body sanctions, yet at the same time stigmatizes with the hateful name of vice. Do you realize of what temper of steel a poor woman must be made to live in this way? With how many insults people demand she pay for the weaknesses she has discovered and the brutalities she has satisfied? Under what burden of ignominy and injustice must she learn to sleep, to live, to be lover, mistress, and mother, three aspects of the female destiny from which no woman can escape, whether she sell herself as a prostitute or through a marriage contract?

Pulchérie argues against social injustice, against the lot of poor women, but above all against society's hypocrisy, the discourses elaborated to justify barbaric exploitation. For all the humiliations of her own life, she has retained a spiritual strength. If there is a heaven and a hell, Pulchérie argues, heaven will be for those who have suffered but also continued to live—and to love. Despite the degradation of the fallen, they will be saved because they have, amid their misery, found "blessings to bestow on God." Hell will be for those who, having seized the best things in life, have failed to appreciate their worth. Self-denial, the refusal of pleasure, on the other hand, is life-denying, and will stir up the wrath of God: "In the midst of the horrors of social degradation the courtesan . . . will have made a profession of faith by remaining true to sensual pleasure, while the ascetic Lélia, in a life of austerity and respectability, will have repudiated God at every moment, shutting her eyes and her soul to the blessings of life."

If Pulchérie speaks for the lives of women like Sophie-Victoire, Lélia is to some extent the young Aurore. What Pulchérie identifies in her sister is an incapacity to love what is real: "You, my shy sister, you were indignant if I showed interest in a man; you were responding only to the elusive beauties of nature, to a sound or a colour, but never to a clear or tangible figure. A distant song would make you shed tears. But as soon as the bare-legged shepherd appeared on top of the hill you would avert your eyes in disgust."

Lélia is a strange and in some ways difficult novel, and much of it is relevant to a later period in Aurore's life. But Pulchérie articulates thoughts that Aurore undoubtedly considered when, in late adolescence, she came to know her mother, herself, and society better.

Forbidden from visiting the convent and gradually denied every freedom by her mother, marriage was the only possible escape. But however desperate her present life, Aurore was unwilling to forfeit future freedom by submitting to an arranged marriage. The Villeneuves initially sought to maintain contact with her. The longer Aurore remained part of her mother's household, they knew, the less likely it was that an appropriate husband would be found, dowry or no dowry. René called to invite Aurore to dinner. With typical and spectacular haughtiness, Sophie-Victoire claimed that the Countess should have come in person to deliver any such invitation. His response was one of absolute commitment to the recognition of the status quo: "Never would his wife set foot in her house."[7] For years Aurore would see nothing of her favourite cousin, the cousin who had claimed, to her astonishment and delight, that her vocation was that of a novelist. She did not forget his predictions.

Auguste, René's brother, also called on Aurore. He was explicit: "You walk out with your mother, with her daughter, with the husband of her daughter, with M. Pierret. People have seen you in the street with that whole group. It is an impossible society." Given her position, the Villeneuves, he implied, could not be expected to find her a husband. Coldly, he advised her "to marry herself off as best she could. What does it matter to me if you marry a cabdriver. If he's a decent man . . ."[8]

Aurore must in many ways have despised the Villeneuves' attitudes. For one thing they were attitudes that her father had clearly not shared. She recognized a new freedom as a result of having been abandoned by that family: "finally free, through force of circumstance . . . to marry according to the dictates of my heart, as my father had done, when the day comes that I should feel so moved." In the meantime, however, she continued to suffer. She again experienced the dreadful appeal of suicide. She became increasingly uninterested in food, and stomach cramps physically prevented her from eating anything more than small amounts. As she began to rapidly lose weight, she felt soothed, and expectant: "I was unable to prevent myself feeling a secret joy, telling myself that this death by hunger would come without my complicity." She had made no conscious intellectual choice. Some other mysterious part of her being had snapped, and slowly and peacefully her body would waste away until too frail to support life. Fortunately, the Roëttiers du Montaleau, *dite* du Plessis, intervened.[9]

This family, unlike the Villeneuves, were friends not of Mme Dupin but of her son. James had been a fellow officer of Maurice's, and they had campaigned together in Italy. Friends of Maurice were friends of Sophie-Victoire's, and she readily accepted their invitation that she and Aurore visit them at Le Plessis, their estate fifty or so kilometres from Paris. James had run into Aurore and her mother in Paris, and had no doubt been alarmed by Aurore's condition. He had been equally sensitive to the nature of the relationship between mother and daughter. Given that Aurore would marry with a respectable inheritance, he was confident that a suitable husband could be found, and that this was the obvious solution for all concerned.

The Roëttiers family was in many ways unconventional, and in ways that bore certain parallels with Aurore's paternal family. Of the five Roëttiers daughters, four lived at home. They, as Aurore had done, often dressed in men's clothes and enjoyed considerable physical freedoms, riding about the countryside. There were usually numerous guests staying at Le Plessis, many James's unmarried army colleagues. The atmosphere was of an almost constant house party. Aurore and her mother arrived on 21 March. Sophie-Victoire soon returned to Paris: she had always disliked the country, and no doubt felt that there was nothing for her at Le Plessis.

Aurore was quickly restored to life. She rode, she read in the extensive library, she enjoyed the company of the Roëttiers daughters. In many ways it was a return to the life she had led at Nohant, embellished by youthful company and high spirits, ever encouraged by James and Angèle, whom she soon referred to as "father" and "mother." But beyond restoring an equilibrium which had been dramatically lost, her stay had a further and more specific end in view: the arrangement of an appropriate marriage. Interested young men paid court to her. One, to whom she was strongly drawn—she was suddenly made aware, to her consternation—wanted her not as his wife but as his mistress. The experience, she would write, made her conscious of the "chimera of happiness."[10] From Paris various names continued to be suggested by her Uncles Maréchal and Beaumont, and even Pierret. Aurore wanted at least to have seen her intended. These men, she could only assume, were interested principally in her relative wealth, and she refused them.

The course of her life was thus in a sense suspended for a number of months, but in April 1822 the Roëttiers returned to Paris, and Aurore to her mother. A certain urgency began to make its presence felt. The Roëttiers, who continued to enjoy social and cultural events in the capital, frequently invited Aurore to join them. The contrast between the contented life with her adoptive family by day and the disorganized and unregulated life with her real family first thing in the morning and last thing at night was marked. Time, she must have begun to suspect, was running out. She recognized that the lives of James and Angèle, their daughters and friends, was an enviable one, and one which, through marriage, she might be able to make her own.

One evening, on 19 April, after the theatre (performances began in the late afternoon), the Roëttiers and Aurore were enjoying refreshments on the terrace of the Café Tortoni. Angèle caught sight of an old acquaintance and called out, "Look, it's Casimir."[11] A sublieutenant, tall and thin, with a long aquiline nose, he was quite handsome. He came over to their table and gave news of his father, Colonel Jean-François Dudevant, a close friend of the Roëttiers. There had long been a light-hearted, not altogether serious agreement between the Roëttiers and Casimir that one day they would give him the hand of their eldest daughter. Who was Aurore? he asked. Angèle joked that the young lady was indeed their daughter. He then claimed, when Aurore's real identity was revealed, that she must be his betrothed. For Aurore, no better script could have been written, no introduction to a husband better stage-managed. For her, in the bosom of her adoptive family and happy, the scene had been spontaneous and entertaining. This introduction had been without deliberation, uncalculated on the part of anyone concerned. Unlike previous encounters with potential husbands, this was familiar romantic drama, unreal and unthreatening. It began as a game, and for some weeks it continued as one. It was a play, and their courtship continued playfully.[12]

During a brief intermission that followed the initial scene of their meeting, Aurore made various enquiries about this new player in her life. There were remarkable points in common: they shared the same birthday, nine years apart. Casimir had been born on 5 July 1795, at Guillery in Gascony, and Aurore was still under the misapprehension that she had been born on 5 July 1804. The similarities in their backgrounds were striking. The story of Casimir's parentage was remarkably like that of her half-brother, Hippolyte. Casimir had also been born illegitimate, the son of

Baron Dudevant and Augustine Soulès, a servant. His paternity recognized, as was Hippolyte's, Casimir had been brought up by his father until his marriage two years later, when Casimir had been handed over to the care of the servants. A few years later, in her husband's absence, Mme Dudevant had caught sight of Casimir eating his supper in the kitchens and asked who he was. She and her husband had been unable to have children of their own, and on learning the truth about Casimir, she insisted, on her husband's return, that the boy be brought up by them. Colonel Dudevant agreed.

Whether or not Aurore, at this stage in her life, had formed ideas about the need for equality if intimate relationships are to be successful, it is certainly the case that in terms of social class, and roughly speaking in terms of economic status, there was considerable parity between Casimir and Aurore. What she must have recognized was the parallel between her father's commitment to Sophie-Victoire and the Dudevants' acceptance of the offspring of a relationship similar to that of her own parents. Her father had married in the face of social prejudice and the Dudevants had brought up an illegitimate son, ignoring, in a similar way, social convention. Marriage to Casimir would be symbolic of her loyalty to her father, and mother. Aurore could not have anticipated her mother's overcautious response. She was impressed that Baron Dudevant travelled to Paris to discuss the proposal with her in person. She accepted. But she made a condition: that she be first satisfied that the young man was sufficiently handsome.

Whatever the part played by rational assessment, Aurore's acceptance of Casimir's proposal had not simply been a matter of intellectual reasoning. Casimir reminded her of her half-brother. Time spent with Casimir at Le Plessis was scarcely distinguishable from the time she had spent with Hippolyte at Nohant that summer of physical, sensual, even erotic awakening, not very many months earlier. Aurore had spent from 21 March to 3 April 1822 at Le Plessis without him. But they coincided from 24 April to 28 May and she was explicit about the parallels in her relationship with her half-brother and Casimir. She wrote to Hippolyte in May: "I have a friend here whom I like a good deal, with whom I run and jump and laugh, as with you."[13] From the beginning, in the spirit of the original Roëttiers' game, they referred to one another as "my husband" and "my wife."

After his initial visit to Le Plessis Casimir had returned to Paris. Back at Le Plessis in June, he spoke for the first time of marriage.[14] The marital game was becoming frighteningly real, but Aurore was reassured; and here, of course, there are ironies. Casimir's fraternal manner and the relative asexuality of their friendship tempted her to believe in the rightness of marriage: "He never talks of love and confesses himself little disposed to passion. He speaks of an unfailing friendship, and compares the calm domestic happiness of our hosts with what he believes he can promise to provide."[15]

The Roëttiers probably believed in the appropriateness of their union. What is more certain is that the Roëttiers' union, and their family and household, were models to which Aurore and Casimir consciously aspired. They intended to return to Nohant and establish a pattern of life like that of Le Plessis. But no one expected that it would be Sophie-Victoire, and not Aurore, who would change her mind. The former had grudgingly agreed to the proposal, despite Casimir's disappointing looks: "He isn't handsome," she had told Aurore. "I would have liked a nice-looking type to take my arm."[16] But she had not fully made up her mind, such as it was.

Sophie-Victoire met Baronne Dudevant and discussions took place as to the legal and financial marriage contract. Everything was falling into place. But a fortnight later she arrived "like a bomb" at Le Plessis.[17] She had learnt, she claimed, the full details of the dissipated and shameful life Casimir had led as a student in Paris. The peals of laughter that met these accusations further inflamed the indignant Sophie-Victoire. She left Le Plessis. The marriage was, she declared, cancelled. If one of Aurore's reasons for accepting Casimir's proposal had been associated with a desire to accept a union symbolic of her loyalty to her parents, and to cross-class marriage, such a reason was not recognized by the typically unreasonable Sophie-Victoire.

Early on in her life Aurore had developed a strong sense of loyalty. As a child, her reactions had often been a matter of response to intuition. If she suspected unfair or uncharitable judgement, or judgement based on no more than social prejudice or religious dogma, she instinctively took the side of the victim. Her loyalty to her mother had always been provoked not so much by admiration as by the attitudes towards her, and treatment of her, by the more powerful, or by those interested parties who, without conscience, colluded in the actions of the powerful. During her adolescence, her loyalty became increasingly a matter of intellectual reasoning. She became fully aware of her loyalty to her grandmother only in the latter's decline, when she had lost her authority. The so-called Archbishop of Arles's attitude to her grandmother had been wholly unacceptable. In her weak state, her grandmother had to some extent been manipulated. Her mother's cruel invective against the dead woman was equally inexcusable. Now that her mother had become a powerful player, Aurore no longer felt it her duty to align herself with her.

Sophie-Victoire's cancellation of her marriage was, Aurore believed, humiliating for Casimir and his family, and the Roëttiers. She sided with her husband-to-be, the victim of Sophie-Victoire's wholly unreasonable assessment. She had judged both his appearance and his character; the first was a matter of arbitrary opinion, the second was without proof. Righteous indignation would play a major part in spurring Aurore into action, into gambles that she would often have cause to regret. If her mind had not been wholly made up, her mother's behaviour had confirmed her commitment to Casimir Dudevant.

Hippolyte, who had resigned his commission, and even the Baronne, who made the journey to Paris, were among those who intervened in defence of Casimir and the proposed marriage. No doubt in part out of an ever-active sense of pride, Sophie-Victoire would reconsider the union only if the financial aspects of the contract were adjusted in Aurore's favour. Sophie-Victoire renegotiated a settlement that would allow Aurore to retain—but not control—her inheritance of 500,000 francs. In addition, Casimir would allocate his wife an allowance of 3,000 francs a year. It is one of the ironies of Sophie-Victoire's premarital interventions that they assured Aurore a degree of freedom which would enable her to take another great risk, again motivated in large part by that righteous indignation, only a few years later. In the weeks before her marriage, Aurore considered her mother's stipulations deeply humiliating for Casimir. Retrospectively, she would consider the matter rather differently.

The unusually lengthy and complicated marriage contract was signed on 24 August 1822. The civil marriage took place in Paris three weeks later, on 17 September, and the religious ceremony the same day in the Church of Saint-Louis d'Antin.[18] The date 17 September is also the anniversary of Aurore's father's death. Did this symbolize an intention, on Aurore's part, to attempt at least to transfer her allegiance from her father to her husband? Casimir was twenty-seven; Aurore eighteen. After a few days at Le Plessis they left that beguiling place and its charming society and travelled in the company of Hippolyte to Nohant, to encounter the reality of their union. Arriving "home" towards the end of October, they were received "joyously, by the good Deschartres." But the joy of their union was clouded by diminishing happiness. Reality, increasingly, broke through. Life was not to be cured by marriage to Casimir Dudevant.

He had spoken little of love or passion because he was unsentimental, and unromantic. But Aurore would, after all, be his wife. He was a sublieutenant (although he resigned his commission on 18 October), and not the "bare-legged shepherd" of *Lélia*, while Aurore, like the novel's heroine, would feel that same desire to turn away. For some time, however, this was an impulse that she denied. Instead it was a response that she rationalized by means of all manner of intellectual strategies. But if rationalization is a form of compromise, then it is no surprise that Aurore would soon long for more.

VIII

The Reality of Marriage and the
Precarious Suspension of Disbelief

"My husband was not at all religious but thought
it good that I should be."

For Aurore, the return to Nohant was a return to the past, and to the lingering presence of the dead. The ghosts of her brother, her father, and her grandmother haunted her imagination. Aurore slept in her grandmother's bed, her deathbed and the same bed she had watched over one last time, when empty but for that negative impression of her grandmother's body. The winter of 1822–23 was unusually cold.[1] The birds suffered, and many died. Chaffinches, robins, and sparrows were saved by Aurore, who had some of those that were dying brought to her. She warmed them, fed them, and released them when they had been restored to life.

Aurore was already pregnant. The next generation was on the way—hence her thoughts of the dead, and of death. Her concern for the Nohant birds can be read as part of that not uncommon anxiety experienced by pregnant women, suddenly disturbingly aware of the terrible frailty of the vulnerable. Deschartres had ordered that she rest in bed after she had suffered a fall. She had lost a good deal of blood. She read little and slept a good deal. Her only distraction was needlepoint, an activity which from time to time throughout her life she found soothing, during periods of anguish or despondency, exhaustion or loss of concentration. Casimir, on the other hand, a great lover of outdoor activities, hunted, shot, and rode. Although he spent little time at his wife's side, he was attentive to her whims, sending to Paris for sheet music, and for particular sweets for which she suddenly and passionately longed. Husband and wife adhered to a safe and predictable script. The pregnancy and the young husband's response to it were patently mere cliché.

For the time being Aurore continued, at least outwardly, to abide by convention. The bleeding stopped and she was allowed out of bed. She prepared for the birth, and wondered at the strange sensations of pregnancy, writing in a letter to Émilie de Wismes dated January 1823, "You cannot conceive of the pleasure you experience, feeling your child stirring within your being."[2] But however conventional her response to pregnancy and the practicalities of preparing for the birth, she continued to consider intellectually the social estate of marriage. In her letter to Émilie, written only a few months after the wedding, she does not limit her communication exclusively to descriptions of the odd and powerful experience of pregnancy. In addition, she wrote at length of the difficulties which arise out of the inevitable differences in character and taste of those joined in union. "In marrying, one of the two," she concluded, "must renounce himself or herself completely, abnegating not only their will, but even opinion, in order to see through the eyes of the other, to enjoy what the other enjoys. . . . All that remains to be asked, then, is whether it should be for the husband or the wife to *recast* his or her being according to the mould of the other." Her answer was a pragmatic one, considered only within the narrow limits of contemporary social reality and convention: "As *it is the bearded party that is all-powerful,* and in any case men are incapable of such commitment, it is necessarily incumbent on us to bend compliantly."[3] This should be done in "the name of God and marital happiness"; it would, she wrote to Émilie, no doubt bring wonderful rewards. Her half-brother would not be required to make similar adjustments. He married Émilie de Villeneuve on 22 March 1823.

At the end of May 1823, as the expected time for the birth approached, Aurore and Casimir decided to move temporarily to the capital in order to employ a Parisian doctor for the delivery. They broke their journey at Le Plessis, arriving on 2 June. However different Aurore and Casimir may have been, the delights of this place and its people were something in which they both revelled. But their stay could only be a brief interlude. In Paris they rented a small apartment from a former chef of Napoleon's in the Hôtel de Florence, 56 Rue Neuve-des-Mathurins (now 26 Rue des Mathurins). On 30 June a son was born, and his name would be Maurice. He was baptized on 24 July at Saint-Louis d'Antin.[4]

Aurore marvelled at her baby, and was determined to breast-feed little Maurice. This, highly unusual for a woman of her social status, was something her grandmother had done, under the influence of Rousseau's prescriptions for maternity, as had, less surprisingly, her mother. Sophie-Victoire was impressed by Aurore's decision and wrote unusually encouraging letters. If Sophie-Victoire regarded Aurore's books as symbols of her loyalty to one social and intellectual group, her breast-feeding was surely symbolic of a very different sense of solidarity.

Deschartres arrived to inspect the first representative of another generation, and, taking the baby on his lap, announced, as though only to himself, that the time had come to leave Nohant. He liked the new master of Nohant well enough. He described Casimir in a letter, displaying a touch of typically provincial racism, as "mild, with a little Gascon petulance." He did not, he wrote, display that other characteristic of his region, "garrulousness." They can have had little in common, one scholarly with notable intellectual pretensions, and a lover of conversation; the other very much an outdoor man. Casimir was also keen to modernize Nohant, an estate that had hitherto been managed in an old-fashioned, paternalistic way, à la Dupin de Francueil. With a hint of not uncharacteristic self-pity, Deschartres concluded his letter with the pathetic statement that "the spectacle of the couple's happiness serves only to augment my own sorrow."[5] Deschartres felt himself to be redundant, looked unsuccessfully for a suitable place to live near Nohant, but in the end settled in Paris. He left Nohant definitively on 15 August 1823. His entire adult life, and all its emotions, had been bound up with that of one remarkable family. Moving away from it required adjustments that he turned out to be incapable of making. But for some years he struggled on, alone.

In late summer the Dudevants spent another spell at Le Plessis. Aurore performed in a little comedy, but they could not stay forever. At the beginning of October they returned to Nohant.

Despite Aurore's apparent commitment to making enormous adjustments for the sake of her marriage, the sacrifices she made had not brought the rewards she had suggested to Émilie such self-abnegation would bring. On 28 November she wrote to her again: "I continue to live a solitary life, if it is possible to believe oneself to be alone when in the company of a husband whom one adores. While he hunts, I play with my little Maurice, or I read. At the moment I am rereading the *Essays* of Montaigne, my *favourite* author. You are too new a wife to know this work, but if you have the time to read, I advise you to read this work."[6] More telling is the evidence of her first novel, *Indiana* (1832).

Much of the experience of Indiana, the unhappy young wife, was Aurore Dudevant's. And Colonel Delmare shares some of the traits of Casimir. "The Colonel's wife," Aurore would write of her first fictional heroine, "was nineteen, and if you had seen her huddled under the mantel of that huge fireplace of white marble and burnished copper, if you had seen her, slender, pale, and sad, her elbow on her knee . . . you would have pitied the wife of Colonel Delmare, and perhaps the Colonel even more."[7] Indiana, like Aurore, suffers from melancholy, from an apparently inexplicable dissatisfaction with life. Indiana chooses, like Aurore, to suffer largely in silence. In both cases, however, the domestic tensions occasionally spark tense exchanges between husband and wife. Casimir's treatment of animals was unsentimental, sometimes rough. In *Indiana*, Colonel Delmare refuses the affection of the household dog, Ophelia, who has "surrendered to the magnetic power wielded by the eye of man upon animals." But Colonel Delmare sets about chasing the dog from the room. The Colonel approaches Ophelia and is about to strike her. Mme Delmare cries out. Her response is something Delmare cannot tolerate. "Have I ever reproached you?" she asks by way of an answer to his accusation that her cry was a cry of reproach. Indiana's tone, Sand tells us, "was one of a gentleness we adopt out of generosity when we love and out of self-respect when we do not." The Colonel's tone is of one who "is half-father, half-brother," but, he declares, "there are more bitter reproaches in the tears of some women than in all the damnations of others. . . ." In *Indiana*, Sand wrote of her heroine in this scene: "Had someone closely observed Madame Delmare, he could have perceived in that trivial, vulgar incident of her domestic life the secret sadness of her entire existence."[8] It was in the small acts of daily life, Sand the novelist suggested, that the true depths of unhappiness in marriage were revealed.

The dissatisfactions of Aurore's married life and the intellectual impasse that they represented are written into *Indiana*. But they are transferred with considerable delicacy, and a surprising degree of even-handedness. Two passages are particularly resonant. Of the fictional husband she wrote: "Thus his [the Colonel's] character could not have been more antipathetic to that of his wife, nor his heart and mind less capable of understanding and appreciating her." What was described was essentially no more than a fundamental incompatibility, for which he could not be held responsible. What Sand then revealed of her heroine was closer to a judgement: "And yet it is certain that her slavery had engendered in her woman's heart a kind of mute, virtuous aversion that was not always just. Madame Delmare's doubts of her husband's heart were unfairly exaggerated; he was harsh—she thought him cruel. There was more roughness than rage in his outbursts, more coarseness than offence in his manners. He was not, by nature, a wicked man; he had moments of pity which led him to repent, and in his repentance he all but revealed sensitivity." His roughness was explained, if not wholly excused: "It was camp life that had made brutality a matter of principle." What Sand suggested was that the Delmares' marriage was unhappy because of their differences. "With a less refined, less gentle woman," Sand wrote of Colonel Delmare, "he would have been as timid as a tamed wolf." Casimir, we suspect, would have been better able to sustain a reasonably happy marriage with a less "refined," a less sophisticated, that is to say a less complicated, wife.[9]

A wife with a more moderate and less resilient sense of pride, one less easily excited to righteous indignation, one less questioning, would also have made an easier wife. Again *Indiana* suggests insights into the Dudevant marriage. Later in the novel the narrator intervenes: "Her husband had become almost unbearable. In public he affected the courage and insouciance of a brave man; returned to the privacy of his household, he was little more than an irritable, demanding, ridiculous child. Indiana was the victim of his troubled situation, and I admit, it was largely her fault. . . ." Why does Indiana, or the narrator at least, regard the fictional judgement as a matter of "admission"? Here the confessional breaks through. Sand then explains that

a woman of a more common class would have dominated a man of this vulgar sort; she would have spoken like him while enjoying private thoughts in private, feigned respect for his prejudices, and secretly trampled them underfoot; she would have kissed him and deceived him. Indiana saw many women behave in this manner, but felt so far above them that she would have blushed to imitate them. Virtuous and chaste, she believed herself under no obligation to flatter her master with words, so long as she showed him respect in her actions. She did not want his affection, because she could not respond to it. To deceive,

that was the great crime in her eyes. . . . By ceasing to
be master in his own house, his self-esteem had suffered; but it would have suffered all the more if he had
been master in an odious or ridiculous fashion.[10]

The mature Sand's account of her marriage to Casimir Dudevant in
her autobiography, and in the traces that are visible in her fiction, are not
altogether supported by the evidence of earlier contemporary letters.
These last became, no doubt, a source of embarrassment. They testify to
Aurore Dudevant's capacity for self-deception, encouraged by her intellectual capacity for reasoning away, or postponing, the recognition of stark
truths. The differences between the contemporary documentation and
what Sand reconstructs retrospectively may also testify to the affective
power which her own letters had on her at the time of writing. There is a
sense in which the success of her letters to her husband may have worked
on, even created, her perceptions of their intimate relationship; she fashioned it into something in which, for some time, she was able to believe. Or
at least the relationship which her letters constructed was something which
allowed her, for a period, successfully to suspend disbelief, as the readers of
her fiction would be encouraged, with consummate skill, to do also. While
it is the business of the reader of fiction to suspend disbelief, or at least to
dip in and out of faith in the imaginary, it is a quite different matter in life.
But it is a not uncommon mistake in marriage. The ridiculousness that
Sand the writer of fiction so frequently fears for her characters was something that she often experienced for herself.

But the gap between the dismal account of married life, provided by
her autobiography, and the contemporary evidence also suggests considerable strength of will. Her unhappiness was no doubt elevated, through her
reading of Byron, Chateaubriand, and Rousseau, to a level at which it
could be stoically, even at times deliciously, borne. She was well able to cast
herself as the romantic, and tragic, heroine; but there was realism too, a
determination, a practical and pragmatic will, to make an unsuitable marriage work. The failure of the marriage rendered that will naïve and
embarrassing. But it was the same strength of will, liberated by a growing
confidence in herself and her ideas, that manifests itself again when she
recognized that life offered more satisfying possibilities than Casimir
Dudevant, and that the marriage would have to be openly renegotiated.

During those first years as a wife, expectant mother, and then mother,
Aurore delays her signature when writing to Casimir, detailing tender

affection and the anguish of separation, and describes her own physical longing for her husband's return. There are arousing phrases, intimations of an erotic life imagined, if not lived out: "Adieu my Angel, my dear love, my dear friend, I embrace you. I embrace you a thousand times, I press you in my arms against my heart. How I will kiss you when you return!" Or again, "I embrace you a thousand times, I press you in my arms, I eat you, I adore you, adieu my love, adieu all that I love. . . ."[11] These fragments testify to her commitment to her marriage, to an idea of marriage, a commitment which weakened. But it was to these letters that her lawyer—who by that time was also her lover—would appeal later, during the court proceedings for separation. Although crucial evidence when it came to the legal separation, Aurore Dudevant cannot have regretted keeping these pathetic documents hidden until then.

The pathos arises from the youthful urgency and desperation of which they speak, the compulsion to make her husband an object of archromantic, even absolute, love. At the time, as her letters to Émilie de Wismes make very evident, self-abnegation, self-denial, self-sacrifice, are the necessary means for a woman to establish a successful relationship with her husband. In arguing the complexities and difficulties of marriage during those years, she was arguing first and foremost with herself.

But the evidence of a much later letter to Hippolyte, which can only be read as confessional by implication, suggests, at least, that the self-sacrifice was more than a matter of habit, taste, opinion, and abnegation of self. This giving up of the self was much deeper and more painful to bear. It embraced the physical, the sexual, and the denial of erotic feeling, or absence of feeling. Aurore's choice of words, the simplicity of her language, suggests that it was a self-denial that should not—reasonably—be borne. At the time, Hippolyte's daughter, Léontine, was soon to be married. Aurore advised her father to speak to his son-in-law: "Prevent the one who shares your sex from brutally assaulting your daughter on their wedding night. . . . Men are too little aware that this amusement is a martyrdom for us. So tell him that he must, to some extent, defer his pleasures; make him aware that his wife may, little by little, be taught by him to understand them and to respond to them. Nothing is as awful as the terror, the suffering and the disgust of a poor child who knows nothing and who sees itself raped by a brute."[12] Sand's insights into the relationship between the experience she described *and its consequences for identity* are as striking as the explicit manner of the letter: The "poor child" *"sees itself"* in this scene. The young woman is simultaneously object, she is acted on, and the seeing subject, a *voyeuse*, witnessing from the outside an act of brutality. The girl not only suffers, within her being, but recognizes, from the outside, the degradation, the self-disgust. Self-esteem is dangerously damaged. The novelist participates in experience, feels, but simultaneously has some perspective on experience. Subjectivity and objectivity are blurred, and confused.

Aurore's letter to her brother was written years after her own wedding night. Her first sexual encounters with her husband were no doubt experiences of a largely subjective kind. Her capacity to consider heterosexual activity objectively, and intellectually, developed gradually. There is also evidence suggesting that her full awakening to erotic feeling was as much a matter of intimate encounters with, and love of, women. But this comes a little later.

During the early months and years of her marriage she must have come to suspect that what she had first conceived as self-sacrifice, in the name of God, and conjugal happiness was instead, or in addition, a form of self-destructive masochism, devoid of religious or spiritual significance. The ability to see her marital relationship more objectively was triggered not by private acts but by a publicly humiliating scene. The harsh recognition of the bankruptcy and lovelessness of her relationship with Casimir was not discovered intellectually, nor was it a matter of conscience. For some time she had continued skilfully to prevaricate. Like her grandmother, she could exploit rhetoric to manipulate the truth, as her letters testify. She had been precociously aware of the power of language to distort the truth, and she puts it very lucidly in *Indiana:*

> Nothing is so easy or so common as self-deception among those who lack neither intelligence nor familiarity with all the subtleties of language. It is like a queen turned into a prostitute who, lowering and raising herself, plays every part; . . . it is like a litigant who has an answer for everything, who has always foreseen everything, and has a thousand ways of being in the right. The most honest man is the one who thinks and acts best, but the most powerful is the one who knows best how to write and speak.[13]

By the autumn of 1824, the gap between their epistolary and their lived relationship had widened. During the months at Le Plessis, from May to September, Aurore realized that the gap was a chasm. At this heavenly place Aurore was first confronted by an image of herself which filled her with disgust. There is bathos in the scene—that sudden and ludicrous descent from one level to another. And the element of surprise, of astonished recognition of something she had hitherto ignored or denied, forced the truth out. Casimir, James, and Angèle were taking their coffee outside, on the veranda. Aurore had recently celebrated her twentieth birthday, but she continued to enjoy abandoned play with the children. Often, as her letters testify, she had walked alone in the park, "to dream and to cry."[14] While publicly everyone considered her lively, happy, and brimming over with gaiety and a degree of mischievousness, in private she continued to suffer from an inexplicable melancholy. As they played boisterously that summer evening, sand was flicked into the air, and some grains found their way into Papa James's cup. He called to them, asking them to play more quietly and further away from the terrace. No one heard, and the lively game continued. Casimir then rose, strode deliberately towards Aurore, and delivered a quick slap to her cheek. This time she withdrew to the park not "to dream and to cry," actions which may have been in part romantic and not altogether unpleasurable self-dramatization, however simultaneously acute and real her sense of despair. This time she wept out of "anger."

Retrospectively, it was this act, which may have been intended to do no more than startle her and bring her like a child to her senses, that Sand the autobiographer identified as the catalyst, the point of crisis. For Aurore, Casimir's public display of marital authority went deep, and the wound it inflicted never healed: "From that day on I scarcely loved him, and things went from bad to worse."[15]

In *Indiana*, Ophelia the dog is threatened with violence, but the violence has been displaced. It is Indiana who suffers. At Le Plessis it was Aurore who suffered the slap. The complexities and mysteries of human relationships, and the simultaneities of human experience at given moments, can only be exposed in narrative in a reduced and simplified form. Colonel Delmare's act, like Casimir's, is a symbol that succinctly conveys what can only partially be described in the linear form of words.

In *Lélia* it is of the sin of pride that Pulchérie the courtesan accuses her ascetic sister. Lélia has denied life, Pulchérie argues, not out of "higher" feelings, or beliefs, but out of fear of public humiliation. What Pulchérie knows, and Lélia must accept, is that the public judgement that condemns is often a matter of double standards. Why deny life, Pulchérie argues, for the sake of avoiding such hypocritical judgement? Aurore had accepted private humiliations as a matter of legitimate, even honourable, self-sacrifice. But Casimir's act of public humiliation wounded her pride. She no longer wanted to remain at Le Plessis. She felt ashamed. That society now had a fuller understanding of her marriage, and it was a humiliating insight. But neither Casimir nor Aurore wanted to return home: "We were afraid of Nohant, afraid no doubt of finding ourselves face to face, with such different instincts . . . and personalities that were mutually incomprehensible. Without wanting to hide anything from each other, we were unable to explain ourselves."[16]

The instabilities of the marriage are reflected in the hopeful travelling of the next few years. First they rented a small house at Ormesson, west of Paris. But they needed company. Aurore invited Tante Lucie, Maréchal, and Clotilde to join them. Casimir often spent his nights in Paris. Domestically little changed. Time passed. It was a period in Aurore's life apparently devoid of letter writing. It may be that the correspondence has been lost, or it may be that she wrote little, because she was suffering from depression at the time.[17]

Aurore's life was uneventful, empty. The nation, on the other hand, was witnessing major events. Louis XVIII was interred in the Basilica of Saint-Denis. On 25 October Aurore attended the funeral. Louis was, after all, a distant relative, as was Charles X, who ascended the throne.

That winter, 1824, Aurore again turned to Montaigne. The paradoxes and complexities of human conscience, the potential and pitfalls for self-knowledge and self-deception, for honesty and deceit, these matters continued to fascinate. Could Aurore understand better her responsibilities, understand the nature of marriage, and see how to fashion out of these a better life for herself, her husband, her child? That winter, in December, they left Ormesson. Casimir had quarrelled with the gardener. They returned to Paris on 13 December and stayed with Uncle Maréchal for a couple of weeks before taking their own furnished apartment on the Faubourg Saint-Honoré, no more willing to return home than before. They based themselves in the capital until March.

In Paris Aurore looked to the sage and gentle Abbé Prémord for advice. Older, but as humane as ever, he comforted her, encouraged her, and suggested a retreat. To succumb to melancholy, even stoically to tolerate it, was, he believed, quite wrong. Casimir, either because he believed that such a period of contemplation might cure his wife of her melancholy or because he was glad to have the burden of his wife temporarily lifted, acquiesced in her withdrawal to the Couvent des Augustines Anglaises.

Faith was not a matter of concern to Casimir but, the mature Sand implies, he was aware of the constraints that it placed on believers. Constraints which were to his advantage. As Sand writes, "My husband was not at all religious, but thought it good that I should be."[18]

The return to an institution in which the individual has had a place but no longer belongs is rarely the reassuring experience anticipated. Those colleagues to whom she had been close and who were still there were either envious of her freedom or bigoted. Sister Alicia, who had been her "adoptive mother" and whom she had loved so dearly, allowed Aurore to bring Maurice into the convent. He was posted through an ingenious revolving hatch, designed for parcels. Seeing nuns for the first time, dressed in their elaborate costumes, he had called out with childish spontaneity, "Rabbits! Rabbits!" Sister Alicia was tolerant, and not altogether conventional in the management of her authority. But her advice was predictable, and disappointing. It fell a long way short of the ideal solution Aurore sought. Sister Alicia had no easy or visionary solutions. Aurore had, after all, not only a husband but a son: "You have a charming child. . . . That is all that is necessary to your earthly happiness. Life is short."[19] Aurore's life was, however, to be unusually long and remarkably full. She loved Maurice, but there were a good many others to whom, for periods at least, she was quite as devoted.

Aurore soon realized that remaining in the convent was no more than marking time. The nights were cold and damp, and she was afraid that Maurice's health would suffer. She left, and the family returned to Nohant. The months that followed, and the spring of 1825 in particular, was a time which, looking back, she lived in the awful wake of Deschartres's death. In fact he died three years later. It may be that she misremembered, or it may be that novelistically she felt she could better convey the melancholy of that period by writing Deschartres's death into it. Aurore suspected that he had committed suicide. There is no evidence of this, although his last letters are despairing, and he died virtually penniless.[20]

She also became increasingly concerned, during these months, for Hippolyte's health. His life at Nohant was one of compulsive and relentless dissipation and risk-taking: drinking, shooting, and riding. Casimir often joined him. The growing companionship between Hippolyte and Casimir served to alienate her from both of them. But her husband continued to make not altogether insignificant gestures. He tried to be a "good husband." He sent for a piano, a luxury which went beyond their means. He tried, but failed, to enjoy listening to her play. She was a good pianist, but the distractions of the piano were insufficient even for Aurore. Her melancholy became a source of hypochondria. First she had feared for Maurice's health, if not his life, then for Hippolyte's. She feared for her own health. She had developed a deep cough, breathlessness, and a racing heartbeat. She believed herself to be tubercular.

In June Aimée and Jane Bazouin, friends from Aurore's convent days, arrived at Nohant. They suggested that the Dudevants accompany them on a little holiday to the Pyrenees.

Aurore was beginning to suspect, that summer of 1825, that the hitherto mysterious melancholy, the insufferable ennui that caused a deep ache within her, was all too explicable. Hippolyte had awakened her, that summer before her grandmother's death, to the sensory, even erotic, pleasures of the physical. These last had not been sustained by her sexual relationship with Casimir, by childbirth or breast-feeding. She had needs that Casimir and Maurice had not met. And she had interests that Casimir did not share. The philosophical riddles of life, the theological puzzles, her desire to explore and measure lived experience against intellectual ideas had continued to be very important to her. In her late teens, when she had left the convent and returned to Nohant, she had embarked on adult life. Her philosophical and religious curiosity had been nourished by Deschartres and her grandmother, by Stéphane de Grandsagne, by René de Villeneuve, by Abbé Prémord. After her marriage, she was now aware, her interests had been lost. "You," she wrote to Casimir, "did not share them. I did not tell myself this. I felt it; I drew you in my arms; I was loved by you but my happiness was missing, something that I could not articulate."[21] But these insights are retrospective. They form part of a letter written some months later. There is no evidence that she and Casimir considered, during the spring of 1825, separation. Instead they accepted the Bazouin sisters' invitation and willingly distanced themselves from the locus of their unhappy marriage.

On 5 July 1825, Aurore's birthday, they left Nohant to meet Jane and Aimée in the Pyrenees. They had been invited to join them and their father at the then fashionable spa town of Cauterets, high in the mountains. Believing herself to be suffering from a serious chest condition, possibly consumption, both she and Casimir thought that the clear air might restore her to health. There would be lively company, too. Aurore left with few regrets: "In ten minutes I will have left Nohant. I leave nothing behind that can inspire real regret, if not my brother. But how that old friendship of a bygone age has cooled! *He* laughs, he is happy, at the hour of my departure.

Let's be off, adieu Nohant, perhaps I will never see you again."²² Why does she close the entry in this ominous way? She may have believed that she was dying. But in the Pyrenees, her health quickly restored—supposing it had been seriously weak on arrival—she would soon take extraordinary physical risks. Casimir would accuse her of dangerous bravado, of drawing attention to herself.

It may be that her last diary entry, written at Nohant, suggests that in the wild and romantic setting of the Pyrenees, she had planned to gamble with her life, and defy her husband's authority in more ways than one. She must have expected that he would spend little time at her side. She knew, or at least felt, the inadequacies of their relationship. In *Lélia* the heroine wonders at her commitment to a deeply unsatisfactory relationship. There are echoes of Aurore's letters to her husband. To some extent Lélia speaks for Aurore:

> Why did I love him for so long . . . ? No doubt because of the feverish restlessness produced in me by the absence of any personal satisfaction. Near him I felt a sort of peculiar, delirious longing which originated in the . . . forces of my mind and thus could not be satisfied by any physical embrace. I felt my breast consumed by an unquenchable fire and his kisses brought me no relief. I would clasp him in my arms with extraordinary strength and then fall exhausted beside him, disheartened by my total incapacity to convey my yearnings to him. For me, desire was a passion of the soul which paralysed the power of my senses before they had ever been aroused.²³

In the Pyrenees, at Cauterets, Bagnères, and Lourdes, she would meet two people who would recognize that "passion of the soul." Aurélien de Sèze would arouse, for the first time, the strength of feeling excited by adulterous passion. The later correspondence between Aurélien and Aurore provides ample evidence of their relationship. But it was also at Cauterets that she met Zoé Leroy. Her love for these two people, and the pleasures of a triangular relationship, threw into high relief the inadequacies, the tragedy, the dullness, of her marriage. At Cauterets she became aware of her own capacity to love passionately, and she also became more fully aware of her capacity to attract both men and women to her.

IX

The Call of the Wild

"We come from nature, and we live in,
by, and for nature."

~In the nineteenth century, journeys forced a wealthy, or relatively wealthy, family to spend hours on end together in an enclosed space. The route from Nohant to Cauterets in the Pyrenees—one of some six hundred kilometres—seemed still longer to Aurore and Casimir. Aurore kept a journal, "Voyage aux Pyrénées," from which she allegedly quotes in her autobiography, although the manuscript has never been found.[1] Sand mentions it in a letter to Zoé Leroy, whom she met at Cauterets; Zoé was sent the journal to read, thus becoming one of the most important and earliest members of Sand's audience.[2] Given that those letters—which *have* been carefully preserved—from which she quotes in the autobiography are sometimes significantly altered, it may be that the "Voyage" was also edited, cut, extended, in short rewritten. But there is also the evidence of her letters of the period. At least where the two sources concur, there can be few doubts.

Casimir was, Sand writes, "bored by travel. He wants to have arrived. I understand that; but is it my fault if the journey is one of 200 leagues?"[3] The Pyrenean adventure marked a new departure from the hopeful travelling of Aurore's first years of marriage: she recognized for the first time that Casimir was implicated in her melancholy. They broke their journey at Chalus (Haute-Vienne), some thirty kilometres from Limoges. The journal entry notes: "I read a few pages of Ossian. The sun set me down there, in the very middle of my shadows and my wandering stars; I took the side of reflection, which is no negligible matter for one who wanted to be able to live without thinking about anything. I took fine resolutions about the journey: not to be in the least bit anxious about Maurice's cries, not to be impatient about the length of the journey, not to be saddened by the temperamental moments of *my friend*. . . ." Describing her husband and companion on the journey thus is, the reader of the fragments begins to suspect, at least tinged with irony. By the time they reached Périgeux, where again they briefly rested, Aurore's resolutions had been more narrowly defined: "I have travelled through charming lands; I have seen beautiful horses. This town seems pleasant enough, but I am saddened to death. I have wept a good deal, out walking; but what is the point of weeping. One must become accustomed to having death in one's soul and a laughing face."

Some days later, the animation and colour of a local fair at Tarbes, while recognized by Aurore, failed to lift her spirits: "Tarbes is very pretty, but my husband continues to be ill-tempered." But the sight of the white mountains rising steeply out of the plains, gradually drawing closer, and with that closeness "gaining colour," astonished her: "The surprise and admiration seized me; it was breathtaking to the point of asphyxiation."[4] The diary entries bear close resemblance to Aurore's letters, sent from Cauterets. A long letter to her mother, written in August, described her awakening passion for the mountains which she and her mother had crossed years earlier on their way to Madrid. "I am so captivated," she wrote to Sophie-Victoire, "by the Pyrenees, that I will never dream, or speak, my whole life, of anything but mountains, torrents, grottoes and precipices."[5] The diary entry describing her first morning is fuller, and more crafted. Written into it is a compelling moment of anticlimax, or deferred climax: "This morning, barely awake, I ran to the window. . . . Where then are last evening's mountains? Where can be hidden the cataracts whose thunder I hear?" The moment of climax is allegory. It describes both the landscape as the mists lift, revealing the landscape in all its minute detail and macrocosmic splendour, and, at the same time, a moment of new understanding: "Finally everything was lit up, everything became clear." The French juxtaposes the transitive and the self-reflexive form of the verb ("light up" and "enlighten"). One describes the effect of the light, the other, revelation; one tells of the visual, the other, the intellectual, the emotional, the spiritual: "What I had taken to be the sky was the mist, what had seemed to me to be space, was mass." The entry continues in the third person, "Monsieur *** hunts with passion. . . . He rises at two in the morning and returns in the night. His wife complains. He seems not to foresee that a time will come when she will delight in this."[6]

Like those ingenious trompe l'oeil drawings where opposing images emerge as representations of one object one moment and something quite different the next, Aurore's experience in the Pyrenees threw into relief every aspect of her life and demanded careful—and fundamental—reassessment of reality, of what was substantial, and what was insubstantial, what was space, and what mass. What might at first seem to be an extravagant reading is substantiated by the next diary entry. Marriage is once again the subject. "If a husband," she continues, "frequently absents himself from his wife, as a matter of duty, this she must tolerate. If he distances himself in order to live more fully than is possible at his wife's side, it is a painful experience for the one who is abandoned." "It is also," she writes, a "philosophical lesson," and a "lesson in humility." And, she adds, "an important lesson, no doubt, but a deeply chilling one!"[7]

The journal moves uncannily between third- and first-person narrative. The analysis of marriage may be made apparently objective by the absence of the "I," but the reader is never for a moment deceived. It is Aurore who concludes, "Marriage is fine for lovers, and salutary for saints. Aside from saints and lovers, there is a crowd of the ordinary-minded and peaceful-hearted who do not know love and who cannot attain the saintly. Marriage is the supreme goal of love. When love is no longer, or is not, sacrifice remains. Very good for those that understand sacrifice." And so the journal continues. Is there, she later asks, a middle way between saintly sacrifice and the mundane acceptance of the small material pleasures offered by marriage? If so, it is despair. Suddenly, the "I" breaks in, or rather the "me," as object, displacing the third person. Of Aimée Bazouin she writes, "She scolds me a good deal. She does not understand that one can make oneself dizzy and that one needs to forget. 'Forget what?' she asks me—How do I know? Forget everything, above all forget that one exists."[8] The "dizziness" Aurore describes is bound up with her "follies," a manifestation of a madness that she described in contemporary letters.[9] Aimée was intolerant of this, and impatient with her.

It would be easy to write off her own references to her "follies" as further evidence of romantic self-dramatization. But simply because her discourse is a conventionally romantic one does not mean that it is without substance. Rather her language suggests that she had not yet found a discourse, an explanation, for something that mattered greatly. It may well be that Aurore's idiosyncratic perceptions of marriage, her dissatisfactions, the strength of her longing for ideal love, and the desperation that these, unsatisfied, engendered, made her fear madness. Her mother, she had come to accept, was an "agitated character" who continued to cause Aurore great pain.[10] Her father had, according to Deschartres, experienced periods of deep despair, and had contemplated, if not attempted, suicide. It may even be that he had deliberately diced with death before his fatal riding accident.[11] In short, there was frightening evidence in her heredity. Her capacity to swing from exuberant joyfulness to profound melancholy was, according to her husband, evidence of a sinister instability. Furthermore, her periods of heightened experience, of joyfulness, he equated—and he was not alone in this—not with happiness but with madness: "My husband, like many others, was somewhat astonished to see me suddenly become so lively and so mad. . . ."[12] Aurore had found her mother's emotional instability and unpredictability impossible to tolerate: "I could not get used to her swings from mad gaiety and sombre anger."[13]

Aurore's "highs" may have been like her mother's, but her "lows" were different. Melancholy had not yet turned to anger, and the former is no doubt more self-destructive. Furthermore, she had begun to believe in her husband's judgement of her: "These extremes of mood led certain people to the opinion that I was eccentric. My husband, more indulgent, considered me an idiot. He may not have been wrong, and little by little he encouraged me so strongly to believe in the superiority of his reason and his intelligence, that for a long time I felt crushed by it, and dumb in society."[14] Aurore would not be alone, as a nascent woman writer of the nineteenth century, if she had considered her peculiar understanding of herself, her perspective on society, and so much of the relationship between the individual and the group explicable only in terms of madness.[15]

In the early days at Cauterets, Maurice's health was soon restored, supposing his ailment had ever been anything more than a matter of Aurore's fears; suspicious of the health cures offered by the spa, Aurore could only escape herself through relentless and dangerous physical activity, as she had done with Hippolyte that summer of her grandmother's death at Nohant. But with Hippolyte physical escape from self had been a matter of marking time. Decisions, she had known then, had soon to be taken. Now she had made her choice. She was married to Casimir Dudevant, and they had had their first child. What choices lay open? This was the question she explored with Zoé Leroy. Zoé was the twenty-eight-year-old daughter of a Bordeaux wine merchant. She was not only older than

Aurore but openly rebellious and iconoclastic. No husband had yet begun to shake *her* confidence in her own vision of things. Similar in many ways to Aurore, she assisted, even colluded, in Aurore's first cautious liberation. Their similarity of outlook reassured Aurore that she was not alone in her vision; she was either sane or less insane. Casimir seems to have thought differently: that they were both to some degree mad. He accused Aurore, in Zoé's company, of "making herself conspicuous." Aurore jokingly accused Zoé of the same thing, and the latter's dismissive laugh clearly angered Casimir.[16]

The occasion was a trip from Cauterets to Gavarnie. Zoé and Aurore had set off ahead of the party. "Zoé," the journal entry reads, "is insanely brave. It is intoxicating; here I am on a level with her. We reach a spot called *Chaos,* half an hour ahead of everyone else. We can stop, and contemplate. 'My God,' Zoé says, 'here we are alone, what bliss! Let's make ourselves conspicuous as it pleases us. Let us look and admire.' Zoé is uplifted. There is good reason. I love this enthusiastic nature, generous mind, intelligent heart. . . . Of what do we speak? Ah! so many things . . . ! Love, marriage, religion, friendship, how do I know?" It is Zoé, the journal alleges, who articulates a provisional interpretation. It is not that they are mad: "We have a bit more intelligence and perspective than a good many others who think of nothing, and it's too bad for us!"[17]

Zoé Leroy threw into high relief the conformism of the Bazouin sisters, their passive collusion in the mores of a society that denied them physical freedom. They had spent their stay at Cauterets in the hands of the resort's doctors. They drank the waters, and bathed in them. Aurore thought it likely that their health would be damaged by the experience. Zoé, on the other hand, like Aurore, was keen to explore. The archromantic setting stimulated wide-ranging and intimate discussions. But what they discussed did not remain on a purely theoretical level. As Aurore became more clear about her mistakes—of having confused the substantial and the insubstantial, what was matter and what mattered—her behaviour changed, and Zoé encouraged her. What emerged was a triangular relationship, typical of so many relationships in which Aurore would be, and had already been, involved. For some months she had in many ways shared her marriage with her half-brother, and had found herself the displaced observer of other lives being lived more fully. This time it was Zoé who assumed the position of *voyeuse,* and Aurore became involved in the action.

There are few mentions of Aurélien de Sèze in the journal, and these are brief and often cryptic.[18] But the letters that Aurore and Aurélien exchanged when they had left Cauterets, Aurore for her parents-in-law at Guillery, Aurélien for Bordeaux, provide ample evidence of the strength of feeling each excited in the other.[19] The young man, Aurélien, was a twenty-five-year-old magistrate. He had come to Cauterets to be with his fiancée, Mlle Laure Le Hoult, and her family. Later he would describe his fiancée to Aurore as "very beautiful but without ideas." He had quickly recognized that, however unconventional Aurore's beauty, she was very far from deficient in the realm of ideas. Aurélien de Sèze was the nephew of one of Louis XVI's advocates, and as conservative and Catholic as his family. He was deeply struck by Aurore's conversation: "No one speaks like you, no one has your accent, your voice, your laugh, your way of seeing a thing and of expressing the idea. No one sees this but me." Aurélien claimed that Aurore's intellectual side, bound up in every aspect of her unusual personality, had attracted him above all: "Your qualities, your ideas, your talents, your quite perfect simplicity married to such a superior mind, such wide instruction, are the things I love in you. . . ." And as if to clinch his point, he all but invites Aurore to misconstrue his final remark, "Even if you were ugly, I would love you."[20]

Aurélien was slight, elegant, articulate, and, despite his youth, not ignorant in the techniques of seduction. Casimir continued to devote his time to that other kind of pursuit: hunting. Zoé encouraged intimacy between the abandoned wife and bored fiancé. The Bazouin sisters were shocked that Aurore showed few signs of discouraging Aurélien's advances, but both Aurore and Aurélien shared a similar notion of honour. Aurore was married, and Aurélien engaged to be married. Both no doubt knew that they were playing a relatively safe game. What they enacted, as well as their speeches and even soliloquies, remained strictly scripted. What they lived was high romantic drama: alone in a boat on Lake Gaube, Aurélien carved the same first three letters of both their names, "Aur."[21] The implication was that their love had been predestined. And there were moments of physical intimacy. Aurélien confessed his love, and urged Aurore to make a similar confession. The codes of love required that she feign indifference.[22]

Offended by Aurore's apparent coldness, or uncertain as to the consequences of what had been initiated, he distanced himself from Aurore. A few days later he accompanied the Le Hoult family on an excursion to Gavarnie. Aurore might have delighted in the pain of separation, and have reflected indulgently on the melancholic despair into which she had been plunged. Instead she insisted that her husband escort her to Gavarnie. The

Bazouin sisters were outraged at the scandal Aurore was exciting. Casimir gave in to Aurore's pleading, and they soon caught up with the Le Hoult party. Aurélien was again overwhelmed by Aurore's vivacious company, and no doubt flattered by her extraordinary audacity. On their return to Cauterets, at a dance, they found their way into the garden. Aurélien spoke of his decision to renounce his love for her. Whether or not intended to provoke him, she encouraged him to remain faithful to his decision. But could they not, she suggested, remain friends? The evening was mild. The music no doubt drifted deliciously out into the night air. The company was some distance away, in the brightness of the festivities. They were concealed by the darkness. Taking Aurore in his arms, he pressed her to him. He was, Aurore would later claim, by way of excuse or triumphantly, "no longer master of himself."[23] Aurore pulled away from him, but Aurélien detained her further, insisting that the moment of physical intimacy he had initiated should not be read as a sign that he had compromised his, or her, honour. He swore fidelity, platonic fidelity. Reassured, she confessed the reciprocity of her feelings. But the improvisation that had replaced what Aurore had no doubt believed to be her script frightened her.

She fled—to Casimir. He had spoken harshly to her, she said, referring to their conversations when she had sought to persuade him to accompany her to Gavarnie. She wanted Casimir to know that she had suffered too. She was also concerned to impress on her husband the nature of her relationship with Aurélien. He, she insisted, considered her a "dear sister," and was taken precisely by her "purity," a purity which, by implication, he would not seek to sully. Casimir, it seems, said little. But they would, he made clear, advance the date of their departure.

Towards the end of August signs of autumn were already visible in the high Pyrenees. On the high plateaux the mists continued to lift during the day but descended earlier and earlier in the afternoon. Visitors began to leave: the bathers first. The walkers lingered for a little longer, admiring, as Aurore admired, the mysterious changes in the light, the dramatic effects of the mists. Aurore watched the people too, the tourists, the herdsmen, "tanned by the sun and looking more like Arabs than Frenchmen walking in groups in their picturesque costumes. . . . Behind them came their herds, cows, sheep, goats, calves, and chickens. A good number, born in the mountains during the course of the season, and never having seen men other than their keepers, were overcome by terrible fear as they passed through the hamlets. . . ."[24]

Aurore and Aurélien made one last trip, this time to the grotto at

Lourdes. The setting could not have been more romantic, and Aurélien's words no less so, if Aurore's record is accurate, " 'It is against this imposing natural backdrop of this imposing nature,' he told me, 'that, in saying adieu, I want to deliver a solemn sermon, to love you all my life as I love my mother, and my sister, and to respect you as I respect them.' He pressed me to his heart, and that is the greatest liberty that he has ever taken with me."[25]

But however innocent the relationship between Aurore and Aurélien may seem to contemporary eyes, even comic, or tragicomic, in the discrepancy between what was spoken and what lived, Aurore's intimacy with Aurélien was to change her ideas, and indeed her behaviour, fundamentally. And the triangular relationship, in which Zoé continued to play a significant part, was sustained for some months. There were further meetings, but more importantly numerous letters were exchanged. Aurore not only corresponded with Zoé, she sent her the journal. And in her letters to Aurélien she embarked on what was essentially her first attempt at autobiography. She wanted him to know who she was. She wanted to explain herself, and their epistolary relationship was a safe one. But she had found another audience, a male reader—and there were further meetings too.

At the beginning of September 1825 Aurélien returned to Bordeaux, and Aurore and Casimir travelled to Guillery, near Nérac, in Gascony, to stay with Casimir's parents. Aurore and the Baron enjoyed each other's company, but relations with the Baronne were strained. She no doubt suspected that her son was not sufficiently in control of his wife.

Aurore once again suffered that exaggerated loneliness aggravated by unsympathetic company. "The young people," she wrote in a letter to Zoé, "*are hunters*. By this, implicit in the term, I mean an ugly being who does nothing but eat at table and fall asleep in the salon, etc." Her husband, she wrote, hunts while she ages. In the same letter she accepts impatiently Zoé's invitation to La Brède, where the Leroys had a property. The Dudevants, Aurore suggests, will pick Zoé up in Bordeaux, en route.[26] They made the trip to Bordeaux between 4 and 10 October. As she would write some weeks later, in an extensive letter to her husband, the so-called *lettre-confession* of November 1825, "I felt an extreme longing to go to Bordeaux." She claims, but gives no explanation as to why, "I felt that I would be seeing Aurélien for the last time."[27]

While they were staying in Bordeaux, Aurélien called on Aurore and Casimir. The latter was out, and Aurore spoke to Aurélien of her unhappiness, her regrets. Their first moments of physical intimacy had, or so she claimed, been initiated by Aurélien. This time it was Aurore who rested her head on Aurélien's shoulder. At that moment the door to the room opened, and Casimir strode in. Aurore threw herself at her husband's feet, begging his forgiveness. Casimir was above all concerned, Aurore alleged, whatever the nature of her relationship with Aurélien, that there be no scandal.

The next day it was not just the group that had planned to stay at La Brède—Zoé, Aurore, and Casimir—that set off from Bordeaux. Aurélien joined the party. The company could not have been more happily augmented for Aurore. The presence of her husband no doubt heightened the intensity and thus significance of fragments of stolen contact: whispers, glances, even moments of physical intimacy. And it may well be that Aurore was secure in the knowledge that Casimir's presence would prevent any spontaneous passionate outbursts, on her own part or Aurélien's. Her relationship with Aurélien could, in short, continue to be enjoyed within safe boundaries. The Romantic drama could continue; reality, in the form of passionate sexual contact, would not break in.[28]

Aurélien, it seems, found the situation just a touch frustrating. He wrote at length to Aurore, blaming himself for the progress of their friendship, their love. She was to assure her husband that it had all been his fault. He pleaded with her to convince her husband of the "purity" of their relationship, and to promise him that they would never again meet. It was more than Aurore could bear. She confided in Zoé, who, ever concerned to facilitate the continuing intimacy between the two lovers, sought Aurélien out. He too was plunged in despair; she led him back to Aurore. Aurélien's hopes remain obscure. His dogmatic Catholic faith and his conservatism may well have ruled out adultery, or he may now have known that the consummation of love, for which he may have longed, would never be fulfilled. Friendship may not have held the charms that it held for Aurore. But she had her way.

Aurore believed that the purity of their friendship was something that "the good and generous Casimir" could not refuse them. Their relationship would be like that of "brother and sister"; Casimir would share their happiness. She was prepared to reason further and even more preposterously: it would be *for Casimir* that they would come together once more: "We will re-unite for the sake of *his* happiness."[29] Aurore, once again, exploited rhetoric, even logic, masterfully, and to her own advantage. Casimir's first response to her proposals, when he returned from his habitual hunting, was a little irritation. But he quickly excused his initial out-burst: he was exhausted from his day's activities. What continued to concern him was the fear of public judgement.

As soon as Aurore's relationship with Aurélien had started to draw attention, in the Pyrenees, Casimir had been primarily concerned to avoid humiliation of one kind or another. Aurore had written to Aurélien quoting his words: "What must above all be avoided," he implored, "is drawing attention to what has happened." Sand interpreted his perspective: "It seemed to me that he was divided between the need to believe me and a sense of shame which made him fear being tricked."[30]

The strength of feeling between Aurélien and Aurore did not render Aurore's programme for platonic love altogether workable. Again separated, during the autumn of 1825, Aurore at Guillery—from mid-October 1825 until the end of January 1826—and Aurélien in Bordeaux, the epistolary relationship continued unabated. Aurore kept a letter-journal for Aurélien, sending bundles. Other more urgent letters were dispatched one by one, and delivered by Zoé. Aurore's letters begin with noble pronouncements. To the contemporary reader these read as something close to parody: "We are pure. Our feelings . . . have attained a celestial brilliance. . . ." But Aurore was also concerned, and able, to introduce erotic nuances, and light, arousing linguistic touches which would later become one of the many reasons for the commercial success of her fiction. Sexual frustration is written into her descriptions of her husband's somnolence; and while he sleeps, she remembers past experience, and imagines. The effect that her fantasies have on her is extreme. Frequently, she is compelled to go out into the open, in the hope that "the night-wind refresh my burning head." Still more daringly, she makes plain to Aurélien that her sexual relationship with her husband has ceased: "He reproaches me for pushing him away."[31] A month later, in the *lettre-confession*, she would confirm the breakdown in the marriage: "Your caresses made me suffer. I was afraid of acting insincerely if I returned them, and you thought me cold."[32]

The famous letter to her husband was not written unsolicited. On 6 November 1825, just before leaving Guillery to inspect the Nohant estate, Casimir discovered the letter-journal that Aurore had written for Aurélien. He was outraged and angry, he felt humiliated. He left for Nohant the same day, returning on 20 November. What Aurore proposed in her letter of 15 November, in paragraphs written with consummate skill, is that her husband, "the good and generous Casimir," allow a triangular friendship, one from which they will all derive pleasure. Casimir would, she assured him, remain apparently in control! His "choices," however, were strictly limited. In well over twenty pages of small handwriting Aurore sketched out Casimir's impossible position. If he failed to display the "nobility," the "generosity" which she attributed to him, and refused her proposals, she would, she claimed, die. What Aurore wanted was, on the one hand, to continue an "open" correspondence with both Aurélien and Zoé, while leaving open the possibility of meeting at some future date, and on the other to encourage Casimir to develop more intellectual interests. She would do her utmost not to give in to feelings of melancholy, and he would do his utmost not to give in to bad temper.

The letter was delivered to Casimir on his return. He had no choice but to accept, or feign acceptance of Aurore's proposals. For all her words and Casimir's assent to them, life had changed little. That winter, at Guillery, where the doctors had advised her to stay until the weather improved, melancholy descended on Aurore once again. Whether her depression was the cause of her ill health or vice versa is impossible to know. "I have a constant headache," she wrote to Zoé. "An hour of work kills me. . . ."[33]

Aurore and Casimir finally made their long-planned trip to Bordeaux at the end of January 1826. Aurore saw a good deal of Zoé and of Aurélien, although rarely alone. What mattered most about Aurore's relationship with Aurélien was less the time they spent together, however, than the psychic life that Aurore lived out, and wrote about, in her letters. These became increasingly long and full. Most importantly, they metamorphosed, as the relationship developed, from documents that record life into documents that transform life. Remarkably, Aurélien gradually became aware that his role in the relationship was, at least in part, to have acted as a catalyst for Aurore's writing. As though previously held back by a robust dam, the force of emotion Aurore experienced meeting Aurélien in the Pyrenees swept that barrier away.

The death of Casimir's father on 20 February called them back to Guillery. They made one final trip to Bordeaux from mid-March into April. There are no letters from the period, no doubt because she saw a good deal of Aurélien, her main correspondent of the period. Aurore and Casimir finally arrived back at Nohant on 6 April 1826.

She had allegedly started her journal of the Pyrenean adventure on leaving home nine months earlier. But there is an aimlessness about the early entries. That summer she found two confidants: Zoé and Aurélien. They perfectly complemented each other. Her friendship with them encouraged her writing, and that autumn she wrote long letters, almost daily, to Aurélien. By the end of October 1825 he had already become an absent presence: "When I write I even believe that you are behind me. You are reading over my shoulder, laughing at the weaknesses of my style, you find my ideas good, my feelings true, and you take my pen from my hand to correct me."[34] Still more tellingly, Aurore had recognized the therapeutic function of reconstructing her past in words: "I have never told anyone, and up until now I doubted the adage that a trouble shared is a trouble halved. But to confide in you my life story is to drink the waters of oblivion. It seems to me that hiding these memories in your heart is committing myself never to bring them into the light of day again and never again to taste their bitterness."[35]

Aurore had discussed her reading with both Zoé and Aurélien, and the latter's literary tastes, crucially, turned out not always to be to her liking: "After your eulogy, I took up once again *The Monk*, that dark novel that I had abandoned halfway through, bored and disgusted by the crimes and absurdities that mark every page. . . ."[36] In an earlier letter to Zoé, Aurore contrasted lovers of "dark novels" with those who prefer "gentle reveries," "*those* that *we* love, my dear Zoé."[37]

There is, in all the vagaries of these months away from Nohant, a strong element of playing at life, of evading serious decisions by attempting to build absurd safeguards. Yet at the same time, Aurore was discovering new capacities and propensities in herself—she was, after all, still in her early twenties. She carried within her the pain she had always known, and she was quite unable to conceal from herself the deep misery and disillusion which her marriage to Casimir had brought her. For all its silliness, the essentially immature timidity and romantic evasions of her relationship with Aurélien, it had inspired her to *write,* to reconstruct her past, to see herself in a new and clearer light. And her relationship with Zoé had reassured her that her own dissatisfactions, her own longings, were far from unique. When she returned to Nohant she welcomed, for the first time, the settled feeling that the familiarity of the place and people nourished. The dead lay there, but in their rightful place; her life lay ahead. She started to write in earnest, and now her writing would no longer *translate* life into words but offer new interpretations, new scenarios that she might one day dare to live out. She was no longer willing, in short, to suppress or sublimate her vision of things in the interests of marital peace and idle, if pleasing, fantasy.

X

The Travesty of Marriage

"A man and a woman are so close to being the
same thing that I scarcely understand the
endless distinctions and subtle arguments
which society produces on the subject."

When Aurore and Casimir (and baby Maurice) arrived at Nohant early
in April 1826, Aurore knew that this was a more permanent return. Their
financial position was unstable: there would have to be considerable
retrenchment. Aurore wrote to Louis-Nicolas Caron, whom she had met at
Le Plessis: "We're truly down-at-heel this year. We're building granaries
and it's ruining us. The inheritance has not made us rich."[1] Baron Dudevant's death had brought them virtually nothing. Casimir's father, it
emerged, had left almost the entire inheritance, which was not inconsiderable, to his wife, who also had a substantial fortune of her own.[2]

While Aurore realized that their financial position ruled out further
hopeful travelling, she no longer equated life at Nohant exclusively with
her marital unhappiness. The extreme solution of self-denial had failed.
But her discussions with Zoé had encouraged her to believe, or at least to
take seriously, her inner feelings of instinctive revolt. The "singularizing
of the self" which Casimir had criticized was not something she was going
to abandon. It had been a reaction to understandable feelings, feelings
which were not going to go away.

By the spring of 1826 Aurore had formulated a new and more workable solution. What she now sought was a reasonable compromise. The
angle of her vision had broadened, as though the vast vistas and wild

mountainscapes of the Pyrenees had provided her with a wider-angled lens. Aurélien had awakened other parts of her being. He had also become a crucial audience who had allowed her to begin the process of articulating her experience of life, explaining the girl she had been and the woman she had become. She now had to consider what her past suggested for her future.

The life Aurore picked up on her return that spring was closer to the life she had left off on her grandmother's death, half a decade earlier. Recognizing that a conventional approach to marriage had failed, aware that the birth of Maurice had been a revelation but had not transformed her life, she knew that neither her husband nor her son could offer the salvation she sought; nor had her relationship with Aurélien de Sèze made a significant difference. The questions she had relentlessly sought to answer in her late teens were questions to which she needed to return. She had failed to silence the persistent and disturbing intellectual and spiritual riddles of life of which she had been precociously aware.

Aurélien and Zoé had become, and remained by correspondence, essential sounding boards, as her grandmother and Deschartres had been. Returning to Nohant was a return to a familiar place and an old self: "There is real pleasure in finding oneself under one's own roof, in the midst of one's people, one's animals and one's furniture. Nothing of all this is indifferent, above all when one comes to it of one's own volition, in search of solitude and repose. This country brings back my entire life. Every tree, every stone retraces a chapter of my life story. You understand, my friend, that I am breathing, with satisfaction, the air that I needed. . . ."[3] The mountain landscape that she had told her mother would be the unique locus of her dreams, her conversation, in other words the landscape of the mind that she would always inhabit, had not been forgotten, but there is a sense in which it now represented escape. Aurore recognized it as a place of romantic stimulus, of fantasy, and she reconnected with the reality in which she was intimately and indissolubly bound up. And writing offered the obvious means to explore that self outside the self, rooted in the place. She focused not on the awe-inspiring grandeur but on the detail. What she heard, and wrote about, were "these little frogs who have but one note in their throats, but who each have a unique tone, and who gather, at night, in the corner of the meadows to sing an air to the moon. . . ."[4] Aurore's descriptions of the unfamiliar landscape of the Pyrenees had been closer to cliché. Now she was struggling to find her own voice, as she listened to the unique voices of the place. Sensory experience remained affective, but what mattered to her was the real meaning of it.

Aurore re-established a daily pattern much like that of her late teens. She resumed her medical ministrations to the local people, concocting herbal remedies and tonics. The plants were not simply the metaphorically charged stuff of poetry: they had real material potential, because she had known them since early childhood. Aurore even took over from Casimir the management of the estate, which years earlier she had shared with Deschartres. Initially she was only in charge while Casimir was away, but she then managed the estate for a more extended experimental period.

What made Aurore's new and practical married life at Nohant tolerable, however, was the continuing presence of an increasingly fictional Other:

> The sense of spiritual solitude was deep, absolute; it would have been fatal to a tender spirit, and a youth still at its prime, if it had not been filled with a dream that had taken on the importance of a passion, not in my life, because I had sacrificed my life to my duty, but in my thinking. An absent being with whom I conversed unceasingly, to whom I reported all my reflections, my dreams, my humble virtues, my platonic enthusiasms, a being who was excellent in reality, but whom I adorned with all the perfections that are not those of human nature, a man who, in fact, appeared before me, for days, sometimes hours, during the course of the years and who, as much a fantasy as I was myself, had never, in the slightest degree, troubled my religion, nor my conscience. It was here that I found the support and the consolation for my exile in the real world.[5]

In a language reminiscent of her descriptions of the still more youthful Corambé, she suggests that Aurélien had been transformed into a new incarnation of her androgynous childhood god. But Aurore's "exile in the real world" was not altogether devoid of interest.

Only weeks after being back at Nohant, on 24 May 1826, Aurore wrote to Zoé, full of self-reproach for not having put pen to paper sooner.

She has been busy, she explains by way of excuse: "Nohant, up until now so deserted, has suddenly become fashionable."[6] It is likely that the allegedly sudden and dramatic change was more a matter of Aurore's widening perspectives.

When Aurore and Casimir had first returned to Nohant after their marriage, Aurore had not renewed her friendships with her childhood companions. Some were still children and Casimir had little patience for those, in their teens, who remained childish—and bohemian. Some of them were now political allies who had to be tolerated.

The bohemian group that attracted Aurore was a youthful one. She herself was now twenty-two. Charles Duvernet was a few years younger, blond, and melancholic. Alphonse Fleury, although only seventeen, was exceptionally tall, with intensely blue eyes and an exaggerated blond moustache. Aurore called him "the Gaul." Alexis Duteil was one of the two members of the group who was older than Aurore. He was thirty, married, and a lawyer. His face was pockmarked, but his quick-wittedness and eloquence made him excellent company, and something of a leader. Duteil was the principal animator of social gatherings. Jules Néraud, nine years older than Aurore, was a naturalist and a poet. He too was married. More than a decade earlier he had visited Madagascar, a naturalist's paradise, much of its flora and fauna unique to this distant and vast Indian Ocean island. Aurore referred to him as "the Madagascan."

The La Châtre band shared an impatience with the provincialism of the place. The younger members of the group were students in Paris, who returned during the holidays, and the older members had seen more of the world. Aurore delighted in their company. Conversation was interesting, risqué, as were their activities. Sometimes she dressed in a blouse and men's trousers so as to feel more fully part of the group. And it was precisely the freedom to circulate that attracted criticism. Each member was drawn to their boyish companion, and they recognized, beneath her manly dress, an exceptional woman. Jules Néraud made no effort to conceal his feelings, and delivered posies, *poésie*, and amorous missives. Aurore returned the love letters, and explained that she was a little in love "elsewhere." She warned Jules that his wife might find the evidence of his adulterous feelings. She did. Mme Néraud promptly wrote to Mme Dudevant, accusing her of "*hypocrisie, coquetterie*, and all that ends 'ie.'" No doubt this was an allusion to *nymphomanie*. Aurore reported the contents of Mme Néraud's letter in a letter to Casimir.[7] No doubt, while needing an outlet for her indignation, she also supposed that her husband would be less likely to believe the rumours he would undoubtedly hear if she had already forewarned him.

During the summer of 1826 she also re-established contact with Stéphane de Grandsagne, the close companion of her adolescence. He had been unwell and left Paris to convalesce in the country. Aurore described him in a letter to Zoé that autumn as "half-mad."[8] But "madness," so much feared in her adolescence, was becoming a complex and shifting metaphor, and something other than the "derangement" with which she believed her mother to be increasingly afflicted. Aurore was coming to associate "madness" with a visionary attitude, and the courage to realize that vision, regardless of society's judgement. Stéphane, a man with enormous drive, was willing, she believed, to pursue his vision even to the point of self-destruction. Aurélien, Aurore had recognized, was in some ways a visionary, but his convictions would never be translated into action where they came into conflict with society's vision. Despite her love for Aurélien, she was beginning to lose faith in him and to shift her allegiance.

Reconnecting with Nohant, and with the past, she had sought to refashion her own image of herself. In dialogue—real or imagined—with Aurélien, she simultaneously refashioned him.

As with Aurore's epistolary relationship with her husband, contradictions between the imagined and the real had become visible in their exchange of letters. The stability of their spiritual union was threatened by differences of literary taste. With Zoé, however, instinctive spiritual responses were shared. Sympathetic accord with Zoé may have encouraged the extrapolation of further differences with Aurélien. Later she wrote: "The absent being, I could almost say the *Invisible Being*, whom I had made the third defining point of my existence (God, him and me) was tired of my aspiration towards sublime love. . . . His passions had need of another source of sustenance, beyond the enthusiastic friendship of an epistolary relationship. . . . I felt that for him I was becoming a terrible chain, or that I was no more than a mental amusement. I loved him for a long time to come, in silence, and despondent."[9]

But the evidence suggests that in this there is significant displacement. He may have longed to consummate their love, but considered this to be beyond the codes in which he ardently believed. He may have had lovers in Bordeaux, but if so, it is highly unlikely that these women would have been married, and of Aurore's class. Aurore, however, would soon consummate an adulterous passion, but not with Aurélien de Sèze. First, she recognized in Aurélien, or fashioned him into, a man who held social dogma superior to the promptings of individual conscience. Aurélien, whether she was right or wrong in her construction, was deeply wounded: "You ask me, my dear friend, whether I have fixed ideas about everything. I believe it almost useless to reply to such a question now, unless I am intent on overturning the pedestal on which you seem to want to place me. In you there is reason, wisdom; you fashion in your imagination a being according to this type, and when you have made it, *when you have yourself made it,* you say, 'It's this type!' No, no, I don't have fixed and reasoned ideas about everything . . . etc."[10]

The political differences between them had also become more visible. It is one of the many ironies of this period of Aurore's life that her marriage was in some ways sustained by shared political sympathies. Aurore was a republican, and a liberal. And so, unlike Aurélien, was Casimir. But it was above all the ideas and beliefs of Stéphane de Grandsagne that interested Aurore.

Stéphane's gaunt features, his bold condemnation of banality, the mediocre, and the conventional, his informed earnestness, his considerable scholarship, his immense resilience and determination, impressed Aurore deeply. She had loved him years earlier, but then she had been wary of his iconoclasm, and above all of his atheism. His absolute commitment to his scholarly work, and his project to create a "library for the people" of some two hundred volumes, which he would quickly realize, was the tangible proof of his ability to create something new and exciting.

In July 1826 Casimir travelled to Bordeaux. Aurore stayed at Nohant, and travelled to La Châtre to see two plays, on the eighth and ninth. In September Aurore's dear friend and surrogate father James Roëttiers arrived, and so did Hippolyte.

That autumn Stéphane returned to Paris, to his research and writing. "When he left," Aurore wrote ecstatically, "when he pressed my skinny hand, it seemed to me that he was making an appointment with me in the other world."[11] On his return to the capital, Stéphane continued to work relentlessly, and his health continued to deteriorate. Hippolyte, who had left Nohant and was staying with his wife in their Parisian apartment, responded to Aurore's request for news. "I found him in a pitiable state," Hippolyte replied, "suffocating, and with a high fever." Stéphane apparently "opened his purse to everyone. . . . His damned head is on fire, he works, fifteen to twenty nights on the trot, drinks litres of coffee. . . . He has something of the sublime in his imagination. . . . Volumes are being born under his pen."[12]

Life at Nohant was cheered by the presence of both Roëttiers: they arrived in November to spend the winter with the Dudevants. But Aurore's thoughts were turned to Stéphane in Paris, and to the challenges to which he could choose to rise—because *he* was a man.

In the second fortnight of January 1827 Aurore made a brief trip to Paris. In March she acted in a play performed at the home of friends. On 12 April the Roëttiers left, but returned in May. Their close friend Louis-Nicolas Caron also came to stay. He was a businessman and Aurore enjoyed his company. They corresponded for a couple of years, but later on he was loyal to Casimir.

Aurore's letters during the late spring of 1827 speak of her sense of loyalty to Stéphane, regardless of his alleged faults. To her brother she wrote, "I will be there when others have turned away," and expressed her sense of powerlessness to help him, this last a function of "the differences between the sexes, status, and a thousand other things. . . ." Her support could only be "all but negligible."[13]

Her correspondence at this time referred more and more to her growing recognition of the consequences of having been born a woman rather than a man. Sometimes she jots down a bitter aside. Sometimes she reflects at length. There are explicit conditional introductions, "if I were a man," and at the other extreme more subtle, often ironical asides, "as I am no more than a mere woman." She was beginning to turn those earlier self-destructive urges outwards.[14]

During the summer of 1827 (12 to 22 August), Aurore and Casimir went for a short holiday, again for the sake of Aurore's health. They travelled to Mont-Dore in the Auvergne so that she could drink the waters. It may be that Stéphane's energy and drive encouraged her to continue her writing, against her instincts, but, as almost always, she ponders for whom, to whom? The question of audience is always the necessary first concern of her writing. Her audience had to be sympathetic. Could it be for her mother that she would write? "Oh my mother," she wrote, "what have I done to you? Why do you not love me? . . . I will weep in silence." Can it be for Zoé? But she would be likely to show anything she wrote to Aurélien: "I do not want to be remembered." Is it for Stéphane that she will write? He would, she feared, approach her writing as a "pedant." The recognition that she had no clear audience led, apparently quite naturally, to thoughts of suicide, "But there is Maurice!"[15] She was coming to associate writing with making life bearable.

On their brief holiday, Aurore continued to attract the attention of other men, and no doubt encouraged them. But there is a not altogether characteristic cynicism in her jottings. This is an ephemeral milieu. The sentences frequently trail off into suspension marks. Like the *transhumance* of the sheep of the Auvergne, travelling up and down the mountains in herds with the seasons, men and women come and go at the resort.[16]

Casimir tolerated Aurore's flirtatiousness, no doubt to allow for his own cavorting. But any tacit agreement they may have made did not imply real equality, or genuine mutual tolerance. During an excursion on horseback that summer at Mont-Dore, Casimir's mount refused an obstacle, and he whipped the animal's muzzle. The horse backed up and Aurore, who was walking beside it, was knocked to the ground. She made some critical remark, to which Casimir replied that he would do as he pleased. If Aurore did not shut up, she would receive the next blow. Without replying, Aurore walked away.[17]

Despite telling moments of extreme tension, the letters that Aurore and Casimir exchanged that year continued to be civil, even warmly affectionate. Aurore's confession had allowed for a degree of understanding. They had established an unspoken agreement to allow each other degrees of reciprocal, but unequal, freedom, they remained husband and wife, and they had a child to whom both were devoted. Some of Aurore's longer letters suggest that Casimir, too, was an important audience for her writing. On their return to Nohant, shared political concerns continued to sustain a working partnership.

During the elections of October 1827, the Liberals and Bonapartists formed an opposition group against Charles X's Bourbon monarchy. In La Châtre Casimir and Aurore and their friends supported the local opposition candidate, François Duris-Dufresne. Casimir played a particularly active role in the organization, renting a house in La Châtre in which to entertain, while Aurore organized dances and dinners for their candidate.[18] But the social life that they encouraged was far from conventional. Superficially, the dinners and dances conformed to expectation. The guest lists, however, were more daring and, by mixing different social groups, fundamentally subversive of the provincial society around them. In November the opposition candidate was duly elected.

During the campaign Aurore had stayed in close touch with Stéphane.

In October Casimir travelled to Paris, and some weeks later, after Casimir's return, Aurore went to Paris, escorted by Stéphane's brother, Jules. Again Aurore's ostensible reason for the trip was her health: she consulted various eminent physicians. On 5 December she arrived in Paris. On the eighth Aurore wrote with uncharacteristic desperation to Casimir, to inform him of her return to Nohant. "Look after yourselves," she writes to Casimir and Maurice; "always love me. I need it."[19] On 14 December she was seen by a Dr. Broussais. Aurore then delayed her departure. A visit by Stéphane and his brother apparently required her to stay on a few more days. Then she was able to book only a single seat in the carriage from Paris. As the Grandsagnes were to accompany her, she told Casimir that they would have to wait until the following Wednesday, the nineteenth. They would be arriving at Nohant on Friday, 21 December 1827.[20] The dates are crucial. On 13 September 1828—nine months later—she would give birth to a daughter, Solange.

Aurore spent the whole of 1828 at Nohant. It was a quiet year in some respects. In January she hosted a soirée in La Châtre. It may be that this was in an effort to distract herself. She was deeply depressed. On 2 February 1828, aware of her pregnancy, she wrote to Zoé Leroy. Humility and self-loathing, not visible in any earlier letters to Zoé, are written into her anguished words: "I no longer ask you to love me as before. Like a wounded animal who dies in a corner, I am no longer able to seek solace and support from those who are like me."[21]

In April Caron arrived back at Nohant and stayed for six months. Married life was easier when they had guests. By May her pregnancy became a topic of discussion within the triangular relationship formed by Aurore, Zoé, and Aurélien. Zoé had learnt of Aurore's condition from a mutual friend. Why, she asked Aurore, had Aurélien not informed her of Aurore's pregnancy? Aurélien, Zoé claimed, had insisted when she reproached him, that he had indeed informed her.[22] Aurélien's own letter brims over with sadness, and resignation.[23] But there is irony too, and overt condemnation of Stéphane de Grandsagne. Aurélien accuses him of "pseudo-philosophy," of attempting to attract attention and admiration by means of teasing paradoxes in his thinking and behaviour. It is in that same letter that Aurélien claimed that she had fashioned him into a fiction, and then condemned the figment of her own imaginings.

In her autobiography, Sand claims that the baby was born "before term." But there is every reason to presume that this baby was conceived during the winter of 1827, when Aurore was in Paris seeing Stéphane.

Solange was born on 13 September and Aurélien was at Nohant. He even signed the birth certificate. But the subsequent letters exchanged between Bordeaux and Nohant are no more than civil: their intimate relationship had come to an end. The restraint in Aurélien's letters contrasts with Zoé's overt descriptions of his heartbroken state. Aurore's behaviour after Solange's birth implied that Aurélien's rigid social vision, and the morality bound up in it, was something she had begun to despise.

Aurélien, on the other hand, was plunged into despair. But Aurore had little sympathy. She felt that his principles, his notion of honour, were confused and compromised by cowardice. Zoé described Aurélien's feelings of hopelessness in a letter to Aurore. "He sits at the piano," she wrote, "playing with only two fingers." Aurore's reply, written in December 1828, was metaphorical, but unambiguous, "You have to play the piano with two fingers if you can't play with five."[24] Musical incompetence, even impotence, alludes to something more intimate, more fundamental.

Stéphane, by contrast, had both visionary political views and a potency that fuelled his convictions. At the beginning of 1829 Aurore continued to entertain, and to mix the societies of La Châtre. She persuaded the subprefect of the town to hold a ball. The local music master and his wife were invited; such an invitation was deemed scandalous. But the pièce de résistance of the evening was the performance of a composition written by Aurore and Duteil. Arranged for piano and violin, the lyrics of the song, and its blunt refrain, made Aurore's identification of the enemy overt. The chorus, sung no doubt with enormous gusto, was simply "Vex the bourgeoisie!"

But amid the frenetic and subversive activities Aurore did not feel that her thinking had been in any way resolved. Like the compulsive horse-riding with Hippolyte in her late teens, and the risky gallivanting in the Pyrenees with Zoé, her periods of hyperactivity suggested rather a desperate attempt to escape the self. That self was, according to Aurore, as muddled, as confused, as anguished as ever. In a letter to Charles Meure, a lawyer in La Châtre with whom Sand corresponded for a number of years, she defined her intellectual position by means of self-parodying and hyperbolic enumeration worthy of Balzac on a good day: "noble, liberal, Jacobite, an émigrée, a partisan of the despotic, of the Republic, devout, atheist." And further to increase the effect she closes not with a single, or even repeated "etc.," but with no less than five.[25]

The year of 1829, unlike the previous year, was full. She travelled a good deal—and she wrote prolifically. On 12 March she drafted *Voyage*

Aurore Dupin (de Francueil), later George Sand, in a portrait by her tutor
René Deschartres

*"Like all violent men Deschartres liked open resistance . . .
and became meek, even feeble, with those who were not afraid of him."*

above: Louis-Claude Dupin (de Francueil)

"The grandfather whom I never knew."

right: Aurore de Saxe, Aurore's grandmother, natural child of the Maréchal de Saxe, and the wife of Maurice Dupin, in a portrait from the mid–eighteenth century

"My grandmother was serious in her interests, with a strong sense of order."

bottom: The Maréchal de Saxe, Aurore's great-grandfather, circa 1748

"He looks like his mother . . . his blue eyes are gentler and his smile more open."

*"Nohant, where I grew up, where I have spent
most of my life, where I hope to die."*

Aurore Dupin and her half-brother Hippolyte Chatiron, natural child of Maurice Dupin, by their grandmother Mme Dupin (de Francueil)

Maurice Dupin

"My father's instincts were adventurous, chivalrous."

George Sand's portrait of her mother, Sophie-Victoire Dupin (*née* Delaborde), circa 1833

"My mother always lives slightly apart, closed in on herself."

George Sand, lithograph after Alcide Lorenz

*"Should God have bestowed greater strength
on women than on man—No."*

George Sand and Ledru-Rollin, anonymous engraving

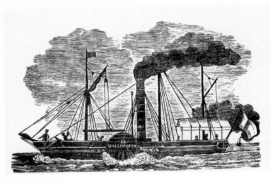

El Mallorquín, anonymous engraving

George Sand's drawing of the local priest's visit to the "family" at Valldemosa in 1839, with Chopin, Maurice, and Solange

The Charterhouse at Valldemosa, drawing by Joseph-Bonaventure Laurens

Alexandre Manceau,
drawing by Grandsire

George Sand by Manceau

The house at Gargilesse, painting by Véron, 1859

Frédéric Chopin by Eugène Delacroix, 1838

Gustave Flaubert, painting by Eugène Giraud

*"You have never been young! Oh how different we are.
I have never ceased being young, if to be young is to love."*

Lina Sand (*née* Calamatta),
photograph by Nadar

Maurice Sand,
photograph by Nadar

Solange Clésinger (*née* Dudevant),
by her husband

Jean-Baptiste Clésinger,
photograph by Nadar

above and below: Solange by Mercier, and
Maurice by his mother

*"My son was more like me, a woman—
much more than my daughter who
was like an unsuccessful man."*

right: Casimir Dudevant, Aurore's husband

*"He did not speak of love, and declared himself
little disposed to spontaneous passion."*

Aurélien de Sèze, anonymous portrait

"I loved him for a long time to come,
in silence, and despondent."

Marie Dorval, lithograph by León Noël,
circa 1835

"She was not a body, but a physiognomy, a spirit."

Pietro Pagello, age twenty-eight, in an
engraving

Louis-Chrysostome Michel (Michel de
Bourges), lithograph by L. Massard, 1835

"He despises devotion because he believes
it his natural right . . . to dominate,
to possess, to absorb."

Alfred de Musset's self-portrait with his stronger-stomached mistress George Sand, sailing from Marseilles to Genoa

Stéphane Ajasson de Grandsagne, lithograph by Achille Devéria, 1832

"He was handsome and lacked neither knowledge, nor intelligence, nor vision."

Jules Sandeau, pencil by George Sand, 20 March 1831

"But we were both too inexperienced, he [Sandeau] and I, to be able to work together."

top: J. Jacottet, engraving of the new road to
Cauterets, 1842

*"The road follows the mountain torrent and
leads up to its source, at Cauterets."*

middle: George Sand's drawing of her romance
with Musset in Venice

bottom: Proclamation of the Republic of 1870,
anonymous engraving

George Sand, photograph by Nadar, 1866

M

Monsieur MAURICE SAND, Baron DUDEVANT, chevalier de la Légion-d'Honneur & Madame MAURICE SAND - DUDEVANT; Monsieur CLESINGER & Madame SOLANGE CLESINGER-SAND; Mesdemoiselles AURORE & GABRIELLE SAND - DUDEVANT; Madame CAZAMAJOU; Monsieur & Madame OSCAR CAZAMAJOU; Madame veuve SIMONNET, Monsieur RENÉ SIMONNET, substitut du Procureur de la République à Châteauroux, Monsieur EDME SIMONNET, employé de la Banque de France à Limoges, Monsieur ALBERT SIMONNET, employé de la Banque de France à Bourges; Monsieur & Madame DE BERTHOLDI, Monsieur GEORGES DE BERTHOLDI, Mademoiselle JEANNE DE BERTHOLDI; Monsieur & Madame CAMILLE VILLETARD & leurs enfants

Ont l'honneur de vous faire part de la perte douloureuse qu'ils viennent d'éprouver en la personne de

MADAME GEORGE SAND
BARONNE DUDEVANT
Née Lucile, Aurore, Amantine DUPIN

leur mère, belle-mère, grand'mère, sœur, tante, grand'tante & cousine, décédée au château de Nohant le 8 juin 1876, dans sa 72me année.

George Sand's funeral announcement

"What of the journey? No matter. Time and space were no longer of significance. I awoke elsewhere, that is all I know, I awoke in a world whose name I do not know and of whose time I had no notion."

chez M. Blaise (*Trip to M. Blaise's*).²⁶ It tells of a journey, various encounters, conversations involving storytelling, and a frightening period when the travellers lose their way. The nature of the fantastic was also written in. Some of the experience may have been dreamt by the characters, or hallucinated. Or it may be that madness had temporarily descended on the teller of the tale—and his companions. The same ingredients are blended into a longer story, probably written a few months later—*Histoire du rêveur* (*The Story of a Dreamer*).

But real life continued. Casimir was openly enjoying the pleasures of a mistress, Pépita, one of the Dudevant servants. On 6 May 1829 the Dudevants travelled to the southwest: Casimir had to attend to a commercial business which his father had left him. Aurore, once again, saw Aurélien. Casimir would later comment on the affair in blunt terms: "Every morning Mme A.D. visited M. A. de S. . . . while alleging that she was ill and visiting the baths."²⁷ From Bordeaux they went on to Guillery, then back to Bordeaux.

They finally returned on 30 July, and Hippolyte and his family also arrived at Nohant. Maurice was now six, and Aurore was considering his formal education. She employed a twenty-one-year-old tutor, Jules Boucoiran, who arrived at the end of October. There is no way of knowing the nature of the relationship that developed between employer and tutor—but Aurore's letters are not without teasing ambiguities. Detailing various commissions that she would like Jules to undertake on her behalf, she adds, in a letter written in April 1830, "If you are not in a hurry, I'll settle up with you myself, in person, and I'll embrace you too for your trouble. . . . Adieu, my child, I am giving you the opportunity of doing something for me. I would like to be able to do the same for you. . . ."²⁸

Only a few weeks after his first arrival at Nohant, however, Aurore had sent him back to his previous employers. Women, some might argue, exhibit their most manipulative and Machiavellian sides when protecting the interests of their children.

A letter of September 1830 makes explicit the rumours that had circulated in La Châtre: she was being described as a "female Don Juan."²⁹ Aurore may well have been concerned less for her own reputation, which she no doubt accepted had been established forever, than for Boucoiran's. They did remain in close touch, however. In May 1830, when Aurore was in Paris, Jules tutored Maurice.³⁰ Aurore and Jules remained close friends even when Maurice was handed over to another tutor, and they continued to correspond for years to come.

Tensions between Casimir and Aurore mounted as the year 1829 drew to a close. She criticized his handling of finances: Casimir had invested some 25,000 francs in what turned out to be a wholly fictitious boat. He had been duped. Furthermore, he shared a mistress with his crooked business partner, Edmond Desgranges. Aurore wrote a firm letter in December 1829: "One should not conclude a business deal at the end of a meal when one is unfortunate enough not to be sober, and I am convinced that you did this with a glass in your hand."[31]

Daily life was bleak. A degree of escape was offered by her prolific letter writing, and her friends' requests for more substantial texts encouraged her, once again, to attempt writing a novel. But this time writing would be something more than therapy. She was beginning to believe that writing might offer a degree of financial independence. She rearranged her writing room, but she did not allow the creation of a stimulating writing space to absorb too much energy. Instead she quickly established a regime, and worked with characteristic feverishness. She describes this period in her autobiography: "At that point what had been my grandmother's room was mine, because it had only one door and thus could not be used as a corridor whatever anyone's pretext. My two children had the large adjoining room. . . . My room was so small that with my books, my herbs, my butterflies and my stones (I always enjoyed natural history without ever learning anything), there was no room for a bed. I compensated by hanging a hammock. . . . My desk was a wardrobe with a drop-leaf, like a secretaire. . . ."[32]

Sand then described the beginnings of her more serious attempts to write in a disciplined way. In typical novelistic fashion, she implicates a grasshopper in the story. The insect lived on the windowsill of her room, a companion during her long hours of solitary writing. But an unfortunate incident occurred: a maid crushed the grasshopper to death. She had also included the event in a novel which she had written in October 1829, for Jane Bazouin, a work which she believed to be worthless and which has never been published.

She read the death of the insect as an augury. Unlike the grasshopper, she would not allow herself to be crushed to death at Nohant. She would find another way out. Writing offered imaginative escape, but it also suggested possibilities for real escape. And the physical freedom of her subversive capering in La Châtre not only offered material for prose accounts, it also served as a metaphor for more fundamental shifts in consciousness.

Aurore first tried to make sense of her life, and who she was, in her letters to Aurélien de Sèze, and the autobiographical voice echoes in the works of the late 1820s, and on throughout her prolific writing. Particularly remarkable is the structural correspondence between the *Mémoires inédits* (*Unpublished Memoirs,* written at some point between 1827 and 1829) and *The Story of My Life* (begun in 1847). The overlaps suggest that while Sand is looking backwards while composing *The Story of My Life,* the life had been lived in expectation that it would conform, to a large degree, to a self that had first been constructed in the late 1820s.

In the late 1820s—but no doubt reworked, as always, from a vantage point much later in life—she wrote a short prose piece, "Nuit d'hiver" ("Winter Night"), which describes escapades with some of her now late adolescent friends from childhood. The story tells of delightful mischievousness, disguise, subversiveness. Hippolyte and Aurore set off, dressed as a young peasants, to awaken friends. They enjoy larking about, and "gaiety" is the object of the escapade. Halfway through the story, there is a brief and compelling paragraph, set apart: "My mask falls. I continue without realizing it, but no one recognizes me. They are all so far from thinking of me! Could one ever suppose . . . And me, a character so earnest inside, and possessing a sang-froid often put to the test, I don't think that it is I. No, it is not I, but the other . . . ?"[33]

Aurore continues to spend time, in this early autobiographical fragment, with her childhood friends, many the sons of artisans employed years earlier by her grandmother. Assimilated into the crowd, she and her companions enjoy the "peasants' ball," which is in full swing. The story describes a return to childhood, to a time when, prepubescent, Aurore circulated freely among every social group, every class. As an adolescent, while in male attire on horseback, she had continued to enjoy this freedom. Now married, a mother, and cross-dressed, she again describes in a story, what is essentially a return to the classless utopia to which she believed she had belonged as a small girl, a world which she would re-create and embellish in her mature fiction years later.

Meanwhile her husband's pitiable handling of their finances allowed her to assume greater control of the estate. She dismissed Pépita in February 1830, only to see her soon replaced in her husband's passions by Claire Mathelin, Hippolyte's wife's maid.

On 26 April 1830 she travelled to Paris, with Maurice. She saw Stéphane, and from Paris she travelled to Bordeaux, where she met Zoé and Aurélien on 14 May. She left there on 17 May. Again, her letters to her husband are surprising in their frank openness. Of her relationship with Stéphane she wrote on 20 May from Paris, where she had arrived back the day before, "We'll see how long this honeymoon lasts." Of Aurélien she wrote, "He has changed dramatically, he is old, and sad."[34] But the joy of renewing contact with former loves was only one of the stimuli that she sought. She also visited the sights of Paris. The Jardin des Plantes, the Luxembourg Gardens, and the Louvre delighted her.[35] But she had to return to Nohant and arrived back on 18 June.

The following month would see the July Revolution in Paris. Unexpected political dramas would coincide with a romantic meeting, and a dramatic upheaval in Aurore's day-to-day life.

XI

Petit Jules

"How good it is to turn life into a novel."

∼In the summer of 1830 Aurore described the atmosphere at Nohant, complaining in a letter dated 20 July of the "permanent stagnation" of life. But if "Tuesdays resembled Wednesdays, and Wednesdays Thursdays," she could always invent more exciting lives in writing. In the same letter she asked Jules Boucoiran to send her some notebooks, "not just one or two—twenty."[1] She was about to begin writing in earnest.

What she did not know, and could not have known, was that political upheaval would soon transform France, and that even events in La Châtre would enliven her otherwise predictable routine at Nohant. And once again the pace and complexity of political change, nationally and locally, would coincide with dramatic events in her private life.

Aurore's conception of place had undergone a transformation on her return to Nohant from the Pyrenees. Her reflections on place were intimately bound up with a new perspective on identity, and this implicated others, both alive and dead. Her sense of fusedness with others involved a complex notion of time which, in its turn, was bound up with the notion of history. And historical events were soon to become very much a part of her life. Thus the timeless melancholy of a place outside history had become the urgent historical now. She was caught up in Nohant's past, her past, and projecting the now into the future, and imagining what the now would look like with hindsight. Whatever was wrong inside her, and outside, might be transformed. Life, with all its very real and painful inadequacies, became exciting. There was hope. "Fever is in the blood," she wrote, describing society. "I feel within me an energy," she wrote of herself. Bookish learning and intellectual debate had thrown up impossible contradictions, hopeless paradoxes. Experience, on the other hand, involvement in political change, might be transforming. "The core of one's being," she wrote, "develops with events."[2]

Political unrest was brewing. In an attempt to enhance national pride an expeditionary force had been sent to conquer Algiers, expanding the colonial venture overseas. The action was successful and France embarked on what was to be one of the most complex and intractable disasters of her history. Algiers fell on 5 July 1830, but this distant victory did little to boost the image of the unpopular Charles X. Further royal ordinances, which reinforced royal prerogatives, incensed the Liberal bourgeoisie, which began to conceive of a Second Republic. The parliament to which those who had been elected in July were to be admitted, including the Dudevants' candidate Duris-Dufresne, deputy-elect of La Châtre, was dissolved before its first session. For three days, the "Trois Glorieuses," the barricades again went up in Paris. Again Aurore rode excitedly to La Châtre to hear the talk and to pick up letters from Boucoiran, who was staying in Paris. Locally there were rumours of a royalist regiment descending from Bourges on La Châtre. Casimir, Hippolyte, and some 120 others organized themselves into a national guard.[3]

Aurore was deeply stirred by what was happening politically, but her feelings were confused. In a single letter she wrote of her desire for a return to peace, "times of quiet reading and days of rest," while at the same time describing a hitherto unknown sense of energy. She was particularly worried about her aunt and uncle, the latter an inspector in the royal household. She was less anxious about her mother's safety than her mother's mad fears. She closed one of her letters to Jules Boucoiran with an explanation of the possible receptions he was likely to receive when visiting her mother: her behaviour had become wholly unpredictable.[4]

But Aurore's experience of that dramatic summer of 1830 was to be one of gradual political disillusionment. The revolutionary will had been translated into nothing more than a bourgeois monarchy: Louis-Philipe replaced Charles X after his abdication. On 15 August 1830 Aurore wrote to Charles Meure: "Are you happy now?—For myself, yes and no. If the new order of things suits as people think, long may it live. But what if we have fooled ourselves? What if we have mistaken words for ideas? What if, without due reflection, we have left plenty of room for a *future* return to absolutism? Well? Who knows? . . ."[5]

She was more certain as to the course her own life should take. The July Revolution coincided with her first meeting, on 30 July, of the novelist Jules Sandeau—his significance in her life is visible in the first syllable of his surname, which she would soon assume not just as her *nom de plume* but as her identity, forever. They had met at a time when conversation had been dominated by talk of revolution in the capital. News of events in Paris had been fragmentary, often contradictory. Aurore rode daily into La Châtre to hear the latest details. It was summer, and amid the political excitement there were village dances, and picnics with Aurore's friends. Sandeau, the precociously able son of a teacher in La Châtre, had returned from Paris for the holidays and was swept up in the group.

The youthful love affair between Aurore and Sandeau was written less ambiguously into his fiction than into hers. His physical descriptions were more explicit and fuller when describing the young hero of his novel *Marianna* than when describing his heroine. There is a striking self-consciousness, if not self-confidence, about the young man's alluring appeal: "His body was supple and flexible, like the body of a woman."[6]

When Aurore and Jules first met, she was twenty-six and he was just nineteen. For Sandeau, Aurore was his first love. For Aurore, as Sandeau was no doubt aware, his youth was wonderfully endearing. Her "petit Jules," as she described him, was "as adorable as a hummingbird from the perfumed savannahs." What she wanted was to examine him with a novelist's eye, an eye that can see, or invent, everything: "If you only knew how much I love him, the poor child! How, from the first day, his expressive look, his sudden and candid movements, his timid gaucheness with me, made me want to see him, to examine him. I do not know the nature of my curiosity, but each day it became greater."[7] And it was her eyes, if Sandeau's *Marianna* can be read, in this instance, simply autobiographically, that struck Jules above all. In the two-volume novel the narrator describes the hero's response to seeing the heroine for the first time: "The expressiveness of her eyes, at once burning and . . . throwing into relief some inner turmoil, at once terrible, relentless, unacknowledged." What attracts the young man is less what is seen and known than what the visible tantalizingly suggests of the hidden and secret, that which might, or might not, be open for exploration.

More surprising than the various inversions of gender in Sandeau's novel was the role that the voyeuristic came to play in real life. In a letter to Émile Regnault, written towards the end of May 1831, Aurore described the genesis of her intimate relationship with Jules. The prelude to each of their meetings, she explained, was a game of hide-and-seek in which both took a turn hiding, and watching the other, unseen: "It was there . . . that he would arrive from La Châtre and sit down, out of breath, exhausted. . . . He would find my book and my scarf, and when I arrived he would hide in a neighbouring alley and I would see his grey hat and his cane, on the bench." The delight in the lovers' attraction to each other's possessions was something Aurore wanted to describe to Émile, but she was conscious that her correspondent might laugh at their obsessions: "There is nothing silly about these little things if one is in love, and you won't laugh, will you, if I tell you all these little things. There was nothing, down to the red lace tied about the brim of this grey hat, that did not cause me to tremble with joy. . . ."[8] Aurore frankly acknowledged the voyeurism in their behaviour, and their fetishistic desires. There was also a degree of exhibitionism in Aurore's wish to describe her anticipation and excitement to a third party. Writing about her experience for others to read is, the reader begins to suspect, the most arousing and satisfying act of all: "How good it is to turn life into a novel."[9]

At the end of that full summer of 1830, the bohemians of La Châtre returned to the capital, and Aurore longed to join them. Paris was the centre not only of political action but of intellectual debate and aesthetic revolution. She wanted to be part of it. But she was a women, married, and a mother.

Between 1827 and 1830 Aurore had written a good deal: "Winter Night" (probably 1828–29), *Trip to M. Blaise's* (probably March 1829), *Voyage en Auvergne* (*Journey to the Auvergne*, between 1827 and 1829), *Voyage en Espagne* (*Journey to Spain*, probably 1829), and *La Marraine* (*The Godmother*, written in October 1829). The notebook containing *The Godmother* also includes a number of other texts. The dating of Aurore Dudevant's early writings is problematic. Some material remains lost, or has been destroyed. But as the delay between imaginative ideas and writing can never be fully known, what matters is the sense that can be made of the body of writing which Aurore had composed prior to leaving Nohant. Too many biographers and literary critics have suggested that Aurore served a brief collaborative apprenticeship with Sandeau and then, in 1832, wrote *Indiana* in a matter of weeks, a novel that rocketed her to notorious fame.

During the closing years of the 1830s she also read a good deal. But whereas in her late teens she had been drawn above all to philosophical and theological works, during this period she read mainly literature: Balzac, Byron, Chateaubriand, Hoffmann, Hugo, among many. In *Les Confessions*, which are contained in the same notebook as *The Godmother*, Aurore writes with reference to Rousseau. As she would claim in *The Story of My Life*, twenty years later, the purpose of autobiographical accounts is to instruct, to give insights into the human heart that will allow the reader to measure their own ideas and actions against those of the writer. Where Rousseau's concern was to provide a study of human character, the emphasis in Aurore's early *Confessions* and later *The Story of My Life* was on interesting, and assisting, the reader. She does not, in either the early or later text, insist on her uniqueness. Unlike Rousseau, she is at pains to present herself as an example of the human condition. As in Rousseau's *Confessions*, however, veracity and frankness are subjects of considerable concern. Aurore's *Confessions* trace a progress from impotence in the face of ethical and philosophical problems as presented by other thinkers to a commitment to self-examination. She no longer fears the influence of other writers, purports not to be concerned by her critics, and describes her future explorations: these will be firmly based on a true knowledge of the self.

But for all the excitement of the *Confessions*, there remains anxiety. Veracity, frankness, truth, are still matters of concern; and self-knowledge, always threatened by pride. There is even an anxiety written into the structure of the *Confessions*, which suggests that to write about oneself is, de facto, a matter of egotism, if not pride. In Aurore's piece, the narrator only comes to talk about herself apparently by accident.

The narrator begins by telling of her intention to write her memoirs, describing and commenting on the kind of autobiographical writing popular at the time. But she has decided to abandon her attempt. This discussion reminds her of a conversation about Rousseau which had been interrupted by the friend's loss of a tie-pin and the fruitless attempts to find it. The description of the hunt is told in wonderfully burlesque fashion. What was fortunate about the loss of the tie-pin was that, by interrupting the conversation, it prevented her friend from destroying her admiration for Rousseau. She then goes on to compare his life to her own, and the three stages through which she has travelled. Thus, surreptitiously, the narrator outlines the memoirs that she had earlier claimed she had abandoned. In *The Story of My Life* it is of pride that she accuses Rousseau. His self-accusation is motivated, she argues, not by a desire to expose his true faults, but by a humility inextricably bound up with self-protection, if not self-aggrandizement. The sleight of hand of Aurore's *Confessions,* the round-about way that she comes to talk of herself, suggests a more profound anxiety with regard to writing about the self. It may well be that it was only her desperate financial position, later in life, that prompted her to do just that—and at very considerable length.

The confidence and excitement of the *Confessions* may show that she felt liberated from the massive theological, moral, and epistemological problems that had dogged her thinking as an adolescent. She may have decided that she was not truly an intellectual. Or she may have come to realize that what concerned her was not the wider questions concerning the nature of the human condition, but the truth in the detail of day-to-day life. The latter was the stuff not of essays, always threatening to move towards pedantry, pretension, and polemic, but of creative writing.

In her early fictional writing, commitment to truth again surfaces as her primary concern. The reader is constantly reminded that the text *is* only fiction; hence the parallel between these early texts and eighteenth-century authors such as Sterne. The reader is invited, "If you are in a hurry, skip this chapter." And there is a playful desire to manipulate the story in conspicuous ways.

The thirty-six chapters of *Mémoires d'un villageois* (*Memoirs of a Vil-lager*), contained in the same notebook as *The Godmother,* are constructed around a wholly improbable plot. It tells of Julien, a country boy whose father is—in a melodramatic flash—eliminated by lightning in the second chapter. But Julien is protected by a "fairy godmother," Louise, daughter of the lord of the local manor, eight years his senior. The consummation of love between an adoptive mother and son occurs in Sand's later fiction, and here there is implicit anxiety as to the propriety of such a union. Julien ends up marrying Blanche, Louise's adopted child, and Louise elopes to South America with a Spaniard. Nothing in the preceding chapters has prepared the way for the denouement. But what the text suggests is not that Aurore was incapable of constructing a more plausible narrative, but that she is anxious not to have the reader believe in something that is mere fiction. Her primary concern is to explore moral questions, but in view of her audi-ence, there is a profound worry as to how this can be successfully achieved.

This is essentially what she expressed in a letter to Jane Bazouin describing the difficulties she had with her first work of fiction, which has not survived, and which may itself have been no more than a fiction. Her irony is, initially, targeted on herself: " 'What indeed was I lacking?' I had Hâvre paper of excellent quality, goose quills that wrote by themselves and ink even blacker, perhaps, than that used by Montaigne." Aurore suggests that her real difficulty is in writing a *new morality* into her fiction: "I began by having my heroes descend into the tomb, amongst the tears of those close to them." The source is, of course, autobiographical, recalling her own descent, encouraged by Deschartres, into her family tomb at Nohant on the eve of her grandmother's burial. She continues:

> As this scene was the most touching and pathetic, I couldn't resist the temptation to describe it first. Then, I gave a family to these interesting characters, but without having first thought to march them to the altar, thus having a good friend to whom I described this scene believe in good faith that I was seeking to introduce a *new morality*, quite different from that observed up until now.
>
> He decried the boldness of my innovation.
>
> I hurried to conclude the marriage of my lovers, and this, making me think that I hadn't yet thought to bring them into the world, led me to see that the more I advanced, the more I had still to do.[10]

However comic Aurore's account, and however fictitious her interlocutor may have been, it was, nevertheless, just such a *new morality* that shocked and thrilled the readers of the first novel she wrote without a collaborator, *Indiana*.

What is implicitly derided, among other things in this account, is a desire for a certain kind of realism. But Aurore Dudevant's concern, even at this early stage in her writing, was not to depict things as they were, but to depict things as they might be. If she had experimented with a quasi-realist mode to describe the improbable in *The Story of a Dreamer*, probably written in 1829, here she explored the possible, within a quite fantastic mode. There is no sense of anxiety concerning the reader's credulity, because there can be no mistaking the fantastic for the real—at least until the end, when the main story turns out to have been a dream.[11] But the realm of dreams allows for the exploration of the psychosexual, a subject which fascinated Aurore early on, and which continued to fascinate her throughout her life.

As in almost all of Aurore's early works, the narrative is framed. The first narrator, a woman, converses with a second, a man. It is the latter who recounts the story proper. But there are exchanges between the woman and the man at the beginning, again briefly in the first chapter, and at the end. Implicit in this use of two sexually opposite narrators are certain anxieties. And these find a parallel in the male narrator's story.

There are four chapters. The first tells of a traveller intent on scaling Mount Etna in order to witness the sunrise, and Sicily spread out beneath him. He, like so many of the characters of Sand's later fiction, refuses the help of a guide, and is warned by locals of evil spirits. Unable to sleep, and troubled by the vision of a face on the other side of his campfire, which he then recognizes as his mule, he decides to continue his ascent without sleeping. It is only in the second chapter that we learn the traveller's name, Amédée (Amadeus), and this allusion to a composer coincides with the hero hearing the voice of a trained musician singing in the forest. Although the traveller is no longer anonymous, the disembodied voice in the trees remains unknown, and sexually indeterminate, "a mixture of what is most harmonious in the musical abilities of each sex."[12]

The song is an invocation to the spirits of Etna, "an inspired and savage poetry that displayed the characteristics of improvisation." Amédée answers the singer with a song of his own, but when Amédée meets the singer, there is no resolution to the question of sexual indeterminacy. The singer mounts Amédée's mule, which starts to bolt. Amédée clings to the body of the singer, a frail and girlish form that exhibits, however, unusual strength. The scene ends with the mule throwing itself and the two figures down a ravine. But in the third chapter, two "men" have arrived at the summit. Amédée, not altogether surprisingly, is afraid that he has lost his sanity. The singer denies that they fell: the rarefied atmosphere had caused temporary delirium. At the edge of the volcano the singer reveals himself to be a spirit: Etna is his king. As lava flows around them, Amédée clamours to accompany him into the foaming crater: "Do not leave me to waste away in real life, to which you do not seem yourself to belong." The scene is terrifying: Amédée sees "the crater vomiting torrents of liquid fire . . . and throwing heavenwards volcanic explosions whose detonation was deafening." But Amédée is apparently fearless. His only desire is to be consumed: "Angel or devil: carry me off into the vortex that I see already enveloping you." As the lava envelops them, the young man is transformed into a woman and Amédée pursues her into the heart of the volcano. Seeing his own body half consumed, he welcomes the flames: "A pure spirit, he felt the heat of the fire, not as a burning pain, but as an indescribable pleasure."¹³ Inside the volcano, he kisses her, and it is as though he has been struck by lightning; he awakens, as from a dream, and finds himself recumbent, beside the campfire of the first chapter.

The Story of a Dreamer explores the relationship between the corporeal and the ethereal, the mundane and the spiritual, real life and dreaming, dissonance (a chromatic scale in the third part is unattainable) and harmony. But the whole story, told by a man to a woman, is also shot through with arousing eroticism, orgasmic images of molten lava that verge on parody, and an implicitly sexual pleasure merged with delicious masochistic pain.

The end-point of the story should be one of implied resolution achieved through consummation. And the bodies of Amédée and the androgyne *are* consumed, but physical contact on the albeit limited level of a kiss only serves to hurl Amédée back from the brink of final and absolute consummation, to real life and the smouldering and lustreless flames of his all too domestic campfire.

Distinct traces of the writing project to which Sand would be more and more fully committed emerge from this and other early texts. Anxiety about the self and its implications for narratorial authority surface frequently. The self is at once an ego, and therefore ever subject to the sin of pride, while it remains sexually and erotically confused, uncertain. Scholarly, intellectual writing is constantly threatened by pretension, pedantry, and polemic. And fiction, if it is to be believable, must subscribe to given social codes, codes in which the writing self no longer necessarily believes.

The fictional codes of the fantastic had allowed for the composition of a successful, whole text in *The Story of a Dreamer*. But what it described was failure. Had it not been for the need for money, Aurore might have concluded that philosophical writing was pretentious and ultimately fruitless. Fiction, on the other hand, if it was to be accepted by the contemporary reading public, could not be true to her own vision, not of how things were, but of how they should be: "I forgot about the need for money," she wrote, adding to a list of the requirements for writing which she had earlier composed, "and what a useful stimulus it is, I don't doubt. The first time I write for the public it will be a wondrous accomplishment, for I know no one who can be encouraged as much as I am by the disposition towards enthusiasm which comes from not having a penny to one's name."¹⁴

Although she playfully parodied her sense of Romantic melancholy in her letters that autumn, the weeks and months after Sandeau and the others had left for Paris were lonely and empty: "You would laugh if you saw me emerging from my room, not like Aurora with purple wings, gracefully reaching out to harness the horses of the classical Phoebus . . . but like a stuffed marmot that the Savoyard takes out of its box and makes dance by beating it with a stick to get it going and make it look cheerful."[15]

What she had been waiting for, that lonely autumn of 1830, was a catalyst, an excuse to leave home. It was not long coming. In December she wrote to Boucoiran explaining that she had "found a packet addressed to me while looking for something in my husband's desk. This packet had a solemn air about it that struck me. *It read:* 'Only open after my death.' I didn't have the patience to wait until I was widowed. . . . Good God! What a testament! Maledictions, that's all. He'd listed all his ill-humoured and angry thoughts about me, all his reflections on my *perversity,* all his feelings of disgust at my character, and he was leaving that as evidence of his tenderness . . . !"[16] Aurore also described her response to reading the testament: "My decision was quickly taken and, I can confidently add, *irrevocably.* You know I don't misuse the word. I don't use it often. Without waiting a further day, still feeble and ill, I have announced my intentions. . . ." What she had announced to Casimir she quotes in her letter to Boucoiran: "I want an allowance, I am going to Paris forever, my children will stay at Nohant." This, it quickly emerged, was a position exaggerated for the sake of successful renegotiation: "It was a bluff. . . ."[17]

XII

Becoming Sand

"The stormy sea of literature . . ."

᭜Leaving Nohant that January of 1831, Aurore was not distancing herself for a brief holiday, but for three months, and by a regular arrangement. What Aurore and Casimir had agreed (or Casimir had been obliged to concede) was a pattern whereby Aurore alternated three-month periods in Paris with a similar time at home. Aurore was abandoning, at least temporarily, a desperately unhappy marriage; she was also distancing herself from her beloved children. Maurice and Solange were even younger than she had been when her mother had all but signed away her maternal rights to her grandmother and left her at Nohant. Her mother had also moved to the capital. Although Aurore intended to return three months later, she may well have reflected on the uncomfortable parallels between the manner in which her mother had abandoned her, and the terrible suffering it had caused her, and her own treatment of her children. Nor had she forgiven her mother.

Solange, aged two, was too young to understand that her mother was leaving for an unusually long time. Maurice, on the other hand, deliberately provoked by his uncle, was, for some time, inconsolable. Hippolyte, who tended to take Casimir's side whenever there were disputes between the Dudevants, apparently sought to upset Maurice as much as possible, in a miserable attempt to dissuade Aurore from leaving.[1] The promise of a full hussar's uniform transformed the immediate childish nightmare of his mother's departure into a not too distant dream—owning the longed-for outfit. His mother would have the outfit sent to Nohant at the earliest opportunity. Maurice calmed down. Curiously, Aurore had worn a similar outfit at a similar age.

Aurore's maternal feelings were certainly troubled. Hippolyte had tried to manipulate her plans. Writing to Boucoiran, Aurore describes a letter her brother had sent her, and her own response to it. Hippolyte's letter was written with the clear intention of arousing a considerable degree of maternal guilt. He was determined to hurry the young woman back to her poorly treated, if not wronged, husband, and dangerously neglected children. At least such was her brother's male view. In her letter to Boucoiran, Aurore wrote: "I am sad; from afar an attempt is being made to hurt me. A letter from my brother, who is sour to the point of bitterness, contains the following: 'The best thing you have created is your son; he loves you more than anyone else in the world. Take care not to dull that feeling.' Therein is a good deal of cruelty. It is tantamount to saying that one day I will not even find my child's tenderness left."[2] This letter was written at the beginning of March 1831, two full months after Aurore's arrival in Paris. Her decision to leave Nohant had not been taken without grief, but the decision once made, she was determined to do all that she could to make something of the gamble that she had undoubtedly taken.

Initially Aurore lived at 31 Rue de la Seine in her brother's apartment on the fifth floor. Whatever his reservations about Aurore's move to Paris, he was not, clearly, wholly obstructive and he gave his half-sister until the end of March to find her own accommodation.[3] From the Rue de la Seine Aurore moved in with Sandeau, to his flat at 21 Rue des Grands-Augustins. The wide views down to the Seine, across the roofscape of Notre-Dame and along the impressive length of the Pont Neuf, were magnificent—and memorable. In her novel *Horace* (1841–42) she described the "apartment . . . made up of three rooms. . . . My balcony crowns the final storey of the house. . . . We could see, with one glance, the best part of the Seine's course, the length of the Louvre, yellow in the sun and sharp-edged against the blue sky; all the bridges and *quais* right up to the Hôtel-Dieu. Opposite us the Sainte-Chapelle . . . and a little further on the fine tower of Saint-Jacques-la-Boucherie raised its four gigantic lions up to the heavens; to the right, the façade of Notre-Dame completed the canvas."[4]

Sandeau also wrote the apartment into his fiction, but his description was of the interior. Already curious inversions of gender are visible.

Aurore relished the grandeur of the exterior and the wide urban views, while Sandeau's account in *Marianna* was of the domestic detail of their homely nest. The romantic, not to say clichéd, emotions of the novel's hero and heroine as they hurry up to their hideaway are presumably based on lived experience: "Madly they clambered the narrow and tortuous stair, and it was never without joyous transports that they took possession of their little room. . . . It was a modest retreat, high up near the sky, but the street noises never reached it. . . . There was neither carpet nor curtains, but the presence of flowers created an eternal springtime. . . ."[5]

Aurore's life was full: on the one hand, she lived the bohemian communal student life of her circle of close friends and enjoyed the delights of a fully fledged love affair, and on the other she sought to establish herself as an individual and a writer. She entered into the first with abandon, allowing herself to be delighted by the city, its life, its excesses, its hidden delights.

But for all the frenetic and spontaneous activity of the now, she kept her sights carefully focused on the longer term too. Looking towards the future, she made her way with determined caution, calculation, and discipline. This kind of double existence sustained her and kept the life-ache at bay. Driven by excitement for the future, she saw below her balcony the grandeur and beauty of the Seine as it twisted and turned through the city, not that mesmerizing blackness that had invited when she had been lured into the Indre years before, on horseback, when out with Deschartres.

Sandeau's Parisian circle, which had been hers too at La Châtre, was made up of the familiar names: Félix Pyat, law student and journalist; Émile Regnault, medical student and Sandeau's—and Aurore's—most intimate male friend; Fleury "the Giant," Gabriel de Planet, who had founded a club for exiled Berrichon men living in Paris; and Gustave Papet, whom they called "Milord," the only wealthy member of the group, who frequently picked up the communal bill. For young people with intellectual, political, and artistic interests—and pretensions—it was an extraordinarily exciting time to be in Paris. In the previous July political events had come to a head, and in 1831 cultural manifestations reflected a similarly revolutionary spirit. In February 1831 Hugo published his weighty *Notre-Dame de Paris,* later that year Michelet published his extraordinary *Introduction à l'histoire universelle* (*Introduction to Universal History*), and a few months later a theatrical event of similar influence took Paris by storm. With the adored Marie Dorval in the lead role, Dumas's *Anthony* was staged, a play which explored, even justified, ways of living involving notions as subversive as bastardy, adultery, and the murder by a lover of his lover in the interests of preserving her honour! Aurore implied that she and her circle of friends were at the première, but Aurore was not in fact in Paris at that time.[6] She did, however, see numerous later performances.

This level of full participation in contemporary cultural events was only possible because she had quickly assumed male attire. The stalls, which were relatively cheap, were open only to men; women occupied the more expensive seats on the balconies or in boxes. Contemporary fashion dictated that young men wear ankle-length military coats with square shoulders and no belt. Aurore ordered one, made up in thick grey material with matching trousers and waistcoat. Interest was added by a cravat and hat. This was a practical and comfortable outfit and she was confident that it would wear very much better than any equivalent woman's outfit. What she delighted in most, however, were her hobnailed boots, the hard male footwear of the day. They quickly took on symbolic importance, and attained the status of an essential metonym, that tangible element of the whole which summed up the meaning of the entire outfit; the boots were resilient and hard-wearing, they protected her from the wet and dirt of Paris, but above all allowed her free movement. In icy conditions they functioned almost like skates, facilitating movement across a wintry Paris:

> I can't describe how delighted I was by my boots; I would willingly have slept with them, as my brother did when he was very little, when he was given his first pair. With their little metal heels I was firmly grounded on the pavement. I flew from one end of Paris to the other. I felt I could have gone round the world. There was nothing to harm my clothes and I went out in all weathers, I came home at all hours, I went to the stalls of all the theatres. No one took any notice of me or questioned my outfit. Apart from the fact that I wore it well, the absence of any style in my clothes or coquettishness in my physiognomy discouraged any suspicion. I was too badly dressed, and my look too simple (my habitual look, preoccupied and unashamedly stupid) to attract or sustain anyone's interest. . . . Not to be noticed as a *man*, one has first to be used to not being noticed as a *woman*.[7]

The physical freedom that her appearance allowed her symbolized a more fundamental freedom. As in so many areas of her life, voyeurism played a part. Dressed as a man and having perfected a facial expression which allowed her to pass quite unremarked, she could circulate and *see* without being seen. This invisibility she experienced as miraculous and inspiring. Her relationship with Paris was in a sense an exaggerated version of what it had been when she looked down from her remote cramped cell in the convent attics. Then too she had been alone and unseen, but seeing. But she had also been far above the thick of things. Now the angle of perception could move from the high edifice of their apartment down into the narrow winding streets of Paris. Smells were strong and sounds distinct and multiple. Now she was down there, but equally invisible, and wonderfully unidentifiable.

Just as the idea of voyeurism recurs in Sand's life, so does the notion of the intimate relationship between voyeurism and anonymous androgyny: "I was no longer a *woman*, nor was I a *man*. I was jostled on the pavements like a *thing* [my emphasis] an impediment to busy passers-by. It didn't matter to me; I had no business. No one knew me, no one looked at me, no one stopped me: I was an atom lost in that immense crowd. . . . In Paris [unlike La Châtre] no one thought anything of me, no one saw me. There was no need to hurry on in order to avoid banal comment; I could invent an entire novel . . . without meeting a single person who would say 'What in heaven's name are you thinking about?' This was worth more than a cell, and I could have said, like René [Chateaubriand], but with quite as much satisfaction as his sadness, that I was walking *in the desert of man*."[8]

In a letter to her mother, written in the summer of 1831, she explained that it was not primarily the society and entertainment of Paris that she needed, but simply "to be alone in the street."[9] Her consuming passion was to see, to listen, to accumulate ideas, to witness emotion that would nourish her writing.

Like Lucien Rubembré, the hero of Balzac's *Illusions perdues* (1837–39) whom the author chose to lodge in the same building as Aurore and Sandeau, and like the heroes of all those other nineteenth-century "Sentimental Journeys," Aurore in her masculine attire could travel to Paris to discover both the world and the self, and to take risks in matters amorous and material.

Aurore was equally anxious to participate in contemporary action, and as part of her Berrichon circle she experienced the full excitement of the cultural and socio-ideological battles raging in the wake of the political instabilities of the previous year. She also quickly disposed of most of the money she had brought to Paris. However much she was swept up in the activities of her bohemian group and with Sandeau, Aurore did not for a moment lose sight of her own individual position. In particular she wanted to bring Solange to Paris and explored the possibility of Maurice boarding at a Parisian school so that she could maintain closer contact with him. In the meantime Boucoiran's renewed presence at Nohant since 20 January 1831, as Maurice's tutor, ensured that Aurore had news of her children and indeed information about her husband's activities, as her letters of the period testify.[10]

What she needed, if she was to move her children to Paris, was greater financial independence. Writing, she was quickly convinced, offered her the best chance of making substantial sums of money. Within less than a week of arriving in Paris (on 6 January 1831), she arranged an interview with Henri de Latouche, another Berrichon. She had brought a letter of introduction from Mme Duvernet, the friend from La Châtre.

Latouche, who had recently bought the *Figaro* for a paltry sum, was a man of few illusions when it came to the chances of literary success. He was a disappointed man, a misanthropist, who had himself tried his hand at poetry, theatre, journalism, and the novel. He had failed in each, with the exception of a single novel, *Fragoletta* (1829). A prose work more different from anything Aurore had conceived, let alone written, is hard to imagine. It is essentially the story of a hermaphrodite. The novel he condescended to consider was Aurore's *Aimée*. No copies survive. But in a letter to the loyal Boucoiran, she described what she conceived as a gap—which would threaten her readers' belief in the people and world of her novels— between her fiction and the way contemporary readers see the world: "I have been wholly unsuccessful; my work was considered unbelievable by the people whom I have approached for advice. In all conscience they told me that it was a work whose morality and virtue would be found improbable by the public. It's true." Whereas a few years earlier her response might well have been an indignant one, a self-righteous condemnation of the lowness of public opinion, by March 1831 her attitude had changed dramatically. Now she had come to appreciate that commercial publishing required fiction which would satisfy the tastes of a wide reading public. Aurore's letter continues unashamedly: "The lamentable public has to be served according to its tastes, and I am going to do what fashion requires. It will be bad. I wash my hands of it."[11]

Aurore had first called on Latouche only days after her arrival in Paris. There are a number of accounts of their meeting. Aurore had already heard a good deal about the man. Hyacinthe-Joseph-Alexandre, *dit* Henri, de Latouche, almost twenty years her senior, had been successful and gained a reputation as an adviser and editor working with aspirant young authors. He had, most famously, encouraged and in a sense copy-edited Balzac's first literary efforts.[12] The *Figaro,* very different today, was then a journal of only four pages. It was, however, highly regarded as an intelligent satirical paper with a polemic relentlessly directed against the bourgeois and reactionary government of the day. Latouche's manner was intense. He spoke with enormous precision which a new acquaintance would find pretentious only for a moment. His fiery eyes suggested hidden passions. Latouche listened with great concentration as Aurore read out *Aimée,* the novel she had brought to Paris to launch her writing career. His attention may have suggested to Aurore that the work had a compelling power. When she finally reached the end of the manuscript Latouche simply pronounced the work detestable. Sand adds in her autobiography that he was, of course, right. He told her, however, that she ought to be able to do better, and that one day she might write something decent. "But," he added, "you have to live in order to know about life. The novel is life told with art. You have an artist's nature, but you fail to take account of reality, you live too much in a world of fantasy. Be patient, allow time to pass and experience to accumulate, calm down. These two sad guides [time past and experience] come all too quickly."[13] But he offered practical support too, and suggested that Aurore join the staff of the *Figaro* as a columnist. He would pay, he said, seven francs a column for copy appropriate for the paper. So the autobiographical account reads.

At the time, however, only days after the meeting, she described a less dispiriting reception: "He told me that it was charming, but that it would not generally be considered credible. I replied that he was right and he added that I would have to redo it all, to which I replied that it would be quite possible so to do. He then said that I would have to start again. I simply added: 'All right.' "[14]

The contemporary account, however tailored, translates her response: one of determined resilience. She was not yet, so early on in her Parisian adventure, ready to give in. With hindsight, she adds the advice about the need for wide experience and for a mature understanding, even vision, of the real world in which the novelist lives and writes. Whether or not Latouche articulated this advice, Sand clearly saw, looking back, that this was what was sorely absent from *Aimée,* which she destroyed. It could also be that she wanted to suggest that Latouche had encouraged, even sanctioned, a life lived beyond conventional boundaries in the interests of literary creativity, thus absolving her from the judgements that might otherwise be made on her.

At the time, Aurore was not wholly convinced by Latouche's assessment, or she was willing to persuade herself of the usefulness of a second opinion. She was also quite clear that what she needed was a literary patron—someone who believed in her. In this she was, of course, quite right. Without contacts in the literary world, the chances of success were negligible. Duris-Dufresne had various literary friends and acquaintances and even suggested Lafayette. Aurore, not always modest, on this occasion thought it aiming too high. A meeting was then arranged with M. Kératry, author of the Gothic *Le Dernier des Beaumanoir* (*The Last of the Beaumanoirs*). The novel contains, among other scenes written to titillate, a graphic account of a priest brutally and delightedly raping a young woman. Aurore was not overly impressed, but she wrote to Boucoiran around the time of her meeting with Kératry: "Literature is in the same mess as politics. There is a hesitancy, an uncertainty that everyone feels. What's wanted is something new—to achieve it something hideous is created in its place. Balzac is at the very top for having painted the love of a soldier for a tigress and of an artist for a eunuch. . . . What's it all about, Good God?" Aurore declared, adding, "Monsters are in fashion. Let's do monsters."[15]

Aurore had called on Kératry on 4 February 1831, at eight o'clock in the morning, the time apparently set by her host. In the room in which she was received was a bed, and a woman, considerably younger than the white-haired Kératry, lying outstretched under a sumptuous red silk cover. Aurore's first *faux pas* was to mistake her host's wife for his daughter, whom she had assumed was unwell and hence in bed. The literary man spoke with economy and directness: "Women," he declared, "ought not to write." Why, Aurore then asked, had he summoned her so early in the morning if this was all he had to say? Her host then accompanied her to the door, declaiming his theories on the inferiority of women and their incapacity, even among the very most talented, ever to produce anything worth publishing. "Believe me," he concluded, "don't make books, make children." "Good heavens," replied Aurore, "follow the precept yourself if you think it so worthy."[16]

It is hard not to believe that Sand embellished this story. Yet the essence of the meeting is no doubt truthfully captured in the carefully ordered sequence of events described in the autobiography. Kératry was playing games, and Aurore's growing sense that women were quite unfairly excluded from the Parisian publishing scene aroused her indignation, that response which so often in her life rallied her considerable energy and strong, not to say pigheaded, determination.

And while waiting to see her first stories in print, in the *Figaro* (3 March), *La Revue de Paris* (March), and, she hoped, in *La Mode* and *L'Artiste,* she would have, she explained, to continue in the "lowest profession," working as a journalist on the *Figaro*. She described herself as a "workman-journalist," "boy-copyist."[17] She had not yet made up her own mind about morality and monsters in fiction, how, in short, to write what she wanted to write while interesting a wide public, but she was becoming preoccupied by the injustices of being a woman, and she was determined not to return to Nohant having failed.

Working as a journalist was not what Aurore had come to Paris to do. More and more she wanted to find a way into the world of literary publishing. But when she joined the editorial team at the *Figaro* she was, all the same, breaking new ground. She was the only woman on the staff. And she recognized in Latouche, with his wide experience of writing and publishing, a man who, by comparison with the likes of Kératry, was singularly unprejudiced when it came to matters of the differences between the sexes—and their writing talents.

With her usual quick-wittedness Aurore realized, not long after her arrival, that there were two literary matters in particular that she needed to consider carefully: morality and monsters. The morality of *Aimée* had been judged naïvely adolescent. And there had been a paucity of monsters. In both these matters Aurore's novel would clearly have left the contemporary reader sadly disappointed. She was not willing to write pastiche. Soldiers with sexual appetites for animals, and eunuchs were not subjects she cared for. But she was not going to let her apparently idiosyncratic attitude to such things seal *her* literary fate. Instead she turned to questions of ethics and mystery.

She returned to the convent. The strong emotional attachment that Aurore had for that place and its people was not reciprocal. She realized that "nuns cannot and should not love with their hearts. They live an idea and attribute real importance only to those exterior conditions which form the necessary framework for that idea." The sisters and the convent could no longer be part of her life, and she no longer part of theirs. This she realized would be her last visit to a place where for the first time in her life she had found a degree of stability and happiness. She described her leave-taking in her autobiography: "When I had had a good look round and, as it were, chewed and savoured for the last time the nooks and crannies of my convent and my beloved memories, I left, telling myself that I would never again pass through that grille behind which I left my most saintly tender-nesses." Had she visited one more time, she writes, looking back, "questions about my interior self would have been raised, about my projects, about my religious disposition. I didn't want to discuss these. There are people one respects too much to contradict and to whom one wants only to bring a calm blessing." She had learnt a useful lesson, and one that only those that have lived within religious communities can really learn, and that is that our humanity is inescapable and that no place and no vows can perfect us while on this earth. In other words, she was no longer romantic about the life, and hearts, of nuns. She continued in the same passage of the autobiography, and tellingly, "I put my beloved boots back on when I arrived home. . . ."[18]

Other parts of her life demanded careful reappraisal. She had embarked, as Latouche had recommended, on a re-examination of much of her past. It was a brave venture, destroying in a sense many of the reassuring myths of her youth. She now had a good idea of the reality of the convent. As she writes in The Story of My Life, "After the convent, there remained other things in my heart, in my life, which I had to do away with." Aurore was systematically dismantling the "fantasy world" which Latouche had claimed was too much her refuge. Of the Bazouin sisters she wrote, "These two young heiresses, who had become countesses, and more orthodox than ever in all things, now belonged to a world which would have had nothing but mockery for my bizarre manner of existence; my independence of mind would have been anathema." She had few regrets: "I returned to my mansard and to my utopia without sadness, aware that I had left behind certain regrets and certain memories, but satisfied that there was no further emotional attachment to break."[19] The mature Sand, writing her life story, showed considerable insight into psychology.

To visit, years later, the places and people that have mattered in the past, in the full and certain knowledge that gaps, even chasms, will have opened up which will make intimacy and mutual understanding limited if not impossible, takes a degree of courage, and strength. But Aurore had to feel even more grounded in her present position. She could no longer straddle two, even numerous, worlds, and so sure was she of the necessity of being decisive that she re-examined, in order to deny, the reality of much of her past.

She now knew that living out the Christian ideal within a community, like the nuns in the Couvent des Augustines Anglaises, required and created sacrifices which in some ways came terrifyingly close to contradicting the Christian ideal. The Bazouin sisters, on the other hand, had reminded her of the stifling and reactionary nature of opinion among women of her age or at least her class. What she could now write into her fiction, or at least experiment with in her fiction, with a degree of integrity, was a much broader morality. As for monsters, her mind had not yet been made up, but financial constraints must have made her aware of the danger of ruling them out of her fictional universe too peremptorily.

It is hard to believe, as most of Sand's biographers have suggested, that Aurore learnt much of direct literary relevance to her writing while on the staff of the *Figaro*. But she learnt a great deal of a more practical kind. The company was stimulating; it was at the *Figaro* that she first saw Balzac.[20] And she certainly learnt the discipline of writing, or struggling to write, for eight hours a day at a desk in a busy and distracting large office, rather like a noisy schoolroom, presided over by a charismatic and liverish schoolmaster.

With her nose to the grindstone, and suffering the frustrations of working for a stern editor who frequently tore up work he felt to be substandard or inappropriate, Aurore continued to write fiction and, remarkably, to believe, or at least cause others to believe that she believed, in a better future. In February she wrote to Boucoiran:

> I don't believe in all the sorrows that people predict for me in the literary career on which I'm trying to embark. You have to know and appreciate what motives drive me and what goal I'm pursuing. My husband has fixed my *living allowance* at 3,000 francs. You know that's not much for me, when I like to give money away, and not to bother counting. I therefore think only of improving my well-being through some earnings, and as I've no desire to be known, I won't be. I will attract neither the envy nor hatred of anyone. Most writers are nourished by bitterness and bat-

tles, I know, but those that have no other ambition
than to make a living, live in the shade, peacefully.[21]

By the beginning of March she was not only increasingly convinced of
her ambition to write for a living, she was also willing to articulate her
ambition, at length. She wrote to Boucoiran, "I am more determined than
ever to pursue a literary career, despite the distaste I sometimes see in it,
despite the days of laziness and fatigue which come to interrupt my work;
despite the modest life I am leading here, I nevertheless feel that my life
will from now on be complete. I have a goal, a task, let me utter the word, *a
passion.*"[22]

Storytelling, an imaginative life filled with fantasy and make-believe,
and writing, had taken up much of Aurore's mental energy from earliest
childhood. Now that she was in the capital, working for Latouche and not
only very much in touch with the world of writers but also gaining a better
sense of commercial publishing, Aurore's letters radiate a sense of mad
hope that something that has always been so much part of her might be liberated and presented to the world. What is more—and this remained all-
important all her life—writing would bring the financial independence
which in turn would buy her a freedom that mattered to her more, she
claimed, than literature. Writing was a passion, but equally a means to an
end: feminine independence. A subversive act in itself, if the views of men
like Kératry were taken into account, it was an act which simultaneously
allowed for what many considered equally subversive: life as a free and
wholly independent being. But she had first, as Latouche had advised, to
live, to experience, to allow time to pass. In the same letter to Boucoiran
she describes delightedly the full life she is leading, "We go to performances. . . . For me it's the chance to make useful and entertaining observations. You have, if you want to write, to see everything, to know
everything, to laugh at everything. Oh! Good gracious, long live the life of
the artist! Our brief is *liberty.*"[23]

A couple of days later, in a letter to Charles Duvernet she revealed a
still more astute understanding of how a writer gains notoriety, and
thereby sales. A satirical article she had written had been published alongside others in the *Figaro* (5 March 1831). Mocking the "citizen-king," the
issue of the paper had been confiscated pending a court case. The articles
had been published anonymously, but Aurore was prepared to maximize
publicity: "If particular articles are challenged in the courts mine will be
one of them. I'll declare myself the author and have myself imprisoned.

Long live God! What a scandal there will be in La Châtre! What shock and despair in my family! But my reputation will also have been made and I'll find an editor to buy my platitudes and nitwits to read them. I'd pay 9 fr. 50 c. for the pleasure of being sentenced."[24]

She had also identified something crucial about her disposition. In February she had written to Duteil:

> I am shattered. . . . But I am still hopeful and then the funny thing is, isn't it, that the more literature becomes a passion, the more obstacles one encounters, the more one sees the difficulties, the more one feels the ambition to surmount them? You're quite wrong by the way if you think that a *desire for glory* has gripped me. That's an expression that makes me collapse with laughter. I've a desire to make some money, and as there's no other way, aside from making a name as a writer, I'm trying to make one (a fantasy one).[25]

Something of her extraordinary vigour and determination emerges from her insistence that what fuelled her ambition was precisely the difficulty encountered along the way: "If I had foreseen half the problems I now find, I would never have embarked on this career. Well! The more I encounter, the more resolved I am to proceed. However, I'll soon be going *back to the family,* and perhaps without having managed to get my boat in the water, but with the hope that I will do better next time, and with plans for work that are more arduous than ever." Aurore then described a trait that she had not recognized in herself until she had embarked on writing commercially: "You have to have a passion in life. I was bored because I didn't have one. . . . A difficult life, and often one that is quite needy, like the life I am living here, chases the *spleen* a long way off. I am well, and when you see me again you'll recognize a thoroughly pink state of health."[26]

In her teens, intellectual enquiry had led her in circles. Spiritual contemplation, the pursuit of a mystical attitude that had absorbed much of her time towards the end of her stay at the convent, had not surmounted the bleakness of Mère Alippe's agonizing death. Attempting to transform the inner imaginative life that had always been hers into successful commercial publishing was a preoccupation, she had come to realize, that was all-absorbing to the point of either dispelling the life-ache or at least displacing it with other more immediate literary pains and spasms.

On 8 April she left Paris and travelled home via Bourges: the cathedral made a great impression on her. She was ecstatic at the thought of being with her children again. When she arrived home on 12 April she was delighted to see them and she was relieved to have distanced herself from the *Figaro* and the gruelling life of an apprentice journalist. But she was also determined to use the time and calm of Nohant to produce something that would catch the eye of a publisher, and the appetite of the public. In short, she would write something marketable, something that would create a name that would in turn become a commodity for the future. She was determined, but she was setting her sights high.

XIII

Paris from the Provinces

"Those who are filled with a true love for
their art have nothing to fear."

⁓Aurore regretted leaving her newly established Parisian life, but not to
the point of failing to appreciate the familiar rural beauty and peace of
Nohant: "The countryside here is truly beautiful; in the evening perfumes
waft into my room: lilac, and lily of the valley; then butterflies come: yellow ones with black stripes; nightingales sing under my window. . . . It is
delicious. . . ."[1] But she was anxious about Sandeau, afraid that her absence
would plunge him into gloom and inactivity. "All day I have been asking
myself . . . what sad reflections will preoccupy him this evening, alone by
the fireside. I am counting on you and Alphonse [Fleury] to console him,"
she wrote to Émile Regnault in April 1831.[2] She missed Sandeau, to whom
she wrote almost daily, and she missed Paris and her circle of friends. The
letters between Aurore and Sandeau have been lost, but many of those
exchanged with Émile survive, although pages have been removed and
passages excised here and there. He had become the familiar third party in
Aurore's latest triangular relationship.

Whatever her regrets, by distancing herself from the place where she
had loved freely, from Jules and the others, she gained the necessary perspective imaginatively to resurrect both: "I surprise myself constantly
dreaming of Paris: those steamy evenings, the pink clouds above the roofs,
and the pretty willows, such a tender green, which surround the bronze

statue of old Henry, and those poor little slate-grey pigeons that make their nests under the old grotesques of the Pont Neuf."³ In the same letter she describes her capacity to conjure up, for her own comfort, the company she so much loved: "My exclusive source of happiness here, when the children are asleep, is shutting myself up in my workroom, and of thinking, at my leisure, of that little room on the *quai* where I envisage you all: Jules—in his tattered, grimy artist's coat, his cravat under his bottom, his dishevelled shirt—stretched out on three chairs . . . ; Émile, praising you in the way you eulogize. . . . Ah! damn them, those who prevent us from living at Nohant as we live in Paris!"⁴ From the calm of Nohant, her Parisian life took on a new and more powerful reality.

But she was lonely, or dramatized her loneliness for want of any other source of drama. Despite her children's "tenderness" and their "kisses," she wrote, "I am terribly alone here where nobody understands me."⁵ She lacked sympathetic adult company, and the bourgeois society of La Châtre struck her as still more small-minded, pompously hypocritical, and generally repellent than before she had first struck out and moved to Paris for those initial three months. But she was delighted to be back with her children and quickly became involved in their day-to-day lives. To their grandmother she wrote, "They are two loves. Solange has grown as beautiful as an angel. There is no rose sufficiently fresh to give you an idea of her freshness. Maurice is still thin, but he's well, and you couldn't know a more likeable and affectionate child. I'm also very pleased with his progress and application in his work."⁶ But never did the delights of Nohant and the company of her children, nor the more mutually tolerant relationship that had developed with Casimir, tempt her to reconsider her decision to live so many months of the year in the capital.

Curiously, it is in letters to her mother that Aurore is most explicit about the changing nature of her relationship with her husband. Aurore met her mother infrequently, but a good many letters testify to their epistolary closeness. It may be that Aurore was unwilling to spare the time to visit her mother, given the demands of her own life in Paris. It is also possible that a relationship based on letters allowed Aurore greater control over the pace and rhythm of their encounters. She was able to stay in touch while protecting herself from her mother's wholly unpredictable and often deeply hurtful outbursts. Aurore was becoming more and more committed to the unconventional, but her mother's peculiarities were something quite other, something closer to real madness.

The letters are not the pro forma letters of an otherwise neglectful daughter writing out of a sense of duty. There is an intimacy, and even a residual childish rebelliousness, in Aurore's tone. Sophie-Victoire's life had been hard, and Aurore must have suspected that her mother thought that her daughter was making her own life a good deal more difficult than it had to be. In a letter dated 31 May 1831, Aurore is at pains to explain what it is that she needs. "It is not society, liveliness, performances, clothes that I need. . . . It is freedom. . . . The freedom to think and to act is my primary need." The way of life that had evolved was, she insisted, entirely fair. "I am therefore wholly independent; I retire when he rises, I go to La Châtre or Rome. . . . I return at midnight or six in the morning, all that is my affair. . . ."[7]

Despite the confident tone of her letters written home to Boucoiran before leaving Paris, now back in the provinces and considering her return to the capital, she had lost some of her earlier optimism, and she contemplated other ways of making an independent living. Writing may have become "a passion," as she had written to Boucoiran, and one that chased away misanthropy and despair, but she had begun to doubt that it would become a source, or a sufficient source, of independent finance. Her lack of confidence in the commercial success of both her own and Sandeau's writings led her seriously to consider alternatives.

In particular she continued to explore the possibility of making a living as a painter. Her skills as a watercolourist and draughtsman were considerable, as remaining works testify. Her sense of colour, form, and line are remarkable. In a letter to Regnault, written in May, she describes the progress she is making in her artistic training and presses him to find her clients for her portrait painting.

In her autobiography she enumerates her initial thoughts about making a living:

> I tried translating: it took too long, I was too scrupulous and conscientious; pencil or watercolour portraits took only a few hours: I caught the likeness very well, I drew the little heads well; but they lacked originality. . . . I worked fast, but my eye did not discriminate well enough, and I learnt that they earned you only ten sous a day; dressmaking: I thought of my mother. . . . At one point I thought I had had a good idea. I had painted flower and ornamental birds in miniature on snuff boxes and cigar cases. . . . I was

advised to try a host of different objects, fans, tea cad-
dies. . . . I struggled on but the vogue passed, I had
reached a stalemate. Yet despite myself I continued to
feel that I was an artist. . . . On one of my brief visits
to Paris I went into an art museum. . . . I returned the
next day, and the day after. . . . I observed, I was overcome, I was transported into another world. . . . It is
in a great painting that one sees what life is. . . . It is
the vision of nature and humanity seen through the
prism of genius. . . .[8]

Having abandoned Sandeau in Paris—as she saw it—she became
more worried about his health. Her letters to Émile implored him to take
care of "my little Jules," or he will fail to eat well and collapse from
hunger.[9] Fears for Jules's health and doubts about the possibility of either
of them making a name as a writer made her return to Paris one charged
with anxiety and doubt—but with excited anticipation too.

Then, quite unexpectedly, the great Honoré de Balzac wrote to
Sandeau, congratulating him on the short story "La Prima Donna," which
had been published in April in the *Revue de Paris*. It was signed "J. Sand,"
but Aurore claimed she had not contributed to it. The future suddenly
looked more hopeful, and Aurore wrote confidently to Émile Regnault, "I
see the young one pretty well set up to earn his own living and mine."[10] But
no sooner had financially reassuring news reached her than she was
informed of another unstable fact of life: Jules was apparently interested in
a young German girl, or so Regnault thought fit to warn her. Aware, as
always, of the dangers of hypocrisy, Aurore clung to what she described in
her letter of reply to Regnault as the "freedom of affections."[11] She was no
doubt hurt but equally felt confident that her passionate physical relationship with Sandeau would resume once she was back in Paris. A further
practical problem had arisen, however. Hippolyte and his wife would be
leaving Nohant to return to Paris in May, and Aurore would need to find
another official address. Hippolyte may well have timed his stay in Paris so
as to complicate, and possibly scupper, Aurore's plans for her return. He
sided increasingly with his brother-in-law.

The degree to which Aurore lived her life as fiction emerges strongly
from a delightful letter to Émile. It is unnecessarily long and absurdly
detailed, and was written in response to his kind offer to find her—and
Sandeau—suitable accommodation. It would have to consist, Aurore had

made categorically clear, of more than one single room. She described the kind of floor plan the apartment must have, in order to ensure the movement of people around it, the potential to circulate reminiscent above all of an archetypal French farce. Inordinately long—for all practical purposes—Aurore's letter translated her anticipated delight in all the possibilities for unexpected developments. Her entire family might become involved, she fantasized: "I have a mother, an aunt, a sister, a brother, etc., who will certainly arrive to *bother me*. . . . If I have only one room, I will run the risk of being blocked, unable to avoid them, or caught in flagrant offence, embracing little Jules."[12]

Here Aurore's capacity for voyeuristic experience has been replaced by a kind of fantasy of exhibitionism. "I want to have a way out to allow Jules to escape at whatever time it might be, because the fact is that my husband might fall, I won't say from the sky, but from a carriage, one fine day at four in the morning and having nowhere to stay might do me the honour of landing up here. Imagine how I would become if I heard him ring and felt his gentle presence on the other side of the door! He would break it down a good bit before I would have opened up. . . ."[13]

Regnault announced that he had found what he hoped to be an appropriate three-roomed apartment at number 25 Quai Saint-Michel. Aurore replied enthusiastically: "I love the three-rooms . . . but will a way out be possible? If we can't make it possible I'll arrange things so that the room behind remains unknown. . . . It'll be the black room, the mysterious room, the ghost's hideaway, the monster's lodge!"[14]

On 2 July Aurore left Nohant to visit Orléans cathedral, or so she told the family.[15] But near Orléans, at Étampes, Sandeau and his friends were waiting for her.[16] They stayed until 9 July, when they returned to Paris. In a letter to Hippolyte, she claimed she was visiting a friend's wife at Étampes, and would then be spending a couple of days at Latouche's country house. Aurore's half-brother was not deceived for a moment. He immediately wrote to Casimir, advising a pragmatic attitude to his marriage, one that came relatively easily to him:

> I have just received a letter from Aurore. Let us support one another as we make our way through a life strewn with pitfalls. Your wife wants her freedom, dissipation, movement. You haven't been a bad husband to her, and it's a just truth acknowledged here and at home. Let her do what she's doing. If she ends

up in a mess it's not your fault, or my fault, or her family's. Since she's doing exactly what she wants, what's left for you to do? To do what you enjoy, not to become bored, swallow your tongue, look after your wealth, your children. Your wealth is well established, your children are looked after and instructed at Nohant. . . .[17]

When Aurore had left Nohant at the beginning of the month, she had been particularly distressed that she was leaving Maurice behind. At the same time, life in Paris with Jules, she wrote in a letter to Charles Duvernet when she had arrived back, was the tonic she needed: "I had a great lump in my throat climbing into the carriage, and when both Maurice and you, whose look had sustained me, were lost from view, I cried bitterly. But as I approached Étampes my heart beat, life flowed back into me. I felt it burning with impatience and leaping with joy. If you could only know the state he was in, waiting for me, the poor child! Oh how could I regret and suffer after so much true love, fervent passion! I am too happy, in truth, too happy. I am afraid of dying and not enjoying it for long enough."[18]

They moved into 25 Quai Saint-Michel on 15 July. Aurore busily arranged the new flat. It was on the fifth floor with a marvellous view of the Paris rooftops, including the double towers of Notre-Dame, the ornate spire of the Sainte-Chapelle, and the Seine below. To furnish it appropriately Aurore had to borrow from her mother, Latouche, and Duris-Dufresne (deputy of La Châtre, re-elected for the third time on 5 July). She had had to sign what amounted to a hire-purchase agreement with the furniture suppliers. The flat became Aurore's first salon. Balzac would arrive, puffing and panting, enthusiastic as ever—generally about his own projects. He continued to encourage both Sandeau and Aurore to write, but came to the little flat mainly to find a sympathetic audience and talk at great length, as perhaps only nineteenth-century novelists could, about himself:

> Everyone knows how he burst with self-satisfaction but it was so legitimate that everyone excused it; how he liked talking about his works, telling their stories in advance, making them up as he talked, reading rough drafts or proofs. . . . He talked about himself and only about himself. On a single occasion he forgot himself and told us about Rabelais, whom I had yet to read.

Check-Out Receipt

Alameda Free Library
Main Branch
1550 Oak Street
Alameda, CA 94501
Tel: 510-747-7777
www.alamedafree.org
Checkout Date: 09-11-2016 - 15:46:55

Patron ID.: xxxxxxxxxx3995

----

1 George Sand : a woman's life writ la
33341003455830   DueDate: 10/02/

2 Bouvard and Pecuchet.
33341003818605   DueDate: 10/02/

Total Items: 2

Balance Due: $

Effective July 8: Main Branch will c
at 10 AM on Wed

Check-Out Receipt

Alameda Free Library
Main Branch
1550 Oak Street
Alameda, CA 94501
Tel: 510-747-7777
www.alamedafree.org
Checkout Date: 09-11-2016 - 15:46:55

Patron ID.: xxxxxxxxxx3995

---

1 George Sand : a woman's life writ lar
33341003455630   **DueDate:**   10/02/

2 Bouvard and Pecuchet.
33341000381805   **DueDate:**   10/02/

Total Items: 2

Balance Due: $

Effective July 8: Main Branch will o
at 10 AM on Wed

He was so marvellous, so astounding, so lucid, that we said to ourselves . . . "Yes, yes, definitely, he will live the future of which he dreams; he knows only too well who he isn't, not to be able to make of himself a great individual."[19]

This was the life Aurore wanted. Four days after moving into the flat, she wrote to Duvernet: "To live! How sweet it is! How good! despite worries, husbands, boredom, debts, relatives, gossip, despite bitter pain and tedious difficulties. To live! it's intoxicating! To love, to be loved! It is happiness! it's heavenly."[20] At the end of that summer Aurore and Sandeau embarked on *Rose et Blanche,* for which they had secured their first significant contract. It would be signed "J. Sand," a joint pseudonym invented by Latouche.

That autumn, on 2 September, Aurore returned to Nohant as arranged. Sandeau was to catch up with her some weeks later, having spent some time with his family. Aurore worked with energy and determination. The novel was to be in five volumes and she often worked overnight until six o'clock in the morning: she all but completed an entire volume in a single week. When Jules arrived, he stayed from 18 to 21 September with Gustave Papet, in his château in Ars, a little way from La Châtre. Casimir and others had apparently insisted that he not stay at Nohant.

But public opinion was not going to be allowed to deprive them of the delights of their sexual union. On the contrary, the stealth necessary and the collusion of a third party, if not two third parties, made the act all the more compulsive and erotically satisfying. On 20 September, the morning after the night before, Aurore wrote two letters, one to Papet and one to Émile. To the former she wrote,

> How good you are! How you love Jules, and how my heart thanks you. So you spent the night in the ditch, under a bivouac, like a poor soldier, while we, egoists of happiness, we could not bring ourselves to prise ourselves away from one another. Oh it wasn't for want of saying thirty times: Come on, we must, Gustave is there, poor Gustave! Jules can tell you that in the middle of our maddest transports, we blessed you, your name mingled with our kisses, all our thoughts were of you, because you were in our hearts with our

love. . . . Your solicitude, watching over our happiness, made it all the more exquisite. . . . But my poor friend, while waiting we were giving you rheumatism. My God, how egotistical is love alongside friendship! Forgive us, love me. I embrace you a thousand times.[21]

To Regnault she wrote in a not dissimilar vein:

Dear Émile, I am truly mad, but truly happy. . . . During the last three days I have lived three years. What do you say? . . . You love me too much to reproach me for so much happiness. Gustave didn't complain. He devoted himself, he buried himself up to the neck in our folly. He was under a bivouac in my garden ditch all the time that Jules was in my room, because he came that night, under the nose of Brave [the dog], my husband, my brother, my children, my maid, etc. I had calculated everything, anticipated everything. Jules ran no other risk than being peppered with gunshot climbing up to my window, which is only six feet off the ground. . . .

Aurore then continues still more intimately, explaining that a few nights earlier she and Sandeau had quarrelled. But the lover's dispute ended in bed—the passion of that night is described to Émile in intimate and graphic detail: "And that night he was there, in my room, in my arms, happy, beaten, embraced, bitten, groaning, crying, laughing. It was a rage of joy such as we have never before enjoyed. . . . Tonight I want him to come again. Twice is not enough. More would be overly imprudent, my husband could not miss realizing. . . . But up until now he doesn't know. He's busy with his wine harvest. He sleeps at night like a pig." Her writing was going well too: "And admire me! Lower the flag, in the midst of this deliriousness, these torments of impatience, burning palpitations, work is progressing. I have made enormous corrections to the second volume yesterday evening." It is one thing to express hitherto unknown depths of happiness to a close friend, even to suggest the bliss of a delirious intimate encounter; but Aurore's letter goes a good bit further. As a final coda to her description of her wild happiness with Jules, she writes: "I am an imbecile,

I am scarred by bites and beatings. I can't stand up. I am in a frenetic bliss. If you were here I would bite you until the blood flowed so that you could participate a little in our enraged love."[22]

Amid this sexual activity Aurore continued to work frenetically on *Rose et Blanche*. Jules, on the other hand, began to show signs of finding the pace too much. Aurore was dismayed. Fleury and Duvernet, motivated perhaps by jealousy, or by real fear for Jules's health, advised Aurore to slow down, and even accused her of demanding too much of her young lover. Regnault chose not to interfere and Aurore was touched by his loyalty to her, writing in a letter, "You see I was right to say it, you're worth more than the others. . . . Their intention was good, I know . . . but they don't understand me as you do! They don't know what an hour of happiness is, because it's easy for them to say, 'abandon it.' It's a function of only having *loved badly*." And she continued: "They always want to compare me to the women they have known who ceaselessly implore them to respect their secret and to maintain their reputation. I leap to my feet when they give me all that morality. . . . I've steered my way through enough of life to know the real depths. . . . Self-respect is a function of friendship just as loyalty is in shared wine. Friends forgive our unhappiness, our weakness, our boredom, the inconveniences caused . . . everything: except being lost to public opinion, which then reflects on them. . . . They would rather lay their heads a hundred times on the blade of the guillotine. They'll give their lives, but never sacrifice their name, what nonsense!"[23]

Meanwhile Aurore was forced to recognize the deterioration in Jules's health, detailing his day-to-day life to Regnault, who was after all a medical student: "He's doing everything he could to kill himself. He's not sleeping. During the day he does no work, taking little strolls like a dog, and in the evening he deprives himself of sleep to make up for lost time. And that's how he lives. I have other quarrels with him that are difficult to explain. We'll talk about them, you and me . . . there's nothing we can't talk about. I am in despair. . . . The whole of La Châtre has but one fear. Everyone thinks him consumptive. . . . Every night I have visions of him in a hearse, I am sad enough to die myself."[24]

Another tantalizingly incomplete letter to Regnault, written from Nohant at the beginning of October 1831, is missing the entire third page. The tone of what remains suggests that it was deliberately excised. Again it is confessional and full of intimate descriptions of her erotic relationship with the frail Jules:

These details are miserable, I do apologize, but you don't know what a terrible anxiety it is, what awful remorse I feel—to see the being to whom one would give one's life dying in one's arms. To feel him becoming thinner, exhausted, killing himself day by day, and telling oneself that one is leading him toward death, that one's caresses are a poison, one's love a fire that consumes without giving life, a fire that destroys, devours, that leaves nothing but ash, it is a terrible idea, Jules doesn't want to understand. He laughs at it. He despises the idea as if it were a childish fear . . . and when in the middle of his transports, the idea seizes me, freezes me, he replies that it is the death he wants, the kind of death he wants to die. . . . Then he makes all the promises I want him to make. He promises as he falls asleep, exhausted. When he wakes he's forgotten everything.[25]

Despite, or because of, the drama of her private life, and whatever her fears and their effect on her, Aurore continued to work feverishly. By mid-October she had finished her chapters of the novel and travelled to Paris, arriving on the eighteenth with the manuscript in her bags. By the end of the month, Aurore was correcting proofs. The production process was of course less technically sophisticated than today, but remarkably swift all the same.

On 17 December the *Figaro* announced the publication of *Rose et Blanche*. But just as her star was about to rise, she became embroiled in something of a quarrel between Latouche and Balzac. The latter was becoming more and more successful, while Latouche, who had done what he could to help Balzac at the start of his career, was clearly not going to succeed as a writer, but rather as an editor and critic. Latouche was afraid that Aurore, whom he considered to be his protégée, relied more on Balzac's advice. He was annoyed and expressed his indignation to Aurore. Balzac, on the other hand, warned Aurore of Latouche's possessiveness, dramatically and ominously declaring, "Watch out! You'll see that one fine morning, quite unexpectedly, and without knowing why, you will discover in him a mortal enemy." Latouche had suddenly and inexplicably taken against him. Aurore judged Latouche's criticism of Balzac inappropriate, and Latouche's belief that the rift could never be healed, equally inappropriate. She tried a number of times to reconcile the two:

> The first time he leapt to the ceiling. "What, you've seen him? . . ." I thought he was going to throw me from the window. He calmed down, sulked, returned and finally gave me back *my* Balzac, seeing that my sympathy took nothing away from what I felt for him. But every time I established or accepted a new literary relationship, Latouche embarked on the same tantrums, and even those to whom I felt indifferent he judged to be his enemies—unless he had introduced me to them. I've hardly spoken to Balzac about my literary projects. I had little faith in them or didn't think to see whether I was capable of something.[26]

Aurore no doubt hoped that all this was a sign that she was being taking seriously, of being important to people as influential in their different spheres as Balzac and Latouche. The publication of *Rose et Blanche* was accompanied by favourable reviews early on, attracting publicity and ensuring that readers were well disposed to it. Some reviews were more mixed, but the novel sold well despite the alleged "ambiguity" of the work, described in a review in *L'Artiste*. The heroine had, it claimed, a "suspect and lascivious head, planted gauchely on a pure and decent body."[27] Likewise, Aurore's recent fantasies, detailed to Émile, may have been more exciting than her actual activities with the frail Sandeau.

The reviewers were no doubt aware that the work had been co-authored but they may have misread the ambiguities that rose from the collaboration. The story of Rose, the actress, and Blanche, the nun, is also the story of two of Aurore's not wholly compatible personae. Nor did Aurore entirely disown the more sensational passages of the novel. Her mother, who read it sometime after its publication, reproached her for the lowness of some of the scenes. Aurore replied meekly, "I am delighted that my book amused you. I wholeheartedly accept all your criticisms. . . . I told you that I didn't write this work alone. There are all sorts of farces of which I disapprove but which I tolerated to satisfy my editor, who wanted it to be *bawdy*." This, in fact, is not altogether true. What the editor had repeatedly asked was that the novel not become too "high-flown"; but he had also invited her to "write as badly as she could!"[28] Aurore's letter to her mother continues: "I don't like the naughtiness either and there is none of this in the novel I am writing at present, to which I am adding nothing but my collaborator's name on the cover. . . ."[29]

The bawdy, farcical, and seamier details of *Rose et Blanche* were not, Aurore alleged, aspects that she would willingly have introduced. But she was increasingly aware of what made a work *sell,* and she was soon to set about writing one without Sandeau's collaboration, and without the editorial constraints that Latouche had imposed on *Rose et Blanche.*

On 14 January 1832 Aurore arrived back at Nohant. She and the children fell ill. But she must have been thinking through her next novel, and was soon working feverishly. The book she was writing was, she explained in a letter to Émile (27 February 1832), neither "romantic . . . nor frenetic";[30] rather it told of "ordinary life, like bourgeois life." But if this was to be realism, there was, she knew, a danger: "I'm afraid I'll bore people, as life bores." But if sex is admitted as part of life, then certain aspects of the story, she was also aware, would be far from unexciting. Much less sexually explicit than *Rose et Blanche,* and because of its convincing subtleties, the eroticism of *Indiana* is infinitely more stirring than that of its predecessor.

She was writing the novel, she implied, because she believed in it, but she expected it "to please very few people." Her most irksome anxiety concerned the heroine of the novel, supposedly an archetype of womanhood, yet remarkable too. The heroine of *Indiana* set something of a precedent. She was, in a sense, an early female hero, like many more who would be written into later novels of the nineteenth century. Aurore's own description of her heroine hints at contradictions, and sums up the difficulties with which the novelist had to grapple. Indiana, at this stage called Noémi, was, she wrote,

> a typical woman, feeble and strong, wearied by the weight of air, capable of supporting the sky, timid in the flow of life, brave on days of battle, refined, adroit, and astute at making out the delicate threads of common life, foolish and stupid at distinguishing the true sources of her own happiness, mocking all men, while allowing herself to be duped by a single man, lacking in self-esteem, while overflowing with admiration for the object of her love, disdainful of all the

vanities of the century on her own account, while allowing herself to be seduced by the man who unites them all.[31]

She recognized the apparent contradictions and wondered if she was making her heroine convincing. What drove her on was the knowledge of the reality of such a woman.

Aurore was trying, for the first time, not to write in the way she assumed to be professional, but from the depths of her whole being. Life as a Parisian journalist had been hard and demanding. Life as a real writer was to prove harder still. This kind of writing was not just physically and intellectually exhausting, as writing for Latouche had been; it drained every part of her being.

XIV

An Exquisite Dissection

"I don't know how to do things by half measures."

⤳The internal struggle that nourished Sand's writing frequently manifested itself in ill health. Her descriptions of her poor physical state always somehow suggest an important psychological corollary, in part because of their inordinate length. She wrote melodramatically to Émile Regnault: "All the while I feel suffocated, I can't do the round of my room without feeling faint, I can't stand up without my legs feeling weak at the knees. I have an appetite, and I want to eat. I could eat all day long if I gave in to it, because my stomach's burning and tormenting me, but all foods fail to tempt me and besides I am all the more breathless if I've eaten. . . . Don't let me die, my dear Émile . . . I'm not of an age to die. . . ."[1] But when Regnault suggested that he should come to Nohant to minister to her, Aurore protested that, added to the company of her husband and half-brother, this would make things intolerably contentious: they would try to convince him that her illness was entirely psychosomatic. Still more awkward to deal with would be their assumption that he was her lover. Aurore wanted to describe her ills, and no doubt exaggerated them, but she shrank from making life at home any more complicated. In response to the loyal Émile, Aurore quickly tried to reassure him that her health was steadily recovering: "I am eating, sleeping, and I feel better apart from occasional pains in the heart and stomach. I play with my children, love you, think of you. . . ." And by way of an afterthought she added, "Am writing a novel."[2]

There is a whiff of coy embarrassment in the offhandedness of her last-minute admission. To write for money out of absolute financial necessity was one thing, a matter of simple survival. But to write without a collaborator, and to excise from her writing those sensational elements that encouraged commercial success, was to write something very different, and much more intimate. She must herself have suspected, if not an emotional cause for her ill health, at least that the torment of writing exacerbated her pains and made them all the more difficult to bear: "Now that the first steps have been taken, I can go at my own pace, without tormenting my mind. If sometimes I put passion in, it's because I don't know how to do things by half measures."[3]

In *The Story of My Life* Sand looked to explain the creative process that had produced her first novel, *Indiana*. At the time, she claimed, she was more concerned *not* to do certain things, than clear about what it was she was seeking to achieve. She wrote, she claimed, "with neither a plan nor hope." She had resolutely banished from her mind all precepts and examples that she had been taught. Nor, she said, did she look within herself or others known to her for her characters: she was too romantic to see herself as a fictional heroine. "I have never found myself beautiful enough, nor attractive enough." She also maintained that there was insufficient "logic" in her character or actions to be transformed into a credible figure. It would have been pointless, she claimed, to seek to embellish herself or dramatize her life, concluding, "My *I*, when I encountered it face to face, always left me cold." Other writers, she continued, might be able to draw on themselves, but she was not in a position to do this, because she was made of "a material that is too highly coloured." Describing two sides of herself, the serious and the childish, she argued that had she based a fictional character on her more earnest side, the character would have emerged more like Alexis in *Spiridion* (1838–39), one of her far from naturalistic novels, than her heroine Indiana. If she had based a character on her more frivolous, light-hearted side, she would have created a wholly unbelievable person to whom it would have been impossible to give words or actions that would have made any sense at all.[4]

In these crucial passages Sand presented a view of herself as heterogeneous and in many ways inexplicable. She argued that the characters in novels have to make more sense than she can make of herself—as a real individual. At the same time, she proposed an ideal character, at the heart of the fiction:

> The novel should be a work of poetry as much as analysis. There have to be true situations and true characters, real characters even, grouped around a figure destined to embody the emotion or idea of the book as a whole. This central figure generally represents the passion of love, because almost all novels are love stories.

She was not arrogant enough to assume that her approach was the only one. "Balzac," she wrote, "has shown that it is possible to sacrifice the idealization of the subject in favour of the truth of the picture, the criticism of society and even of humanity." He had summed up these differences between their two approaches in conversation, when he had said to her, "You look for man as he ought to be; me, I take him as he is. Believe me, we are both right. Both paths lead to the same goal. I also like exceptional beings; I am *one*. . . . I need them to develop my vulgar characters. These vulgar creatures interest me more than they interest you. I enlarge them, I idealize them, in the reverse sense, in their ugliness and their stupidity. . . ."[5]

Sand claimed to draw very little directly from her knowledge of herself or others, and that she had no theory of the novel when she started to write. Only looking back with considerable experience was she able to construct anything like an aesthetic philosophy. What motivated her initially was not an idea, a vision of what the novel could be, but a powerful inner energy:

> I felt, when I began to write *Indiana,* a very strong and very particular emotion, which did not resemble anything that I had experienced when working on my previous attempts. But this emotion was more painful than agreeable. I wrote in a great spurt, without a plan, as I said, and literally without knowing where I was going, without even being aware of the social problem I was treating. I was not a supporter of Saint-Simon, I have never been, although I have had real

sympathy for some ideas and certain members of the group, but I did not know them then, and I was in no way influenced by them.

Saint-Simon was a social reformer and intellectual whose ideas about the repressiveness of marriage and the social merits of "free love" attracted a significant following among the more liberal thinkers of the day. Sand was less concerned with the institutional injustices of marriage, and more aware of the suffering experienced by so many women who had chosen to live within it:

> I simply felt within me, like a circumscribed and passionate feeling, the horror of brutal and mindless slavery. I had not experienced it, I was not experiencing it, as is obvious from the freedom I enjoyed and which no one disputed. Thus *Indiana* was not my story, unveiled, as has been said. It was not a complaint made against a particular master. It was a protest against tyranny in general, and if I personified that tyranny in a man, if I framed the struggle within a domestic context, it is simply that I had no ambition to write anything other than a novel of manners. That's why, in a preface written after the book, I defended myself against the charge that I had wanted to attack institutions. . . . Critics pointed it out to me and encouraged me to examine the question more closely.

What Sand insisted on was the reality of the *feelings* that were the origin of the novel. The novel form had presented itself as a "receptacle" which allowed her to unstop the emotions that had "slowly accumulated during the course of a life of reflection." But initially the vessel turned out to be the wrong size or shape for the content: "It found itself squeezed, and this sort of combat between the emotion and the execution held me, for six weeks, in a mood of determination quite new to me."[6]

The intense emotion Sand described as the stimulus to write *Indiana*, and the struggle to translate the emotion into a satisfactory form, sustained her. But she felt that something was slipping away from her. The discipline of novel writing, once she was properly on with the project, banished Corambé forever. Her freewheeling poetic spirit, her imaginative muse, the comforting source of her daydreaming, left her: "But my poor Corambé took flight forever, as soon as I started to feel myself on that road of perseverance leading to a specific goal. It was of an essence too subtle to be bent to the exigencies of form. As soon as I had finished my book, I wanted to rediscover the usual vagueness of my reveries. Impossible! I could write at length about this phenomenon of half-hallucination which had happened within me my whole life long, but which wholly vanished, and quite suddenly."[7]

On 1 April 1832 Aurore made her way back to Paris. She had a completed manuscript of *Indiana* with her, and she also had Solange. In her letters from April 1832 onwards, often addressed to Maurice at Nohant, Aurore enthusiastically described the gay time she and Sandeau were having with Solange. In a letter dated 7 April she describes a visit to the zoo at the Jardin des Plantes: "She saw the giraffe and claims she had seen lots of them before, in a field at Nohant!"[8] Light-hearted anecdotes that convey Aurore's delight in the company of her daughter, and wholehearted enjoyment of the childish activities undertaken ostensibly to amuse Solange, contrast with the bleak discussions of the cholera epidemic which ripped through Paris and other French cities that same year. Aurore caught a benign form on 13 April. Her decision to bring Solange to Paris must have been one she regretted, but Solange escaped contagion. That April, on a single day, 800 deaths were recorded among a population of some 650,000. Altogether the epidemic took the lives of roughly 18,000. In her own apartment block, 6 people died on the lower floors and Aurore feared for the scourge. It climbed "floor by floor."

Living under the shadow of a devastating epidemic, Aurore nevertheless pursued publication. On 2 May she signed a contract with Dupuy (sometimes Henri, sometimes Ernest, possibly two brothers) for *Indiana* and publication was announced on 19 May. While the manuscript was with the printers, Aurore considered under what name the work might be published. Sandeau, who was impressed by the manuscript, was no doubt dismayed that during the period in which it had been written he had produced very little. He was clear that the novel should not be published under their joint name, "J. Sand," as he had had nothing to do with it. But as the pseudonymous author had already established a name, there was a commercial argument for using it. Sandeau and Aurore consulted Latouche, who had originally devised the name.

It was not as though the author of *Indiana* had an obvious *nom de plume*. Her mother-in-law and, more surprisingly, her mother were both unwilling to see *their* names on the covers of printed books. Sand tells how she visited her mother-in-law in part because the latter wanted an explanation for Aurore's long periods of absence from her husband at Nohant. When Aurore had explained that Casimir did not object to their arrangement, Mme Dudevant went on to ask whether it was true that she "intended to *print* books," to which Aurore replied, "Yes." Mme Dudevant then declared it "a funny idea," to which Aurore again replied, "Yes," refusing, characteristically, to be provoked. When Mme Dudevant then came to the point and expressed her concern that *her* name might be printed on the covers of published books, Aurore assured her that this would certainly not occur.[9] Whatever persona Aurore imagined as the author of *Indiana*, it was clearly not one who bore the name Dudevant.

Sophie-Victoire had been critical of *Rose et Blanche* and would, Aurore must have supposed, have strongly objected to seeing *her* name on the covers of *Indiana*. But Aurore's choice of a name was not simply by a process of elimination. She had felt a form of possession take hold of her when composing *Indiana*, an experience which had been exhausting and disturbing. And she had emerged, having finished the novel, somehow changed. Her phantasmagoric experience, orchestrated by Corambé, had stopped. In creating *Indiana*, she had re-created, or been re-created, herself. That new writing self could, quite appropriately, have been given a new name. Further, Aurore described the novel as the product of something other than her rational, controlling self. It was thus suitable that the author of *Indiana* carry a name other than her own, and remain pseudonymous, just as the real author of *Indiana* remained in a sense unknown to Aurore.

Latouche suggested that she retain the surname "Sand," for commercial reasons, while adopting a new first name. She chose "George" without reflection "because George seemed synonymous with Berrichon," no doubt because of Virgil's *Georgics*. It could be that she adopted the English "George," rather than the French "Georges," out of some sense of loyalty to the English nuns at the convent.

The question of a name seems little to have preoccupied her. She was clear that she wanted to remain anonymous: what the specific name on the cover might be mattered little. What was significant was that the *change* of name represented the beginning of a new life, the life of George Sand:

> I was baptized unknown and unaware, between the
> manuscript of *Indiana*—which was, at the time, my

whole future—and a thousand-franc note—which was at the time my entire fortune. It was a contract, a new marriage between the poor apprentice poet that I was and the humble muse who had consoled me in my troubles. God preserve me from disturbing anything I have left to destiny. What's a name in a world that has been revolutionized and remains revolutionary? A number for those who do nothing, an ensign or chit for those who work or fight. The one I've been given I have made myself and alone . . . by my own labour. . . . I don't feel that anyone should reproach me, and, without being proud of whatever it might be (I have only done my duty), my clear conscience sees nothing to change about the name that designates and personifies it.[10]

While writing *Indiana*, Aurore had expressed various anxieties about its reception: was it too dull, as dreary as real life? Was the protagonist believable, sufficiently typical? Whether by coincidence or design, Latouche was in the Saint-Michel apartment with the author when the first copy of the work was delivered by the printer. Flicking through the pages, stopping to read a paragraph here or there, he contemptuously declared it a pastiche, "school of Balzac." Arguing that "this element and that" amounted to nothing more than a poor imitation of that other celebrated author, he declared that what she had produced was neither Balzac nor herself. Typically, she said nothing but waited for him to leave to read the novel properly.[11]

In her autobiography, where she described Latouche's initial reaction to her work, she wrote nothing about her own feelings. Did she despair, fearing that he was right? Or was she confident that when he took the necessary time to read the novel in its entirety, he would change his mind? She did not have to wait long to hear a fuller account of his reactions. When she awoke the next morning a note from Latouche was waiting for her: "I did not want to leave for the country without first returning to ask your humble forgiveness, George. Forget the nonsense I said yesterday about the beginning of your book. Your book is a masterpiece. I spent the night reading it." And he went further than declaring it as good as the work of the most highly regarded writers of the day: "Balzac and Mérimée," he wrote, "are dead beneath *Indiana*. Ah! my child, how happy I am."[12]

Reviews were enthusiastic, but Sand was surprised and disturbed by some of the interpretations of the novel. In the *Journal des Débats* (16 May 1832), an anonymous reviewer described the novel as a "heady story full of interest which is imprinted with all the weaknesses and also the qualities of the modern period." The degree to which the novel was discussed as emblematic of its age, while highly encouraging in terms of sales, also seems to have disturbed Sand. She had unknowingly articulated some of what had only been spoken about in fragments before. Her novel had given shape, form, and persuasive power to certain contemporary preoccupations.

In the *Figaro*, on 24 May, another anonymous reviewer, very probably Latouche, wrote: "It is the story of modern passion, the true story of women's hearts, hearts which alone have retained their primitive passions while men have lost theirs. . . . A chaste and delicious work, simple, true and touching, and written with exquisite purity of expression." Félix Pyat, in *L'Artiste* (27 May), wrote: "You have never witnessed a more penetrating analysis, a more exquisite dissection, a more thorough autopsy of the human heart. . . . The characters are true and drawn with that vigour of expression that you admire in *Le Rouge et le noir*. . . . The expression is always there to serve the idea: strong, elegant, simple."[13] In June, in *La France Littéraire*, a certain "E.D." declared the book "worthy of being singled out as one of the best novels of the period."[14] A more penetrating review was published in the *Revue des Deux Mondes*, dated 1 June, by Jacques Lerond. The reviewer deemed it a work which conveyed a sense of erotic power, on the one hand, and delicacy of feeling on the other, and accounted for this combination by suggesting that it must be a collaborative work between a woman and a man: "There is, in this book, at once a sensual love, a spirited voluptuousness, and exquisite delicacy of feeling. One would suppose this brilliant but unharmonious material to be the product of two distinct workmen . . . that a young man's hand tightened the strong, vulgar tissues, and that a woman's hand embroidered onto it silk and gold flowers." In her autobiography Sand commented, "The papers all spoke of Mr. G. Sand enthusiastically, but insisting that a woman's hand must have glided across it here and there to reveal to the author certain delicacies of heart and mind, while declaring that the style and discrimination were too virile to be anything but a man's. They were all somewhat Kératry."[15] The reference is, of course, to Kératry's alleged recommendation when Aurore first went to seek his advice on arrival in Paris: "Don't make books, make children." The reviewer may have known of the earlier collaboration behind the name "J. Sand." It is possible, however, that he was aware of certain androgynous elements which are part of the novel's fabric.

Praise had been hyperbolic. Sand was frightened by the heights—literary, social, political, feminist—to which she had suddenly been raised. In a letter to Charles Duvernet that July, in the wake of endless reviews and articles about *Indiana*, she wrote: "The success of *Indiana* frightens me a good deal. Until now I thought I was working aimlessly and never merited the least bit of attention, but fate has ordained otherwise. I have now to justify the admiration directed at me and which I don't merit. This truly makes me abhor the position I'm in. It seems to me I'll no longer take pleasure in writing."[16] Was this simply exaggerated modesty, and self-dramatization? It may have been to some extent, but it is also possible that, having written the novel fired by emotional rather than intellectual energy, by strong feelings rather than well-defined ideas, she had revealed to her readers part of herself that she scarcely knew, a self that was deemed by many of the critics to be quintessentially contemporary in its anguish, and in its passion.

Indiana, signed "George Sand," is narrated by a man. The novel's story can be briefly told. The eponymous heroine is a young Creole woman from the Île Bourbon (now La Réunion) in the Indian Ocean. She is unhappily married to Colonel Delmare, an irascible and domineering veteran of the Napoleonic wars. Their home is a small château on the outskirts of Paris, where they live with their dogs, including Indiana's dog Ophelia, and Sir Ralph Brown, Indiana's cousin and protector. Their close neighbour, the suave Raymon de Ramière, is conducting a flirtation with Noun, Indiana's maid, but Indiana herself soon falls in love with him. Ramière is an out-and-out cad who calmly swaps the maid for her mistress. Noun, heartbroken, commits suicide. The opportunistic Ramière, satisfied by his conquest, then leaves Indiana for a wealthy heiress. Indiana is saved from a suicide attempt by her devoted cousin. Sir Ralph and Indiana then survive a mutual suicide pact and Indiana, now widowed (conveniently), sails back with Ralph to their native tropical island, where they live in a hidden valley (Bernica) devoting their time to buying the freedom of old and infirm black slaves, much to the colonists' dismay.

What quickly emerges even from a short summary is the characteristic straddling of two otherwise distinct fictional modes: realist in the first section, and improbably idealist in the second. For the 1833 edition of *Indiana*, Sand removed those comments made in the original 1832 preface, affiliating its author to the realist school: "The current trend is to depict a fictional hero so ideal, so superior to the common run. . . . These heroes bore you, I'm sure, because they are not like you, and after a while, craning your neck up to watch them float above you, makes you dizzy. I place mine firmly on the ground and they live the same life you do."[17] This declaration of adherence to the realists' hero (which may or may not give off a whiff of double-edged irony) did not accompany the second edition, presumably because Sand realized that her allegiance was more complex. She wanted to depict ordinary life while suggesting possibilities for *something better*. Thus Sand's fiction is a form of idealist writing and Indiana's passionate love story necessarily exhibits implausible extremes that are not compatible with nineteenth-century bourgeois realism in order to be compatible instead with fictional idealism.

Indiana stands apart from other unhappy, dissatisfied, even sadomasochistic, nineteenth-century female protagonists in France (most obviously Emma Bovary, Indiana's most illustrious descendant) because Sand's heroine's quest for ideal love is bound up in a vision of an ideal world. Emma Bovary's fantasies are about the rich and elegant and the sumptuousness of their material wealth and relative freedom. Indiana dreams of a society in which men no longer deprive women of their freedom and, in parallel, slaves are no longer owned by their masters. Indiana's fantasy is that "a day will come when everything in my life will be changed, when I shall do good to others, when someone will love me, when I shall give my whole heart to the man who gives me his; meanwhile, I will suffer in silence and keep my love as a reward for the man who will set me free." This may be difficult to take seriously at the turn of the millennium.

What remains immediately compelling is the concatenation of the sadomasochistic, erotic, moral, and political, which can be excavated beneath the bland discourse of Sand's preface and the archromantic discourse that she requires of Indiana. Sexually the split between realism and idealism is written into the split between two types of woman: Indiana, the upper-class, virginal woman (given by her violent father to her violent husband, she expresses her resistance, wholly improbably, by refusing to consummate the marriage), and Noun, the working-class, sensual hedonist. From a feminist point of view, there is a split too between the challenging of "barbarous" and "unjust" laws that govern women's existence in wedlock, in the family, in society, and the representation of women that uses conventional patriarchal imagery. The plot, however delightfully improbable it becomes, is less engrossing ultimately than the symbolic strata which are tantalizingly glimpsed and suggest Sand's complex psychic, sexual, and imaginative world: she frequently described her own thinking as "illogical."

When Indiana returns to France she arrives in Bordeaux in the midst of the July Revolution and just as Ramière has decided, in what must be a pointed political allegory, to side with money in the form of an heiress to an immense industrial fortune. Indiana, and here it is a moral allegory, has no political conscience: "In the whole revolution she was personally interested in only one detail; in all of France she knew only one man. She fainted on the pavement, and came to in a hospital—several days later."[18] As though in punishment for an egotistical denial of political history, she is quite literally denied an identity. She is entered "on the books there [in the hospital] and also in the police records, under the rubric *unknown*."[19] An important aspect of her sexual identity is also assaulted—her beautiful black hair, brilliantly fetishized elsewhere in the novel: "But, when she was ready to tidy her hair, she sought in vain the long and magnificent tresses which she had once had; during her illness they had fallen under the nurse's shears. Now she noticed this for the first time; her all-engrossing thoughts had diverted her mind completely from small matters."[20]

As twentieth-century psychoanalysis suggests, our psychic life takes place in a space where time is nonlinear. Castration—represented here in the cutting off an emblem of feminine beauty—has always taken place already.[21] Before Indiana's ultimate humiliation, when she throws herself at Ramière's feet only to learn that he is married, Indiana has not apparently noticed her grim surroundings. But when she returns to her hotel after her encounter with Ramière and his new wife, the narrator presents her. The passage is steeped in symbolism and worthy of comparison with other accomplished nineteenth-century novelists—Dickens, Balzac, Dostoevsky—for whom the boarding house is a symbol of poverty, disenfranchisement, solipsistic melancholy. Sand is unique in describing a *woman's* experience of such a place:

> I do not know that there is anything on earth more terrible than life in a furnished boarding-house in Paris, especially when it is situated, as was this one, in a dark, narrow street, and only a dull, dispersed light crawls, unwillingly as it were, over the smoky ceilings and grimy windows. And then there is something chilling and repellent in the look of the furniture, to which

you are unaccustomed and to which your idle glance
turns in vain for a memory, a comforting contact.

The dispossessed traveller becomes an anonymous object in the commodity market of the nation's largest urban economy. Sensory experience conjures no memories, no meaning. Sounds from the street below are no more than "discordant, endless noise."

The narrator of *Indiana* then addresses a hypothetical reader in the provinces: "you, ill-starred provincial, who has left fields, blue sky, greenness, a house, a family. . . ." He will come to the city at his peril, "to shut [himself] up in this dungeon of the heart and mind." It is no more than a place of death:

> Exhausted before you have seen a fraction of this constantly mobile population, this impossible labyrinth, you seek refuge, overwhelmed by all you have seen, in the cheerful entrance of a furnished boarding-house, where, after settling you hastily, the only servant in the house—often a character of immense proportions—leaves you to die in peace. . . .

Things cannot get much worse. Sand has still more to say: "*But to be a woman and to find oneself in such a place,* abandoned by everyone . . . to be without money . . . with a past which offers up not a single happy memory untouched by bitterness . . . with a future which offers not a single hope to distract one's thoughts from the emptiness of the present, is the extreme point of misery and hopelessness." Sand then reintroduces her heroine: "And so Madame Delmare, making no attempt to refuse a destiny whose time had come, to refuse a broken, ruined life, submitted . . . without the slightest effort to die an hour earlier, to suffer for an hour less."[22]

If many of Flaubert's female readers believed that Emma Bovary had been based on themselves, how many of Sand's women readers shared Indiana's aspiration towards ideal love in an ideal society? What guaranteed its success above all, however, was the novel's brilliant critique not so much of marriage as of the physical, even sexual, frustrations and emotional and spiritual disappointments of women's relations with men whether inside *or outside* marriage. This tension between women's desires and mundane experience was read as an allegory by many of Sand's male readers. It stood for a universal conflict: that of the individual constrained to live within the false and life-denying rules and codes of society. In a fifteen-page article in the *Revue des Deux Mondes* (15 December 1832), Gustave Planche lauded every aspect of the novel, in particular its "generative force, the conflict between love and the law, the irreconcilable conflict between passion and society."[23]

Certain scenes and insights stand out and no doubt go some way towards explaining further the novel's extraordinary success. One scene closely parallels some of Sand's descriptive letters which detailed her sexual activities. In her letter to Papet, who had kept watch for her and Sandeau, she had assured him that his name (he is the third party) was on their lips as they enjoyed each other. The parallel scene in *Indiana* is a long passage in which the caddish Raymon de Ramière continues to enjoy the sexual favours of Noun, Indiana's maid, after he has sworn his love to the chaste Indiana, who has refused him any physical contact. Furthermore, it is in Indiana's bed, in her sumptuous boudoir, that Raymon and Noun sport. Raymon's sexual pleasure is heightened by imagining that he is making love to a double, a woman who is by turns Noun *and* Indiana. Sainte-Beuve claimed that no male author would have dared to lay bare so daringly the duplicities of men's psycho-sexual lives, and he went on, in an article in *Le National* (5 October), to speculate on the sex of the author—while knowing full well. Cynical like Stéphane de Grandsagne, Raymon was modelled also on Aurélien de Sèze. Indiana will give herself to Raymon if he forgoes all that she is willing to forgo: wealth, reputation, duty, principles, family, etc. She is willing to "sacrifice everything." Raymon, on the other hand, like Aurélien, calculates the costs as too high and marries another woman. Further evidence that Sand re-created aspects of her relationship with Aurélien are suggested by certain parallels between the fictional names of *Indiana* and Aurélien's family names. His brother was another Raymond, and his sister another Indiana.

Aurore had claimed, before the publication of *Indiana*, that what she wanted was essentially a quiet life. She needed to make some money as a writer in order to retain independence from her husband and to live reasonably comfortably. She would not, she had written to Boucoiran, ever be tempted to seek success or glory in the eyes of a wider public.[24] Whether or not she was sincere it is difficult to know. She had certainly written *Indiana* expecting only limited success. Her heroine, she had feared, was insufficiently believable. And the novel told largely of everyday life, which might well, she supposed, bore the reader. Her anxieties were quite unfounded, and as that year drew to a close Planche astutely wrote in an article, published on 15 December, that the supposedly anonymous "G. Sand" was now facing a daunting task: that of writing a second novel that would again take the public by storm as had the first novel. Editors would now put pressure on the author, and the public had high expectations of "G. Sand's" future novels.

The events of the summer of 1832 had, however, provided ample distraction from her professional concerns as a writer. She had experienced the events of June as a rite of passage. As if until that point she had, in a sense, been playing at life, she wrote: "The sixth of June . . . brutally catapulted me into real life."

The revolt of June came hard in the wake of the cholera epidemic, uniting Liberals and Republicans, the *petits bourgeois* and the working class in opposition to Louis-Philippe. On 5 June the streets of Paris were filled with mourners participating in the funeral of Maximilien Lamarque, a popular Liberal general. Sporadic shouts of "Long live the Republic" quickly metamorphosed into a mesmerizing chant: "Down with the Bourbons! Down with Louis-Philippe." Soon the troops appeared and the barricades went up. Sand, late the same afternoon, had been with Solange in the Luxembourg Gardens. She was suddenly distracted from her intimate maternal play by shouts. "The soldiers," she heard people cry, "are firing randomly on everyone."

Once home, Sand stuffed her mattress against the window to prevent the force of a stray bullet from spraying broken glass into the room and, barricaded into their apartment, she tried to calm and reassure Solange. Below them chaos took over for forty-eight hours. The first night, on a neighbouring bridge, a column of soldiers marched on a group of insurgents. Their mutilated bodies were thrown into the Seine below. Sand heard their cries carried in the night air. During two days some six hundred people were massacred. All that struck Sand was the hideousness, the horror, the waste of violent death. Such was her shock that she forgot all political reason, writing simply that she felt a profound disgust "for the monarchy, the Republic, a horror of all men."[25] To have witnessed the scale of illness and death caused by the cholera epidemic was sickening. Aurore wondered how she would ever find the heart to write again. In a letter to Laure Decerfz, a childhood friend and the daughter of her grandmother's doctor, that June she wrote: "You will understand that amid these real tragedies art is forgotten, lost, exterminated. . . . If we had ten years of political calm, literature would no doubt enjoy a period of growth. . . . But 6 June killed *Indiana* . . . and has thrown me back into real life and it seems impossible to me *now that I will ever again dream of novels.*"[26]

She was quickly shaken out of her melancholy, or at least temporarily distracted from it, by none other than Victor Hugo. The most famously successful of contemporary novelists, he was piqued by the praise lavished on "G. Sand's" *Indiana*. In particular he was unwilling to let pass a judgement that declared it "the finest novel of manners that has been published in French for twenty years." The very next day Hugo published a counter-attack, declaring with delightful brashness, and quite unashamedly, that it was ridiculous that *Indiana* be regarded as the greatest book. "What about mine then?" he asked of the reviewer. "Do you take *Notre-Dame de Paris* to be a whore?" Sand was, it seems, delighted by his pique.[27] Hugo's article was to inaugurate a not altogether humourless rivalry that lasted until Sand's death.

On 28 July Sand and Solange left Paris to return to the comparative peace of Nohant. Sand was exhausted by political events, by the excitement and startling surprises of *Indiana*'s success, and by her increasingly con-frontational relationship with Sandeau: she wanted him to write more. In her baggage, needless to say, was a contract for her next novel, *Valentine*, signed two days earlier with Dupuy. It was for an edition of 1,200 copies and she would earn twice what she had received for *Indiana*. Tensions between Sand and Jules had gradually been growing. Jules found it diffi-cult to settle to work but George was not altogether sympathetic. The hor-rors of June, and Jules's aimlessness, depressed her. Both filled her with a tragic sense of waste.

At Nohant, settling down with few anxieties, it seems, to work on her next novel, she felt liberated. Jules had returned to his family at Parthenay. He knew that he would not be welcome at Nohant and wrote somewhat pathetically to Papet: he would not be troubling him for a bed. Nor would he be asking Papet to sleep in the ditches of Nohant, keeping watch while Jules and Sand enjoyed their intimacies. But he asked Papet to visit Nohant: "See Aurore, see her often. . . . Tell her that I love her and that I have no other life than hers." He hoped that when they all reassembled in Paris in the autumn, their bohemian and communal life would resume. He must have known that Sand would have finished another novel and would have more time for him, more time for carefree living: "I'll smoke my cigar, you will caress Solange, and Aurore will make *plum pudding* [in English]," he wrote longingly to Émile Paultre. What he yearned for most was a return to the domestic comfort of his life with Aurore. In the meantime, he concludes typically, "I'll settle down to work tomorrow."[28]

While Jules fantasized about autumn hot puddings, Aurore quickly re-established her writing routine and fantasized about "free love" in her novel *Valentine*. There is then an overlap between what might be construed as the novel's ideology and the ideas of Claude de Saint-Simon. During the July Revolution the disciples of Saint-Simon had publicized their mentor's ideas more widely, advocating a more equal distribution of wealth through, for example, the abolition of inheritance laws. They argued for the enfranchisement of women, and even for the equality in law of the sexes. Most sensationally—the term "sensational" is a nineteenth-century one—they argued for the abolition of "the tyranny of marriage" and the practice of "free love."

That *Valentine* would be discussed as part of a wider debate originally fired by Saint-Simon could only improve its chances of commercial success. The novel subverts class: the eponymous heroine, who belongs to a comfortable class, falls in love with the son of a peasant. He is impulsive and wholehearted in his loving. Further, the novel is more explicit in its condemnation of marriage than *Indiana*. But it was arguably not mere churlishness that motivated Sand to distance herself from the Saint-Simonians when they sought to make her a figurehead of their movement. *Valentine* can be read not as the fictional working through of a theory, but rather as a fictional exploration of an idea that had long concerned her: the possibilities for love between different social groups. She continued to romanticize her aristocratic father's marriage to her lowly mother. *Valentine* celebrates the intimate encounter of individuals who are motivated by love and who abandon social convention because of amorous conviction. Raised to a theoretical level, or abstracted into a politics, *Valentine* became, Sand recognized, problematic. As she repeatedly argued, she was not an advocate of "free love" but an advocate of the individual's right to act in accordance with conscience. The power of love, the life-reinforcing energy born of love, was not to be denied. In certain circumstances this might lead to "free love," but that was a quite different matter from advocating a way of life based on the *principle* of free love. A further reason why Sand was reluctant to side with any party, in addition to her shyness, was a sense that her ideas and commitments were changing rapidly. She was still trying things out and unwilling to be a card-carrying member of any pressure group.

The exploration that *Valentine* represented came to a swift conclusion within two months of embarking on the novel. Writing was often for Sand a kind of hopeful travelling, and arrival, in the form of finishing a work, brought disappointment, even despair. Exhausted by the intensity of her writing, she fell into a depression. Her relationship with Jules, she had to admit to herself now that she had time to think about real life, was far from happy. Free love lived out had not been successful, and soon even her Berrichon friends, her bohemian circle, would lay the blame for the relationship's failure squarely at her feet. Every member of Sand and Sandeau's group seemed to see things from his point of view. They were all men. Literary success, it must have seemed, had made more difficult her membership of a society which she had come to depend on as a kind of extension of her family. Financial independence had allowed her to free herself from her husband, but the relationship she had established in place of her unhappy marriage seemed doomed. From Nohant she described the places that had been important to them soon after they had met and fallen in love. What they had meant then, and how they had felt in those places, threw into high relief their present unhappiness: "All that country is now empty, bleak and without charm," she wrote on 11 September 1832.[29] Aesthetic and temporal subjectivity blurred and, she continued: "Where are those days of youth, of greenness and poetry . . . ? The frightful drought of this year has devoured everything. . . . I looked for [the tree] where you wrote my initials. It has disappeared. . . . Everything passes, and it is folly to become attached to the places where one has been happy. Happiness leaves, places change and the heart ages."[30]

When Sand returned to Paris at the end of October 1832, they tried once again to re-establish their relationship. But things were difficult. As Aurore had written portentously (11 September 1832): "For others a habit of laziness might establish itself, and a tepid apology be exchanged. But between us, if there were a serious wound, there would be no possible way back. One has to hate, to the same degree that one has loved the being to whom one has given oneself unreservedly, when the poison of ingratitude enters the heart."[31]

On 25 October she left Jules and moved to 19 Quai Malaquais. Their domestic relationship had come to a stormy end, but they maintained close contact for some months. In November *Valentine* was published and again Sand won eulogies from both the critics and the public. Her private life, however, was desperately unhappy. She returned to Nohant in November. Not only had she had to admit that her relationship with Jules was over forever, but in separating herself from him she had lost the comfort and intimacy of most of her Parisian friends. Continued support, however, was offered by Gustave Planche, an influential literary critic whom she had first met in 1831 or 1832. He wrote a tremendously flattering review of *Valentine* which he sent to her at Nohant, and he acted as an astute intermediary between François Buloz, publisher of the *Revue des Deux Mondes*, and Sand.

On 1 December she left Nohant with Solange. Discussions continued with publishers. She negotiated cautiously—and well. Initially Buloz had offered her a contract for regular contributions to the review. At the same time, the *Revue de Paris* made a similar offer. Sand offered Buloz a short story, no doubt to keep her options open. He refused. What he wanted was a commitment from "G. Sand" to produce copy regularly for his review. Her name appearing in an issue would guarantee a certain number of sales. The contract he offered her was much too good to be refused: a retainer of 4,000 francs a year in exchange for thirty-two pages of copy every six weeks. She formally committed herself to the agreement on 11 December. Given how quickly she wrote, she must have felt that this was an obligation that she could easily meet and that it would buy her financial stability in the years to come. Planche, now very much in love with Sand, arrived with the final contract for her to sign. Sand liked Planche, but he was not a man with whom she would fall in love: he was more interested in theories of art than in artistic creativity, quick to recognize "beauty only in the grand and severe. . . . He was antipathetic to the pretty, the gracious, the agreeable."[32]

Indiana continued to sell well. On 3 September she had signed an agreement with Dupuy for a third edition. Yet for all her success, both literary and financial, Sand felt isolated. She longed to be understood. As the year drew to a close Sand had completed a number of experiments: living away from Nohant, exploring a relationship based on "free love," and dramatically appearing on the literary stage. Much of what she had lived had been written into the fiction, and the writing had been a tremendous success. Life, on the other hand, had fallen short of her ideal.

But as 1833 opened, a new experiment presented itself, still more daring than anything she had as yet dabbled in. In January she met Marie Dorval, one of the most celebrated and beautiful actresses of the day. She was drawn to Marie Dorval by a strength of feeling she had never before experienced. She longed for intimacy with her.

XV

Exploring Another Self

"I loved valiantly."

⤳By 1833 Sand's commitment to spending three-month stretches alternating between Paris and Nohant had completely lapsed. She spent almost the entire year in Paris, leaving only for a week—to stay at Fontainebleau. And then, on 12 December, she left for Italy.

Her dwindling commitment to Casimir was balanced by further ambitious writing projects. On 8 January 1833, as though to guarantee a full and productive year, she signed an agreement, again with Dupuy, for her third substantial novel: *Lélia.* A renegotiated contract increased her earnings to more than double that of *Valentine* and five times what she had received for *Indiana.* The publicity it would attract would be on a quite different scale from the attention lavished on *Indiana* and *Valentine.* Female sexuality would be written into the work in a way that no writer had hitherto attempted.

Within days of signing the contract, Sand met Marie Dorval. That year Sand would be caught up in scandal and gossip, because of her novel and because of her relationship with Dorval. And the two are closely linked. Sand's fictional writing often suggests an intimacy with the writer that emerges from an anguished sense of urgency, or an overwhelming strength of feeling. The subtle power of her words suddenly conjures up the intensity of lived experience so that the reader actually encounters the woman. But this is always brief and fleeting, as though the moment of recognition is also the turning point. The voice becomes shy, even self-conscious, and dies away.

Sand had listened as a child to Berrichon tales, spoken by the firesides of the little cottages on the Nohant estate. The sense of intimate encounter with the author, experienced when reading Sand, gives the occasional sensation that the novel, like a tale, is being told aloud.

Sand's relationship with Dorval is undoubtedly written into her fiction. One piece, "La Marquise" ("The Marchioness"), composed the previous year, suggests that she had explored—imaginatively—the nature of lesbian sexual encounters. She herself may not have recognized the peculiar relationship between a writer's imaginative life and what can *then happen* in the real world. It is as though a fictional experiment influences, prompts, even sanctions what later actually occurs. Sand had clearly experimented with various ideas before she fell in love with Marie Dorval.

Marie-Thomase-Amélie Delauney was born on 6 January 1798. She was illegitimate and her parents were both players in a touring theatre company. Marie followed them onto the stage. A Romantic actress through and through, her performances exuded pathos, but also simplicity and a sincerity of emotion that melted her audiences. She was just fifteen when she married. Her first husband, Allan (by all accounts a second-rate actor), used the name Dorval. Little is known of their relationship, and he died not long after their marriage. Dorval was married again, in 1829, to Jean-Toussaint Merle, a playwright and journalist, and although she had other lovers, most notably Alfred de Vigny, Merle seems to have turned a blind eye to these.[1]

The letters that Dorval and Sand exchanged, those few that survive, testify to the strength of their feelings, and to the respect, admiration, and, above all, mutual curiosity which they felt. They were very different women and each, it seems, believed that there was much to be learnt from the other: to some extent each wanted to be more like the other. From the moment of their first meeting, in mid-January 1833, they felt an extraordinary sympathy, born in part from the shared recognition of the difficulties of both their lives. Both lived relatively independently of their husbands, to a degree that was rare for women of their era. Both welcomed the support of the other woman. But to what extent did Sand embark on this relationship out of a calculated desire to explore a closeness that would necessarily be quite different from what she had known before? To what extent was she drawn by a sense of the forbidden, different from those transgressions that she had already committed? To what extent had she given up hope of establishing a satisfactory relationship with a man? Just how intimate was her relationship with Dorval?

In the previous December, Sand's "La Marquise" had been published but little remarked on.[2] The Marquise of the story has married at sixteen, been widowed six months later, rendered frigid by the ineptness if not brutality of her husband, and left sexually frustrated by her lovers. She falls passionately in love with an actor, Lélio, and disguises herself as a man in order to pass unnoticed at the theatre and see him play. Watching him, her "forehead is bathed in sweat" because of the strength of feeling his slightest gesture arouses in her. When they embrace and exchange a single kiss, the Marquise's capacity to love is suddenly liberated. When they part, Sand wrote, "Lélio started to weep like a woman." The gender inversions are striking. The Marquise had been dressed as a man, and the actor moved to "feminine" tears. There are parallels between the Marquise and Dorval, and between Sand and the Marquise.[3]

The following winter it was Dorval whom Sand watched from afar. Just as Lélio, in the short story, serves to arouse passion in the Marquise, a passion repressed by earlier encounters with decidedly masculine men, so Sand describes Dorval's performances as expressive of a hidden or sublimated self: "If this woman appeared on the stage, with her broken frame, her nonchalant gait, her sad and penetrating gaze, well, do you know what I imagined?—may God forgive this innocent and vain fiction—*it is as though I am watching my soul;* that this pale form, sad, and beautiful, is my soul that has reclothed her so as to appear to me, to reveal itself to me, and to men."[4] Sand felt that she was incomplete, even in some way crippled. In a fictional exchange between Dorval and Sand (Mario) in a short chapter devoted to the former in Sand's *Questions d'art et de la littérature,* the first asserts, "Your character is both sombre and intense; people reproach you for being haughty and defiant, I think it is more that you are timid." Mario (Sand) replies, "I am perhaps all those things. . . . I don't know what words might convey what is cold and incomplete in my nature; I myself don't know how to express anything. There is a paralysis . . . in my brain which prevents my feelings from finding expressive form."[5]

Sand and Dorval had first met in January. A few weeks later, on 27 March 1833, Sand reflected on what she described as Byron's "secret."[6] In 1846, editing her autobiographical work, Sand claimed, somewhat unconvincingly, that she could no longer remember what she had meant by this. The three-page reflection on Byron, apparently written in the early hours of the morning, explored the idea of living with a secret, as allegedly sketched out in conversation by Sainte-Beuve. He, Sand writes, spoke eloquently of the grandeur of those who choose to keep part of themselves hidden, but not because this hidden self is in some way culpable. The examples Sand gives are of the man of faith who conceals his religious convictions, or the soul who loves secretly. Sainte-Beuve went on, Sand claims, to comment on "less sublime" secrets, defined rather as "social" secrets. "He found," Sand writes,

> more poetry and refinement in the precarious situation of some men for whom an unrecognized crime, or a sadness denied, has forced them to turn in on themselves, to deny themselves consolation, isolating themselves from all intimate, and thereby dangerous, situations; in short to hide a venomous wound in the depths of their soul and to fight courageously against a fatal and menacing consequence, forever at their bedside. Byron's alleged crime has often excited speculation. This crime surrounded the great poet with a magical halo and excited, within the minds of credulous poets, a naïve superstition: they prostrated themselves before the near-divinity of Childe Harold.

Sand argued that no one, however much he or she may live "in a bourgeois manner, free from persecution or attention," is exempt from "a stain, a fetter, a concealed fault, or a hidden misfortune."[7]

> I would say that the man who is sufficiently pure, or happy enough sincerely to give an account of his whole life without blushing with shame, or trembling from fear, that man, I would say, is very rare among us. Oh! We! We are not great men; and in our sad and gloomy life there is no glory, nothing intoxicating comes to counterbalance the insurmountable burden which weighs down one side of our destiny. It has to be carried in silence and without false glory, because society reserves vulgar punishments and insulting prescriptions for those of us who dare to brave it to the point of calling society to judge. Openness, far from

having washed us clean in the eyes of men, is a further blemish which they feel it their right to inflict on us.[8]

What gnawed at me before, what will always gnaw, is the need for sympathy.[9]

In the summer of 1833 Sand wrote a short piece, "Jour de pluie (sur Marie)" ("Day of Rain [on Marie]"). It begins, "Let me love her. I know who she is and what she is worth. Her faults, I know them, her vices. . . . Ah! there's your grand word! You are afraid of vice. But you are petrified and you do not know it. . . ."[10]

Her relationship with Dorval created a scandal. Only after both women's deaths, however, was the public fantasy of their relationship written unambiguously into fiction. In his *Confessions,* Arsène Houssaye wrote with characteristic sensationalism:

> At that time Sappho came to life again in Paris. . . . It was then that a superb woman, who was infatuated with the abyss and who made more than one man dizzy, fell into the open arms of a great actress who devoted her life to passion. Every midnight, after the actress had kindled flames and desire in every heart, either at the Boulevard du Crime or at the Comédie-Française, she returned to her little room, decorated in blue, to find that strange woman seated in front of a blazing fire with a kettle on the boil ready for tea, a cigarette in her mouth, waiting for her prey.[11]

In all the more or less fictionalized accounts of Sand and Dorval's relationship, there is one point about which every writer agrees. One woman emerges, in each account, as a predator, and the other as prey. What varies is which woman was cast in which role. Houssaye continues: "It was a most amorous dialogue. The dark-haired woman [Sand] ran her hands through the golden hair. The blonde woman ran her hands through the dark hair, and the hair mingled with their kisses and their bites." Houssaye transforms the couple into a perfect example of the archetypal lesbian pair:

> Never did Sappho speak so beautifully to handsome Phaon, never did Errine answer Sappho in a more caressing voice. The nocturnal hours were more radi-

ant than the daylight hours. Both women, alight with the fire of passion, were possessed by the unexpected, insatiate for love. It was more than the licentiousness of the heart, it was the voluptuous indulgence of the Orient, of India, of Japan. The two priestesses of love parted at daybreak, still drunk with fulfilment which would soon fade like a dream. And the eloquent woman had that day more eloquence. And the woman of the theatre had, that day, more affection in her voice, more fire in her looks, more belligerence in her passion. . . .[12]

Houssaye's extravagant account of Sand and Dorval's intimate relationship was written some fifty years after "the event." But it is likely that much of Houssaye's fantasy passed through the minds of Sand and Dorval's contemporaries. No one was privy to their private activities, but a number of their friends witnessed the strength of feeling that each inspired in the other.

In her autobiography Sand described their first meeting with what might be read as a naïve frankness, calculated to disarm. Sand had written to Dorval to congratulate her on a recent performance. "My letter," Sand wrote in *The Story of My Life*,

must have struck her by its sincerity. The very day she received it, just as I was telling Jules Sandeau about it, the door of my garret burst open and a breathless woman rushed in, flinging her arms about me and crying out, "Here I am." I had never seen her before except onstage, but her voice was so familiar that I had no difficulty in recognizing her. She was more than pretty; she was charming; but she was pretty too, but at the same time charming to the point of making prettiness superfluous. Her face was more than a mere face, it was an expression, a soul. She was still slim, and her figure was like a delicate reed floating on some mysterious gust of wind.[13]

At this point Dorval was Alfred de Vigny's lover and it was thus two couples who dined together when Dorval invited Sand and Sandeau.

Vigny, it seems, was quick to recognize the threat that Sand might represent. In his diary he wrote:

> She must be twenty-five or so. She reminds me of Judith in the museum [the apocryphal seductress and killer of Holofernes]. Her hair is dark and curly and falls freely over her collar, rather like one of Raphael's angels. She has large black eyes, shaped like those of mystics whom one sees in paintings, or in those magnificent Italian portraits. Her face is severe and gives little away, the lower half is unattractive, the mouth ill-shaped. She has no grace of bearing, and her speech is coarse. In her manner of dress, her language, her tone of voice and the audacity of her conversation, she is like a man.[14]

Sand had initiated the friendship and continued to press Dorval for some definite response, while at the same time expressing her anxiety that she was unworthy of friendship with the lovely Dorval:

> Do you think you could put up with me? You do not know yet, and neither do I. I am so awkward, so stupid, so slow and tongue-tied, particularly when my heart is full. Do not judge me by appearances. Wait to see whether you can feel compassion and affection for me. For my part I feel I love you with a heart brought back to life and rejuvenated by you. If it is a dream, like everything else I have wished for in life, do not steal it from me too quickly. It does me so much good.[15]

Sand's amorous discourse has to be measured against contemporary letter-writing convention. Women commonly wrote sentimental letters to one another and expressed their love freely, and such exchanges do not necessarily imply a sexual relationship. Sand's letters to Dorval, on the other hand, are quite unlike her letters to other women friends. Nor did her friendship with other women ever excite the interest of others in the way that her relationship with Dorval did. Gustave Planche, in particular, wrote only a couple of weeks after the two women had met, to "warn"

Sand of Dorval's lesbianism: "My warning against Mme D. must have seemed incomprehensible, mad. The vehement responses you made last Thursday during lunch made quite plain how you feel. I had told Jules why I was so concerned about your embarking on this dangerous friendship. I realize that it is an unforgivable assumption on my part, but what would you have me do? Whatever the voice of reason I would feel guilty if I had not revealed to you what I have learnt. . . . A friend of mine who is on intimate terms with J——te [Juliette Drouet] and who has no reason to doubt what she has to say, tells me that Mme D. once felt the same passion for J——te that Sappho felt for the women of Lesbos."[16] Sand apparently dismissed this warning with "virile force." She may have discounted Planche's allegations as mere gossip. Or she may well have been excited by the possibilities they conjured up. In either case what she had heard in no way discouraged her from seeking intimacy with Marie.

Sand's natural attraction to Dorval was no doubt further exaggerated by her friends' response to her separation from Sandeau. Everyone, it seemed, was on his side. Balzac invited him to stay and Regnault openly blamed Sand for the failure of the relationship. Sand turned instinctively to Dorval for support: "You, surely, would not condemn me when I am to be pitied? I am sure you will not. Women do justice to women because they understand one another. You will surely not condemn me in my hour of grief. Alas it was nobody's fault. It was fate."[17]

Vigny continued to be disconcerted by his mistress's growing closeness to the peculiar George. Dorval alleged that it was Sand who was pursuing her, while at the same time castigating Vigny if he failed to show George appropriate respect when they met in company. The two women met as often as possible and exchanged letters and notes if prevented from seeing one another for more than a day or two. That their relationship was more than one of close friendship is also suggested by the evidence of Sand's "À l'ange Lélio" ("To the Angel Lélio"), altered to "À l'ange sans nom" ("To the Angel Without a Name"). This blends androgynous, sexually indeterminate images into a compelling account of love, passion, and intimations of satisfied desire:

> Here is the day breaking, come . . . the window is open . . . I am waiting. . . . But here you are! Bless you, son of the sky, give me your forehead to kiss . . . your hair that is an arm's length long. . . . Why don't men have long hair?

You who have no name, come. . . . You speak no
language, you give nothing away, not a single word.
How I love you when it is so, and how well I understand you!

Paradoxes accumulate: the "son" is, by implication, more like a woman,
and understanding depends on the absence of speech. The androgynous or
sexless "angel" allows for increasingly explicit lesbian fantasy:

Place your cool hand on my shoulder, it is hot with
love, but no man's lips have pressed on it: your perfumed breath, your damp hair alone can refresh it.
These perfumes are intoxicating . . . spread them out
on me, strip the leaves from your damp crown.
. . . That's enough. I should die. I want to live
another day and see you again. Adieu . . . leave
quickly . . . lest anyone see you, because they would
steal you from me and I would be obliged to give
myself to men. Adieu, let me kiss your snowy neck
and your forehead. . . . Give me a feather from your
wing so that I may have proof of your passage, a sou-
venir of my inebriation.

To suggest that the "feather" is a covert reference to hair, even pubic hair,
would be reductive of the passage's subtler sensual suggestiveness. This
gradually accumulates, strengthened by numerous references to associated
images.

But the inadequacies of heterosexual physical closeness are less coded:

I prefer thistledown to a man; on the first one blows
and it disperses in the vagueness of the air, the other
never steals away, nor evaporates by any method. . . .
Angel of the morning, leave then. I'm falling asleep.[18]

In the weightless gravity-free zone that Sand constructs here, what is
experienced is an intoxicated excess of pleasure, followed by rest. There is
neither speech nor violence. Some of the pleasure of Sand's experience of
intimacy with Dorval is conveyed here, but the text remains a fiction, and
its origins in specific lived experiences remain to some extent mysterious.

In between her numerous meetings with Dorval, Sand worked on *Lélia*, went to the theatre, and supported her literary friends. On 8 February Balzac sent her his *Histoire intellectuelle de Louis Lambert,* keen to hear what she thought of it. On 9 March she read part of *Lélia* to Sainte-Beuve. By the beginning of March Sand's relationship with Sandeau was causing what she describes in a contemporary letter as *"affreux chagrins."*[19] By the end of the month their relationship had come to an end. Sandeau left for Italy on 26 March. Three weeks later Sand wrote to Laure Decerfz: "So it is that for some time I have felt a deep bitterness in my heart. . . . Then I started to see Mme Dorval, in intimate circumstances, the famous actress of whom I have so often spoken. . . . When, coming out from the dressing rooms, we are able to chatter in front of my fire . . . we regain lost time and we live a great deal in few hours."[20]

On 17 April Sand was much cheered by Maurice's arrival. He had come from Nohant with Casimir, and was to enter the Collège Henri IV as a boarder. He would soon be ten and Sand would be able to see more of him. On 5 May Sand sent the opening chapters of *Lélia* to Sainte-Beuve: they were published on 15 May in the *Revue des Deux Mondes.* On the thirtieth she attended the first night of Vigny's *Quitte pour la peur,* with Dorval in the lead role.

At some point towards the end of April she met Prosper Mérimée: author (of *Carmen* most famously), archaeologist, and epicurean. Sand's sexual experiment with Mérimée is one of the most extraordinary stories in French literary history. Knowing that Sand's relationship with Sandeau had foundered, and more importantly having read parts of *Lélia*, Sainte-Beuve had suggested Mérimée as a consoling figure. Sainte-Beuve had been deeply struck by the pessimism of the passages of *Lélia* that Sand had given him to read. "To be a woman," he wrote, "to be under thirty years of age and believe that there is nothing outside these chasms you have sounded; to carry within you this vision which would devastate our temples and whiten our hair—to carry it so lightly, easily, to express it in such sober discourse—that's what I admire above all." Sand replied that he should not confuse the author of *Lélia* with the novel's eponymous heroine. Meanwhile Sand continued to see Marie, writing her short notes that frequently end, "Come and see me soon."[21]

At the same time, she made the mistake of believing Mérimée's assurances that he could make her happy—in bed. It was to be the most sexually stereotypical of all Sand's relationships and certainly the most disastrous. She was tempted by the hope that this man had a privileged understanding of life and love, and that in union with him, she too would be initiated into the secrets that had so far been kept from her: "On one of those days of boredom and despair, I met a man who had doubts about nothing, a calm and strong man, who knew nothing of my nature and who laughed at my sorrows. The strength of his vision fascinated me for eight days, I thought he knew the secret of happiness."[22]

This was the most humiliating of all Sand's encounters, and the misery of the experience itself was compounded by Dorval's indiscretion. She turned to Marie for solace, deeply injured by her recent sexual fiasco. Marie, it seems, could not help telling Dumas, and he in turn told everyone. The story circulated around literary Paris and Sand's alleged words to Marie, "I had Mérimée last night, it was nothing out of the ordinary," were on everyone's lips. While the story titillated Paris, Sand felt more broken-hearted and humiliated than ever.

According to Sand, "The experiment failed completely. I cried with pain, disgust and despair. Instead of finding a friendship that would allow me to unburden my feelings of resentment and discouragement, I found only bitter and frivolous mockery. That was all, and the whole story has been summed up in . . . words that I did not say [it was nothing], that Mme Dorval neither betrayed nor invented, and which bring little honour to the imagination of M. Dumas."[23]

Mérimée, it seems, had believed himself to be the sex therapist that Sand needed. He was the first of a number. He sensed, or knew, of Sand's dissatisfaction with previous sexual relationships and no doubt believed that her disappointment was bound up in her choice of lover. Sandeau, for example, was delicate and effeminate. He was also ineffectual, as Balzac eventually recognized: "Jules Sandeau was one of my mistakes. You could never imagine anyone as lazy, anyone as nonchalant. He is without energy, without will. The finest feelings expressed in words, no action, nor anything in reality. . . . He has not, in three years, completed a half-volume. He despairs of friendship as he has despaired of love."[24] Sandeau did, however, remain a friend of Sand's and later became, somewhat improbably, Marie Dorval's lover.

Mérimée, on the other hand, did not remain a close friend. His account of their brief relationship was written into *La Double Méprise* in a way which allows for a direct comparison of the real and fictional couples. It is a straightforward tale which dramatizes sex and gender difference, and exposes the hero's thinking while the heroine's feelings, her broken hopes and disappointments, remain obscure, mysterious.

Sand's experience of the relationship was to appear in the later drafts of *Lélia*. What for Mérimée had been an almost comic and wholly contained fiasco became, in *Lélia*, a crucial experience relevant to a number of the layers of the text. Here, the relationship between Sand's life and the novel is more perplexing and complicated than the relationship between "À l'ange sans nom" and her relationship with Dorval. The beginnings of the novel had been adumbrated in an early work on the character of Trenmor, who reappeared in *Lélia*, and whom Sand first mentions in a letter of December 1832.[25]

Lélia was her most controversial novel when it was published, and it has continued to arouse speculation and critical commentary. It is a long and complex work, part novel, part prose poem, interspersed with philosophical monologues and dialogues. It explores moral questions, the quest for happiness and not just sexuality but sex, even in a technical sense that suggests, for example, the importance of sexual positions. And all this is written very much from a woman's point of view. In *Indiana* and *Valentine*, the omniscient narrators remain distant.

Lélia begins as a love story, but *in medias res*. Sténio, who is twenty-four, loves Lélia, who is thirty. But love, Sténio observes, makes his lover unhappy. "Why," he asks, "does love cause you such pain?" Lélia is unable to respond to Sténio's desire. Lélia's love is gentle, maternal even, and when she addresses him, she calls him "my child." Something about Lélia also frightens Sténio. Lélia turns to Trenmor for advice. He is a mystic, a stoic, who has spent years in prison for some minor misdemeanour. He advises Lélia that she must either push Sténio away or distance herself from him. Otherwise she will destroy him. Much remains ambiguous, but there are suggestions that it is Sténio's incapacity to satisfy Lélia sexually that deeply saddens her and excites the frail Sténio to greater and greater physical exertion for which he is ill equipped. Lélia seeks refuge from the scene of her sensual frustration and disappointed feelings in "a large abandoned monastery, half destroyed by the battles of the Revolution." There she struggles to establish an inner calm through a life of "resignation and regularity."[26] But as she watches the stereotypical romantic sunset and meditates, she is aware that she has failed:

> Sometimes I watched the sunset from the top of a half-ruined tower. What remained was encircled by the monstrous sculptures which had previously adorned Catholic places of worship. Beneath me these

bizarre allegories stretched out their heads, blackened
by time. They seemed to stretch towards the plain and
silently to watch the flow of waves, centuries, and
generations. These fantastic scaly serpents, these
lizards with their ghastly bodies, these chimeras full of
anguish, all these emblems of sin, illusion, suffering,
lived a life that was inert and indestructible. . . . While
I contemplated these beings embodied in masses of
stone, which the hand of neither man nor time had
been able to dislodge, I recognized myself in these
images of eternal struggle between suffering and
necessity, between rage and impotence.[27]

Lélia retires to reflect, and then returns. She meets her sister Pulchérie, with whom she has had no contact for a long time. Pulchérie has
lived, in a wholly conscious if not calculated way, for pleasure, and she is
unashamed; she is a courtesan. The dialogue between Lélia and Pulchérie
is urgent and compelling, and forms the central section of the work.

This scene where the two sisters meet and explain their lives and ideas
about life has sometimes been reduced to an autobiographical lesbian confession. It is more complicated. Pulchérie's confession is an interesting
one. She tells how as a young girl she awoke to erotic desire, and explains
that Lélia played a crucial role in this, a role which she has never dared to
admit to her sister. They had both fallen asleep, outside, in a romantic pastoral setting. Pulchérie first dreams of a "man with black hair." When she
awakens it is Lélia who is lying beside her. "I thought you resembled this
beautiful black-haired child of whom I had just dreamt, and, trembling, I
kissed your arm." Pulchérie allows the eroticism of her dream to prompt
action, although no more than a gesture, in real life. Having been awakened
to her own sexual desire, Pulchérie embarks on numerous sexual adventures—with men. Lélia, on the other hand, remembers the scene that her
sister describes as insignificant. Pulchérie changes, while Lélia remains
somehow trapped in her body, unable to respond. Later she loves Sténio
but it is the androgynous side of their union that Lélia celebrates:

Lélia remembered when she had loved him most. It
was when he was poet rather than lover. In those first
days of their affection, Sténio's passion had a roman-

tic, angelic quality. . . . Later his eyes would grow animated with a more virile fire. His greedy lips would seek and demand kisses. His poetry would express more savage outbursts of feeling. Then the impotent Lélia had felt frightened, fatigued, and almost disgusted with this love she did not share.[28]

André Maurois was the first of Sand's biographers explicitly to propose that Sand suffered from sexual frigidity, although precisely what he means by this is never explored. At what might at first sight appear the opposite extreme, suggestions have been made that Sand suffered from so-called nymphomania. But what Sand's fiction reveals rather is a sexual ideal in which the erotic encounter transcends the sexual and becomes a symbol of an ideal and complete union, and a desire that the sexual act be one in which both parties assume degrees of abandon and control. Sand certainly had an idealized and romantic view of sex, but in her non-fictional writing she discusses sexual difference, and her conviction that much has been made of little. This also emerges implicitly from her fictional accounts of unsatisfied female desire. Lélia regrets the egotism of Sténio's passionate self: his lips are "greedy," he "demands" kisses. Sexual difference depends here on the feminine idealization of love: "I experienced an inexpressible state of sadness and joy, of despair and energy. . . . Had I been a man I would have loved combat, the odour of blood, the pressures of danger. Perhaps in my youth I might have sought to reign by intelligence and to dominate others by powerful speeches. As a woman I had only one noble destiny on earth, which was to love. I loved *valiantly*."

Masculinity, and male sexual desire, are bound up with control, power, and domination, and this translates directly into the question of sexual positions:

Sometimes in my sleep, susceptible to those rich ecstasies that consume ascetic minds, I felt myself carried away with him on clouds by balmy breezes. Then I swam in waves of pleasure, and passing my arms . . . around his neck, I would fall on his breast murmuring vague words. But he would awake. In place of that angel who had rocked me . . . I found this man as brutal as a wild beast, and I would flee. . . .

But he would pursue me. He did not want to have been awakened from his sleep for nothing, and he would take his pleasure on the bosom of a woman who was fainting and half dead.[29]

Lélia's life has reached an impasse. She explains to Pulchérie that for a time she responded spontaneously to strong feeling, but that her "caprices . . . have become rare and lukewarm." Now she suffers from boredom and has turned in on herself "with a calm and sombre despair and no one knows what I suffer. . . . Among all these men, there is not a single one whose intelligence is sufficiently broad to understand that it is a great misfortune to have been unable to become attached to anything and no longer to desire anything on earth."[30]

The "rage and impotence" that the fictional Lélia has experienced finds a corollary in Sand the novelist's frustrations with genre, and the conventions of narrative open to her. While struggling with the unwieldy novel, she recognized her incapacity to encode convincingly in language the complex taboos associated with female erotic experience. *Lélia* has to be read either as allegory—a story that tells another hidden story—or as realism, as a true-to-life narrative about "real" people in a "real" world. If *Lélia* is read as an allegory, then the hidden story is about oppositions—between doubt and faith, scepticism and belief, imaginative experience and brute experience, culpable and innocent behaviour. If, on the other hand, it is read as a work of realism, then it is essentially a graphic confession of sexual dissatisfaction (and impotence), and a bleak howl of frustrated despair. It is no wonder that the first edition sold like hotcakes.

The ambiguity about the genre to which *Lélia* belongs—or the various genres to which it somehow fails properly to belong—was recognized by Sand. She wrote: "*Lélia* was and remains in my mind a poetic essay, a fantastical novel, where the characters are neither completely real, as the exclusive aficionados of analyses of manners wanted, nor completely allegorical, according to the judgement of some synthetic minds."[31]

Sainte-Beuve, following a similar line of analysis, argued that Sand's allegory failed because of an indeterminacy, an uncertainty that threatens the secure boundaries between different forms of representation. Sand confessed: "As for Lélia I must admit that this figure appeared to me through a fiction more gripping than those that surround her. . . . This predilection for the proud suffering character of Lélia drove me to commit a serious artistic error: giving her a completely impossible existence, which, because of the semireality of the other characters, seems shockingly real, by dint of wanting to be abstract and symbolic."[32]

Contemporary critics responded vociferously to the new George Sand novel. They were divided—and extreme—in their views. Sainte-Beuve wrote:

> This time, George Sand, taking off the vast virile coat in which she had enveloped herself with so much courage and energy, wanted to show herself more than a woman, that is, in her thinking, twice as much as a man, and she has fallen into the gravest excesses. . . . George Sand, having gone back to being a woman, in this book which is written against women, should thus pay the penalty of this disguise.[33]

Sainte-Beuve devoted a substantial part of his review to questions of sex and gender. "We especially like to see," he wrote, "a noble effort on the part of women to enter into a more equal intellectual partnership with men, to handle all sorts of ideas and to express themselves where necessary in more serious language."[34] Sainte-Beuve was something of a lone voice; most men, it seems, wanted to stay on top. Latouche, it will be remembered, had written to Sand to congratulate her on *Indiana;* his choice of words was telling: "Balzac and Mérimée *lie dead beneath Indiana.*"

Another critic of *Lélia,* writing in *Le Petit Poucet,* called it a "work of lewdness and cynicism." Capo de Feuillide wrote two damning articles and claimed that the novel contained "the prostitution of soul and body"; both he and Léon Gozlan wrote that *Lélia* was not a book to be read by women! It would, they argued, contaminate and corrupt them. Feuillide even went as far as to compare Sand with de Sade.[35] He warned:

> The day you begin *Lélia,* lock yourself away in your study. If you have a daughter, a tender flower whom you want to protect from the breath of vice, whose soul you wish to keep virginal and innocent, send her out to play with her girlfriends in the country. If you have a young wife whose love you cherish, allow her the costume of her choice so that she can take herself

to a ball; if your daughter stays at home and picks up
Lélia she runs a greater danger than if she is away
from home, and as for your wife, no amount of flirtation at a ball will stain her purity as much as the corrupting pages of that book.[36]

No real experience, he argued, could be as corrupting as the psycho-sexual
change that might occur in the mind of the reader—high praise indeed.

Feuillide's first article was published on 9 August 1833; on the fifteenth Planche wrote in Sand's defence, but on 22 August Feuillide wrote a
further review, provoking Planche to challenge him to a duel. The ever-
loyal Planche was intent on defending George's name. She, it seems, was
somewhat embarrassed, as it was a gesture that would suggest to all Paris
that she and Planche were having an affair. They were not, but Planche
may have hoped that this impression would be given. The duel, which took
place in the Bois de Boulogne, was as undramatic as Planche's friendship
with Sand. No serious injuries were sustained.[37]

When *Lélia* was published in book form on 31 July, Sand was twenty-
nine, and while Lélia's life ends in the hands of a murderous priest (who
strangles her), and Sténio drowns himself, Sand had to stand up valiantly
to the severe criticism—both literary and highly personal—which her
astonishing work excited. Musset, one of a relatively small number of critics who lauded the novel, claimed it would provoke a literary revolution.
He had also become more than a little fascinated by its author. Earlier that
year, before the Mérimée fiasco, Sainte-Beuve had suggested introducing
Sand to Musset, but she had replied: "With regard to the matter, having
reflected, I don't want you to bring me Alfred de Musset. He is very much a
dandy. . . ."[38]

They finally met in June, and soon began an exchange of letters. Musset wrote: "Before *Lélia* you might have remained Mme So-and-So. Now
you are George Sand."[39] Musset may have overestimated the revolutionary
influence of *Lélia*. Their relationship, on the other hand, was to have a profound effect on both of them.

XVI

Musset and Madness

"Art is an aspiration, eternally impotent and incomplete."

~In the days and weeks that followed the Mérimée fiasco, and with *Lélia* finished, Sand felt profoundly weary. The late spring and early summer of 1833 brought worries about the health of the children: Maurice had flu and Solange, more seriously, whooping cough. Sand's mother was also in a peculiarly difficult mood, and accused Sand of calling to visit only at times when she knew that her mother would be out. Of all the visions Sand had had of life in Paris, few had been happily realized. All that remained, it seemed, was for her to confront her responsibilities as a mother and daughter, and to continue to write in order to maintain financial security. On 20 May 1833 she wrote to François Rollinat, one of her oldest and most loyal friends, now a lawyer in Châteauroux: "My heart has aged twenty years and nothing in life now smiles on me. There are neither deep passions nor sources of acute happiness left for me. Everything has been said. I've rounded the cape. I am in dock."[1] But Sand was not the kind of woman to stay away from the stormy ocean for long. Outside the harbour walls the extremes of the marine climate raged, offering endless possibilities of adventure, and Sand soon steered her way back out into the open sea.

When Sainte-Beuve had first suggested introducing Sand to Alfred de Musset she had refused. But on 19 June 1833 Buloz finally succeeded in bringing them together at a dinner he gave for the contributors to his now highly successful *Revue des Deux Mondes*. The occasion was, presumably, one that lent itself to pretension, as members of the journal's "in-group" vied with one another to be witty and entertaining. When there was a social expectation that participants be articulate and amusing, Sand often withdrew into her shell. Fortunately, the other guest on whom eyes were turned, in addition to Sand, was Alfred de Musset, and he had been seated next to her. He was more than half a decade her junior, strikingly handsome in ways that were often to attract her. His features were delicate, he was slim, and his elegance was youthful and unfussy, rather than mannered. His curly blond shoulder-length hair was tinged with auburn and his skin pale. More importantly still, despite his precocity and early successes, his overwhelming ebullience and sense of fun, he exuded a nervous vulnerability that Sand experienced as quite irresistibly attractive.

But he was no innocent, as Sand knew all too well. His erotic appetite was no secret: he moved between the thrills of young prostitutes and their seamy world, and the attentions of older society ladies in grand and sumptuous residences where he was pampered. His enjoyment of each of these societies, Sand the novelist must have suspected, was no doubt informed by his knowledge of the other. He also smoked opium and was fascinated by it. In 1830 he had published a French version of De Quincey's famous *Confessions of an English Opium Eater*.

Sand knew to be on her guard and left conversation to the suave young man. He was more than willing to fill the gaps left by her silences. She listened. But although shy in terms of conversation, Sand had dressed conspicuously. Her outfit was not calculated to pass unnoticed. Musset commented on a little jewel-encrusted dagger which dangled, rather provocatively, just below her waist. During the course of the evening, Sand chose to conceal it in some hidden corner of her person: she had been embarrassed by his questioning and had removed it so that no one would mention it again. She had answered Musset's teasing questions, explaining that she wore it in the interests of self-defence: had she removed it as a sign that she did not want to defend herself against him? Or was she inviting him to some intimate and daring game of treasure-seeking?[2]

The playful mutual curiosity of that first encounter was maintained for some days. By the end of the dinner Musset had promised Sand a fragment of an unpublished poem, and Sand had promised him the proofs of *Lélia*. When he wrote to her some days later, he had reread parts of *Indiana* and had in turn written "a few lines of verse" inspired by the scene "where

Noun receives Raimond [misspelt by Musset] in her mistress's room."[3] The nature of Sand's sexual experience and the ways in which, imaginatively, she reconstructed her erotic life already fascinated him. How much of *Indiana* was based on real experience, how much had been dreamt, how much was a matter of directed and deliberate fantasy? Had she experience of "these pleasures devoid of happiness" that she described, or had she imagined them? His poem asks unambiguously "where had you seen that terrible scene where Noun half-naked on Indiana's bed is intoxicated by Raymond? Who then dictated it to you, that burning page where love vainly seeks, with a quivering hand, the adored ghost of its illusion? Is this sad experience lodged within your being? Is what Raymond suffers something you remember? And all those feelings of ill-defined suffering, pleasures devoid of joyousness, so filled to the brim with gaping emptiness, did you dream that, George, or is it memory?"[4]

George was unwilling, she replied, to reveal her "sad secrets"; he was a youth, "a poet only twenty years old" (in reality twenty-three).[5] Musset continued to be tantalized by the relationship between this older woman's experience (which might be more or less extraordinary and extravagant) and her imaginings (which she might or might not want to realize). They continued to exchange poems and letters. Whatever her earlier resolves, which may have been no more than deliberately provocative game-playing, she closed one letter with an invitation: "If one day you were to be wearied and disgusted by activity, if you were tempted to enter the cell of a recluse, you would be received with courtesy and cordiality."[6]

While Musset needed a high level of activity and excitement but wearied quickly, she needed to reflect on, and savour, pleasure. She also needed a regular working life, to maintain both her emotional equilibrium and her financial independence, while he was far from industrious. Both, in short, had been attracted to the other by their differences. Having read *Lélia*, Musset was still more determined to know Sand better. He wrote proposing a friendship "without consequences and without rights, and consequently without jealousies and quarrels."[7] He had no doubt inferred from both *Indiana* and *Lélia* that such an open relationship might tempt Sand more than any other arrangement. He may also have realized that love, for Sand, also needed to be part of any intimate relationship. On 26 July he confessed his feelings. "My dear George," he wrote, "I have something foolish and ridiculous to tell you. . . . I am in love with you. I have been since the day I first called on you. I had thought I could cure myself by knowing you as a friend."[8] On the twenty-seventh he wrote again, casting himself very much as a hapless and helpless victim and closing, "Adieu, George, I love you as a child loves."[9]

Sand may have feared, early on, that a liaison with Musset would never work. Or it may be that she held back in order to encourage him further to fall in love with her. In any event, she finally invited him to call on her at midnight on 28 July 1833. That night their relationship was consummated, and Sand would claim that "without your youth and the feebleness that your tears caused me, we would have remained brother and sister."[10] The relationship would be seen by both as in some sense "incestuous."[11] Either they were, in some imaginative sense, more like brother and sister, or like mother and son. But the retrospective casting (the following year) of their sexual relationship in this way was simply an attempt, and one full of pathos, to add a last *frisson* to an adventure that had very rapidly lost its excitement.

One of the most tragic aspects of their intimacy, which still remains mysterious, is bound up with Musset's mental instability. Within a couple of weeks of their first night together, they left Paris for a brief sojourn in Fontainebleau. It was August and the stifling heat of the capital had been unpleasant. They stayed in the Hôtel Britannique from 5 to 13 August, and expected to enjoy the romantic setting of the forest and moonlit walks. One night when they were out, Musset suddenly and dramatically threw himself to the ground, utterly possessed by some terror unknown to Sand. He had seen a ghost in the scrub. George had seen nothing, but was quite as terror-stricken by the sight of Musset so profoundly affected by what she supposed could only be a vivid and petrifying hallucination.[12] When Musset recovered his senses, he tried to make light of the whole event. He even sketched a cartoon of the scene, depicting himself lost and disorientated. Beneath his own portrait was the caption "Lost in the forest and in the mind of his mistress." Under the sketch of George he wrote, "The heart as rent as the dress."[13] Sand had experienced periods of deep depression, knew of her father's propensity to despair, and considered her mother increasingly deranged. But in her mother's case it was more a matter of a disordered personality—Musset's madness, if madness it was, was of a very different order. And still more terrifying.

The little holiday in Fontainebleau came to an end and the lovers returned to Paris. Sand's reputation following the publication of *Lélia* became difficult to live with. But she was, it seems, very much in love with Musset. Her fright at his hallucination may even have developed her interest. Both were intrigued by the relationship between outer and inner self. On 25 August she wrote to Sainte-Beuve: "I am in love and this time seriously, with Alfred de Musset. . . . It is a young man's love and a youthful friendship."[14]

The attention that Sand attracted in Paris in the wake of the publication of *Lélia* was becoming wearying and Sand longed to be alone with Musset: seeing Italy, a setting for Romantic writing, could only enrich their work. Not long after returning to Paris from Fontainebleau, Sand was proposing another more ambitious journey, to Venice: she hoped its exoticism would spur Musset to creativity and great productivity. Maurice had settled into his Parisian boarding school and Solange had been dispatched back to Nohant. To fund the venture, Sand negotiated a number of financial deals with Buloz. Contracts with Buloz were still more attractive than what Dupuy could offer. She sold him *Metella*, which she finished at the beginning of October, and *Le Secrétaire intime* (*The Private Secretary*), completed a few weeks later.

The thought of the Italian trip spurred on her writing. So too did the stimulus of meeting Béranger, an immensely popular poet of the people, and a Berlioz concert on 24 November. On 9 December she clinched a financial agreement that would allow for the Italian adventure. Buloz agreed to an advance of 5,000 francs for her novel *Jacques,* with an ambitious delivery date. She was also bound over not to publish any other novel until *Jacques* was out. She committed herself to delivering the manuscript by May 1834, in other words only six months later.[15]

Dickering with publishers was more straightforward than negotiating with Musset's mother, who considered the realization of the Italian escapade to be dependent on her willingness to give or withhold her consent. Initially she deemed the project too dangerous.[16] No doubt she was more aware than Sand of Musset's capacity for losing control over his daily life, his eating, drinking, and sleeping, and that this in turn seriously affected his mental equilibrium. Sand, ever persuasive, assured Mme Musset that she would look after him like a mother.[17] On 12 December 1833 Sand and her young poet set out on what would be one of the most rewarding, and at the same time most difficult, periods of her life.

They expected to enjoy the anonymity that travel offers lovers. But who should they meet, only days into their journey on the boat that was to take them from Lyon to Avignon, but Henri Beyle, also travelling to his beloved Italy as consul in Civitavecchia. Beyle, who is better known by his pseudonym Stendhal, found a flattering audience in Musset, who was delighted by the older man's caustic wit, satirical tone, and airs of a man-of-the-world. Sand was less easily seduced. Not only did she want to be alone with Musset, now she was in the company of a man who was almost a parody of the Parisian writer. It was from just such personifications of weariness that she had wanted to distance herself.[18]

Fortunately, Sand and Musset's itinerary diverged from Stendhal's at Avignon. On 20 December 1833 they set sail from Marseille alone, for Genoa. While Sand had found Stendhal's company exhausting and upsetting, she found the sea voyage invigorating and exciting. Alfred, who had shown himself to be more robust in Stendhal's company, suffered terribly from seasickness. His doggerel translates his irritation—and sense of humour: "George is up on deck/Smoking a cigarette/Musset, on his back/Has a stomach ache."[19]

Once on Italian soil, they travelled on from Genoa to Livorno, via Pisa to Ferrara, and then Venice. Casimir, to whom Sand wrote regularly, displayed an unusual astuteness with regard to his estranged wife's temperament: "You see with a cold and calm eye, and so to speak with the eyes of a good philosopher, monuments, sites, and all kinds of luxury that have made so many other hearts palpitate, astonished so many heads, and dictated so many fiery pages."[20] What Casimir failed to understand is that passionate writing, "recollected in tranquillity," flows from a controlled pen: Sand was observing, recording, and storing up.

On 1 January 1834 Sand and Alfred arrived at the Hotel Danieli. Only three days into their "honeymoon," Sand was stricken by intestinal troubles and had to retire to bed for a fortnight. Nineteenth-century Venice was not a healthy place and a month later Sand was still complaining of persistent bouts of dysentery. Musset had also been struck: "I have just been ill for five days with a frightful bout of dysentery. My travel companion is also very unwell. We keep quiet about it, because in Paris we have a crowd of enemies who would delight in it, saying '. . . They went to Italy to have a good time and they've got the runs.' . . . My heart's as sick as my stomach."[21]

While Sand was used to tending the sick, Musset had neither experience nor, it seems, the inclination to care for her during the worst bouts of her illness. Instead, the moment he was fit, he explored Venice and made the most of what the city had to offer, including its women. Tension between them increased. Financial difficulties loomed. Musset had relegated all financial responsibility to Sand, and now he was no longer by her side but gallivanting about the city while she either wrote or collapsed under the onslaught of the illness. A further bout of ill health, Musset was afraid, might be "a serious disease," caught from one of the women he had frequented.[22] Sand wanted to move from the Hotel Danieli, which had turned out to be expensive, but Musset's health had suddenly deteriorated to the point of making this inadvisable. The nights of 4–5 and 7–8 February were particularly frightening. On the fourth she implored Buloz for a further 1,000 francs to cover medical expenses. Musset, she wrote, "is suffering from a nervous inflammatory fever."[23]

The precise nature of Musset's illness, or illnesses—it may be that an underlying disease had been exacerbated by the dissipations of his life in Venice—remains mysterious. The doctor employed to care for him was a charming Venetian of twenty-seven. He was one of those few Italians who are strikingly blond. Both his hair and complexion were fair. Something of a dandy, Pagello expected to inspire confidence in his patients in the same way that he quickly gained the confidence of women. Sand was immediately struck by his charm. Musset, on the other hand, took an immediate dislike to him and refused to follow his medical advice. Sand, anxious that any underlying nervous disease not be overlooked, explained to Pagello that his way of life—wine, women, and song—might explain some nervous condition that manifested itself from time to time. Pagello was soon to witness the outward signs of Musset's inner torments. His hallucinations months earlier were trivial by comparison with the bouts of derangement and raving madness that now overtook him.[24] Sand watched in horror as two strong men tried to restrain him from gambolling naked about the room, ranting and shouting.

Pagello and Sand struggled to calm Musset and nurse him back to health. As soon as he regained his mental stability, however, he suffered from an attack of bronchitis. Sand, who was longing for a return to normality and exhausted by the horrors of Musset's illness, nursed him for eight days and nights without even undressing. She feared his madness and was desperate that at the least sign of hallucination she be there, ready to frighten away his demons and reassure him of her love, and of his strength in the face of whatever madness might periodically overcome him.

By the end of the eight days Sand was exhausted, even fearing for her own mental stability. She felt profoundly lonely, and uncertain about the future. What was she to make of the inspired young poet who had so much loved her? The same young man had quickly found other pleasures in Venice the moment she had become ill. And what of his madness? How serious was it? What was its force, its temporal life, its limits? She could not know. As good as alone in a foreign city, and rapidly running out of money—Musset's medicines had cost some twenty francs a day—she badly needed someone to whom she could turn for comfort and support.

Dr. Pagello had remarked on Sand, silhouetted against the window of the Hotel Danieli, before he had been summoned to Musset's bedside. Or so he later claimed. Something of a rake, he was charming and sensitive to the needs of the women to whom he was, however temporarily, committed. Sand was quick to see her attraction to Pagello in metaphorically incestuous terms. Musset was her son, Pagello her father.[25] Their relationship began at the end of February.

Sand's letters to Pagello are delightfully, breathtakingly, frank: "Born under different skies . . . we have neither the same thoughts nor the same language; have we even similar hearts? . . . The generous sun which has browned your forehead, what passions has it given you? I know how to love and to suffer. And you, how do you love? . . . Do love's pleasures leave you breathless and stupid, or do they throw you into a divine ecstasy?" Elsewhere she simply wrote, "I love you because you please me." More tellingly, she claimed, "I don't want to know your name."[26] She of course knew his name. What she suggested is a kind of sexual anonymity, an erotic relationship that would elevate the physical and minimize linguistic communication. Could it be that she was seeking quite deliberately to achieve satisfaction in a quasi-anonymous sexual encounter? The appeal to anonymity and the desire for silence are both highly reminiscent of Sand's "To the Angel Without a Name," where she had celebrated her intimacy with Dorval. Musset tormented her—albeit in his less lucid moments—with her sexual inadequacies. Had she decided to experiment with Pagello in the hope of discovering an erotic life that had so far eluded her?

In any case, it seems likely that the complexities of her relationship with Musset (their struggles precisely to *understand* fully and invent a common language) seem to have exhausted her capacity for amatory ingenuity—or else she felt disillusioned with the poetry of love. The excitement of a relationship at once real and phantasmagoric had proved frightening as much as stimulating. Musset had fine words but he had not behaved in a way that was consonant with them. She looked to Pagello for certain reassuring gestures. She seems not to have feared rejection. Given her exhausted state, it is fortunate that Pagello read her intelligently and responded warmly. Just as Sand's letters had been honest and straightforward, so they planned their affair paying particular attention to its practicalities. Above all, Musset must not know of their relationship. "Are we sufficiently sensible," Sand wrote to her newly conscripted lover at the end of February, "and sufficiently happy, you and me, that we can conceal our secret for another month? Lovers are not patient nor good at hiding themselves. If I had taken a room in the inn, we would have been able to see each other without causing him to suffer and without exposing ourselves to his sudden outbursts of rage."[27]

Sand felt the injustices of her relationship with Musset acutely, and wanted him to know how she had suffered in her illness when he had disappeared to find pleasure elsewhere. But quite apart from this, Sand was strongly attracted to Pagello. He was an expert in love and provided her with precisely what she wanted. He was reassuring, judicious in his demands, entertaining if called on to be, otherwise quiet and calming. He was the tonic that she needed, and she gradually felt a happiness that she thought had left her forever, quietly returning: "To be happy for a year and then to die. This is all I ask of God and of you," she wrote to Pagello.[28] She sensed that their easy and contented relationship could not last. The patient for whom they were both responsible proved a complication in their lives. He either saw, or took it into his head that he had seen, Sand on Pagello's knees, kissing. And why, he asked, was there a single cup of tea on the table? The two of them must have shared the same cup, an obvious and incontrovertible sign of intimacy.[29]

It is in many ways remarkable that there remains so much evidence of the nature of the tensions between Musset and Sand. How, Sand would ask Musset, could he reproach her for her behaviour considering how he himself had behaved? He had, she would remind him, accused her both of being a flirt and—one day when he had been attacked by fever and delirium—of never having known how to give him the pleasures of love. How could he now reproach her for having found love elsewhere?

Clearly Sand's relationships with Musset and Pagello could scarcely have been more different. The first was enormously complex and fluid. Different forms of intimacy were involved—at once intellectual, erotic, emotional, nervous, phantasmagoric, psychic, playful, childish. At times they established a degree of equality, but this never lasted. Sand found this friendship enormously invigorating, but also exhausting, even frightening. It was impossible to sustain, and tended towards repetition, rather than moving on to embrace new experiences.

But however contented and happy she was in the arms of the reassuring Pagello, and however unsustainable her actual relationship with Musset, it remained a passionate one at least on paper. Sand had forgiven

Musset his infidelities, but Musset was not, it seems, about to forgive Sand. Nor, on the other hand, did he show any signs of wanting to distance himself from Sand, or for that matter from Pagello. Just as Musset had, from the very beginning, been as, if not more, intrigued by the woman he *imagined* as the author of *Indiana* and *Lélia* as by the woman he had come to know, so he seems to have speculated about Sand's relationship with Pagello, one about which he could only conjecture. Whatever his feelings of bitterness, Musset had no intention of leaving George Sand.

Musset and Sand moved from the Hotel Danieli at the beginning of March 1834. Their rooms had no doubt become inseparably associated with illness, even madness, and unfaithfulness. They moved to an apartment on the Delle Rasse, where the arrival of an enormously wealthy and dissipated young friend of Musset's, Alfred Tattet, further added to a feeling that the atmosphere of their relationship was freshening up. Pagello was largely responsible for having helped Sand through one of the bleakest periods of her life, but work, and the necessity of work, had also played a large part. As she wrote to Hippolyte on 6 March that year, anxious to tell him about herself, while at the same time to encourage a conversion in her lackadaisical half-brother: "The love of work can save us from everything. I bless our grandmother for having made me acquire the habit. The habit became a faculty and the faculty a need. I have managed to work for thirteen hours at a stretch without making myself ill. . . . I regret that my financial needs compel me to churn things out without replenishing my stocks. I long for a whole year of solitude and complete freedom so that I could pile into my head all the great works of foreign literatures that I know little or not at all. . . ."[30]

By March 1834 Musset's health was much restored. He even seems to have felt that his relationship with Sand could be reinstated. Sand wrote, "He thinks he desperately wants us not to separate and he is showing me heaps of affection."[31] Sand's affections, however, were now firmly attached to Pagello. As far as Musset was concerned, she had taken fright. But when the time came for his departure from Venice at the end of the month, Sand and Pagello offered him a little notebook as a present, inscribed "À son bon camarade, frère et ami Alfred, sa maîtresse, George" ("To her good mate, brother and friend Alfred, his mistress, George"). He was accompanied as far as Mestre by both Sand and Pagello.[32] Sand had already considered some kind of more permanent triangular relationship. The correspondence between Sand and Musset in the weeks that followed his departure from Venice testify to the ideas that both envisaged of some kind of *ménage à trois:* "Oh why can I not live between you two, making both of you happy, without belonging to either!"[33]

Sand made clear than her relationship with Pagello was much more limited and circumscribed than her intimacy with Musset: "This brave Pagello has not read *Lélia,* and I truly believe that he wouldn't understand a jot. . . . He treats me like a woman of twenty and he crowns me with stars as though I were a virgin soul. I say nothing to destroy or suggest his error. I allow myself to be regenerated by his gentle and honest affection. For the first time in my life, I love without passion."[34] It must have been clear to Musset that the door was still very much ajar. But on 4 April he had written much more calmly to Sand, "I still love you, George. . . . I know that you are close to a man that you love, but nevertheless I am contented. . . . I am only a child, but I have two grown-up friends and they are happy." What Musset suggests is that he can derive some vicarious pleasure from the happiness that Sand had found and no doubt this was made easier by his own awareness of the inadequacies of his sexual relationship with Sand. He wrote explicitly on the subject to the editor/publisher Hetzel. "Exhilaration," he wrote, "that's something she doesn't want to give me, exhilaration, you understand, what you find with all girls. I insulted her, I accused her of not wanting it."[35]

Musset was writing at a time when his pride must have been wounded, but the surviving correspondence does suggest that whatever the strength of passion manifest in words, in ideas, in mutual fascination, this did not translate into a successful physical love. This is most obviously apparent in their mutual inclination to describe their relationship as one between a youth of one generation and an older woman of another. The actual age difference was only six years.

In practical terms Sand's relationship with Pagello was ideal. He was, she wrote, "an angel of gentleness, goodness and devotion." In short, he was an exemplary companion for an author under increasing pressure to write. By the beginning of March she had finished *Leone Leoni:* its hero is an irresistible and schizophrenic young man. She had also written the first half of *André.* On 29 March Musset left: Sand travelled with him as far as Mestre and then toured for a week, returning to Venice on 5 April. This trip inspired her *Lettres d'un voyageur* (*Letters of a Traveller*), which Buloz thought excellent. The first was published in the *Revue des Deux Mondes* on 15 May.

Needless to say, much of the anguished experience of her previous months in Venice is translated into the text. But it is not, as the title might suggest—and did to contemporary readers—a kind of travelogue, that typically nineteenth-century account of a journey in foreign parts. What is striking is the range of emotion experienced by the traveller—a young cigar-smoking man—as he walks along the foothills and through the beautiful valleys of the Brenta. Here Pagello and Sand walked not long after Musset's departure. The "Letters" describe, with a vividness that suggests the immediacy of Sand's experience, the full sensory delights of that part of the world: the scent of almond and peach trees in bloom, the dazzling snow on distant mountaintops, the delights of those first breakfasts of fresh coffee and aniseed-flavoured bread and mountain butter, eaten out of doors on a mountainside thick with primroses.

That spring she delighted in the feeling of life rushing back at her, making her sensory experience one of dizzying joyousness. All this was thrown into high relief by her tortuous relationship with Musset. But there is more in the "Letters" than the transposition of an idyllic relationship with a handsome Mediterranean, and delightful landscapes. In the "Letters" the young doctor who initially accompanies the narrator is dismissed, and replaced by an absent poet who becomes the letters' addressee. And what the "Letters" convey most forcibly is the human capacity mysteriously to travel from states of ecstasy to despair. The emotions had been lived, and remained fresh at the time of writing: what would Musset make of it?

With her usual shrewdness, she wrote to him in advance of its publication: "I have written you a long letter about my trip to the Alps which I intend to publish in the *Revue* if you don't object. . . . I wrote it down as it came to me without a thought of all those who are likely to read it. I have seen it only as a framework for my love for you, a pretext for silencing those who won't fail to say that you have ruined and deserted me."[36] While it is true that Musset was known to be something of a rake, it is not as though Sand's own reputation was without blemish. Not only had she already written three novels that suggested her iconoclasm and some licence in her private life, she had also abandoned a husband and two children and gone to live in Italy. It is also true that while the "Letters" present Musset largely in an admirable light, there are equally hints of debauchery, pride, and something of a split personality. Musset cannot, as some have suggested, have been blind to these criticisms. But he always accepted that he had in many ways behaved appallingly towards Sand. He wrote back, having read the "Letters," and described the book as "sublime." He was not about to ask her not to publish something that he believed to be in some sense true, and he too would draw on the same shared experiences in his own *La Confession d'un enfant du siècle*. Musset was least childish when looking at things from the perspective of a writer.

Fortunately, Buloz was still more enthusiastic about the "Letters" than Musset and suggested that Sand stay on in Venice to write further instalments. One reason why the idea appealed to her was that she was writing in the first person (as a man). All her heroines—Indiana, Valentine, Lélia—had been partially autobiographical recreations, but she had not been able, within these relatively complex narratives, to express her ideas in the way that the form of the first "Letter" had allowed. She desperately needed money, she was happy with Pagello, and she had, for the first time, an opportunity to write more freely. She may not have been fully aware of her need to explore her own ideas in published written form, but twenty years later she would comment: "I felt I had many things to say and that I wanted to say them to myself and others. My individuality was in the process of taking shape. . . . I was so wholly preoccupied that I had to examine it and to work it, so to speak, like a metal in fusion thrown by me into a mould."[37]

When Sand and Pagello arrived back in Venice she stayed first at Ca'Mezzani, Corte Minelli. On 29 April she rented the first floor of a house near the Bridge of the Barcaroli. On 6 May she completed *André,* and worked unstintingly on *Jacques.* But it was her Italian letters that mattered to her most. On 30 May she was able to send Buloz half of the first volume of *Jacques* (further bundles were sent on 14 June, 26 June, and 4 July). Meanwhile she was broke and enormously relieved to receive a letter and money sent by Boucoiran on 15 May. The "Letters" came easily to her, and she continued the series.

In the next two instalments there are only occasional reminders that Musset is her imagined audience. But aside from these brief apostrophic utterances her concern is above all to convey, in as immediate a manner as possible, Venice in the spring. She was enraptured by the city and some of the lyrical passages of the second letter brilliantly, and hauntingly, convey the completeness of her infatuation. Descriptions of music floating across the water, the relationship between the sounds of different instruments and the rhythms of her prose, work superbly together. But there is extraordinary range in the "Letters" too. The domestic banter of the doctor's household, the chatter in the cafés, the arguments between the gondoliers: this cacophony of sound mingles with the easy harmonies of the music. In addition, there are comic vignettes, and analyses of the class structures of Venice: the poor, Sand maintained, live more easily here than in many cities. There are also passages of religious commentary, preaching toler-ance. Finally there are intimations that everything that is described has been assimilated through a process of comparison. The "type" against which Venice and its people are measured is France, or the Vallée Noire, or Nohant. And the ache of absence begins to make itself felt. In the final scene of the third "Letter," alone in the quiet and antiquity of Torcello, the traveller walks along the scented lanes, "more beautiful, alas, than those of the Vallée Noire." The regret is not that—measured in this abstract way—home has been found wanting, but that home *is far away*. It will soon be time, the reader feels, for the traveller to return.

Despite Sand's happiness, Musset was an ever-present absence. Whether as the audience she is addressing in her "Letters" or as an imag-ined third party in her relationship with Pagello, she did not forget him. She was surprised at her own sudden restlessness: "All my real needs, I have at my disposal." By this she meant sky, water, the sun, and a peaceful love affair, but she protested too much. The underlying source of a certain discontent bubbled to the surface.

From Sand's correspondence it is clear that she derived very real plea-sure from her weeks in Venice after Musset's departure. Her intimacy with Pagello, his family and friends, was a source of great happiness—and, simultaneously—grist to a writer's mill very much in need of material. Mérimée, somewhat surprisingly, rightly remarked how "admirable" it was that Sand could write not as a tourist but rather as someone "who had asso-ciated with the common folk and studied their idiom."[38] These months were also a respite, a period of calm after the torments of life with Musset. She was also conscious of the freedom she enjoyed to move about anony-mously. Yet even in Venice, as the months passed, she began to be recog-nized, at least as the mistress of Dr. Pagello. Pagello's former mistresses stirred up trouble and the time came when many of the advantages of stay-ing on in Venice had disappeared.

She had known all along that at some point she would have to return to "real life," to life in France, and reappear there as the public figure she had become. She was missing her children, and the date of Maurice's school prize-giving presented itself as something other than an arbitrary date at which to aim.

In late July she and Pagello set off, intent on making the most of the journey back to Paris. They stopped at Lakes Verona, Garda, and Iseo, and then travelled on via Milan. They saw the Alpine lakes, travelling to Chamonix and Geneva. On 14 August they arrived in Paris. Three days later she saw Musset, and on the twenty-fourth left Pagello in Paris to return to Nohant with Maurice and her mother to see her daughter and husband.

She was delighted with her children, particularly Maurice, who was rapidly growing into a striking-looking and interesting young man. But from that August through the autumn and winter she was to face mortifying unfinished business, both in Paris and at Nohant.

XVII

Pagello, Paris, and Politics

"I have always condemned the woman who seeks to
be happy at the expense of a man's well-being."

It is a testimony to Pagello's devotion that he left Venice to return with Sand to Paris. Days before his departure he wrote to his father, who strongly disapproved of his attachment to a married French woman writer. His letter revealed his own awareness, or at least hope, that his infatuation might soon be over: "I am," he claimed, "at the last stage of my folly and I must run though it with my eyes closed as I have run through others. Tomorrow I leave for Paris where I will leave George Sand and I will return to embrace you, worthy of you. I am young and I can rebuild my career."[1] He may have sensed that he and George had arrived at a point where their lives—however happy they had been together for a brief period—would soon naturally diverge.

The reappearance of Musset in their lives, only days after their arrival in Paris, did more than a little to strengthen his resolve. Sand and Pagello had arrived back on the fourteenth of August, and on the seventeenth Musset called. Pagello, who had tolerated Musset on home territory, found his presence very much more difficult to bear now that he was the outsider. Sand recognized his psychology and wrote, "He who had understood everything in Venice, has understood nothing from the moment he set foot in France, and here he is despairing. Anything that comes from me either wounds or irritates him."[2] Pagello no longer exercised the control over

236

their relationship that he had in Venice, when he had played host. Now she was in control, and however uncertain he was as to the precise nature of Sand's intentions with Musset, it was very clear that Musset remained very much in love with Sand. At the end of the month Sand left Paris. From Nohant she wrote to Boucoiran. She was low: "I feel a growing sadness and loathing for life. My soul has turned sterile and nothing will stir it sufficiently to produce something good in this life. Have I not already fulfilled my duty? And if weariness has destroyed me, am I not free to go?" She also devoted a lengthy paragraph to her smoking requirements. She detailed the quantities and type of tobacco she would like him to send, and reminded him to buy papers too. She begged him to do all he could to have the package to her as quickly as possible. It is only tobacco, she wrote, "and nothing else that can stimulate my nerves and brain in a way that gives me strength and stimulation."[3]

She needed time to take stock of her position, and she had, perforce, to make some gesture of compliance with regard to the pact she had made with her husband. What had been initially agreed was that she would spend three-month periods in Paris. She was now returning to Nohant having spent six months, with two lovers, in Venice.

Anxious about the reception she might receive from Casimir, she took Maurice and her mother with her to Nohant. She also wrote ahead inviting her old La Châtre friends—Papet, Fleury, Duvernet, Duteil—to a reunion. This took place at the end of the month. Cushioned by the crowd, Sand had less reason to fear her husband. He, however, was in good spirits and even went as far as to invite Pagello—who had looked after his wife so well in Venice—to join them at Nohant. He refused. He must have wondered what his reception at M. Dudevant's home would be, and he must have been aware that his relationship with Sand was as good as over. He took the opportunity of meeting various doctors in Paris, guided by the ever-helpful Boucoiran. Sand felt it incumbent on her to see to Pagello's professional needs. She even pretended to sell various paintings that he had brought from Italy, so that she could give him money without wounding his pride.

But Sand was saddened too by the failure of her relationship with Pagello. For a period she had clearly thought it close to her ideal, a relationship that was at once peaceable and passionate, where each allowed the other considerable freedom, while only feeling fully alive in the other's company. Pagello had been, Sand wrote "generous and romantic." In Paris he was a different man, "feeble, suspicious, unjust."[4] She acknowledged that she too had played a part in the decline of their relationship. She expressed disappointment mingled with anger—and self-loathing: "Here I am, insensitive," she wrote to Musset, the man who throughout her passionate affair with Pagello (one in which silence and anonymity had played such an important part) had remained her crucial audience. The numbness of her feelings for Pagello suggested that she had used him. She described herself to Musset as "an accursed sterile creature."[5] From Baden, where Musset had gone after Sand's departure for Nohant, he wrote, "I will not die until I have written my book about me and you. . . . Posterity will repeat our names, like those immortal lovers . . . like Romeo and Juliet, like Héloïse and Abelard. One will never be spoken of without the other."[6]

But Sand did not forget the miseries of her intimate relationship with Musset. Whatever the strength of her feelings for him, whatever his importance to her as a *reader*, she was unwilling to offer any encouragement in the matter of a renewed sexual relationship. That failure remained all too vivid and she still felt the wounds. She was, she told him, broken. Were it not for her children, she would throw herself into the river. That summer Sand turned thirty, and felt old. She read Mme de Staël's *Réflexions sur le suicide* and found it mortally boring, to the point that she felt twice as drawn to suicide intellectually as she had been before starting to read it. She was encouraged and rejuvenated, somewhat paradoxically, by her intense irritation at the author's philosophical pretensions.[7]

At the beginning of October Sand returned to Paris, and at the end of the month Pagello left to return to Venice, to his father, his career—in short the life he had all but abandoned in order to enjoy those blissful months with France's most famous contemporary woman writer. Sand had returned to the harsh grey realities of the north; her Venetian life, lit by the bright light of the Adriatic, faded into the past, and with it Pagello.

On 13 October Musset returned to Paris. She gave in, and allowed their relationship to begin again, but tried not to allow it in its former intensity. That autumn she met Franz Liszt. She was immensely drawn to him, and he, it seems, to her. That the relationship remained one of platonic friendship is evidence that Sand had consciously or unconsciously embarked on a new phase of her life. Her earlier absence of caution was replaced by a more considered and measured approach to life, to friendship, to love.

This new balance was encouraged by the range of commitments Sand now had. She had the "Letters" to complete, and delivered the fourth for publication in the *Revue des Deux Mondes* that autumn (15 October). She had further contracts to discuss with publishers, she was responsible for two children, and she was anxious to make up for what she considered lost time. Musset was more relaxed: "I have nothing to do but to love you." He did, however, continue to take one other activity seriously: he drank more and more. And despite Pagello's physical absence from Paris, he continued to be a significant player in their complex relationship.

Pagello had committed an indiscretion before leaving Paris. His pride wounded by the recognition that he mattered less and less to Sand, in conversation with Tattet he claimed that he and Sand had been lovers before Musset's departure from Venice. When Tattet took it upon himself to announce this indiscretion to Musset, the latter's anger was quickly translated into the most fearful abuse against Sand. When Musset became enraged, particularly when he had been drinking, he became a quite monstrous figure. Between 23 and 25 October, Sand and Musset had re-established their intimate relationship. Only days later, Musset announced its end—in furious and melodramatic terms.

Sand was transported back to those first weeks with Musset in Venice. The intensity of his feelings had, despite her caution, been vented on her once again. She was shocked and distressed, desolate and utterly despairing. She implored Musset to believe her: she had not slept with Pagello until after he had left Venice.[8] Musset would not believe her. Sand abandoned all pride and sought, desperately, to win him back. "O my blue eyes," she wrote, "you no longer look at me! Beautiful head, I will never again see you inclined against me, that I might envelop you in a gentle languor. Small body, supple and hot, you will never again stretch out on me. . . . Adieu blond curls, adieu white shoulders, adieu all that I loved, all that was mine."[9]

Sand and Musset's relationship had always been a warring one. There had scarcely been even brief periods of peace. The phases of the relationship were known to all of literary Paris, and others besides. Musset justified his position to one set of friends, Sand to another, then Musset to the group to whom Sand had spoken, and Sand to the group to whom Musset had first spoken, and so on. On 22, 25, and 29 November Sand poured out her heart to Eugène Delacroix, who had been commissioned by Buloz to paint her portrait for the *Revue*. She had cut her long hair—a sacrificial gesture—and had sent it to Musset. Musset ceased to reply to her imploring letters, whose rhetoric became increasingly complex and baroque. Sand spoke to Sainte-Beuve and spent long evenings talking to Dorval. No one could console her, or advise her how to win Musset back. Her one solace, work, could no longer save her. She was unable, for the first time in her life, to write fiction. She had committed herself to writing her *Unpublished Memoirs*, and Duteil had negotiated a contract, dated 5 December 1834, on her behalf for her first *Oeuvres complètes* (*Complete Works*). She might be able to look back, but she felt unable to write imaginatively.

On 7 December 1834 Sand returned to Nohant. She had, she claimed in letters to her friends, decided definitively never to see Musset again. To Sainte-Beuve she wrote calmly that she had exchanged letters with Musset. His had been "a little affectionate letter, full of remorse for his violence." She had replied sending a leaf from her garden, and he had then sent a lock of hair that she had requested. But now that they were back in touch Sand resolved not to become seriously involved again. "I do not want to see him again, it causes me too much pain," she told Sainte-Beuve.[10]

Less than a month later, however, on 31 December, she returned to Paris and wrote to Tattet, the catalyst for the couple's last separation, announcing that Musset had returned to her. Is there a note of triumph? In the same letter she invited Tattet to witness the spectacle of their rediscovered joy. Sand was often reluctant to admit defeat: most often she would seek to win the round. Thus she wrote to Tattet: "Alfred is, once again, my lover. As I presume that he will be delighted to see you here, I beg you to come to dinner with us on the first free day you have. If I forget my offence, may our friendship be restored."[11]

The spectacle of the couple's happiness was, however, short-lived. Even before the month was out the terrible scenes they had known so often before began to repeat themselves in an irrepressible pattern. Sand despaired and wrote to Musset: "Do you want us to go to Franchard and together to blow out our brains?"[12] By the end of February Sand was at the end of her resources. She knew that the relationship with Musset would have to end definitively, that it was a union which, however idyllic for certain brief periods, would quickly and inexplicably turn hellish; she could no longer bear to risk it. She wrote to Musset: "No, no, enough! You poor unhappy one, I loved you as I love my son, it is a mother's love, my wounds still bleed. I pity you, I forgive everything, but we must leave one another."[13] This time she meant it. On 6 March she left for Nohant. Musset knew, when he learnt of her departure, that this time she had ceased to play games. She had not told him of her intention to leave because she did not want to embark on further discussion, further terrible scenes. By 6 March 1835 the passionate affair with the mysterious Musset was, in the conventional sense, over. For both, however, it was a relationship whose depths of passion and anguish, of exhilaration and despair, of mutual understanding and mutual incomprehension, would feed their writing for years to come. Thus in another sense an intimate and very private, even secret, relationship was sustained in their writing and their reading of each other's work.

The gossip in Paris about her relationship with Musset was more than she could bear. Her return to Nohant was, as so often before, a return to calm. But her need for quiet was accompanied by an equally fervent desire to continue to explore intellectual questions. At Nohant she was settling in for a period of retreat, although her old friends Rollinat and Duteil were nearby.[14] She wrote to Boucoiran asking him to send her various essential materials: books, including a complete Shakespeare, the works of Plato, the Koran, some sheet music which he would find on top of the piano—and her hookah, which she had left behind in her haste to leave Paris. She carefully described how the water pipe was to be safely dismantled.[15]

Sand was clearly planning to think long and seriously, and *Mauprat*, which had initially been conceived as a short story, started to take the form of a novel. The themes and underlying concerns look backwards and forwards in her life. Musset is present in the theories of neurosis and even psychosis which can only be averted by passing through the strait gate, and deep into the realm of the symbolic. Here, later theories of psychoanalysis are strikingly prefigured. Looking forwards, *Mauprat*'s frame of reference is a large one. Although overtly feminist, like *Indiana*, *Valentine*, and *Lélia* before it, *Mauprat* explores social and political questions at greater length, and the relationship between private happiness and the state of health of the group. This is visible most obviously in Sand's ideas about a common language. What Patience, the philosopher-sage of *Mauprat*, dreams of is a hybrid language incorporating both popular and cultivated idioms, one that would allow everyone, without simplifying their ideas, to inhabit the world and to explain it through the language of their dreams. The most obvious influence of her affair with Musset on *Mauprat* was, however, her conviction that "love's ideal is most certainly everlasting fidelity."[16] Sand was in a reflective mood, keen to think, once again, about life's principal conundrums. She was beginning to think less about the problems of the individual, and more about the relationship between individuals in a social context.

In November 1834, in response to an admiring letter from Marie Talon, a young woman reader of *Lélia*, inquiring as to her position in relation to Saint-Simon's thinking, Sand had claimed that *Lélia* was "without doctrine" and could not even be read as a "profession of personal faith." Six months on, Sand's interests were turning increasingly to politics. Civil unrest in various cities, in response to the repressive regime of Louis-Philippe, brought politics to everyone's lips. At the end of Sand's letter to Marie Talon she had insisted that what was needed was not so much a "new faith" but an urgent war on "corruption, that is, destruction."[17]

It is not surprising that her next intimate friend should be a man who attracted her precisely because of the power and persuasiveness of his political ideas and by the sheer force of his rhetoric, by which she was, for a time, wholly convinced. Of her initial impressions she wrote, "The first thing that struck me when I saw Michel for the first time . . . was the extraordinary shape of his head. He seemed to have two crania fused one to the other, signs of high intelligence were as prominent at the prow of the powerful ship as were signs of generous instincts at the poop."[18] The adventure on which she embarked aboard this impressive vessel was very different from, but quite as stormy as, that from which she had released herself not many weeks earlier. She had been working hard and needed to steer from the harbour of Nohant into stormy seas once again, this time aboard the good ship Michel. She had recovered her optimism, and believed her transport quite unsinkable.

Sand first met Michel on 9 April 1835, in Bourges. She was introduced by Fleury le Gaulois, her childhood friend. Louis-Chrysostome Michel, known to all as Michel of Bourges, was a lawyer, a resolute Republican, and a militant, who had married a rich widow. When Sand first met him he was thirty-seven, but he gave the impression, with his thick trunk and large head, his broad chest, his stomach and liver problems, of a man considerably more mature in years. His carefully considered dress was calculated to suggest his political views. He wore what were essentially peasant's clothes, including clogs, set off by an impeccably white shirt, evidence of his professionalism and cleanliness. He had read *Lélia,* and like most of its readers he had been deeply impressed by it.[19] On the evening of their first meeting, Michel apparently pulled out all the stops and held forth with great eloquence and interest until the early hours of the morning. Planet, who was used to Michel's lucidity, declared to Sand, "I have never before seen him like that. I have been living by his side for a year, but it is only this evening that I have come to know him. He finally opened up completely, for you."[20] When Sand left Bourges, Michel's eloquence pursued her. "His letters follow with a rapidity without time for replies. This ardent soul has resolved to take hold of mine."[21] The speed with which Michel dispatched his letters did not allow their correspondence to settle into a conversation. He wanted to win her over, but he was not interested in dialogue.

When Sand left Nohant to travel back to Paris on 3 May, she looked forward not only to seeing Michel, who would be up from Bourges again, but to being introduced to a new circle made up of his Republican friends, including Emmanuel Arago, Armand Carrel, Armand Barbès, and Pierre Leroux, as well as François-Vincent Raspail and Alexandre-Auguste Ledru-Rollin, both of whom would stand in the presidential elections of 1848 and be beaten by Napoleon. Sand was the only woman invited into the group, and so as to feel less conspicuous, she reverted to wearing her "boy's outfit." Once again the metaphorical use of the notion of incest, and indeed homosexuality, was suggested to describe Michel's relationship with Sand. He had always imagined the author of *Lélia* and *Lettres d'un voyageur*, he wrote, "in the guise of a young boy, a child-poet whom I would make my son."[22]

Sand had called Musset her "child." Pagello had been her "father" but, no doubt feeling vulnerable away from his native Venice, he had begun to abuse his paternal authority, denying freedoms which she thought legitimate. While Michel imagined Sand as his "son," she imagined him as an absolute monarch. "You were born king," she wrote, and she was but "his most humble servant and faithful subject."[23] Such are the ironies of the metaphorical language used by Sand the increasingly committed Republican.

Michel was in Paris to defend the accused in a celebrated case, known as the "*procès monstre*." It was monstrous not only in the unreasonableness of the accusations but in the number of accused. One hundred and twenty-one workers were standing trial for allegedly conspiring and provoking disturbances in Lyon and other cities a year earlier. The government of Louis-Philippe wanted to make a characteristic clean sweep of the opposition.[24]

Meanwhile Michel and Sand spent increasing amounts of time together. The sixth of the *Lettres d'un voyageur* (11 April) is dedicated to Michel, who was rapidly becoming more and more dedicated to Sand's children. He would take Maurice out on exeats from his boarding school, and Solange to the Jardin des Plantes. They also enjoyed a bubbling social life. They saw a good deal of Planet, Fleury, Arago, and Liszt, and talked endlessly about realizing their socialist vision. Sand felt that she was absorbing a great deal in the ideal social context in which to learn. The idea of any official involvement in a group or movement did not appeal to her, and she politely turned down Adolphe Guéroult's invitation, made on behalf of Enfantin, to become more involved with the Saint-Simonians. Saint-Simon had died in 1825. His disciples, led by Enfantin, called for the emancipation of women, proposed an androgynous definition of God, and founded a remarkable utopian community. Sand continued to want to discover, rather than lead.

The bourgeois domesticity of her life with Michel and the others was disrupted, however, by Michel's sudden arrest and prosecution, following the publication of a critical article. He was sentenced, on 4 June 1835, to a brief period of imprisonment and a 10,000-franc fine. On 19 June Sand left Paris, leaving the children in boarding schools.

Later that summer, after a period at home recovering from illness, Michel left again to travel to Nohant on 24 June. He stayed for a few days while Casimir was away. Sand accompanied him back to Bourges on Casimir's return. At the beginning of July she left for Paris, travelling via Châteauroux and Bourges, where she again saw Michel. At the end of the month Michel was arrested again, and Sand returned home.

Life at Nohant was becoming strained, but Casimir came and went. During his absence, Michel returned to Nohant, in the middle of August. Most of September Sand was in Paris, where she and Michel spent a good deal of time together. On 12 September Michel fell ill, and it was to Sand's apartment that the doctor was summoned.

Her return to Nohant coincided once again with Michel's imprisonment in Bourges for having failed to serve the whole of his previous sentence. Sand returned to Nohant the day before he began his sentence.

Sand was less and less able to bear life at home. She disliked the way Casimir treated Maurice, in particular. Casimir's life and ideas had stagnated, while her own vision had continued to widen. She knew the Parisian revolutionaries—Ledru-Rollin, Barbès, Hippolyte Carnot—and she had met Marie d'Agoult, Franz Liszt's lover, another woman who had left her husband and children because of her commitment to an adulterous relationship. Liszt, in turn, had introduced Sand to Abbé Félicité de Lamennais, a Catholic priest who had broken completely with Rome, adamant that the Vatican was concerned above all with earthly power. He was as convinced in his faith, however, as he was in his criticisms of the institution of the Catholic Church. Surrounded by iconoclastic friends, or in touch with them by letter, Sand felt frustrated by her life at Nohant. Although Fleury, Duteil, and Papet frequently visited, as often as not Casimir's presence interfered with the social atmosphere. Tensions between husband and wife erupted into quarrels, even fights, as on one night (19 October) when Casimir's criticisms of Maurice prompted Sand to defend her son. She asked him to go to his room, reassuring him that his father did not know what he was saying. Casimir heard her dismissive remarks and worked himself into a spectacular rage. He even fetched his gun, shouting, "You'll see what I'm going to do to you." Sand's friends successfully disarmed him and she retired to her room. She felt the full weight of the humiliation, born of the exposure of her deeply unsatisfactory family life, and she felt shamed by her husband's uncontrolled behaviour.[25]

The following day Sand wrote to Michel, her lover and now her lawyer, sketching out the legal separation she wanted to obtain from her husband. On 21 October she consulted Rollinat in Châteauroux, and then visited Michel in prison. A brilliant man of the law, and no doubt further spurred to professional excellence by his personal interests, Michel prepared a brilliant case. In the meantime Sand returned to lodge with the Duteils in La Châtre; a return to Nohant would, in the eyes of the law, signify a renewal of the marriage.

On 30 October 1835, Sand filed her official request for separation. On 2 December Casimir's failure to appear before the court filled Sand with joy: the process would be straightforward. But there were to be further twists and the judicial case would be longer and more complex than anyone could have anticipated. The autumn and winter were lived under the oppressive inconclusiveness of numerous court hearings. Sand tried to work, and signed a contract with Buloz for a further novel, *Simon*, hoping that the obligation to write might motivate her. The year-end was gloomy and the judicial events of the new year wholly uncertain. She longed for resolution. She forced herself to work.

At the beginning of 1836, and looking ahead to the court case (which would not finally be resolved until the end of July), Sand felt trapped. In a letter to Maurice she described herself working every night until seven in the morning. "I'm like an old lamp," she wrote, and "I'm nailed here. . . . I'm forced to be. . . . In the first place I've no money. . . ."[26] Some things remained constant.

On 15 January *Simon* started to appear in the *Revue des Deux Mondes*, while the court hearing took place from 14 to 22 January. Michel argued that Sand's marriage had been destroyed by Casimir's dissolute and immoral ways, and more specifically by his acts of adultery. The judgement was to be announced ten days later. Sand braced herself, but the judgement was postponed for a fortnight because Casimir had failed to attend court.

In the middle of this anguished period of waiting, Sand had to cope with the emotional disturbance caused by Musset's publication of *The Confession of a Child of the Century*, which came out on 1 February 1836. She was deeply moved by the fictional exploration, and extrapolation, of their love affair. But it was a torture to relive the relationship while reconstructing it according to her former lover's point of view. She wrote to Marie d'Agoult: "I started to cry like a child when I finished the book. Then I wrote some lines to the author, to say I don't know what: that I had loved him a great deal, that I had forgiven him everything, and that I never wanted to see him again."[27] Reflecting on the experience some months later (in May), she again wrote to Marie, at greater length:

> If you want me to talk old history, I will tell you that this *Confession of a Child of the Century* moved me deeply. The smallest details of that unhappy intimacy are so faithfully, so minutely reported, from the first to the last hour. . . . I started to cry like an ass when I turned the last page. . . . For a long time I believed that passion was my ideal. I was mistaken or I chose badly. I believe in yours, and am convinced that having known a passion as complete and beautiful as yours you could not survive its loss. If you had my past in place of your present, I think you would, like me, put calm before all else.[28]

On 16 February the court finally announced the official separation of Aurore and Casimir Dudevant. Casimir did not mount a defence but accepted the judgement, and some financial support in the form of the income from the Hôtel de Narbonne. The La Châtre tribunal thus found in favour of Sand: Nohant and the children were deemed to be hers. She returned home triumphant and felt that the place, for the first time in a very long while, breathed that familiar calm for which she longed: "I am savouring for the first time since my grandmother's death the calm of contemplation; no conflicts surface."[29] But the calm turned out to be no more than a brief lull: her half-brother was soon stirring up trouble, inciting Casimir to appeal. He lodged the first appeal, against formalities, on 8 April, and a second, against defamatory evidence given against him, on 14 April. The hearing would resume on 10 May.

Whether or not she initially considered giving in to Casimir's demands out of court, Sand quickly announced that it was a matter not simply of personal but of familial pride, and more particularly of filial duty, to defend her interests. She wrote to her mother, holding her head high: "I am my father's daughter. . . . If my father had listened to the fools and idiots of the world, I would not be the inheritor of his name."[30] Meanwhile Hippolyte wrote to Casimir: "What conduct: for our friend Duteil to believe that after such a judgement you would not appeal. . . . [Aurore] is furious. . . . For my part I would like you not to involve me in the affair. . . . *You have enough evidence without me.* I will help you with advice and some *fairly crucial* details. . . . There are people at your side who with a single blow will ensure that you win your case. You need to loosen their tongues, I'll make this possible at the top of my voice."[31]

Between two of the court hearings Sand had become involved in one of her most liberated love affairs, in March and April 1836, when Michel was not particularly attentive. Charles Didier had first met Sand on 2 February 1833, and his *Journal* testifies to his changing attitudes towards her. Initially, he notes at the end of the entries, "Don't think she's capable of passion," or "Would she be capable of passion?"[32] Didier was born in Geneva but had moved to Paris aged nineteen, intent on making his way as a writer. He had been drawn into Hugo's *cénacle,* a group of Romantic poets, and became Hortense Allart's lover. Allart was an outspoken feminist and pamphleteer. Sand knew of Allart's writings and commented on her *Women and Democracy in Our Times,* in a letter to Marie d'Agoult in February 1836, that it was full of interest and fine ideas but the author was clearly a "pedant; I don't like her."[33]

Allart's lover, Didier, was more difficult to dismiss. His interest in Sand is reminiscent of Musset's. Didier, like his predecessor, was fascinated by the relationship between the writer and the woman, by the life and the fiction. He noted in his *Journal* on 9 August 1833: "Read [*Lélia*] furiously and straight through, very late, fall asleep shattered." And the following day's entry reads: "*Lélia* finished . . . find my novel stupid compared to *Lélia.* I won't say all this to Mme Dudevant, disposed as she is to take little interest in her admirers." Two days later, the passion that he had considered inconceivable in the woman had bowled him over in her writing: "I feel, once again, and more than ever, the effect of *Lélia.* I am not jealous . . . but I feel feeble, a poor writer, a small artist next to such a powerful and passionate form. Why write? To eat."

Didier's musings were written the year of *Lélia*'s publication. There are, thereafter, few and only insignificant mentions of her until the entry for 26 March 1836: "In the drawing room I discover George Sand. I go back home with her and Arago. I spend the whole day there musing. Charles d'Aragon, Arago and I stay to supper, have tea and chat all night.

A fantastic night. We do not leave her until five in the morning; it was broad daylight. Arago was grey. . . . They are both in love with her. I was there, watching, my head in the cushions of the divan, and she, sad and not very talkative, passing her fingers through my hair . . . calling me her old philosopher." Over the next month the diary entries become increasingly detailed in their descriptions of the growing intimacy between the diarist and George. But despite their physical closeness, Didier's entries continue to record his inability to feel he knows her. A comic parallel suggests itself: the diary entries might be those of an anthropologist, even a zoologist living alongside his subject: "I study her, observe, ill at ease, troubled, doubting. This complicated being remains unfathomable from more than one point of view, and I fear her impetuous changeability. I am still studying her. I don't understand. Is she loyal? Is she playing a game? Is her heart dead? Problems without solutions."[34]

While Didier's fascination and infatuation are clear, Sand's feelings remain more mysterious. Was she looking simply to be comforted, and distracted, during a bleak interlude between the two court hearings? It would seem so. On 3 May 1836 she left Didier's apartment to travel to Bourges and La Châtre, a week before the hearing was due to commence.

Meanwhile Casimir had drawn up a magnificent list of recriminations against his wife. Needless to say, he lists alleged infidelities. But there are stark entries of an altogether different sort: "September 1830. She writes novels." This is the real resentment. And sure enough, five years later, the effects of the earlier attack make themselves seen: "Mme D. affecting the manners of a young man, smoking, swearing, dressed as a man and having lost all the feminine graces, has no understanding of money." But if the most serious accusation is, according to the rhetoric of the courtroom, best kept until last for greatest effect, then it is again writing that is her greatest crime: "Author of *Lélia*. Political witness *Revue des Deux Mondes*."[35] The novel, the lawyers suggested, although presumably only obliquely, testified to an unsavoury psycho-sexual life and explored ideas about what women might want to acknowledge about their own bodies, their own eroticism. Her political ideas, as expressed in the *Revue*, were also, they implied, unbecoming to a woman. Both sets of ideas, about the private and the public, were deemed wholly unacceptable, and evidence of Sand's essential immorality.

Surprisingly, the court once again found in Sand's favour. The fact that it had been Sand who had initially pressed for a separation, and that Casimir had initially objected to it, made the trauma he was now alleging he had suffered somewhat unconvincing. Casimir, fearing that he would lose everything, appealed once again, this time to the tribunal in Bourges, the capital of the province. On 10 and 11 May 1836 Michel successfully persuaded the jury that the domestic setting of Casimir's infidelities had first poisoned the marital relationship: "The conjugal home was profaned and it was you who profaned it. You introduced debauchery and superstition," Michel alleged of M. Dudevant. Further he accused Casimir of "representing his wife as the vilest prostitute." Sand sat in the court dressed in white, no doubt to suggest her rightful claim to moral superiority, and soon heard the judge find in her favour. She won possession of both Nohant and her children. She had been right to believe in Michel.

However, life for her children, and particularly Maurice, was becoming difficult. His mother's strong and very public political views did not ease his social relations with his colleagues at his college. On one occasion he had been invited out by the young Prince de Montpensier, son of Louis-Philippe. George wrote a typically uncompromising letter: "However good the son of a king might be, he is destined to be a tyrant. We are destined to be reviled or rejected, or persecuted, by him." Maurice replied: "Don't worry . . . the blood that flows in my veins, my old Georges [*sic*], and in yours will prevent me from loving aristocrats. . . . My father is happy that I am going to [the Prince's balls] and he says that it will be useful to me when I am grown up, if I want a job in the government, I say nothing, but inside I say NO, NO . . . long live the Republic, long live justice, equality, long live my old Georges, long live my old Michel!"[36]

Living with his mother's political views must have been nothing by comparison with the strains imposed on his life by her not-so-private private life: "The other day," he wrote to his mother, "someone said that d'Arago [he meant Arago] was my father and your husband, in short they said all sorts of things, because you are a woman who writes, because you are not a prude like most of the other boys' mothers. . . . They call you, I can't tell you the word because it is too wicked, P. . . . I have told you despite myself, but you must know what is happening in the heart of a good son and a true friend."[37] Maurice was sufficiently astute to see that it was the fact that his mother *wrote* that was at the bottom of the prejudice and hatred meted out to her. Despite the maturity of his perspective, he suffered. Sand began seriously to consider removing Maurice from his college and educating him at home with private tutors.

Meanwhile she was busy editing her *Complete Works*. *Lélia* was significantly changed by the removal of a number of intimate autobiographical passages. And in her private life, the letters exchanged between Didier and Sand suggest that the relationship was foundering. By June 1836, according to Didier's *Journal,* things had turned sour. Sand had accused Didier of treating friendship as "a contract full of clauses," while Didier accused Sand of a "calculated coldness . . . a sort of prostitution of the heart."[38] It is true that Didier invariably calculated and recorded with some desire for precision the number of hours he had spent alone with Sand. She, on the other hand, clearly wanted to maintain considerable independence, despite their "union": "I do not ask for the support of anyone," she wrote, "whether to kill someone or pick a bouquet, correct proofs, or go to the theatre. I have been there alone dressed like a man, out of choice, and when I want beautiful flowers I gather them on my own, barefoot, in the Alps. . . . If ever I make a name I will owe it to myself alone."[39] What emerges here, apart from a trenchant desire to refuse conventional male gallantry, is a desire to control her literary life: going alone to the theatre when it pleases her, correcting her own proofs without interference, and making her own name for herself. Her early collaboration with Jules Sandeau had no doubt made her wary of becoming too involved, as a writer, with a lover who also wielded a pen.

Didier enjoyed one final sojourn in his mistress's arms at Nohant. It lasted five days (18 to 23 June). After his departure Sand enjoyed walks alone in the countryside around Nohant, and bathing in the Indre, an activity that would be a source of great delight and comfort well into her old age. But she was also suffering from disillusionment with Michel de Bourges, a man whom she admired enormously. In a letter to Marie d'Agoult, she wrote of men of Michel's stature (he is nowhere mentioned explicitly by name):

> Where there is, in a person, strength and insight, goodness is scarcely to be found; because experience and observation have engendered suspicion and hatred. Souls devoted to the most noble principles are often the most severe and embittered. . . . We hold them in esteem, we continue to admire them, but we can no longer love them. . . . I have had enough of *great men.*[40]

But it was Michel who was charged with the responsibility for freeing Sand from her despotic husband. On 25 and 26 July 1836 the public seats were soon all taken in the courthouse. Sand wryly noted that the public supposed that she would, on entering the courthouse, be wearing "red trousers with pistols in my belt."[41] Casimir's lawyer Louis Antoine Thiot-Varennes delivered a wonderfully moralizing address. Again an appeal was made to the alleged evidence of her writing: it revealed profound unhappiness. But the solution that Thiot-Varennes proposed was delightfully stupid: "Your works are filled with bitterness and regret which devour your heart. . . . Everywhere you asked for goodness but found it nowhere. Well! I want to show you the way: return to your husband, return under that roof where your first years passed calmly and peaceably, find your way back to the path of righteousness and virtue; submit yourself to the gentlest laws of nature: beyond these all is but error and deception; it is only on the path that you will find happiness and peace."[42]

The court case, like so many celebrated judicial hearings, focused on urgent debates of the day, arguments about the rights of husbands and wives, about the estate of marriage and its financial corollaries, about happiness and the individual's right to seek contentment. Michel argued eloquently that Casimir's position was profoundly contradictory and therefore suspect. He had sought to describe his wife as nothing more than a "vile prostitute," while expecting her to return to him. She was, Michel argued, a good mother, despite having expressed certain views in her fictional writing that might not be universally shared.

The drama of the hearing reached a point of climax which quickly became one of anticlimax. The judges were split, five and five. The public vociferously backed Sand. The hearing was then adjourned in order to reconsider further. But the next day Casimir, no doubt discouraged by the public response, withdrew from the legal battle and agreed to an out-of-court settlement. Sand wrote to her mother on 30 July describing the new life that now lay ahead, a life as clearly separated from her husband as she can have hoped it might be: "Dear Mother, everything is over and I am finally calm and free forever. . . . M. Dudevant leaves me at liberty, for the rest of my life, to look after my wealth and to live far away from him. I am abandoning to him the income from the Narbonne property, on condition that he pay for Maurice's education and that, from the age of twenty on, he will give him an allowance of one hundred louis. I keep Nohant, and my daughter."[43] These were what mattered to Sand, and no doubt remain the prerequisites of satisfactory divorce for women today.

XVIII

Maurice's Notorious Mother

"My body is still dislocated from another terrible
but delicious weariness: I retain the stigmata
in a thousand places. . . ."

⌇Michel de Bourges was, it seems, more interested in the judicial case that could be constructed to defend George Sand in continuing legal proceedings against her husband than in the woman herself. Although the legal separation had been finally granted, for years there would be further wranglings in court over property and the children. The technical challenge that she represented continued to interest him. They had planned to live together, and openly, after Sand's separation, but the intention was never realized. Sand was bitterly disappointed and not a little disillusioned by the great Republican lawyer. By the summer of 1836 she recognized that her hopes would never be fulfilled. "There was a time," she wrote to Charles d'Aragon in August, "when I carried an ideal of happiness in my head, in which I no longer want to believe and to which I have the good sense no longer to aspire. My heart is full of kindly affections and I have tied myself to someone [Michel] in a way that you well know will not bring domestic happiness."[1]

Sand had been deceived before, but this time her sadness and sense of regret were aggravated by anxieties about her children. Maurice wrote to her from his college, essentially asking whether the allegations reported in the press at the time of the hearing were true or not. His colleagues had taunted him with all this, which they—or their parents—had read in the papers. "In the *Gazette des Tribunaux,*" the distraught boy pointed out to his mother, "it said that one day you were in Bordeaux, and having met some young people you did something that a lady should not do. When you returned home you told your husband everything and he forgave you and that finally, in Italy, you had started again. . . ."[2] Sand thought it best to provide Maurice with the "evidence." She expected a good deal of her son. What he had to show was contempt for such nonsense: "The silence of scorn ought to save you from these deplorable hypotheses. Read the n[umber] I am sending you carefully. I'll send you tomorrow's as soon as I receive it, keep this one, don't lose it, it is the only copy I have. . . . It is a very dry summary of an address that lasted four or five hours. But all the same it will give you the idea."[3] No doubt, had Maurice ever received the *Gazette,* it would have been an early and important lesson in the vagaries and prejudices of the press, but it was confiscated at the college on the grounds that it did not make appropriate reading for a schoolboy.[4] Sand was anxious to see Maurice and persuaded Casimir to allow her to have both children for the summer. On 14 August Maurice wrote to his mother to announce that his father was happy that he spend the summer with her.[5] But her plan was not to stay at Nohant but to take them abroad, to Switzerland, to join the youthful Franz Liszt and Marie d'Agoult.

They set off on 28 August 1836. When they arrived at Geneva Franz and Marie had already moved on to Chamonix. But they had arranged for Sand, the children, and Ursule, Sand's childhood companion now in service at Nohant, to meet the party arriving from France, which would be escorted on to Chamonix by Adolphe Pictet, an entertaining scholar, philologist, and soldier. Franz had clearly set out to make the holiday as lively as possible. In the hotel register required by the local police, Sand read, obviously written by Franz: "*Qualities:* musician, philosopher. *Address:* Parnassus. *From where have you come?:* from doubt. *Where are you going?:* to the Truth.*" Sand wrote a not dissimilar entry, but ending on a note of bitterness, "*Issued by:* public opinion."[6] No doubt she could better bear the public's judgement of her than Maurice's distress. She had come to Switzerland to be out of the public eye, to enjoy her children, to cheer herself up. Franz, fortunately, wanted nothing other than entertainment. They encouraged "Puzzi" Cohen, one of his pupils, and Solange to cross-dress, shocking the chambermaid profoundly. Soon the entire hotel was aware that the occupants of room number 13 were quite extraordinary. They rambled in the mountains, they talked endlessly about all the big questions. They argued about Schelling, Hegel, God. Pictet revealed himself as something of a pedant, and overearnest. Sand did not share his views. If he quoted Aristotle, "Art is imitation," Sand quickly corrected him, "Art is creation," and so on.[7]

The party travelled on to Fribourg. Pictet described his companions in his notebook with typical economy, but convincingly. He contrasted Marie d'Agoult's "grace" with Sand's "strength"; the former exuded "reflection and ideas," while the latter exuded "spontaneity and genius." Liszt personified "the spirit of music," playing Mozart's *Dies Irae* on the famous cathedral organ. For all the playfulness of the party, there must have been sublime moments.

In Geneva the city's cultural offerings were enjoyed: Liszt and Sand continued to work, the former composing his *Rondo fantastique,* which he dedicated to Sand, the latter writing *Le Contrebandier* (*The Smuggler*) (published on 1 January 1837). There were, inevitably, certain tensions between Liszt, Marie, and Sand. As Marie wrote in her *Memoirs,* "When she [Sand] came to Chamonix . . . her preoccupations left me cold and awkward; her *pranks* disconcerted me; I felt that I was not at all at ease, and that consequently, I was scarcely likeable; this saddened me, because I desperately wanted her friendship."[8] While Marie's emotional life had been tormented by the relationships of those of the party, Sand's thoughts had often turned to Michel. She wrote to him suggesting that he come and join them in Geneva. She wrote again suggesting that he come to Lyon. She did not read Michel's letter waiting for her at Nohant until she arrived back in the autumn. On 15 October 1836 she wrote a long and remarkably frank letter in reply.

The young man who was accompanying her, Gustave de Gévaudan, whom she had met at Geneva, was, Michel had claimed, a lover. This was not, she was adamant, the truth. She had not, she repeated, been unfaithful to her love for him. Her letter also revealed something of her attitude to sexuality, and her understanding of the libido. She tried to reveal to Michel the contradictions in his approach to their relationship: "Love is, for you, a sickness, for me it is an emotion, you think that you can spit in my face if bile comes into your mouth. According to you, it is a right, an attribute, an inevitable consequence of the love of someone strong for someone weak. You know that I have never accepted such conditions. . . ."[9] She is at pains to convince Michel of her innocence:

> I have told you once and for all that if I had had the
> misfortune of behaving unfaithfully, on some day

when I had been overcome with weariness, physical weakness, or unhealthy need, I would have admitted to you my mistake, and I would have charged you with the responsibility of punishing me by forgetting me forever. . . . Such spite would have been a negligible punishment in comparison with such a glaring, but equally pardonable, blunder, and besides, one which you have committed with your wife since we have belonged to each other.[10]

Again what she identified was the double standard. She had not expected Michel to cut off relations with his wife, but he expected constancy from Sand. Nor, it seems, was sexual abstinence something that she easily tolerated, as her letter made very plain:

That I have suffered a great deal from my chastity I have not hidden from you. I have had deeply disturbing dreams. Blood has risen to my head a hundred times, in the full sun, in the bosom of beautiful mountains [suggesting a subliminal inversion: "the beautiful mountains of my bosom"!], waiting for the birds to sing and smelling the sweet smells of the forests and valleys, I have often sat down, apart [suggestive of parted legs] with my mind filled with love and my knees trembling with desire. I am still young, however much I might say to other men that I have the calm of an old person, my blood is burning and, surrounded by nature, intoxicating in its beauty, love boils within me like the sap of the lifeblood of the universe.

It is only by exhausting herself physically that she can find calm. Her letter described the long walks she felt driven to undertake, but even so, "throwing myself on the bed of an inn, in the evening, I continue to dream that the breast of the man whom one loves is the only pillow that brings rest to both the mind and the body." But, she is at pains to insist, "I have retained my calm."[11] Whether consciously written in or not, there is tremendous subtlety in Sand's language. An erotic current ripples beneath the more practical elements of the argument. Her letter also discusses overtly, and at considerable length, her unsatisfied sexual excitement. She reassures and flatters her addressee: it is for him alone that she longs: "It is of you that I dream when I wake bathed in sweat, it is to you that I call out when sublime nature sings passionate hymns and the mountain air enters my pores like a thousand pricks of desire and enthusiasm."[12]

But strangely woven into Sand's frank and stirring descriptions are angry recriminations. The previous quotation closes one paragraph while the next begins: "After a wait of six weeks, of anticipation, of hope and oppression, you still refuse to come and find me because, according to your Pasha's ideas, I should come to you and submit myself to you like an odalisque. . . ."[13] On her return to Nohant what awaited her had been "the kind of letter an ageing banker might write to a girl whom he has been keeping."[14] Towards the end of the letter she implores more gently, but not without her usual directness: "Try to calm yourself, to heal yourself, to see clearly, to renounce your despotic ideas and to understand that I have quite as much right as you, before God, to walk, to breathe, to sit next to people of the opposite sex. . . . You are a great man, Michel, and yet I am too, because I feel no fear of you, and do not feel that your love is worth being bought with a lie. . . ."[15]

Sand had left Geneva on 1 October. She returned to Nohant for ten days, and then headed back to Paris, arriving on the twenty-fourth, to await Michel. She had left Didier's, and had moved in with Liszt and Marie at the Hôtel de France, Rue Laffitte. She participated in Marie's newly established literary salon and the three of them soon attracted a remarkable group of artists, intellectuals, and politicians: Meyerbeer, who did so much for the operatic tradition, was, like so many before and after him—Gluck and Stravinsky for example—a foreigner. Lamennais, who had been ordained at the age of thirty-four, broke with the Church to become a republican pamphleteer. Then there were novelists, the German Heinrich Heine, and Eugène Sue, one of the most commercially successful novelists in France. His stories, when serialized in the press, would boost circulation remarkably. Visitors also included Pierre Leroux, Socialist philosopher, propagandist, and idealist. Liszt also attracted a varied group of Poles living in Paris: Count Albert Grzymała, the poet Adam Mickiewicz, and, of course, Frédéric Chopin. On 5 November Sand was invited to an exquisite musical soirée at the home of this last.

Throughout November and December Didier pestered her, unwilling to accept that their relationship had come to an end. On 13 December she was again invited to Chopin's. She wore her Turkish costume, complete with slippers. While Liszt and Chopin played duets, she smoked her long pipe, listened quite mesmerized by the frail perfectionist pianist. By the end of the year Didier had finally accepted that his intimacy with Sand had come to an end, as his *Journal* bitterly records. He continued to long hopelessly for her, as she longed hopelessly for Michel—while becoming increasingly intrigued by Chopin.

Meanwhile the cultural activities of the salon continued apace, including a concert that brought together Liszt and Berlioz, a Franco-Hungarian collaboration of wild Romantic fervour. But for all the exquisite musical events and engrossing intellectual conversation, Sand remained deeply unhappy. She was impatient to see Michel. And Maurice's life was becoming increasingly hard to bear at the college, where he was bullied, ostensibly because his mother was the notorious George Sand. At first Casimir was opposed to Sand's proposal to remove him from the school and have him educated by a tutor at home, but he then agreed and Sand quickly engaged a tutor before he could change his mind. The costs of a private tutor, however, stretched Sand's resources. Tension mounted again between Sand and Buloz. She was busy working on her *Oeuvres complètes*, which already stretched to twenty-four volumes. The first was published on 31 December 1836, less than five years after she had begun work on *Indiana*, her first solo novel.

In the new year, back at Nohant, life had to be rearranged to allow for Maurice's schooling. Eugène Pelletan arrived to be Maurice's tutor, on 24 January. Sand nicknamed him "le Pélican" on account of his skinny, stiff physique and misanthropic disposition. Although his teaching would turn out to be unsatisfactory, his arrival marked the beginning of a period in which, no longer anxious about Maurice, except during periods of ill health, Sand settled back into the rhythms of her country house. She was able to put in a considerable amount of work on *Mauprat*, the novel on which she had been working for some time.

Mauprat gradually became a fictional exploration of the possibility of a man being transformed by a woman's love. Like *Wuthering Heights*, published a decade later, with which it bears numerous points of comparison, at the outset the male protagonist is a wild animal: "a wounded wolf" in *Mauprat* ("an accursed beast" in Brontë's novel). The latter is a tragedy, but the ending of Sand's novel is happy, and delightfully improbable: Mauprat is wholly transformed by his cousin Edmée, and they marry and live happily ever after.

As Sand worked to finish the novel, she was also writing desperate letters to Michel. *Mauprat* had essentially become a fantasy version of their
relationship. Hopelessly improbable it might be, but Sand refused to give
up believing that the happiness that she had shared with Michel might be
transformed into something like the marital bliss enjoyed, if only very
briefly, by Mauprat and Edmée. Sand and Michel had, after all, once
planned to live together.

The ending of *Mauprat* may be comically unlikely, straining the suspension of disbelief to the breaking point, but this should not for a moment
suggest that Sand had altogether lost her astute pragmatism in matters feminist. That spring of 1837, Lamennais persuaded her, on a brief visit to the
capital, to collaborate on *Le Monde*. Her first "Lettre à Marcie" was published on 12 February. Several others would follow. These were essentially
fictional letters, written by a man advising a woman who is without money
on matters concerning her life as a woman and the choices and possibilities
open to her. As Sand's relationship with Michel deteriorated, she was no
doubt exploring precisely these possibilities. Lamennais's editorial interference was quickly provoked, however. The third letter, an outspoken
defence of divorce, was heavily cut, as were later letters.[16] The sixth
denounced the patriarchal conspiracy to stifle women's intellectual development: "Women receive a deplorable education. . . . This is the great
crime that men commit against them. . . . They have succeeded in bringing
about the enslavement and degradation of women, a condition they now
claim to be instituted by God, and part of an immutable law."[17]

If there is a distance between her perspicacious sociological and political observations, as explored in the *Lettres* and the fantasy of the relations
between a man and a woman in *Mauprat*, there is equally a gap between
these two and her letters of that spring to Michel. Here all that matters is
that she bring about a reconciliation that will facilitate the renewal of a sexual relationship. Despite accusing him of wanting a union which she goes
as far as to describe as one based on the principle of absolute and brutal
domination like that of a bygone barbaric age, she nevertheless claims that
what she wants is simply to bring him happiness and pleasure. At one point
Sand asks that he deny rumours that he is seeing a certain "Marie." According to local rumour, she claimed in a letter that March, "you are all but
being accused of criminal activity and bestiality."[18] Sand had hoped that
Michel would feel moved to make some effort to see her, but in the event it
was she who stopped off at Bourges on 10 and 11 April, en route for

Nohant.[19] They saw each other a number of times during the two days that she was there. Their coming together was as passionate as ever, but their parting, characteristically, full of reproach and distrust. Michel again accused her of having had Gévaudan as a lover. Sand reproached Michel for his attitude. All she had ever asked of him, she wrote, was that he be happy. He, on the other hand, remained suspicious, quick to accuse, and unforgiving.[20]

There were further meetings between the unhappy Sand and Michel, in Bourges, Nohant, and at a midway point, symbolic no doubt of a mutual desire not to be seen to be the one who makes all the concessions. Meanwhile Michel complained that his meetings with George sparked days of marital strife, and he continued to maintain that he suspected Sand of infidelity. These were mere excuses for his dwindling desire to maintain the relationship. He was clearly an ambitious man; the affair might interfere with his career and he may also have suspected that Sand's feelings for him might not last forever. Despite her extravagant promises, which suggested a willingness to submit to his control, Michel may have known that such a contradiction with her theoretical feminist views would not be lived out within their relationship for long. In a letter written at the same time to a common friend, she expressed her anguish over Michel's infidelities, but also wrote: "I will lift women up from their abject state, both in my life and in my writings." Sand was clearly aware of the potential for contradiction between the lived and the written.

The relationship, remarkably, continued. Their sexual life was passionate, and there are intimations of sadomasochistic activity. Unusually, Sand's private life was for once interfering with her working life, or so she claimed that May: "My head feels broken by the labours of an arid night, cigars and coffee have not been able to sustain my poor nerves. . . . My body is still dislocated from another terrible but delicious weariness: I retain the stigmata in a thousand places. . . ."[21] Here Sand is very clear that Michel was her "master," that her obsession with him was of a quite different order from his interest in her. But she was prepared to submit to him further. In response to her imploring letters, Michel replied complaining of the "double battle" he was fighting—against his wife and his mistress— and described his desire to retreat, hermit-like, to a cabin on the Mediterranean coast! Sand's reply, written that same May, is breathtaking: "You taunt me with the idea that you are going to go and live in a cabin. God will be looking after me if he exorcises your wish. I will soon be close to you; in me you will find the Negro devoted to looking after your body, the faithful dog, happy to elicit at least a useful and recognized devotion. And soon you will understand that the love of a woman is not a *base* thing, and that the low men against whom you regret not being able to measure yourself are not, and never will be, like you."[22]

Marie d'Agoult was once again staying at Nohant and recorded Sand's state in her journal: she was, she wrote, "swallowed up in a weighty state of nonbeing."[23] Sand was aware of the trap in which she was caught and which she had in a sense conspired to create. On 5 June she wrote to Michel: "You maltreat me and insult me, because during the course of our battles you have seen that my love is more solid and deep than you imagined. You are abusing it. This is what we do to everything, and in relation to everything. If we see a flower whose perfume tempts us we crush it in order to enjoy it. . . . Man wants to destroy in order to possess. . . . My heart is full of love, but my head is filled with memories, and experiences. Never have I felt, in such an irrevocable way, that it [our relationship] is an impossible one."[24]

Sand was finally becoming aware, gradually and painfully, of the hopelessness of her love, and its pathology. Her feelings for Michel were not simply and purely those of love. They arranged a further meeting, but this time it was Sand who cancelled it. "I am ill," she wrote, "I cannot travel tomorrow in the heat, and I have not the strength to leave this evening. I would arrive broken, and you would take no pleasure, I imagine, in receiving me in your arms in such a state at the inn."[25] What she wanted was to see whether Michel would encourage her to come in any case. Perhaps she hoped that he would offer to be *her* servant, attending to her, broken and exhausted. But no such offer was forthcoming. Her response was to displace and transpose her correspondence with Michel onto a fictional and altogether more controllable plane, but one that nevertheless intersected intimately with real life. The more reasoned debate was written into her *Lettres à Marcie*. Something rather different appears as a set of fictional dialogues.

Sand's "Entretiens journaliers avec . . . docteur Piffoël" ("Dialogues with Dr. Piffoël"), written between 1837 and 1841, were not published until after her death.

Piffoël is the fictitious name she had adopted in play with Liszt and Marie. Piffoël, some kind of other self, represents the free Sand: "What terrible calm in your soul! Has the flame been extinguished? I greet you,

Piffoël, full of grace, wisdom is within you . . . ! Holy fatigue, mother of all rest, come down on us, poor dreamers, now and at the hour of our death. So shall it be."[26] Sand had regained her calm. Two days later she wrote at greater length, revealing the complexities of her own understanding of what she had lived through: "Must it be that the object we love be as blind, as devoted, as indefatigable and as tender as a mother for her firstborn?—No, Piffoël, [s]he does not need to be all these things. . . ." She denounced self-denial, an attitude she had assumed with Casimir: "I accept you, you *are mine*, and I am yours also, because I have retained nothing of myself. . . . No.—No, Piffoël, doctor of psychology, you are no more than a fool." Men, Sand now believed, despised devotion. What they seek is domination: "To possess, to absorb, these are the only conditions to which he will commit himself. . . . To be loved like a God. . . ." The only path open to women, if this "tyranny" is to be controlled, is, Sand argued, "base flattery."

Sand's "dialogues" allowed her to consider aspects of her own psychology (and Michel's in particular) that were brutally exposed in her relationship with him. But all this mattered for her heroines too: "My dear Piffoël, learn then the science of life and when you dabble in writing novels, try to understand better the human heart." And her writing is shot through with irony: "Never make your ideal woman a strong soul, disinterested, courageous, candid. The public will hiss at you and salute you with the hideous name of Lélia the Powerless! Powerless!" The irony soon falls away, to be replaced by anger—and resilience: "Yes . . . powerless to submit to servility, adulation, baseness, powerless to respond to your fearfulness. Stupid creature, incapable of killing without laws that punish murder with murder and who has neither strength nor vengefulness except in the face of slander and libel!"

Sand had not established a monogamous relationship with Michel. He had undoubtedly wielded enormous control over their relationship, but she remained free to walk away: "When you find a female who knows how to leave you, your vain power turns to fury, and your fury is met with a smile, an adieu, a casting out into eternal oblivion."[27]

What Sand had discovered in herself, while trying to fathom the experiences of those weeks in which her obsession with Michel de Bourges had been so all-consuming, was something more profound, more peculiar to herself, more real, than the Romantic *ennui* of the French, or the *Sehnsucht* of the German Romantics. Exacerbated by that old "ache," she had longed with a quite uncontrolled desperation for mutual acceptance. Reflecting in tranquillity, informed by an acute sensibility and intelligence, and marshalling considerable intellectual honesty and courage, she recognized, in the course of writing the "Dialogues," that she needed to continue exploring the question of power. For the time being, she had to wait, while the "stigmata," both real and metaphorical, healed.

XIX

From the Real to the Sublime

"Why cry and why not cry? All these instinctive
emotions, which are motivated by something
outside reason and will, mean something
certainly, but what?"

That deeper bruising which is not visible to the eye, combined with the
real physical marks left by her relationship with Michel and which perhaps
healed more quickly, explains a period of relative peace in Sand's otherwise eventful private life. Her relationship with Liszt, which was one of
friendship, was nevertheless passionate, and it provided some of the comfort and support which she had hitherto found only in intimate sexual relationships. Liszt's piano playing calmed her and was a source of quiet
strength. In her diary entry for 3 June 1837 she wrote: "When Franz plays
the piano . . . I am soothed. . . ." More tellingly she adds, "All my pains are
translated into poetry."[1] The entry continues, "All my instincts are elevated. It is above all the chord of generosity that must be made to
vibrate."[2] Sand recognized in Liszt a great and tortured creator: "a powerful artist, sublime in the great things, always superior in the small ones, yet
sad, and troubled by a secret wound."[3]

Liszt and Marie had arrived at the beginning of May, and they stayed
until 24 July. The days passed pleasantly, and at night the novelist and composer worked at the same table. That summer, astonishingly, Sand finished
Mauprat and immediately embarked on, and finished, *Les Maîtres Mosaïstes*
(*The Master Mosaicists*). Set in Venice, the novel draws on her own exten-

sive experiences there. More striking is the recurrence within this novel of a "double."

The female double is common in her fiction, as in so much women's writing. Symptomatic no doubt of Sand's awareness of the traditional split between the woman as mother and as whore, in other words "woman" as often represented in fiction written by or from the point of view of male authors. In *Indiana* it is the eponymous heroine and Noun that form this couple. In *Lélia* it is again the eponymous heroine, this time paired with her courtesan half-sister, Pulchérie. A second group of pairs is made up of doubles cast as male/female alter egos, as in *Jacques*.[4]

A third group which begins to emerge, and which is arguably more problematic, is one of male brothers or half-brothers. This pairing, which will be essential to her famous novel *La Petite Fadette,* emerges in *The Master Mosaicists*. It matters more in the later novel, but this earlier exploration of the fraternal is symbolic of a fascination with sameness and difference in a private sense, solidarity and individualism in the public domain. The use of the two brothers is also frequently associated with incest. There is nothing new about the basis of the story.[5]

Sand's productivity in 1837 was remarkable. And while she finished *Mauprat* and embarked on *The Mosaicists,* Liszt transcribed Beethoven's symphonies, completing the first, second, fifth, and sixth.[6]

Didier arrived on 15 June, lovesick and irritating as ever, dismayed by Sand's friendship with the actor Pierre-François Bocage, star of Dumas's *Anthony.* There was clearly no desire on Sand's part for renewed intimacy with Didier. In his torment, his sleep was disturbed by terrible nightmares in which he even became murderous. Sand, needless to say, had been his imagination's victim. Terrified by his psychic torment, Didier left for some days, returning on July 14. Meanwhile other guests had arrived: the lawyer François Rollinat, her lifelong friend, and Félicien Mallefille, the tutor who had replaced the unsatisfactory Pelletan, and Bocage once again. Didier supposed that it was to Bocage that Sand was most drawn. Marie had apparently confirmed this suspicion, and Didier finally decided to leave Nohant on the fifteenth, the day after his return. He noted his leave-taking in his *Journal:* "She takes me in her arms, and I kiss those huge, dry, impenetrable eyes."[7]

Liszt, whatever the impending disasters of his relationship with Marie, could not but make the most of teasing Bocage about Sand and the possibility of establishing an intimate relationship with her. Sand was irritated. On 24 July both Liszt and Marie went on their way, separately. And Marie, who would soon become well known under her publishing name—Daniel Stern—wrote of her hostess at Nohant:

> It has been a useful insight to see, next to George the great poet, George the uncontrolled child, George the weak woman, weak even in her audacity, inconstant in her feelings, in her opinions, illogical in her life, always influenced by the unpredictability of things, rarely guided by reason and experience. I have recognized how childish it was of me to have believed (and this thought often filled me with sadness) that she alone could give Liszt's life everything necessary, that I was an unhappy barrier between two destinies made to fuse with, and complete, each other.[8]

The calm of Sand's platonic relationship with Liszt, and their admiration for each other's work, explain in part Marie's somewhat exaggerated attitude. She herself was more critical of his work, and her encouragement had an urgency that bordered on bullying, compared with Sand's disinterested, fostering admiration. Sand remained a close friend of both Marie and Liszt. Their daughter, Cosima, would marry Wagner.

After their departure, in the newly recovered comparative privacy of her own home, she consummated her relationship with Bocage. They moved temporarily to Fontainebleau, travelling regularly to Paris. In Fontainebleau they stayed at the same Hôtel Britannique to which Sand had retreated with Musset four years earlier. Did Sand return to refresh her memory—for the purposes of fiction?

At the beginning of July Sand had learnt of her mother's rapidly deteriorating health. Sand visited her regularly. Sophie-Victoire made plain that she did not want to see a priest at her bedside, claiming with theological logic that it was unnecessary. She had no fear of meeting her Maker; she had lived a godly life. What she wanted therefore, during her last days, was that there be an atmosphere of good cheer about her bed. Dying would be, Sand believed, a welcome release for her mother.

Anticipating her mother's death was not the only family concern that preoccupied her that summer. There were other more urgent matters that, rather than requiring reflection, demanded physical and emotional energy.

Rumours reached her at Fontainebleau that during her absence, Casimir had set out with the intention of removing Maurice from Nohant. Nothing could have motivated Sand to swifter action. She immediately instructed Mallefille to bring the boy to her.[9] He set off on 13 August, returning triumphantly four days later. The story of the abduction seems, however, to have been no more than rumour.

On 19 August Sophie-Victoire died. Her funeral took place two days later, in the Church of Saint-Vincent de Paul, and the interment at the Cemetery of Montmartre. Sand believed that death had "cured her [mother] of the terrible weariness of living in this world." Sand was no doubt speaking also of her own fatigue. In a letter to Marie, written from Fontainebleau in September, she described a visit to the grave. Her mother, she wrote, "lies in the sun, under beautiful flowers where the butterflies flutter without thinking of death. I was so struck by the gaiety of the tomb which I went to see a few days ago in the Montmartre Cemetery, during magnificent weather, that I asked myself why our tears flow so much there? Why cry and why not cry? All these instinctive emotions, which are motivated by something outside reason and will, mean something certainly, but what?"[10]

Sand was shaken out of her confused bereavement by Casimir's latest actions. On 13 September he descended on Nohant to take possession of his daughter rather than his son. He successfully removed her to Guillery, the family house that he had finally inherited from his stepmother. With characteristic determination and efficiency Sand procured the necessary legal documents from ministers in Paris and arrived in style at Guillery on 25 September with a local police escort, papers in hand.

Sand's account of the escapade suggests a degree of mischievous enjoyment that cannot be wholly explained simply because of the successful outcome. Her stylistic expertise is very evident. The use of short sentences dominated by verbs, and the economical use of adjectives and adverbs, brilliantly conveys the breathless action and its pace: "I race to Paris. I send a telegram. I notify the police. I have a court order issued. I run to the ministers, I make a rumpus, I ensure that everything is in order, and I leave for Nérac, where I arrive in the morning, as fresh as a pickled herring after three days and three nights in a post chaise. . . ."

Sand orchestrated the recovery of Solange and ensured that it was done with due pomp and ceremony: "I cajole the Subprefect, who, moved to pity, climbs up to join me in my cab, the police lieutenant, the bailiff, etc., all the others are on horseback. Imagine the escort! What a departure from Nérac! What astonishment! The whole town, everyone in every street, is on its feet." Solange was handed from father to mother, "like a princess at the border between two States." What the actual exchange between husband and wife may have been no one will ever know. Sand claimed: "We exchanged a few pleasantries, the Baron and I. He warned me he would win back his son, with the law on his side, and we parted, each charmed by the other. . . ." So as to convey a sense of her own self-composure, not to say self-satisfaction, she added: "The next day I was possessed by a desire to see the Pyrenees, once again."[11] Sand was often drawn back to places that had been the setting of earlier dramatic episodes, as though the return might allow her to ascertain better the reality of those experiences.

Back at Nohant that autumn, Sand reflected on her hyperactivity: "Reconsider a moment what has happened during the past three months. . . . Can you even remember? Have you not already forgotten the detail? Your mother dead, your son saved, your daughter abducted and won back—and the rest!—you have been back to Franchard, and with whom? . . . You come back here to do what? What fate awaits you? Who will you love? From what will you suffer? Whom will you hate next month, or next year, or tomorrow?"[12] That autumn (on 30 October) she also heard that the body of Duris-Dufresne, her great friend and political ally from their La Châtre days, had been found in the Seine in Paris.

Sand's conversation with herself may be little more than romantic self-dramatization, but it reveals a woman capable of self-criticism, looking at her life with irony, even cynicism. There is a bleakness too, a deep regret that may explain the focus of her energy over the next few weeks, even months.

She gradually regained her equilibrium, and wrote to Pierre Leroux: "You have made me confess something to myself which has been a revelation, and one which explains a good many things."[13] Leroux arrived for a brief stay at Nohant that autumn of 1837. Sainte-Beuve had encouraged them to meet in 1835, and Sand had been deeply struck by his intellectual originality, his wide-ranging ideas that informed theories religious (pantheistic), political (utopian-socialist), and psycho-philosophical (he had expounded a neo-Pythagorean theory of the migration of souls). Leroux had had to abandon his academic career because of the needs of his family. His wife was probably mad, and certainly seriously incompetent, and he had numerous children. A convinced Saint-Simonian for a period, he had worked on the *Globe,* and then, collaborating with Jean Reynaud, had embarked on an ambitious *Encyclopédie universelle* in the footsteps of Diderot.

Sand knew Leroux's work, and admired the vitality and iconoclasm of his thinking, even though she did not always share his views or believe in his ideas. She was also deeply impressed by his social and intellectual commitment: Leroux's conviction that things mattered, and his discipline, had a good effect on Sand, and acted as a much-needed tonic. She worked quickly and steadily, producing a substantial number of pages of the novel on which she was working, first *La Dernière Aldini* (*The Last Aldini*), then *Orco*, every night. The first part of the former was published in the *Revue des Deux Mondes* on 1 December.

Once again her productivity was reinforced by financial need. Running Nohant, particularly if there were numerous guests, was expensive. She calculated that the annual costs of running the estate, including the fees of tutors for Solange and Maurice, required "an outlay of 25 to 30 thousand francs."[14] In addition, Sand also assisted needy friends, Stéphane de Grandsagne's brother, Jules, for example, who was imprisoned for bad debts.

Inspired intellectually by Leroux, Sand's life at Nohant was also soothed by the presence of Mallefille, who at some point became her lover. A writer (as well as tutor to Maurice), he was unassuming and gentle and disciplined in his work. Eventually Mallefille displaced Michel in Sand's affections. As she wrote to Frédéric Girerd, a friend she had made through Michel, in January 1838, "*I have finally wrestled the dragon to the floor. . . . The tenacious and destructive passion which had taken over my every faculty has finally been cured by another affection: it is gentler, less urgent, less rough too, and, I hope, will be more lasting. M[ichel] is now protected from any grief coming from me. He is in his element: it is what he needs. From time to time he sees people who are friends of mine and tells them that I am the only love of his life. What love! But I am no longer wounded.*"[15]

It was none other than Honoré de Balzac who pronounced Mallefille an inappropriate lover for Sand. He was visiting friends near Nohant in February 1838 and wrote to Sand: "I did not want . . . to return to Paris without having seen either the Lioness, or Nightingale, of Berry, in her den or nest, because you have remarkable strength and grace. . . . Y.d.s. [Your devoted servant] H. de Balzac." Balzac stayed from 24 February to 2 March. He described his visit, in detail and with delightfully undisguised male chauvinism, in a letter to his beloved Mme Hanska. Nohant had turned out to be more of a "lion's den":

I reached the Château of Nohant on the Saturday before Shrove Tuesday, towards half past seven in the evening, and I found comrade George Sand in her dressing gown, smoking an after-dinner cigar by the fireside, in a vast lonely room. She had pretty yellow slippers, decorated with little fringes, stylish hose, and red trousers. . . .

Balzac had a keen interest in physiognomy and considered himself, with characteristic modesty, an expert. He noted:

In terms of her physique, she has doubled the size of her chin, like an ecclesiastical canon. She has not a single white hair, despite fearful misfortunes, her tanned complexion remains unchanged, her fine beautiful eyes are quite as brilliant as ever, she has quite as silly a look when she thinks; but as I told her, having studied her, her whole physiognomy is in her eyes.

He thought her unhappy, and working too hard, which was saying something, given his own industry. Balzac adjusted his working hours while at Nohant, which was the reverse of Sand's writing pattern, and they enjoyed—unless Balzac was tempted to exaggerate—conversations lasting twelve hours. Her unhappiness was, he believed, a function of her inadequate relationships with men: "Here she is, truly retreated from life, condemning marriage and love, because, in one as in the other estate, she has only been disappointed." And he suggested that her requirements were unrealistic: "*Her* male is rare, that's all there is to it. He will be all the more so if she is difficult to love, and consequently it will be all the more difficult to find someone. She is boyish, she is an artist, she is great-hearted, generous, devout, and *chaste;* she has all the main characteristics of a man; *ergo,* she is not a woman. . . . I was talking to an ally." He acknowledged that despite these complexities, she was an excellent mother, and adored by her children, but he criticized her habit of dressing Solange as a little boy. She had allowed Maurice, on the other hand, to glimpse the dissipations of Paris too early. Maurice was twelve but, according to Balzac's sage judgement, already suffered from "a malady, a weariness." Sand, by contrast, "has the morals of a twenty-year-old, because she is fundamentally *chaste, prudish,* and is an artist only on the outside." He reported her heavy smoking, her debts "accrued for *tutti quanti,* friends and lovers. . . ." In short, she was not managing her life at all well. Above all she had chosen an inappropriate lover: "a man who is her inferior. In such a contract, there is nothing but disenchantment and disappointment for a woman with a fine mind; a woman must always love a man who is her superior, or she has to be completely fooled that such is the case."[16] Such were Balzac's egalitarian insights.

Sand was perfectly aware, or at least supposed, that she controlled her relationship with Mallefille. Later, in May 1838, she wrote to Albert Grzymała, "He is the only man who has given himself entirely and absolutely to me, without regret for the past, without reservations for the future. And then, he is such a good and kind nature that there is nothing I cannot encourage him to understand with time; he is a malleable wax on which I have imposed my seal, and when I want to change its imprint, I'll manage it with a little patience and precaution. . . ."[17] His self-abnegation and self-denial no doubt made the relationship an easy one, but it fell a long way short of an ideal of love which Sand claimed to have abandoned as an idea, but which in fact would soon reappear, in the person of her most famous lover, Frédéric Chopin.

Not long after Balzac's visit to Nohant, Auguste Charpentier arrived early in April to paint portraits of Sand and her children. But before what would be the most flattering of all Sand's portraits had been completed, the sittings were interrupted. Further financial negotiations with Casimir had to be managed in Paris. In the event Sand would eventually regain ownership of the Hôtel de Narbonne, although she would have to compensate Casimir. But the real gain was one very much more significant to her than the material one.

Sand arrived in Paris on 17 April and stayed with Charlotte Marliani. Here Chopin often played for a small and privileged audience. There were other meetings too. On 8 May he played at a dinner hosted by Astolphe de Custine, given for a group including Sand, Hugo, Charles Nodier, Sophie Gay (a novelist), and the duchesse d'Abrantès, who had been Balzac's mistress. Two weeks later Sand was forced to return to Nohant. Her financial affairs had been dealt with, and Maurice was ill.

From Nohant she considered the possibility that Chopin might become an intimate companion. She wrote to Albert Grzymała. There were a number of obvious problems: Chopin's love for Maria Wodzinska, and her own involvement with Mallefille. But Chopin was, Sand believed, an "angel." Michel de Bourges, her last great love, had been a "god." Real love Sand always personified in celestial terms.[18]

Chopin's heavenly nature also translated, however, into what Sand supposed was a certain prudishness when it came to matters of physical intimacy. In the same letter to Grzymała, she wrote, "He seems to despise, like the devout, human coarseness and blush at the temptations he has felt, and to fear sullying our love by further rapture. . . . Who then is the unfortunate woman who has left him these impressions of physical love? Has he then had a mistress unworthy of him?"[19] It may be, however, that Chopin's erotic desires were more homosexual than heterosexual. His letters to his close friend Titus Woyiechowski, written in his early twenties, communicate intense, and confused, emotions. His letters are often addressed to "DEAREST LIFE" and end "I have no one but you," or "I want you and I expect you clean-shaven," or "I kiss you heartily, right on the mouth, may I?"[20] He also confided to Titus that he would express in his compositions feelings that he would never articulate in words.

Sand returned to Paris on 26 June. Within days she would embark on what would be the most lasting relationship so far. Her attitude to Chopin's apparent fear of physical intimacy was one of astonished horror: "I have always felt repelled by this manner of envisaging the intimate embraces of love. If the final embrace is not a healthy thing, as pure, as devoted as the rest, then there is no virtue in abstention."[21] Sand did not accept the trenchant division of love into the "purely physical" and "purely intellectual." There was never "love without a single kiss and a lover's kiss devoid of sensual pleasure."[22] To separate the mind and body, Sand claimed, led to "convents and places of ill repute." She believed that the spiritual and the physical were constituent and inalienable facets of our fundamental humanity. Chopin, it seems, soon came to agree with her.

Sand had implored Grzymała to bring Chopin to Nohant: she would ensure that Mallefille had been dispatched on business elsewhere in good time. Less than a week later, she wrote simply to tell Grzymała that she had to be in Paris, again allegedly to attend to other practical matters. Charlotte Marliani had told Chopin that Sand was travelling up to Paris, and he, according to a hastily scribbled note to Charlotte, awaited her arrival with mixed feelings: "What is going to happen? God only knows, I don't feel well."[23]

In the weeks that followed, Sand and Chopin spent a good deal of time alone together, as well as in the company of Charlotte and Manuel Marliani, and Grzymała. Sand rented a tiny mansard room in the Rue Laffitte, under the name of Mme Dupin. Her pattern of work changed little and she signed a new contract with Buloz (and his partner Félix Bonnaire) on 26 July, requiring an annual output of two or three volumes. The agreement gave her publisher exclusive rights to all her work until 1 January 1840. Her writing would first appear in the *Revue des Deux Mondes* and then in book form. She would be paid 5,000 francs per column of a stated length.

By early September Sand and Chopin had settled into a happy relationship. "I am still in the state of bliss in which you left me," she wrote to Delacroix. "There is not the tiniest cloud in this pure sky, not a grain of sand in our lake. I'm beginning to believe that there are angels disguised as men who pass themselves off as such and who inhabit the earth for a while to console and lift up with them toward heaven the poor, exhausted and saddened souls who were ready to perish here below."[24]

But the supposedly "malleable" Mallefille had begun to show signs of resistance, now that Sand had abandoned him. She sent him to Leroux, who, she confidently believed, would quickly persuade him to see things more philosophically.[25] Meanwhile, angelic as Chopin continued to be, Paris was not heaven. What Sand could not bear was the thought of publicity. As Chopin's health was poor and there had been talk of tubercular symptoms, the best solution was to leave Paris for a milder climate. On 18 October Sand and her two children left Paris, travelling via her beloved Le Plessis. Chopin travelled separately for the sake of discretion. They met up in Perpignan at the end of the month, and on 1 November sailed from Port-Vendres, aboard the *Phénicien*, for Barcelona. From there, on 7 November 1838, Maurice, Solange and a maid, and Chopin boarded the steamer *El Mallorquín* and set sail for Majorca.

As they travelled south, what they expected was to be leaving the harshness of the winter and the crowds of the city behind to arrive in a quieter place, blessed with a mild, gentler climate. To their surprise, Palma was overrun by people: civil war on the continent had driven large numbers out and many were seeking refuge on the island. Unable to find suitable lodgings, they stayed briefly as paying guests of a family living in a somewhat insalubrious part of the town. Sand was keen to remove her charges to a healthier home, and with her usual energy and determination she set about finding an ideal nest. A few days later they were making their way to Establiments, a village some eight kilometres from Palma, to a house called "So'n Vent" (the house of the winds). The name would turn out to be unpropitious, but initially both Sand and Chopin believed they had arrived, on 15 November, in an almost tropical Eden: "I am in Palma," Chopin wrote, his delight visible in the desire fully to catalogue the tangible stimuli "among palms, cedars, cacti, olives, pomegranates, etc." He alludes to the value of precious stones, evoking the splendour of his surroundings: "The sky is like turquoise, the sea like lapis lazuli, mountains like emerald, air like heaven. Sun all day long, and hot. . . . At night guitars and singing for hours. Huge balconies. . . . In short a glorious life!" Sand, unusually concise, described the place as "the promised land."[26]

The landscape, the flora, and the climate were the principal sources of pleasure, and a dramatic change in the weather necessarily brought about a complete change in the mood of Sand and her party. The rain set in, the temperature dropped, and their house began to absorb water "like a sponge." They were wrapped in a cold damp layer. Sand described the house as a coat about their shoulders "like a garment of ice."[27]

They had been living an isolated life. As early as December Chopin had been aware of the serious deterioration in his health. He had written to his compatriot, the musician Jules Fontana, with typical dry humour: "Three doctors, the most esteemed on the island, have examined me. One smelt my sputum, the other thumped me to see where the sputum is coming from, the other spoke to me having heard me expectorating. The first said I was going to die, the second that I was dying, the third that I was already done for. . . . It was only with enormous difficulty that I managed to avoid bloodletting and blisters. . . . My illness has wreaked havoc with the *Preludes*."

Although Chopin's cough was the most violent, and he expectorated blood, they were all suffering. His illness was diagnosed as a contagious consumption. They may all have been afflicted: "We became an object of repulsion and terror for the local population."

Gomez, the owner of the property they were renting, decided to evict them on the grounds that they were a source of pernicious infection.[28] He also required them, as he was entitled within the law, to pay for the replacement of virtually the entire contents of the house, on the grounds that it would all have to be burnt. After a brief stay with the French consul in Palma (10 to 14 December), the party made its way to the massive Villa Valldemosa, some twenty kilometres north of Palma, where Sand had arranged to rent three cells and a garden at the all but abandoned monastery. They arrived on 21 December and Sand described it to Charlotte Marliani as "poetry, solitude, everything artistic that there is . . . under the sky!"[29]

Until three years earlier, the community had consisted of thirteen monks, but the order had since been dissolved and the monks expelled from the island. The buildings had not been left entirely uninhabited. There was one former monk still in residence, a self-appointed pharmacist who sold them the medicines they needed at extortionate prices. A second former monk would, at night, haunt the corridors of the monastery, inebriated, brandishing a knife in one hand, a rosary in the other, calling out for a mysterious Brother Nicolas who had left years earlier.[30] They had most contact, however, with a certain Maria-Antonia, who lived in the neighbouring cell and offered her services to them, ostensibly in the name of Christian charity. But, Sand became increasingly convinced, she was stealing food and even their clothes.

Despite continuing ill health and despite the inhospitable company, the austere, dramatic beauty of the place was a source of delight, even awe. Sand described it as the "most romantic sojourn in the world."[31] She was completing *Spiridion* and the monastic setting was no doubt a source of inspiration for the novel, which is essentially a religious one. Very much influenced by Pierre Leroux's ideas, *Spiridion* explores different kinds of Christian belief and doctrine. Broadly speaking, the shift of the novel's focus of attention, from Catholicism to Christian Socialism, follows Sand's own religious development. Sainte-Beuve thought it inaccessible. Rather like *Lélia* in its mixing of genres, the novel explores various philosophical questions—a blend of ideas and fiction that Dostoevsky found interesting and inspiring. But the complexities of the novel's construction certainly confuse some of the arguments.

The story tells of the eponymous abbé; the narrator is a Benedictine monk, Alexis; his audience is Angel, a novice. The novel becomes, however, increasingly concerned with social change. A few years later, after the Revolution of 1848, Sand's ideas about the justifiability of violence would change. After the suppression of the Paris Commune in 1871, at the very end of her life, she would become, broadly speaking, a pacifist. A similar pattern is visible in Tolstoy's thinking. In *Spiridion*, however, change comes about through violence, and those who suffer go as far as to thank their assailants. Alexis, who expires under the rebels' blows, declares, "Liberty can only be bought at the price of social cataclysm and revolution."[32] Sand's Russian readers remembered the phrase. Dostoevsky, Gorky, Turgenev, Belinsky, Herzen, and Bakunin all read Sand with great admiration. Only Tolstoy supported the state's opposition to her.[33] In 1847, when Pauline Viardot, celebrated singer and close friend of Sand's, visited Russia, she wrote to her, "Here all your works are translated from the moment they appear. . . . Everyone reads them, from top to bottom of the social ladder. . . . Men adore you. . . . Women idolize you. . . . All in all you reign, in Russia, more sovereign than the Tsar."[34]

Sustaining the writing of *Spiridion* at Valldemosa was not easy. Never had she had to struggle with so many domestic and administrative responsibilities. Among the thorniest problems was ensuring that Chopin's piano be released by Spanish Customs. Then there would be the very difficult business of organizing its delivery to one of the least accessible residences in the world. They themselves had walked the last stage of the journey, abandoning the cart that had brought them from Palma.

Chopin too was deeply impressed by the drama of their clifftop vantage point. On 28 December he wrote to Fontana, "It's a huge Carthusian monastery, stuck down between rocks and sea, where you may imagine me, without white gloves or haircutting, as pale as ever, in a cell with such doors as Paris never had for gates." If his cell was not altogether hospitable, he looked out on life through "a small window, outside the window orange trees, palms and cypresses." But he also added, by way of a not altogether negligible footnote, that his cell resembled "a tall coffin."[35]

Sand cooked, taught the children, cared for Chopin, and regularly journeyed to Palma, intent on finding the right foods for Chopin, whose cough was as bad as ever and who was now losing weight alarmingly. The local people continued to treat them as lepers: "They call us pagans, Muslims, Jews," and she adds, presumably to distance herself from their racism, "which is the worst as far as they are concerned."[36] Yet whatever the difficulties of life at Valldemosa, whatever the sense of isolation, both Chopin and Sand were able to work well. Towards the end of January Chopin sent to Fontana his twenty-four *Preludes* (opus 28). When Sand had spoken of the "imitative harmony" of one of the pieces, Chopin vociferously denied her "puerile" interpretation. "He was right," Sand later wrote. "His genius was full of mysterious harmonies of nature, translated by means of sublime equivalents in his musical thinking, and not by servile repetition of exterior sounds. He has conferred on a single instrument the power to articulate the infinite. . . . Only Mozart is his superior."[37]

There were periods when Chopin's condition deteriorated and Sand had to care for him. She nursed him with devotion. He was very aware of her belief in him, and admired her remarkable spirit. To Grzymała he wrote: "I see her constantly concerned for me. She has to nurse me single-handedly because God save us from the local doctors! I see her making my bed, arranging my room . . . giving up everything for me . . . looking after the children. . . . In addition, she writes."[38] His condition no doubt exacerbated by fever, Chopin gradually began to show increasing signs of mental instability, not unlike those of Musset. On one occasion Sand had travelled to Palma with Maurice and Solange and their return had been delayed by appalling weather. Chopin waited for them, afraid for them and overcome by what Sand described as "calm despair." He had been caught up in a terrible waking dream, a vivid hallucination in which he had witnessed each of them dead. He himself had been drowning in a lake; "weighty frozen drops of water were falling on my chest, in strict [musical] time." Sand recognized that it was time to leave the extraordinary villa. Chopin "was dying to leave," she noted. "His mind had been flayed alive. . . . The fold of a rose leaf, the shadow of a fly, made him bleed."[39] They left Valldemosa on 11 February 1839, but the journey home was to be a perilous one.

First they had difficulty hiring a carriage because of continuing suspicions about their infectious health. The vehicle that finally took them down the mountain threw them about so violently that Chopin suffered a haemorrhage. By the time they boarded *El Mallorquín* on the thirteenth, he was very seriously ill. The hundred or so pigs that accompanied them on their crossing to Barcelona did little to improve the atmosphere. When they reached the capital Chopin was coughing "bowlfuls of blood." Fortunately, there was a French naval vessel in harbour and he was immediately taken aboard and seen by the ship's doctor.

On 24 February 1839 they finally arrived in Marseille, where Sand arranged for Chopin to be seen at once by Dr. Cauvière, whom she had met in Paris. It is only in retrospect that she seems to have recognized how very dangerous the flight from Majorca had been. It was not simply a matter of physical health. As she wrote to Charlotte Marliani: "One more month and we would have died in Spain, Chopin and I . . . he of melancholy and loathing, I of anger and indignation." Hers was the more resilient disposition.[40]

Dr. Cauvière recommended that they stay in the south until Chopin's health was restored. He prescribed sun and rest. While on Majorca they had been kept very much at a distance, in Marseille, despite their best efforts to remain incognito, every writer, musician, artist, or bohemian soon learnt of their presence in the city and sought them out. Sand fought hard to keep everyone away. It even occurred to her that the best solution might be to spread the news that they had both died. She wrote to Charlotte: "Don't worry . . . if news reaches you from this country that I am dying. . . . If this continues [the pestering] we will send out dozens of notices of both our deaths, so that we are mourned and left in peace."[41]

Whatever the more complex psychological reasons for wanting the admiring public to leave them alone, Sand needed peace to write. Her finances were, once again, in a highly precarious state. She even had to instruct Hippolyte to sell a parcel of land in the Vallée Noire, a course of action which she would have seen as a last resort, but her debts had now reached some 70,000 francs. The costs of the Majorcan episode were very much higher than anticipated and the Narbonne property had needed expensive repairs.

Her letters to Buloz are almost exclusively taken up with financial discussions. Sometimes she complained that she had been poorly remunerated. He, in return, complained that her work had not always been quite what he had anticipated when he had paid advances. *Les Sept Cordes de la lyre* (*The Seven Strings of the Lyre*), for which he had paid an advance of 5,000 francs, and *Spiridion,* which was being serialized in the *Revue des Deux Mondes,* were both too philosophical, too lacking in dramatic action. *Spiridion* also lacked a feminine presence. These were not the kinds of works that her loyal reading public wanted. *Uscoque,* which she had written some time earlier, was much more the kind of novel he had anticipated. It is an adventure story, and the twists and turns of its plot and its lively characters, complete with pirate, made it an obviously saleable work.

The novel had not, however, come easily: "My poor Chopin, although as well as he could be, can hardly bear to be alone. He is bored when there are no playful children, or reading aloud, beside his chair." In the event Sand simply stayed in bed herself, and wrote until the work was finished. The delivery was, she wrote graphically, "by forceps."

Whatever the weaknesses of *Spiridion,* Sand had not been ready simply to write to please an audience which ranged from "grand ladies . . . to their chambermaids. These men [Sand's publishers] are hoping for some short story à la Balzac. Not for all the world will I condemn myself to work in this way eternally. I hope I have escaped that forever."[42]

Her next novel, *Gabriel,* would seem, however, to have been written to satisfy her publisher and her public. Yet it remains one of her most engaging and successful books, praised by Balzac for the sophistication of its psychological insights. Where *Spiridion* treats questions of religion and society, *Gabriel* explores, with extraordinary insight, questions of sex, gender, and society. Gabriel is a princess who is given a boy's education by mistake, and who turns out to be a perfectly competent "prince." Thus the hero-heroine of the novel is a woman, but she has been dressed as a boy, and then a young man, until the age of twenty-five. To please her lover Astolphe, she agrees to dress in women's clothes, but only for three months of the year. Gabriel wants to be a companion and colleague of Astolphe's, as well as his lover. She wants to be like him, and thereby equal to him. Astolphe, on the other hand, wants her to distinguish herself from him. In turning away from her and taking up with a prostitute who becomes his mistress, he implies that what he wants is to mark himself out from, and to dominate and control, the woman who is his intimate companion.

No doubt there are parallels with Sand's relationships with both Musset and Chopin. The former, who was constantly attracted to a dissolute way of life, had always been ill at ease with Sand's independence, resilience, and discipline. He, like Astolphe, struggled to love a woman who was his equal. The difficulty, the reader supposes, is that both men can only love women whom they despise at least to some degree, women who are precisely *not* their social or intellectual equals. Chopin, on the other hand, was clearly comforted by Sand's feminine, her maternal side, while depending on her masculine strengths, her robustness, her courage. When Gabriel dies, dressed as a man, it is with the word "liberty" on her feminine lips. Gabriel's vision of who she is, and who she is allowed to be, is an anguished one. Her androgynous self-understanding is not one that can be easily lived out. "It still seems to me that I am something more than a woman."[43]

The points of comparison between Astolphe and Sand's former lovers, and current love, are more obvious than those between her heroine and herself. Sand's heroines tend to fascinate because they, like their creator, remain in many ways contradictory. The complexities of Gabriel's psycho-sexuality are powerfully conveyed but never explained. But the parallels are quite as evident as those between the real men she knew and those of her fictions. A few months after finishing *Gabriel*, finally returning to Nohant after a brief trip to Genoa with Chopin and the children (3–18 May), she wrote to Charlotte: "I no longer like travel. . . . Or rather I am no longer in a state in which I can enjoy it. I am no longer a boy."[44] What explains the death of her boyish self? What were its consequences? How much did it have to do with the historical moment, and how much the events of her private life? On 12 May 1839 there had been an uprising in Paris, led by Blanqui (condemned to death the following January), Barbès, and Bernard. It had failed. Sand described it as "another fine gust of wind against the monarchy, while waiting for the inevitable shipwreck, but one that would come too late."[45] She felt an urgency, a foreboding about political events, and at home she had two children and the vulnerable Chopin to care for. It must have seemed as though there was little opportunity to express her boyish self. But she hoped that her domestic life had arrived at a point of stability that would last for some time to come.

XX

Creativity and Compromise

"Life is a journey with life as its destination."

There is a certain irony in the comparatively settled domesticity of Sand and Chopin's life together. Their relationship was as close as either of them would come to happily married life. Yet from the outside, friends described their ménage in far from conventional terms. Elizabeth Barrett Browning, who visited them with her husband, dedicated her sonnets to an androgynous figure, "a large-brained woman and great-hearted man who has given herself the name George Sand."[1] And Sand herself had described her relationship with Chopin in quasi-incestuous terms. He was, supposedly, "another Maurice."[2] But whatever the perceived oddities of their relationship, their shared life assumed an ordered regularity. Both worked steadily but followed quite different routines, Chopin retiring early, while Sand worked through the night. His annual pattern had developed a rhythm which Sand had, to some extent, to follow also if she was to be with him. The winters he reserved for teaching and the occasional concert performance, while the summers were spent composing. The former had to take place in Paris, while the latter he now undertook at Nohant. Movement between the capital and their country home suited them both, and the year of 1840 was an exception, spent entirely in Paris. Dr. Gustave Papet kept a careful eye on Chopin's health and he soon came to know Sand's old circle of friends: Duteil, Fleury, Papet, Planet, Rollinat. New friends and admirers also called at Nohant, some staying for long periods. The Viardots were regular guests, as was Delacroix. Others passed through: Sand's former lover Bocage, Matthew Arnold, Emmanuel Arago (lawyer, playwright, and later diplomat), the painter Théodore Rousseau, who drew inspiration from Sand's beloved Forest of Fontainebleau.

The hospitality that was always offered at Nohant was expensive. Sand calculated that life in Paris cost only half as much. Sand had two pavilions at the bottom of the garden of 16 Rue Pigalle prepared for the family. While the work was being done she stayed with the children in Paris with Charlotte and her husband. Chopin's apartment in the Rue Tronchet was damp and uncomfortable. He would soon move out and share one of the two pavilions with Maurice. Sand and Solange shared the other. Balzac, a frequent visitor, described the flower-filled room in which she received her guests, with a magnificent piano in the centre of things. Chopin, he recorded, was always there too, and in the bedroom was an arrangement of two mattresses side by side on the floor.[3]

Buloz, now royal commissioner at the Comédie-Française (and administrator from 5 March 1840), encouraged Sand to continue to write for the theatre, assuring her that very substantial amounts of money could be made. Her first plays had not been great successes, but desperate for money, and keen to provide Marie Dorval with an appropriate role, she responded with *Cosima*. Initially entitled *La Haine dans l'amour (Hatred Within Love)*, it was accepted by the National Theatre Committee on 26 September 1839. Its première would be in the spring. And the part of the play's heroine would be taken by Marie Dorval. That winter she spent long evenings working with Marie on the script. Maurice, now in his mid-teens, was intent on becoming a painter. On 27 February 1840 he was officially apprenticed to Delacroix, but he spent much of his time at home. Solange showed no signs of settling to anything and became an increasing worry. While looking after Chopin and keeping an eye on her children, Sand anticipated the opening night of *Cosima*, and Marie's performance.

The common practice of hiring a group to encourage an admiring reception was not one in which Sand had indulged, but the play's disastrous reception cannot be entirely explained by the absence of a claque. It was poorly constructed and above all wholly lacking in dramatic interest. Because Sand had written it consciously in a bid to make money quickly, she took the play's failure in her stride. She withdrew it after seven performances, and wrote to Marie, "We will laugh. . . . It is the best remedy for all human things."[4] Her unusual sangfroid also arose from having implicated Marie in her failure. She was concerned above all to ensure that the actress did not take the play's disaster too much to heart.

Despite the considerable disappointment of *Cosima*, Sand's fascination with the theatre and theatre people, first excited as a small child at her actress-mother's side, continued, although her next work would be a novel. She became close friends with Pauline Viardot. In the summer of 1840 the "family" was to stay in Paris, mainly for financial reasons; but Sand spent 12 to 18 August at Cambrai with Pauline and, some days later, her husband, Louis. Pauline was a brilliant singer whose career looked poised for success: her contract to sing at Cambrai was an encouraging sign. Her husband had given up his job as the director of a Parisian theatre, primarily to act as his wife's agent and manager. While enjoying the place and people at Cambrai and relishing Pauline's exquisite singing, Sand wrote furiously. By the time she returned to Paris, the next novel was half finished.

But *Le Compagnon du tour de France* (*The Journeyman-Carpenter*) was not the kind of novel Buloz wanted from Sand, nor was her next one, *Horace*. The first was published, but it did not appear in the *Revue*, one of the stipulations of the contract that both author and publisher had signed. Buloz refused to publish *Horace* in any form. The breakdown in relations between Sand and Buloz had been long in coming.

Sand's correspondence that autumn reveals her growing interest and concern for social reform, in particular for class reform. As she wrote to the activist artisan Agricole Perdiguier, "The future of the world is in the hands of the people, and above all the working class. In time the masses will emerge from the blindness and crude ignorance where the so-called *enlightened* classes have held them in chains. . . . It is the [united] country which will be master of the world, the initiator of civilization."[5] The social vision of *The Journeyman* (in which the character Pierre Huguenin is based on Perdiguier), and to an even greater extent *Horace*, was not compatible with Buloz's royalist sympathies. But since the uprising in Paris of 1832 Sand had been haunted by her memory of the screams of terror of the students and workers who were being massacred. She had heard them all too clearly from her balcony. Eight years on she was able to describe vividly the experience of being there.

Yet *Horace* is not a historical novel but a *roman à thèse*. Her concern is to propose a new vision of how things might be. The novel's hero, Paul Arsène, exhorts the masses to revolt, and to work together towards a new order. It was all more than Buloz could stomach. Not only did he refuse to publish the novel, he counterattacked: he commissioned an article for the

Revue that denounced the "communism" of individuals like Proudhon and Louis Blanc. Leroux certainly considered Sand a communist. He wrote to her not long after the *Revue* article appeared: "Because you are a *communist,* and I am a *communist.* It is only Monsieur de Lamennais who does not want to be one, and in this he is wrong." "*Communionism*" was, he thought, a better term, conveying the notion of "a social doctrine founded on fraternity; but the people who always aim at a practical goal have preferred *communism* to designate a republic where equality may reign."[6]

What was clearly needed was a rival publication to disseminate communist ideas and to defend certain ideological notions abused in the *Revue.* Leroux and Louis Viardot, who was something of an entrepreneur, founded and funded the new *Revue Indépendante.* The first issue appeared in early November 1841. Sand had contributed ninety-six pages: the first instalment of *Horace,* rejected by Buloz.

Although the journal struggled to survive, Sand became more and more convinced of the rightness of its politics, and continued to develop her own ideas for social reform informed by a liberal Christianity: while "charity and fraternity" might be widely preached, this meant nothing and was thus simply one of numerous examples of bourgeois hypocrisy. These were ideas which "have never interested people unless they profit from them, and the institutions created by the bourgeoisie prove it." What she envisaged was a very particular revolution, not a class war but rather a "moral revolution" informed by "the religious and philosophical conviction of equality." Hers was a cautious approach. She was all too aware of the dangers of mass movements, of mob rule. It was no good, she urged, simply to incite revolt, declaring, "Bring about a revolution, we'll see afterwards." Rather, she warned, "say, 'Bring about a revolution, be aware now with what we will be faced afterwards. . . . What freedom will the individual have and what authority will society have?' " There were, she deeply believed, a great many questions to be answered before the time for revolution would come.[7]

Sand's growing involvement in social reform was difficult to sustain given her commitment to Chopin. But her extreme left-wing views had not prevented Chopin from being invited to play for Louis-Philippe and his court on 29 October 1839. Chopin's own aristocratic and somewhat reactionary attitude to social and political questions made him unsympathetic to Sand's ideas, and the growing group of proletariat poets who sent their work for her approval and gathered at the Rue Pigalle was not Chopin's idea of congenial society. Even with men whom he considered to be his social equals he displayed a firm commitment to the known and familiar. Of the relationship between Chopin and Delacroix, Sand wrote tellingly, "Delacroix understands Chopin and adores him. Chopin does not understand Delacroix. He admires, he holds dear, he respects, the man; he detests the painter. . . . He is a musician. . . . Michelangelo frightens him, Rubens gives him goose-flesh. Anything he considers eccentric scandalizes him. . . . What a strange anomaly."[8] Sand spent more and more time at the *Revue*'s offices, but she and Chopin spent their evenings together enjoying their new hobby—billiards.[9]

Sand's thinking was leading her more and more towards a belief in a communal philosophy, towards a view of humanity bound up together, a theory that dominates the autobiography. Somehow, without isolating Chopin, she succeeded in mediating between her often temperamental and suffering lover and her devoted proletarian poets: Charles Poncy, a stone carver; Reboul, a baker; Magu, a weaver; Gilland, a locksmith. She was particularly impressed by Poncy's work and did what she could to promote him. He published a good deal, culminating in *Oeuvres du Charles Poncy,* in 1846, for which Sand wrote a preface. Sand felt close to working people with aspirations, in part because she saw herself as someone whose mother had been rescued from poverty and exploitation by a man of vision: her father.

But Sand had never felt convinced by her own attempts at concise essay writing, the kind of material appropriate for journal publication. The results were always, she felt, pedantic, pompous, or platitudinous. Her interest was in communicating her ideas for reform through a medium that allowed for subtlety, for complexity, even paradox. If her ideas were to reach a wide audience, they would have to be written into novels that were simultaneously compelling and moving. And she needed, as always, to make money from her writing. Despite clinching a 28,000-franc contract for a new *Complete Works* on 25 November 1840, by 28 November 1841 she was forced to take out a substantial loan of 10,000 francs to make ends meet.

Meanwhile she struggled to complete *Un Hiver à Majorque* (*A Winter in Majorca*): the two-volume publication was announced on 1 January 1842. As Robert Graves pointed out in the foreword to his 1956 translation, Sand branded the islanders "barbarians, thieves, monkeys and Polynesian savages." Looking back on her stay, Sand felt that it had failed. She wrote into the work Solange's tendency to manipulate others, but what emerges is not a lucid account of the months on the island, but rather, as Graves noted, "the bitterness it left in her heart."[10]

The year continued busy: there were further battles with Buloz, worries over Chopin's health, the bouts of rheumatism that sometimes affected his fingers in particular, and in the summer former lovers appeared at Nohant: Michel de Bourges on 24 June, and Bocage on 12 July.

In the new year the first instalment of *Consuelo* was published in the *Revue*. This novel is arguably Sand's finest, and was certainly her most popular. It interweaves what was a winning combination of themes, including a woman artist-visionary, music, Venice, grottoes, initiation, and the search for a mother. Central to the novel is the question which animated *Lélia:* how can a woman escape the repressive rules that govern society without finding herself outside it? Lélia fails in her first incarnation. In the 1833 edition she is murdered. She failed equally in the less provocative and daring edition of 1839, where she is found wanting by a religious tribunal, removed from her position as abbess and confined to a cell. No doubt Sand needed to write these two earlier versions in order to write the more optimistic later novel.

Initially *Consuelo* was conceived as a novella about the musical society of Venice, and the great musician Porpora in particular. The heroine was to be based on Pauline Viardot. But Sand was soon begged to continue her story, which contains enough material for a dozen novels and was to become a weighty tome.

The first section is dominated by the figure of old Porpora, based in part on Deschartres, and tells of the musical intrigues of Venice. The action then moves to the Castle of Rudolstadt, which is presided over by the half-mad Count Albert. There are delightful comic touches: Count Albert possesses bizarre powers, including those of catalepsy and reincarnation, which offer the novelist easy solutions in what might otherwise become difficult narrative moments. Count Albert is always accompanied by a loyal dwarf who might have issued either from the pages of Mrs. Radcliffe or a film by Cocteau. The politics of the novel are consistent with her preoccupations at the time of writing—in particular a fierce warning against the destructive power of despotism.

Consuelo also explores the relationship between sexuality and the rest of our being—whether it be soul, spirit, or something else. Sand's point is that we are more than our knowable material selves. In the novel physical passion is identified as the only force capable of bringing either a man or woman into full existence. The argument on which this is based is that it is only in love that we recognize our inability to be totally self-sufficient. Sand's heroine renounces hedonistic love, thereby pointing to the fallacy of pleasure and the easy satisfying of erotic desire. Instead she loves according to a code of reciprocity, respect, and equality.

Consuelo and its sequel, *La Comtesse de Rudolstadt*—the latter is arguably inferior as a novel—are also works that most powerfully convey Sand's spirit: her energy, her commitment to hope which is a choice and not a given, her social vision, her liberal faith, her remarkable, generous, even gentle feminism, her belief, above all, that "life is a journey with life as its destination."[11] The pattern of her own days and thinking, about the time of writing *Consuelo,* is perfectly expressed in a letter to Delacroix written in April 1842. What it forcefully conveys is a sympathetic but puzzled realization of the distance between her own approach to life and that of her family. Other people, she observes, find life difficult—for physical, philosophical, or psychological reasons:

> Le Chopinet has had a heavy cold, and is still suffering. My daughter is better; she has had a racing pulse which has still not gone. I am the toughest of all of us. I work at night, ride during the day, play billiards at night, and sleep in the morning. It's still the same pattern of life. I step across any reflections that are too dark with great strides, and when I am in my right mind, I find life *acceptable* because it is *eternal*. You call that my dreaming. I call it my faith and my strength. No, nothing dies, nothing is lost, nothing ends, whatever you say. I feel profoundly and passionately that those that I have loved and seen depart, live on in and around me.[12]

As a child, and in her adolescence, Sand had been profoundly immersed in the self. Now, middle-aged, she had come to believe in the self only as part of a greater humanity. Thus in *The Story of My Life* she would write, "My individuality in itself is neither significant nor important. It only takes on some sense when it becomes a part of life in general, merging with that of my fellow men, and thereby becoming part of history."[13]

Sand and Chopin continued to work well, and to work well together. She believed more and more in his genius and, with typical modesty, described by implication what she saw as the limits of her own literary contribution. She wrote to Delacroix early in 1842: "Chopin has composed two adorable mazurkas that are worth more than forty novels and which speak volumes more than all the literature of the century."[14]

That summer Sand looked for more satisfactory accommodation in Paris. On 5 August they rented two separate apartments in the beautiful Square d'Orléans. They returned to Nohant on 9 August, and were joined on 12 September by the Viardots on their return from Spain. At the end of the month the household travelled back to Paris.

That autumn, on 29 September, they moved into the midst of a wonderful community of artists. Chopin's apartment was on the ground floor of number 9, while Sand's was at number 5. Maurice had a studio on a higher floor, and Solange an adjacent room. Charlotte Marliani and her husband lived at number 7, and the Viardots a few streets away. There were other artistic spirits nearby, and Heinrich Heine and Delacroix frequently visited. They could depend on interesting company for stimulus, but were equally free to withdraw to work the moment they felt so moved. Sand could not have done more to arrange an ideal Parisian life. Good news came too, at the beginning of October: Pauline was signed up by the Théâtre des Italiens, and Liszt was appointed to the Chapel of Weimar.

But however perfect their working and social environment, their relationship can never have been altogether straightforward. Both, after all, were artists, and neither placid by nature. There are, no doubt, aspects of the Sand-Chopin relationship written into later novels. In *François le Champi* (1850) an older woman takes in a foundling, brings him up, and then marries him. In the fiction it is, as a contemporary critic noted, "the perfect incest."[15] But there are equally more obvious aspects of the Sand-Chopin relationship in *Lucrezia Floriani* (1847).

The heroine, a woman in her thirties, mother of four children by three different men (none a husband), falls in love with the twenty-four-year-old Karol. He is disturbed by a sexual relationship that resembles a mother-son relationship. Lucrezia, on the other hand, is unconcerned by the parallels. What she is disturbed by is Karol's unwillingness to allow her any real contact with anyone else. On one occasion Karol and Lucrezia are talking but they are interrupted. Karol's response is as extreme as Chopin's often was: "My God," he cried, pressing Lucrezia's arm convulsively, "we are no longer alone. I am lost! Ah! Now I want to die."[16]

Lucrezia Floriani also reveals some of the tensions between Chopin and Sand's children. Karol is intolerant of Lucrezia's children, and quick to feel jealous. He responds by quarrelling tirelessly with them, and it is his treatment of her children that explains the death of Lucrezia's love for Karol. Chopin's relationship with Maurice, now in his early twenties, had never been an easy one. Maurice's intimacy with his mother was something Chopin found difficult to bear. When, for example, Maurice had had a brief clandestine affair with Pauline Viardot, he had confided in Sand, but not in Chopin. Relationships were further complicated by the behaviour of Solange, who was seventeen, flirtatious, and attractive; Chopin fell in love with her. To some extent Solange's interest in Chopin had more to do with her relationship with her mother. She must have been aware that her mother in some ways despised her.

Sand's loyalty to Chopin was not exclusive. In 1844 she had a brief and very discreet affair with Louis Blanc, the thirty-three-year-old socialist leader. The year after, there was Victor Borie, a twenty-seven-year-old editor of *L'Éclaireur,* a new review founded by Sand and her La Châtre circle. But despite these brief passions Sand did not feel any less committed to Chopin. As she had written to Pierre Leroux in January 1844, "There are . . . certain infidelities that do not destroy an old love."[17]

Chopin was irritated above all by the time and attention Sand devoted to their immediate entourage. This had been extended by her adoption (first temporary, then permanent, from January 1846) of Augustine Brault, a distant cousin on Sophie-Victoire's side. Sand feared that without protection Augustine's life would be much like Sophie-Victoire's, and she even went as far as to pay Augustine's impoverished and avaricious parents for the "privilege" of adopting their daughter. The scenario could have been taken directly from a Balzac novel. Maurice promptly shifted his affections from Pauline to Augustine, much to Sand's relief. But while the appearance of another young woman in the household transformed Maurice's life for the better, Solange became more and more embittered by the supposition that her own mother felt greater affection and admiration for her adopted daughter than her own flesh and blood.

Chopin, needless to say, resented the attention that the plebeian newcomer attracted, and thus a fault line between the two halves of the "family" appeared, quickly to become a gaping chasm. While Sand seems to have been best able to write her more serious, weighty novels when she enjoyed relative peace in her private and home life, when there were tensions and numerous distractions in her household she often withdrew to write those works which seem most truly her own. She needed, as always, to increase her income, as the household at Nohant was growing all the time. But it did not always follow that financial need stimulated creativity, and there were times when it had been an impediment to concentration. Sand had chosen, to some extent at least, whatever the dictates of conscience, to adopt Augustine and add to her expenditure. It is almost as though, either consciously or unconsciously, she increased financial pressure in the hope of further disciplining her writing. The requirement to write was also a defence against the business of daily life, an escape, an activity that required her to turn her attention elsewhere, and to transpose and translate much of her lived emotion to the safe regions of fiction.

At the point when tensions between Chopin and Sand were beginning to be acknowledged by both, Chopin heard, on 25 May 1844, that his father had died. In response to Sand's letter of consolation to his widow, she received a letter which testifies to Chopin's family's acceptance of the relationship between Sand and Chopin. His mother even thanks Sand for *her* maternal solicitations.[18] Chopin meanwhile, hitherto discreet and honourable in his correspondence, began to express his irritation and intolerance of Sand's treatment of the young of Nohant, even criticizing her relationship with Solange.

In mid-July Chopin travelled to Paris to meet his sister and her husband, bringing them back to Nohant on 9 August. On the twenty-eighth he returned with them to Paris. Sand was increasingly excited about *L'Éclaireur,* edited by Victor Borie and François Fleury, Jr. Sand contributed a number of articles that autumn, ranging from "Les Ouvriers boulangers de Paris" ("The Worker-Bakers of Paris") to a piece about Oc, the regional patois. A new pattern established itself: Sand and Chopin tended to travel to and from Paris alone, sometimes a week or two apart.

Chopin returned to Paris on 28 November, and Sand on 12 December. That winter she was tremendously impressed by William Charles Macready's performances in *Othello* (16 December), *Hamlet* (18 December), and *Macbeth* (6 January). And she was working on a preface for Pierre Leroux's translation of Goethe's *Werther:* the publication was announced on 4 January 1845. She received Macready and George Sumner on the twentieth. There were musical delights too: she and Chopin heard Mozart's *Requiem* on 21 March, and Haydn's *Creation* on the twenty-third.

On 12 June Sand travelled back to Nohant with Pauline Viardot. The month was one of serious flooding, not uncommon in the late spring. Pauline left on 3 July, and Sand continued work on a novel, as yet untitled (*Le Péché de Monsieur Antoine*). Sand signed a contract for it on 20 August—with Paul Delavigne, one of a number of publishers with whom she would now work, following the breakdown in relations with Buloz. On 1 September Maurice left for Paris with the first part of the manuscript in his baggage. Around the middle of the month Augustine Brault arrived at Nohant for the first time. Sand's commitment to her would become an increasing source of tension with Chopin. *Le Péché* was finished on 21 October. In November, however unsettled the household, Sand's loyalties pulled in numerous directions, her sense of personal responsibility challenged, she withdrew to write, in just four days, one of her short masterpieces, *La Mare au diable* (*The Devil's Pool*). On 9 November she returned to Paris, exhausted. Unusually, she took to her bed for five days.

She continued to ruminate, believing that social improvement would come. She had no fear of change: "What frightens the delicate and exquisite Chopin doesn't worry me. And for a long time I have known how to wait."[19]

The winter passed undramatically, with money worries and publishing negotiations. But there were trips to the theatre too, and on 20 February Sand, Chopin, Delacroix, Solange, and Augustine enjoyed a spectacular ball at the Hôtel Lambert. In April Chopin was seriously unwell. Mme Marliani and Sand soon caught the same illness. But by May they were all back on their feet. Sand left Chopin in Paris on 5 May, returning to Nohant with Solange and Augustine. Chopin arrived on 27 May. Sand must have regretted planning a four-day trip to the races at Brenne with the girls. There they met a young country squire, Fernand de Préaulx, who promptly fell in love with Solange.

On 14 July 1846 the young Matthew Arnold arrived at Nohant, the first to make a pilgrimage that would be repeated by thousands after him. Despite the tensions between the residents at Nohant, decorum was maintained. His notes do not betray the slightest hint that life at Nohant was anything other than perfect. But in her correspondence Sand makes clear that, privately at least, Chopin's equilibrium was not always maintained. To Chopin's pupil Marie de Rozières, she wrote that July that "his heart is still half here half there, as you know."[20] Chopin had remarkably little self-knowledge. When Sand read him *Lucrezia* Delacroix was also present. The latter recognized, in Karol, some of Chopin. He was deeply embarrassed, but Chopin did not see the parallels. Delacroix observed to Caroline Jaubert, with a painter's capacity for graphic description, "The executioner and the victim astonish me in equal measure. . . . Mme Sand seems perfectly at ease and Chopin continues to admire the story. . . . Truly, he had not understood, and the man continued his enthusiastic eulogy of the novel."[21]

When the novel was published Delacroix's reading of its reference to Chopin was confirmed by others, including Heine, Balzac, and Liszt. Sand continued to deny that the fictional Prince Karol had anything to do with her beloved Chopin. Were there other aristocratic geniuses on whom she had based the character, and did she see Chopin quite differently from others? Or was she sustained, in a very private way, by the monopoly that she knew she would always have, on the knowledge of the relationship between the real and the fictional? Secrecy had always been important to her. This knowledge was something truly, and exclusively, her own.

Solange meanwhile, at the age of eighteen, had, no doubt predictably, fallen in love with the grand Fernand de Préaulx. Although Sand was not explicitly opposed to the match, he was certainly not a man with whom she would find sympathy. "Noble, a royalist and a hunter of wild boars"— none of these recommended him to Sand.[22] Tensions at Nohant grew once again. But in between stormy scenes or periods when passions were cooled in one way or another—composing, writing, hunting—there were times of great gaiety and common merrymaking. The theatre at Nohant was well established and the company staged little performances. Even Chopin, who was an excellent mimic, forgot himself momentarily, to entertain.

The group at Nohant was not a homogeneous one, which no doubt explains both the immensely lively and creative spirit which presided over the place, and the challenging tensions. Sand felt responsible for maintaining a careful balance between creative liveliness and intellectual excitement, and the collapse of amiable social relations. Delacroix had arrived on 16 August, and in September most of the household made two lengthy excursions in the Éguzon region, fishing for salmon in the Creuse. Chopin stayed at home.

That autumn of 1846 conflicts finally came out into the open. Discussions about Solange's marriage to Préaulx were under way, and Chopin was moody. Maurice then announced that he could tolerate life at Nohant no longer. "Life cannot and ought not to be this way," Sand declared in response.[23] But it was Chopin who would leave, on 11 November, full of self-pity and recrimination: "He . . . announces that I no longer love him. What blasphemy after eight years of maternal devotion! But his poor wounded heart is not aware of his delirium. I think that a few months spent far away and in peace will heal this wound."[24]

The new year was dominated by Solange's indecision about marriage. Sand and Solange travelled up to Paris, arriving on 7 February. Sand saw Chopin, and the meeting was pleasant enough, but she had already decided to leave the Square d'Orléans and spend the year at Nohant. While Solange had been on the point of marrying, and was in Paris ostensibly to arrange the wedding, Maurice and Augustine were at Nohant and it was to them that Sand felt drawn. While she was briefly in Paris that spring, the sculptor Auguste Clésinger requested a sitting with Sand and Solange. He wanted to do a bust of mother and daughter in marble. Each attended sessions in his studio and it is very possible that Solange consummated her relationship with him there and then. By the end of the month she had changed her mind about marrying Préaulx and he left Paris, hoping that she might change it again.

Both Sand and her daughter had been warned off Clésinger. But it was one of Sand's strengths—and weaknesses—to rely on her own judgement. Delacroix, Emmanuel Arago, and Chopin, among others, tried to convince her that the man was a fraud, but she dismissed their views as mere prejudice. He was headstrong, Sand appreciated, but this was the source of his strength. He would marry because "this man wants it, because he does everything he wants, within the hour, within the minute, without having to sleep, to eat. Since his arrival two days ago, he hasn't slept for two hours even, and he is fine. This tension of the will, which knows no tiredness, nor momentary lapses, astonishes and pleases me. . . . I admire the power. . . ."[25] In many ways Sand was right. What she had not anticipated was that the strong, energetic man might turn his strengths against her.

Sand returned to Nohant on 6 April with the two girls. Clésinger visited briefly in mid-April. In May he was back and on 19 May he and Solange married in the tiny church at Nohant. Tensions between Solange and Clésinger, Maurice and Augustine and her recently betrothed, Théodore Rousseau, would soon come to a head. When, on 11 July 1847, the violent explosion occurred, it was essentially about money, and Sand's loyalties. She had promised Augustine a generous dowry. Clésinger had, it emerged, colossal debts and had the effrontery to ask Sand to mortgage Nohant to pay them. Instead she invited Solange and Clésinger to leave. Before their departure, Clésinger became abusive, then violent. He accused Eugène Lambert, who was staying at Nohant, of improper behaviour towards Solange, and aimed a blow at him. Maurice intervened. Clésinger then threatened him with a hammer. Sand then entered the fray, taking a hammer blow on the chest. Pistols were brandished, Clésinger was pinned against the wall by a servant, and the curé arrived.

The scene was dramatic, not to say melodramatic. The couple left the same day, and Sand wrote to Marie de Rozières: "This diabolical couple left yesterday evening, riddled with debts, triumphing in their impudence and leaving behind a scandal in the area that they will never live down. In fact for three days I lived, in my own house, with the threat of some murder. I can never see them again, never will they set foot in my house again. They have gone too far. My God I have never done anything to merit a daughter like her!"[26] The extent of Solange's wrongdoing was, however, only now beginning to emerge. As Sand took stock of the feelings Solange had aroused in Chopin, she regretted the way she had brought her up: "I would have done my duty better if I had been brutal and severe."[27] Chopin had transferred his allegiance to her spoilt daughter. He would be "happy, and less ill than he has been during this impossible battle to persuade me to share his sickening prejudices and to enter an unsociable solitude."[28] At the same time, she recognized her new freedom: "As for me, what a relief! What a bond broken! I have constantly fought against his narrow and domineering ideas, while remaining chained to him out of pity, and fear that he would die of grief. For nine years, while full of life, I tied myself to a cadaver."[29] These lines, of July 1847, are among the most bitter she ever wrote, but no doubt go some way to explaining her occasional infidelities. Their sexual relationship had been sporadic, even nonexistent in these later years. What Sand needed was to look back and consider the direction her life had taken so far: she needed to consider the degree to which she should accept responsibility for so much that had gone wrong, and, with the past reconsidered, move forward into the always unpredictable future.

Sand's writing, and particularly her autobiographical writing, was quintessentially both a therapy and an ever-necessary source of income. She could count on her readers' satisfaction, given that her work was read more and more as a window into her private life, which remained as compelling as the romances of her fiction. She was in her mid-forties, and had embarked, in April, on her autobiography, *The Story of My Life*, her most famous and, many would argue, her most accomplished work. What she could not have known at the time was that while she was withdrawing to think about her past, and its relationship with history, the present would simultaneously project France into a new and unexpected future. And Sand would feel compelled to throw herself fully into the historical moment.

XXI

History Past, Present, and Future

"What is termed a political passion is something
I shall never have. I have only passion for the idea."

Shaken by the violence of family passions, Sand drew up a will, on 17 July 1847. She waited expectantly for news from Chopin. Nothing came, and by the end of the month she was beginning to fear that he was seriously ill. She prepared to travel up to Paris, but on the eve of her departure a letter finally arrived. Sand was dismayed: Chopin criticized her handling of the young at Nohant, and in particular her hard-hearted treatment of Solange. On 28 July she wrote in reply, unaware that this would be her final letter to him.

Meanwhile she had to attend to a long-running legal battle with the Société des Gens de Lettres. Sand had fought in the courts against her husband, and on a number of occasions against editors and publishers, but her case against the Société was the most unusual. Sand displayed tenacity of purpose in her legal dealings, motivated in part by the knowledge that unless the case was won, the legal bills would be substantial. Once she had embarked on proceedings, there was nothing to be done but to fight it all the way to victory.

The august authors' institution had, without consultation with the author, allegedly sold the rights to publish *La Mare au diable* to two literary periodicals, *L'Écho des Feuilletons* and *L'Écho des Halles*. Soon after, on 11 November 1846, Sand had decided to resign her membership of the Société in protest, although there is no record of this having been accepted. On 6 February 1847 Sand had taken her case to the Tribunal de Commerce, but her complaint was rejected on grounds of insufficient evidence. On 20 August the case, *George Sand* v. *La Société des Gens de Lettres,* went before the First Chamber of the Royal Court: it was adjourned because Sand could not plead her case without her husband's authorization. She had written asking him for such permission, on 12 August, but he had not given his consent. On 17 December 1847 the court confirmed the tribunal's judgement of 6 February. Sand was determined to appeal. In the meantime there were not inconsiderable legal bills to pay.

Between legal hearings Sand nevertheless found the concentration to write. It is true that she was unwell for a period that September, suffering from heart palpitations, but by mid-October she had completed *François le Champi.* Two weeks later she received a parcel for which she had been waiting impatiently: Louis Blanc's *Histoire de la Révolution française.* Now she had the necessary material for what would become a long historical background to her own life.

By the beginning of November negotiations for her autobiography were under way. Two weeks later Hetzel, her editor, arrived at Nohant for further discussions. He had travelled on the brand-new railway from Vierzon to Châteauroux. He made a second trip on 9 December. The contract was finally signed at the end of the month: Sand would be paid advances of 5,000 francs on 1 January 1848 and 10,000 on 15 March of the same year, to be deducted from payments on receipt of sections of the work. Payment, in instalments due when each fifth was delivered, would total a staggering 130,000 francs.[1] This can be contrasted with Gustave Flaubert's earnings from *Madame Bovary* (1857). His initial contract was for just 800 francs, and even down to 1862, after further editions, his total earnings were only 3,300 francs.

At the beginning of February, Maurice and Eugène Lambert set off for Paris with instructions to remove the contents of the flat in the Square d'Orléans to a smaller and cheaper residence. Maurice moved into 8 Rue de la Condé, and it was here that Sand would now stay when in Paris. The move was motivated by financial worries, but she also knew that her time with Chopin in the idyllic square was over. In mid-February Chopin performed in Paris for the last time.

Maurice had been further charged, while in Paris, with the business of trying to extract, from the Ministry of War, certain records concerning his maternal grandfather, material which Sand needed for her autobiography.

Histoire de ma vie (*The Story of My Life*) is an ambiguous title, or a rich one as the French word *histoire*, of course, translates as both "story" and "history." The work is highly historical, and the text rapidly assumed something of the *Tristram Shandy*. Concerned to provide a full and adequate context in which to situate her individual life, Sand mentions her own birth only well into the work. She wanted to produce the kind of account of her life which would require full treatment of her ancestry, but she had also committed herself to five very large instalments.

The historical present was thrown into relief by the dramas of the Napoleonic period which she was describing as a background. In comparison, the present appeared uneventful. Thus when Victor Borie claimed that France was heading for a period of revolutionary turmoil, Sand could only smile. She was not alone in being taken by surprise when, in just two days, on 23 and 24 February, Louis-Philippe's bourgeois monarchy fell. But she feared that such a revolution should have been carefully planned if one unsatisfactory regime was not to replace another.

What happened, as Sand understood it, is an oversimplification, but the complexities only emerged over time. On 22 February numerous groups of working men and students began to congregate at meeting points throughout Paris. Prime Minister François Guizot, above all, had provoked public protest. Although a Liberal in some areas—he was committed to universal education, for example—he was adamantly against the universal franchise on the grounds that it would lay the country open to mob rule. His foreign policy was cautious, not to say pusillanimous; he was primarily concerned not to involve France in costly wars. At home he sought to build the economy by protecting and encouraging the interests of the wealthy. He believed that as the economy grew, so all levels of society would begin to benefit from the nation's prosperity. In the meantime, however, the poor had become poorer and more numerous. In the cities, and particularly Paris, the urban population divided into a large and growing group of have-nots and a relatively small and secure group of haves. The insurgents, on that first February day, sought to force Guizot out. One group swelled to mob size and poured across the bridge at the Place de la Concorde. It was easily beaten back by a platoon of dragoons, but the following day the crowds retaliated: the barricades went up all over Paris. Red flags were flying. News quickly spread to Nohant but no one seemed altogether clear about the scale and likely outcome of the latest demonstrations. Sand's maternal instincts told her that Maurice would undoubtedly become involved in the violence and she feared for his safety.

The Guizot government was aware that the demonstrators far out-numbered any regular troops and called up the National Guard. But this was largely made up of ordinary men, and most felt sympathetic towards the revolutionary cause. Along with the mobs that they were under orders to disperse, many of them called for Guizot's resignation. The ever-cautious prime minister resigned. Before Louis-Philippe had managed to appoint his successor, a demonstration in front of the Ministry of Affairs ended in the shooting down of around fifty demonstrators. The response was an extreme one. Within twenty-four hours a further fifteen hundred barricades had gone up in Paris. Over four hundred trees were felled and more than a million paving stones were ripped up. Witnessing the fury of a crowd of Guardsmen in front of the Tuileries Palace, Louis-Philippe abdi-cated. It was 24 February 1848. He and most of the royal family fled, first to Saint-Cloud, then to England. The palace was invaded, and the throne carried by the crowds to the Place de la Bastille, where it was burned. Mau-rice was too taken up by the atmosphere in the capital, and uncertainty about the next turn of events, to think to reassure his mother. Delacroix noted in his diary that Maurice "walked out of here [the studio] as though drunk; I didn't believe him capable of such exaltation."[2]

Meanwhile Alphonse de Lamartine and his supporters transferred the seat of power to the Hôtel de Ville and set about forming a provisional government. News of this was occasion for much rejoicing at Nohant, and at the end of the month Sand, accompanied by Planet, Borie, Duvernet, and Duteil, set out for the capital. They arrived on 1 March, intent on mak-ing their contribution to the establishment of a new and better order.

Lamartine was more poet than politician. He was very much a moder-ate, and many of the group over which he presided shared his desire for the re-establishment of parliamentary rule, while others wanted to see their republican and socialist beliefs informing a wholly new political system. While theoretically Sand was a radical in most respects, in practice she deeply feared the potential for anarchic mob behaviour. She admired Lamartine's rhetoric but knew that he lacked the decisiveness of an effec-tive leader. Sand had friends in every schismatic group: Hippolyte Carnot had assumed control of the Ministry of Education, the astronomer François Arago, Emmanuel Arago's uncle, took charge of the navy. Marc Caussidière, now in charge of the police, was a friend from the so-called monster trial of 1835 in which Michel de Bourges had become involved. Louis Blanc was also very much at the centre of things, heading a Labour commission charged with improving the lot of the most exploited and the unemployed.

Sand sought an interview with Ledru-Rollin, in his capacity as minister of the interior. Her concern was to persuade him to make a number of appointments—and to prevent him from making another. She asked that Frédéric Girerd be named commissaire de la République for the department of the Nièvre and Duvernet sous-commissaire for the Indre. Alexis Duteil was to be public prosecutor at Bourges. Gabriel Planet was appointed commissaire for the Cher. This last position Ledru-Rollin had intended to fill with one Michel de Bourges, but Sand persuaded him that Michel had compromised his republicanism by defending a prefect in a lawsuit against an opposition journalist. Sand had come to Paris intent on persuading Ledru-Rollin to make these appointments. But she had also wanted to reassure herself that Maurice was well, and to see for herself what had happened, and be part of subsequent events.

On 4 March she witnessed the funeral at the Madeleine for all those who had died on the barricades. "It was fine, simple, and touching . . . four hundred thousand people pressed together from the Madeleine all the way to the Column of July [the column at the Place de la Bastille]. . . . Not a constable, not a police sergeant to be seen, and yet such order . . . not a foot was trampled, nor a top hat dented. It was admirable. The people of Paris are the foremost in the world."[3] She had gone to the Foreign Ministry in the same building to obtain a passport for Guiseppe Mazzini, the exiled Italian nationalist who had become a close friend. A year later, he would become one of a triumvirate ruling the short-lived Roman republic. His was a cause worth supporting and Sand had taken him up; she had immediately been ushered into Lamartine's room. What she saw from the window was so close to Sand's vision of an ideal post-revolutionary mood that it must have seemed too good to be true, the stuff of idealist fiction.

Already profoundly moved by the day's events, on the same day she met Chopin, once again, at Charlotte Marliani's: he informed her that she was a grandmother: Solange had given birth to a baby girl, Jeanne-Gabriel, born on 28 February. Sand wanted to detain him in the antechamber where they had met, but Chopin offered his hand as a sign that he intended to leave immediately, without further conversation. Sand was deeply wounded. "I was never to see him again," she wrote simply in her autobiography.[4] That same day, Sand immediately wrote Solange a congratulatory letter. But only days later, amid all the dramatic political upheaval, Sand had a more difficult letter to write to her daughter: one expressing her deepest sympathy. Her grandchild had died, just one week old, on 6 March 1848, at Guillery.[5]

Profoundly disturbed by the chaos of events in Paris Chopin was to leave some weeks later (on 19 April) for London. He wanted to escape. Sand, on the other hand, like her son, quickly became drunk with the events of one historical moment after another. In this she was not alone. As she wrote to Charles Poncy: "People are mad, drunk, happy to have fallen asleep in the mud and to have woken up in the heavens. . . . The republic has won through, it is assured, we will perish rather than abandon it. The provisional government is composed for the most part of excellent men, but all of them incomplete and insufficient for a task which would demand the genius of Napoleon and the great-heartedness of Jesus."[6]

Before leaving Paris, Sand composed her first "Letter to the People," which Hetzel her friend and publisher printed. She left, intent on waking up the rural population to events in Paris and their potential importance for those living away from the capital. At Nohant she wrote further "Letters." She was dismayed by the apparent lack of local interest in Parisian affairs and wrote to Charles Poncy, "I have returned here to help my friends as best I can and to revolutionize Berry, which is asleep."[7] But she was not yet discouraged by her involvement in political change. Her assumption that France was in the throes of real change deeply moved her. In the same letter to Poncy she communicated the effect that recent events were having on her: "All my physical ills, all my personal sufferings are forgotten. I am alive, I am active, I am only twenty years old!"[8]

Sand's articles, published in the *Bulletin de la République,* were numerous and rallying. At the beginning of the month Sand saw Maurice installed as mayor of La Châtre amid joyous celebration. On 12 March the Republic was declared at Nohant. On 19 March she wrote her second "Letter to the People" and returned to Paris. In the fourth issue she defined the idea of a republic. It was, quite simply, "the reign of the people": "Citizens, France is embarking on the greatest endeavour of modern times: the foundation of the government of *all* the people, the organization of democracy, the republic of all rights, of all interests, of all intelligences, and of all virtues . . . ! The new idea can take its place in Europe."[9] It was published on 19 March. Sand arrived back in Paris on the twentieth and was immediately drawn into the corridors of power: "Here I am already working like a Statesman," she wrote to Maurice. "I have written two government circulars today, one for the Minister of Public Instruction, and the other for the Minister of the Interior. What amuses me is that all this is for the attention of the mayors and that you will receive, through official channels, instructions from your *mother*. Ah! ah! Mr. Mayor. . . ."[10]

What was needed, however, was more than stirring rhetoric and visionary ideas. To play for time Lamartine announced that elections would take place in April. In her writing Sand explored and analyzed the lot of the country's poorest, and the lot of French women: they had no vote, nor did the peasantry. In an article published on 6 April she argued that it was women who had "necessarily suffered the heaviest part of this oppression."[11] The new Republic, she claimed, would change this state of affairs. Sand was first proposed as a candidate for the forthcoming elections by Ernest Legouvé, a member of the Club de l'Émancipation des Peuples. She refused. There were other groups, however, equally intent on proposing her as their candidate. *La Voix des Femmes,* in particular, founded in March and headed by the prominent feminist Eugénie Niboyet, commented on the irony of Sand's position. She would necessarily be elected exclusively by men, and then speak on behalf of women in the new Assembly. Sand's response was, in many ways, surprising. She published it in *La Réforme:* she had no intention of representing a *cénacle féminin.* Her concerns were for the underprivileged, men *and* women, as she explained in another letter, this time to the Central Committee (Comité de la Gauche), from whose list she also requested her candidacy be removed.

Locally, Sand suspected that those elected would be opposed to the Republic. In the sixteenth edition of the *Bulletin* (15 April), she appealed to the people not to undo the work of the revolution of earlier that year. If the elected government failed to respond to the injustices that had first provoked violence, then violence would be repeated at some later stage. Such a cycle of violence, she implored, was in no one's interests:

> Citizens, we have not been able to pass from a corrupt regime to a lawful one in a day, an hour. . . . If social justice fails to win out in the elections, if they represent the interests of only one caste, torn from the confident trust of the people, the elections, which should be the salvation of the Republic, will be its downfall. . . .

What Sand went on to write would be read very differently in the light of what happened next:

> Then there would be only one road to salvation open
> to the people who put up the barricades, which would
> be to impose its will a second time. . . . This extreme
> solution . . . is it to this that France would want Paris
> to have recourse?[12]

The day after the *Bulletin's* appearance there were further demonstrations on the streets. Had Sand's rhetoric incited the people to violence? It had not been her intention. Schisms among those on the left did nothing to strengthen the cause. The bourgeoisie, joined by conservative forces from the Parisian suburbs, emerged as a stronger body. "Today," Sand wrote to Maurice on 16 or 17 April, "Paris behaved like La Châtre."

There was one last glimmer of hope, provoked by the Fête de la Fraternité, on 20 April. Sand witnessed the scene and wrote to Maurice, "It was truly sublime. . . . I watched for twelve hours and I still hadn't seen enough and, in the evening, the fireworks, the parade of troops, torches in their hands, an army of fire, ah! My poor boy where were you? . . . You must come on 5 May, even if that's when Nohant is razed to the ground. . . ."[13] What she had witnessed was "the most massive human event ever produced!" Scenes of huge, peaceable crowds always elicited hyperbole from Sand. By the time of the elections, however, that fraternal street fellowship had already been replaced by political "malice, rumour, hatred, breaches."[14]

In the wake of the election, and deeply disappointed by the outcome, Sand feared for the future. The precise nature of her suppositions was recorded by Tocqueville, following a remarkable lunch party where he met her for the first time. The party, on 4 May 1848, was attended by numerous writers, including Mérimée and Vigny, and had been organized by Richard Monkton Milnes, the British politician and man of letters who was staying in his Parisian apartment at the time. Tocqueville does not attempt to disguise his first suppositions about Sand, "I had great prejudices against Mme Sand, because I detest women who write, most particularly those who disguise the weaknesses of their sex in systems, instead of interesting us by revealing them to us in their true light."[15] However, he continues, "I liked her. I found her features somewhat big, but she has an admirable expression; her spirit seems to have retreated into her eyes, leaving the rest of her face to matter; what struck me above all was to encounter in her something of the natural appeal of all great minds. Indeed there was a genuine simplicity in her clothes." Tocqueville was impressed:

> I was much struck by what she had to say about this subject; it was the first time that I had entered into direct and familiar contact with someone who could, and wanted to, tell me something of what was occurring in our adversaries' camp. Opposing sides never know one another: they draw in, they press against each other, they take hold of each other, but they never see each other. Mme Sand painted a very detailed and unusually vivid picture for me, of the state of the workers of Paris, their organization, their numbers, their weapons, their preparations, their thoughts, their passions, their terrible intentions. I thought the picture biased but it was not; what followed amply testifies.

Sand had her own interests in disclosing information about her camp. She was afraid of the consequences of "the people's triumph" and, as Tocqueville recorded, "displayed a slightly solemn pity for the fate that awaited us. 'Try to persuade your friends, monsieur,' she said, 'not to push people into the streets by unsettling or irritating them; in the same way I want to counsel patience to those on my side; because—believe me—if a battle breaks out, you will all perish.' "[16]

Tocqueville was no doubt right: Sand's thoughts and feelings were complex, even contradictory. She advocated revolution, and produced propaganda prolifically and passionately, but she abhorred the violence which she recognized as all but inevitable if change was to come about. She feared for the future. Ten days after the literary luncheon where she had met Tocqueville, violence did break out. And across Europe similar discontents were stirring men to action. Paris, it seems, attracted Irishmen seeking independence from British rule, and German and Belgian democrats who wanted to wrest power from their respective leaders. But it was affairs in Poland that had the most direct effect on events in Paris. On 13 May news of the Polish insurrection sparked further protest. The brutal suppression of the Poles by Prussian troops could not be allowed to continue. In the streets of the capital the people called for France's involvement, shouting "Long live Poland!"

The ostensible reason for the march, which gradually absorbed more and more people as they progressed towards the Assembly, was to persuade the country's leaders to send an army to Poland. But the head of steam which took the crowd over the Concorde bridge continued to push people forward in front of the Assembly. The railings were trampled down and the crowds penetrated the amphitheatre. For two hours pandemonium ruled and no one, even those in the chamber who supported the Polish invasion, had a chance to speak at any length. The mindless mob that Sand so much feared was running wild. Sand was outside the Assembly and hoped that some progress was being made in the debating chamber, but a sudden furious drumroll signalled the arrival of the National Guard. It charged into the Assembly, brandishing bayonets. There were numerous arrests—Blanqui, Raspail, Barbès, Leroux, Théophile Thoré. Most were colleagues, friends, or at least acquaintances of Sand's. She had not played any direct role in the organization of the demonstrations, but knew that she would be under suspicion, as a story she told testifies. At a point when events had been at their least predictable, she had seen an impressive-looking woman leaning out of a window, shouting authoritatively to the crowds. She asked someone nearby who the woman was, only to be informed that it was "George Sand."

Deeply saddened, and deeply disillusioned, she and Maurice returned to Nohant on 18 May 1848. "The country people," she wrote to René de Villeneuve, "are calm, because the harvest is *fair and golden,* as they say." Her affair with politics was over. As she explained in her letters, she now knew herself better. What had happened, she wrote, was that passions had been stirred up that were affected by neither "reason nor the heart." "What is termed a political passion," she wrote, "is something I shall never have. I have only passion for the idea."[17] She believed deeply in democracy. And she believed in goodness. She was as unwilling as ever to accept unsatisfactory compromises as means to ends. Action, political action, would always fall short of Sand's ideal. The pen was her subtler and more effective weapon, and one which she continued to wield from the peace and gentle rhythms of Nohant. She wrote to Théophile Thoré:

> I went home determined not to lose a single hair on my head for men like Raspail, Cabet and Blanqui. As

long as these men sign up in our camp, I will abstain. They are pedants and theocrats. I do not want to see the individual crushed, and I will go into exile the day we make the mistake of bringing them to power. . . . They wanted to impose by stealth (and if they could have done so, by force) an idea which the people had not yet accepted. They would have established the reign of fraternity, not like Christ but like Mohammed. . . . Instead of a religion, we would have had a fanaticism. This is not the way that true ideas make their way in the world. At the end of three months of such a philosophical usurpation we would not have been republicans, but Cossacks.[18]

At Nohant, much to Sand's delight there were rumours that it would be the conservatives of La Châtre who might behave like Cossacks. To Pauline Viardot, who had gone to London to rival Jenny Lind, she wrote, much amused by the ironies, "I would even find it rather funny were the conservatives of La Châtre to come over here, and simply out of their fear of communism . . . burn and pillage my home. What an example they would be giving; nor do I despair of seeing them undertake such an action against myself or another, as they would thereby be demonstrating their love of order, their morality, and *respect for property*."[19]

For all her resilient sense of humour, she was in a sombre mood that summer. Provoked by the bourgeois shopkeepers of La Châtre, the locals vented their spleen against her, shouting outside the walls of Nohant: "À bas Mme Dudevant! À bas les communistes!" She belonged, they were led to believe, to a group that was intent on putting to death "children under the age of three, and old people over sixty."[20] And so it went on. Meanwhile Sand withdrew into her autobiography and waited, she wrote, "for the current to take me elsewhere."[21]

Much of Sand's insight into—if not her vision of—the contemporary political and social upheaval was shared, to an extent, by Louis Napoléon Bonaparte himself. During the revolution of February 1848 Napoleon had been back on French soil, after a period in exile in England. He had offered his support to Lamartine, who had promptly sent him back to London. There he bided his time, waiting for events to turn propitious. During the June elections, at the age of forty, he deemed the time right to test the water once again. Representing the working classes, he was successfully elected

in the partial elections of 4 June, but aware that he did not command significant support, he stood down, and awaited a better opportunity.

On 21 June events once again came to a head. The National Work-
shops were finally closed after a period of temporary cessation of work.
The unemployed massed in the streets and marched on the Bastille chanting "Bread or death!" The familiar barricades were not long in appearing.
As Tocqueville recorded, "It was not the work simply of a certain number
of conspirators . . . but the rising up of a whole population . . . trying to
escape from their condition." General Louis Eugène Cavaignac, the new
minister of war, awaited his moment, aware that the people of the streets
would tire, while the army could be successfully entertained for a few days.
Lamartine and Ledru-Rollin desperately tried to gain interviews with
Cavaignac, who knew that the government would soon grant him full
powers. By Monday 26 June the fighting was at its height. Tocqueville
recorded the scene, and what he understood of the psychology behind it: "I
noticed, chatting with them [the National Guards], with what terrifying
speed, even in the middle of a century as civilized as this, the most pacifist
souls throw in their lot, so to speak, with civil war, and how the taste for
violence and contempt for human life suddenly spills forth in these
unhappy times. . . ."[22] The violence, that June 1848, and the scale of human
loss of life, shook Europe. France had been saved from communism, or so
some argued.

Sand's loss of faith in mass public action had occurred earlier, but she
suffered deeply, and felt still further disillusioned, as news of events in
Paris reached Nohant. Suspicions that she herself was in some way intimately involved in these events continued to provoke the people of La
Châtre. There, "a considerable band of imbeciles . . . talk daily of coming
to burn down my home." But, interestingly, whatever the threats or
rumours, members of the same group, if they meet her, "raise their hats."[23]
Sand found solace in her correspondence with Abbé Lamennais, whom she
continued to regard as a visionary among the blind: "You alone . . . have
had the courage, in the midst of such great peril, to articulate the truth."[24]

Telling the truth had not been Joseph Brault's concern. The father of
Augustine, he had published a work entitled *Une Contemporaine: Biographie et intrigues de George Sand*. As soon as Sand had become aware of the
libellous publication, in June, she had filed a lawsuit and had it seized. The
pamphlet (it is a work of just a few pages) alleges that the innocent Augustine was lured to Nohant by the infamous George Sand, seduced by her
son, who promptly ditched her, and that she had then been married off to

the first possible husband, a drawing teacher (Charles de Bertholdi)! So as to make the publication as inflammatory and saleable as possible, reference was also made to Maurice's "affair" with Pauline Viardot, and Sand's relationship with Marie Dorval was "exposed."

It could be that the political and private dramas that Sand had recently witnessed explain the scale and nature of her writing at the time. In addition to her autobiography and essays, she wrote two pastoral novels: *La Petite Fadette* and *François le Champi*. But these are not the escapist fiction one might suppose them to be. The apparent "innocence" of these novels is misleading. A number of substrata can be easily exposed. Incest, in particular, continues to be a major, if slightly hidden, preoccupation. Nor had she abandoned her memoirs in favour of writing something easier. She had finished the final draft of the first volume, but the instabilities of the publishing world delayed its appearance. There were also worries about the volume's length. If Sand had ideas of continuing to write more overtly political work, the time was clearly not right. She dedicated *La Petite Fadette* to "our imprisoned friends; as we are forbidden from talking politics with them, all we can do is to write tales to distract them, or send them to sleep."[25] She may also, however, have lost the impetus for political novels, although *Fadette* is not without significant subversive elements.

Fadette became the second part of a trilogy that began with *La Mare au diable* and was followed by *François le Champi*. If the first was to some extent an exploration of how and why a young man chooses a lover, the third explored the temptations of mother-son incest. *Fadette* tells of a tomboy who is a social outcast. A handsome and well-to-do peasant, Landry, falls in love with her, however, and she marries and bears numerous children. But this conventionally happy ending is undermined by the reader's unease as to how this transformation has come about. Fadette has, essentially, had to renounce her individual identity in order to assume a passive position within the society into which her marriage has allowed her full entry. It is Landry who explains to her: "I'll tell you why people don't respect you in the way a girl of sixteen ought to be respected. It's because you are so unlike a girl and so like a boy in your looks and manners. . . . Well, do you think that it is right and proper, at sixteen years of age, not to be in the least like a girl? You climb trees like a squirrel, and when you leap on the back of a mare with no bridle or saddle you spur her to gallop as though the devil were on her back. It's a good thing to fear nothing, and for a man it is a natural advantage. But for a woman enough is enough, and you look as though you are trying to draw attention to yourself."[26] In a curious twist that complicates a reading that suggests that Fadette can only become part of society by denying her more virile side, Landry suggests that Fadette can then use her intelligence more openly without provoking resentment: "You'll see that when you are a little more like other people they will be less resentful of the fact that you have more insight than they."[27]

But the real story of *Fadette* is arguably about Landry and his twin brother, Sylvinet. Fadette causes the split between the two brothers when Landry falls in love with her, and Landry then turns to her when his brother retires to bed and refuses to get up. Sylvinet's dislike of Fadette has become pathological. Sand invented psychoanalysis numerous times, but nowhere more obviously than in *Fadette*. When asked to cure Sylvinet, Fadette replies, "The only cure I know is reasoning . . . for it is the mind that makes the body ill, and whoever can cure the one will cure the other." First, while Sylvinet is asleep, Fadette lays her hands on his head, then on his forehead. While he sleeps, Fadette has encouraged what would later be called transference. He wakes and asks for her. When she returns to his bedside she begins what we now know as the process of psychoanalysis where unprocessed, uncensored thoughts are articulated. Fadette even adds, "Say it all, Sylvinet, you *mustn't* hold anything back."

Predictably, if the theories of psychoanalysis are presumed, Sylvinet transfers his obsessive homosexual love of his twin brother to Fadette, thus transforming it into an incestuous love. The only way out of all this is for Sylvinet to join Napoleon's army and absent himself from both his brother and sister-in-law. In *François le Champi*, incest is consummated when François weds his adoptive mother and the two apparently live happily ever after. The two novels were written, of course, on either side of the Revolution of 1848, which may well have undermined Sand's faith in the "fraternal bond." The conversation that functions as one of the two prefaces to *Fadette* certainly confirms the idea that times have changed: " 'Do you remember,' he [the fictional interlocutor] said to me, 'that evening we came this way a year ago, and we stopped here for a whole evening? For it was here that you told me the story of François le Champi . . .' 'I remember, and it seems like ten years ago. . . .' "[28]

Similarly, in *The Story of My Life* she wrote, "Everything that has come before was written under the Monarchy of Louis-Philippe. I am beginning work again on the first of June, 1848. . . . I have lived a good deal, I have aged a good deal during this brief interval. . . ."[29] *Fadette* was read to Marie Dorval on her deathbed, and remains one of the most widely (mis)read of all Sand's novels.[30]

Despite her output, Sand's financial worries were as great as ever. It is true that hyperbole associated with Sand's discussion of money worries in her correspondence can make them seem exaggerated, dramatized. But despite sending Victor Borie a substantial sum of money to placate her creditors in Paris, first the contents of the Hôtel de Narbonne were sold, then, on 6 December 1848, the building itself, for a song. Sand's money worries were real.

The public wondered at Sand's political silence. But a number of journals that would otherwise have suggested themselves as outlets for her ideas had ceased publication, including *Le Peuple Constituant* (Lamennais) and *La Vraie République*. She corresponded, however, with a large number of friends and "brothers," including Poncy and Hetzel, to whom she explained her new ideas about the scope and nature of public ownership of property, for example.[31] In a letter to a young journalist that autumn, she had made explicit her reasons for publishing so little of an overtly political kind: "You ask me in what papers I am writing, I am writing in nothing at the moment, at least I cannot speak my thoughts while under a state of siege. It would be necessary to make concessions of which I am not capable. And then, my spirit has been broken, discouraged for a time. It is still ill and I have to wait for it to recover."[32] Sand's idealism had suffered terrible assaults. She was well aware that she needed time for her faith gradually to be restored. But events would soon militate against a speedy recovery. While *François le Champi* had been a dramatic success in its adapted form on the stage, so Napoleon, who had reappeared on the political stage, looked set for victory. Sand doubted it, but was sorely mistaken.

On 4 November a new Constitution, drafted by Tocqueville and Lamartine among others, announced forthcoming presidential elections. A clever blend of nationalism and socialism, Napoleon's campaign went from strength to strength. Sand pronounced her position: "Mr. Louis Bonaparte, an enemy—*in terms of political system and political conviction*—of the Republic as an institution, has no right to run as a presidential candidate. May he have the honesty to admit that he is a pretender [to the throne] and France will see whether she wants to re-establish the monarchy for the benefit of the Bonaparte family."[33] The elections took place on 10 December. Louis Napoléon Bonaparte's majority was overwhelming. Support for Cavaignac, Ledru-Rollin, Raspail, and Lamartine had been negligible. The

Republic that had been of such tremendous importance to Sand would soon be killed off by its first president.

Like a transposed form of the pathetic fallacy, the death of political ideals and institutions was mirrored in the deaths of some of the people for whom Sand cared most. On 23 December Hippolyte died, principally from drink-related illnesses. He had died, as far as Sand's relationship with him was concerned, years earlier. More heartbreaking was Marie Dorval's death, on 20 May 1849. She had failed to recover from the grief she had suffered when her grandson Georges had died. The family wrote to Sand. Whatever their idea of the relationship between the two women, and when death had swept away all but the essentials, Marie's family recognized the depth of Sand's love for Marie: "Ah! dear Mme Sand! how you loved Marie, how you understood her soul!"[34] Sand ensured that Marie's grandchildren were adequately provided for, and for many years Jacques and Marie Luguet spent their summers at Nohant with their grandmother's dear George.

On 20 July 1849 Sand's battle with the Société des Gens de Lettres was finally over: the First Chamber of the Tribunal of the Seine condemned the Société's agents, Pommier and Godefroy, and required them to pay damages of 500 francs to Sand, and 4 francs for every unsold copy of the book published by Delavigne. This was entirely legitimate: sales of the book had virtually stopped, after a quick turnover in the first two months, when the serializations appeared in the press. The two journals had printed 40,000 copies.[35]

Chopin's death, on 17 October 1849, was also a blow very hard to bear. Although neither had sought a meeting since their chance encounter in Paris years earlier, and still conscious of his "jealousies," Sand was ill for several days after hearing that he was gone forever. Hippolyte, her closest relative, had survived only to the age of fifty. Sand, at the close of 1849, had lost two of her former loves: Dorval and Chopin. She was forty-five.

XXII

Eden

"Only very rarely do children die here!"

⚭ There is something disingenuous, although innocently so, about Sand's correspondence during the years after the Revolution of 1848. She emphasizes the importance of gaiety, of entertainment, of fun. But she protests too strongly. Typically, she wrote to Arago, "Dear old chap, the fact is that we are having frantic fun at Nohant."[1] And in a letter to Mazzini she suggested that merriment had been prescribed: "It is our way to be cheerful, because here in France gaiety, apparent light-heartedness is a kind of rule of life. Particularly in certain milieux, you must always laugh when others laugh. . . . *Everyone has a good time here* and I am always cheerful."[2]

While in the country Sand involved herself in the Nohant theatre; while in Paris she regularly saw plays, negotiated contracts, and signed agreements for new editions of earlier publications. Illustrated editions were now beginning to appear. She also submitted plays to various Paris theatres. Privately, her old ache, which she had identified so many years earlier, had never gone away. But now it could be suffered in silence and even act as a measure of the relative happiness of her more mature self. In the same letter to Mazzini she explained, "The hurt of my life is within me. It is part of my secret appreciation of all those apparently highly distracting things, those which set off such lugubrious stirrings in my inner being."[3] Laughter could numb the pain, the ache, and could distract her from it. But it could never be cured. She had written in a draft of her auto-biography a fragment too intimate perhaps for publication:

> I carry within me a great sorrow, which drives me always to love too much and to want too much to be loved myself. Age has taught me not to be so obviously demanding, not to make unnecessary reproaches, to hide my inner suffering, and to blame only myself for the kind of moral loneliness in which I am often left by the best affections. . . . I love gaiety, and am sad if no one shakes me.

She knew that this inner unhappiness had made her difficult to love, and had complicated her own urgent desire to love:

> My inner being is easily affected, but outwardly I appear cold. What I feel most keenly is always what I am least able to explain; as in still water, everything accumulates in me and sinks to the bottom. . . . But as, despite all this, I am never bored by my own company, I have difficulty recognizing that others are tired of me.

She also recognized her own capacity to move on from the period of suffering that followed the ending of a relationship. And that when she was rejected by another, her own feelings towards that other being gradually changed too, bringing freedom:

> When time has been given to that period of secret unhappiness which follows, I recover, and begin to weary of him, and it is this that saves me from behaving in the pestering and vindictive way characteristic of a wounded heart. Mine rebuffs quickly, it is a blessed trait in me. Without this, given all the betrayals I have suffered, I would not have been able to live.[4]

She had come to know herself well.

Two young men were to be loved, and to love, before Sand found another great love. Victor Borie had been her lover for two years before leaving Nohant in 1850; a young German, Hermann Müller-Strübing, replaced him.[5] She was soon confessing to Hetzel, to whom she continued to write highly personal letters, "He often bores me."[6] In an earlier letter she described their behaviour as "like two boys."[7] One obvious difficulty was that his command of French was limited: intimate conversation was one of Sand's great delights. Before long he left Nohant to act as tutor in a neighbouring household. At Nohant he was soon replaced.

Alexandre Manceau, a sculptor some thirteen years Sand's junior, had arrived at the house at the end of 1849. Although not physically robust, he was energetic, enterprising, and willing to express his ideas. "Manceau came, saw, and criticised," Sand wrote approvingly of his response to the Nohant theatre and its actors. But his criticisms were far from mere rhetoric and he was very willing to do what he could to improve at least the structure of the theatre. He set about rebuilding it with enormous energy and childish excitement. The "mysterious 'entente' between souls" which Sand identified as the unknowable reason for love explains no doubt the speed and degree to which Manceau's enthusiasm communicated itself to Sand. To Augustine she wrote in March 1850, "You see the family theatre is turning into something serious."[8] A month later Sand admitted to Hetzel that she was struck not only with Manceau's improvements in the theatre at Nohant, but with him too. In a long letter to Hetzel she explained their growing love. In a telling passage she sees fit to explain that Manceau "never breaks anything." And she adds, "Don't take that to be a joke." She goes on to explain that his manual precision and care are indicative of his disciplined and gentle character. And in her descriptions of Manceau, and explanations, to Hetzel and to herself for their contentedness together, images of androgyny recur. He was, she wrote, both a "caressing cat" and a "loyal dog," and more explicitly she wrote: "He has a woman's care, that of a dexterous, energetic and ingenious woman." Sand believed it to be a calm love, even a reasonable love, but what counted were her feelings: "In any case I love him, I love him with my whole heart, despite my age and his, even despite a horrible lack of trust which has always been a torment in the very depths of my heart, with all my loves. . . . It is as though I have been transformed, I am well, I am calm, I am happy, I tolerate everything, *even his absence,* which is saying a good deal: hitherto I have never tolerated that."[9] For the first time Sand both loved and was beginning to trust; and this was reciprocal.

References to her own age are common in the correspondence. In July she wrote to Hetzel again stressing the success of her relationship with

Manceau. "Yes, I am happy," she writes, but she adds, "I am forty-six years old, I have white hairs, it does not matter. Old women are more loved than young women. I know this well."[10] She may not have been wholly convinced, and the deaths of both Charlotte Marliani and Balzac, in August, served to remind her of her age and mortality. Charlotte had died aged only sixty.[11] Sand already anticipated her old age, but claimed to be confident that she would enter the final phase of her life "with uncommon serenity and one which astonishes me, because it is the age of regrets, and I am astonished not to feel a single one."[12] This was because she felt that her conscience was clear, and because of the companionship of her beloved Manceau. But she needed to justify this most recent shift of allegiance, and wrote in the same letter to Bocage that October (1850), "I have never known how to *organize my life*. I have only thought to organize other people's." As a consequence, she wrote, "I have often caused myself great suffering rather than enduring or accepting inadequate feelings."[13] Sand continued to have a high ideal of love.

But for all the serenity of that relationship, the continuing presence of Maurice caused tensions as always. Although Solange was not to be seen on the stage of Nohant, she had not altogether left the family troupe. She had claimed to Charlotte Marliani not long before Charlotte's death, on 2 August 1850, that Sand had written to her husband to inform him that she (Solange) had been born illegitimate and was not "la fille de M. Dudevant."[14] The feud rumbled on. Sand was appalled by her daughter's relentless accusations and told Maurice that she would rather that neither her daughter nor her husband dine with them: "He [Clésinger] is mad." And of her feelings for Solange she wrote, "I no longer love her, or that is what I believe at least. As far as I am concerned she is a cold rod of iron, an unknown being, a stranger in the world of ideas and feelings where I have my being, incomprehensible as you say, because it is clear that those who live to love cannot understand the interior mechanism of those who do not love." Sand no longer believed that her relationship with her daughter would change: "The young woman has broken our hearts, let us forgive her, but hope no longer."[15]

But new life would always bring optimism. It had been three years since Solange had been at Nohant and she appeared, unexpectedly it seems, accompanied by little Nini, Sand's new granddaughter, and a maid. The scene, when Solange and the baby arrived, was an uncanny re-enactment of that recognition scene orchestrated by Sand's father to persuade Sand's grandmother to accept little Aurore. On 26 February 1851 she wrote to

Hetzel, "My daughter appeared from nowhere last Friday, she left again this morning." She and Nini could come again, Sand had decided, but not to live.[16]

The theatre at Nohant continued to function both as an entertainment for the whole household and as a professional studio in which Sand's plays could be tested. One theatrical success followed another, although there were a good many exceptions. In January *Claudie* had done enormously well. *Molière*, on the other hand, which she had had difficulty finishing, was withdrawn early on. On 5 March 1852 *François le Champi* returned to the stage once again. On 23 November 1849 its hundredth performance had already been staged. *Le Mariage de Victorine*, in November 1851, was another triumph.[17] Of the twenty-four plays Sand wrote *in toto*, only six were out-and-out successes. But her theatre nevertheless attracted enormous attention and her status as a playwright came to be celebrated.

Yet what Sand notes in her diaries during the early 1850s are the happy domestic details. On 26 November 1851, she had jotted, "Production of *Victorine*. Success. I felt extremely calm without knowing why. . . ." What seemed to matter most was not the public success but that the unhappy scene in *Indiana*—where tensions rise as Indiana, her husband, and Sir Ralph sit by the fire—has been replaced by one of contented domesticity. The Sunday entry in her journal simply closed: "I played dominoes by the fireside with Manceau."[18] She was determined not to allow her public success to distract her from the day-to-day appreciation of her private happiness.

Political events, however, seemed once again to be coming to a head. On 1 December 1851, back in Paris, she lunched with Emmanuel Arago, who was convinced that Louis Napoléon was poised for a *coup d'état*. Sand did not, or did not want to, believe that further political upheavals were about to strike France. That same night she passed by the Élysée. All was quiet. "It's not going to happen tomorrow," she asserted. But on 2 December 1851 Sand learnt that Cavaignac and General Louis Juchault de Lamoricière had been arrested, and the Assembly dissolved. Elections would follow. No one was clear as to Napoleon's objectives. Public reaction was slow and equally uncertain. Initially Sand noted, "Oh men! You will destroy but you will not convert as long as your passions speak without listening." The following day the response came. Students demonstrated in the streets and were met by "an army of policemen." On 4 December several hundred students were killed. It was time to leave Paris. Sand recognized her own impotence, and at the same time a more widespread impotence. "Oh! If I were a man I wouldn't leave; but the children must be saved, it is a woman's first duty, a mother's first concern, and in any case what would I do here? All I could do would be to get myself killed." She left Paris, with Manceau at her side, and Nini, and Solange.[19]

The "referendum" of 21 December brought no surprises. Support for Louis Napoléon was overwhelming. But he had to ensure that dissenters were well out of the way by the time of the second "consultation," exactly a year later when he would become Napoleon III, Emperor of all France. On 9 January 1852 sixty-six former opposition deputies were exiled from France, including Victor Hugo, Perdiguier, and Raspail. Others were deported to the colonies, Algeria and French Guiana (including Devil's Island).

However uncertain Sand felt about political action, however hopeless she now considered mass initiatives, she was not willing simply to retreat to Nohant in the full knowledge of the fate of so many of her friends and acquaintances whose sympathies she shared. Her action and the response she solicited were remarkable. Knowing full well that she herself might be imprisoned, or even exiled, she took a decisive and brave step. But it was also no doubt a shrewd and tactical one. To present yourself to the enemy is, in a sense, to make ignominious any action that they may take in response. Somehow denying or suppressing her pride, which was not negligible, she wrote, "Prince . . . I am not Mme de Staël." The latter had been one of Napoleon I's great enemies, and, she continued, "I have neither her genius nor her pride with which she fought the double force of genius and power. . . . I come to you, however, to take a brave step on my part. Prince, my family has been dispersed and thrown to the four winds. My friends from childhood and from my old age, my adopted brothers and children, are in hiding or in exile; your harshness has weighed heavily on all those who have adopted, who accept, or who submit to, the title of socialist republicans. . . ." Napoleon was, she added, "a socialist genius . . . accepted by the people."[20]

Sand's rhetoric ranged from emotive reminders of Napoleon's own experience of imprisonment to shrewd tactical suggestions that clemency would produce political benefits. And she made explicit the risks she herself had been willing to take in writing to him, "I have had . . . to burn my boats behind me, placing myself entirely at your mercy." Napoleon wrote back in person, motivated perhaps by curiosity, or aware that Sand might remain a force to be reckoned with. Knowledge of the enemy can only improve the success of any putative confrontation.

They met on 29 January 1852, and Sand claimed to have seen "a tear, a real tear, in those cold eyes and he stretched out both hands towards me."[21] Sand's friends were far from easy about her approach to Napoleon and feared the advantage that the Bonapartist press would take from their meeting. But Sand protested that what she had requested was a "general amnesty"; she had not pleaded on behalf of individuals. This she did to the minister of the interior. She had a further interview with Napoleon, and successfully pleaded with minister after minister for the release of literally hundreds of political prisoners. Some would otherwise have been executed. She suffered the criticisms of the left and the approval of the right, but she continued to be deeply admired whatever was thought of her approach. Whatever the tactical and symbolic weaknesses of Sand's action, she believed more and more in *life*. Very large numbers of her friends and friends' friends would have been denied their freedom had it not been for her action. In this her idealism is less visible than her pragmatism. What mattered was that all these people should not be prevented from living, and from living fully.

Sand's fame continued to spread, and she continued to receive large numbers of visitors. Both authorized and unauthorized translations were published, and in Belgium, pirated editions had appeared. A convention of 3 November 1851 between France, Britain, and Belgium offered future protection, as discussed in *La Presse*, on 14 May 1852. In February 1852 the Brownings arrived, and a few days later Delacroix, for whom Nohant had become a home away from home; he came and went regularly. She and Manceau lived as wife and husband, and both were happy. Sand's attitudes to marriage are many and not wholly without contradiction. *Indiana* and *Valentine* had explored and exposed the wretchedness that was so often a woman's lot in marriage. Her own marriage she had abandoned without great personal difficulty. She was committed above all to life, and marriage took second place if the two came into direct conflict. Her life, at a certain point, seemed liveable only if she was separated from Dudevant. Yet she was concerned to see Maurice, now thirty, married.

Solange and Clésinger were living apart, and Solange felt very sorry for herself indeed. She wrote to Sand from the convent where she had taken refuge: "Since yesterday I have been a paying guest here. It already seems a long time. Is it thus that the best years of my life are going to be spent? Without family, without friends, without children, without even a dog to fill the void? The loneliness of the fields is bearable. . . . But in Paris, in the midst of movement and noise, alongside people, it gives rise not to boredom, but despair." Artful in her own rhetoric, Sand was no doubt more immune than most mothers to her daughter's complaints. She invited her to Nohant, but her offer was not without conditions. Solange could come to Nohant providing she did not cause "trouble on account of her follies, or despair on account of her unkindnesses."[22]

Sand was dismayed by Solange's ideas about how she might live as a single woman in mid-nineteenth-century France. In her letters to Sand, Solange implied that she considered "pleasure and vice" an attractive couple. Sand replied frankly:

> Why don't you try a little vice and prostitution then, I defy you to. . . . It is not as easy as you think to lose your honour. . . . Men who have money want women who know how to earn it. . . . I have seen young women fighting against strong feelings of both the heart and mind, and alarmed by their domestic misfortunes, because they are afraid of being dragged down against their wills. But I have never seen a single one, brought up as you have been, having lived in an atmosphere of moral dignity and freedom, alarmed by material privations and loneliness. . . . A woman with a heart and good judgement can be afraid . . . of being carried away by love, but never by greed.[23]

Sand had felt that acute sense of loss of honour in her sorry encounter with Mérimée. Solange's sense of honour was one that belonged to another generation, and she was a quite different kind of woman. Sand also offered to look after Nini and bring her up, knowing that the child's presence or absence from Nohant would depend on maternal and paternal whim. If Sand's concern was, above all, to maintain her own equilibrium, the decision to provide a foster home for Nini was a risky one to make. Clésinger, she knew, might descend on Nohant at any moment to claim the child. One of the many roles that Manceau fulfilled was to marshal a group which Sand called their "firefighters," a band of local youths charged with the protection of Nohant and its residents.

Sand, Manceau, and Nini, aged three, soon formed a family. Manceau looked after the little girl in the morning, while Nini and Sand spent time together in the afternoon, often working in the garden. The *Agenda* kept jointly by Sand and Manceau suggest contentment, in their meticulous recording of events, almost invariably noted with great economy: both described the other's current state of health, the weather, good meals, their activities—writing, music, embroidery, dominoes, chair recaning. All the while the endless stream of visitors failed to disrupt their settled domesticity. On 22 December Manceau noted: "Very ill. Letter to Hetzel. Visits from Blanchard, Duvernet and his son François, Mme Hetzel, P. Bocage . . . Mr. and Mrs. Browning, N[apoléon] Bonap[art]e. . . ."[24]

Suddenly, as their domestic life gradually asserted its own calm but steady rhythm, and at about the same time that Nini had begun to feel properly loved and safe at Nohant, her parents arrived and took her away. Sand knew very well that any reconciliation between Solange and Clésinger was unlikely to last, and feared for Nini. By the autumn the little girl had been returned to Nohant and Sand reassured Solange that Nini was well: "She wants to eat like a horse," Sand wrote, suggesting the outward sign of Nini's inner well-being.[25]

Sand and Nini spent long, happy hours on the miniature garden at Nohant. It was ambitious in its design, complete with miniature fountains, grottoes, and mountains; grandmother and grandchild often worked late into the evening, moving rocks in their wheelbarrows: one large, one small. Manceau would sit nearby, reading aloud a novel by Walter Scott or Balzac.[26] Sand looked after Nini and considered how best to order her life. And Manceau looked after Sand, always going to her room in the evening to arrange Sand's desk ritualistically, ensuring that her ink, tobacco, and the glass of sugar water from which she sipped as she wrote were all in place. No one had ever eased daily life for Sand as Manceau did. In all her previous relationships it had been Sand who had gone out of her way to support her lover. Manceau was utterly devoted. Noting in their journal that Sand had woken suffering from a blinding headache that day, he wrote, "All the same I did what I could to distract her: I took her into the garden, planted flowers on the island; I was spiritual, silly, gay, but nothing worked!"[27]

Devoting her time to playwriting at night, enjoying Maurice's marionette theatre and the real Nohant theatre, and above all enjoying the company of Nini and Manceau, Sand led a life in the mid-1850s that was as peaceful as it had ever been. That winter of 1853–54, in the snow, she worked "like a Cossack" and Nini "like a little horse," determined to extend the miniature garden. In January 1854 she described the project as a "monomania," and herself as healthier than she had ever felt before.[28] She was also making final adjustments to her autobiography that spring, and no doubt thinking more and more about Nini's future, and how best she might shape it for her. Nini was soon to turn five, and Sand was busy preparing to celebrate her birthday. What Sand most feared then occurred, quite unexpectedly. Clésinger arrived on 7 May 1854 and announced that he had filed a case for separation against Solange and that he intended, with the full support of the law, to remove his daughter. There was nothing Sand could do but cancel all the preparations that she had joyfully put in place for the birthday three days later. It would be some time, Sand knew, before the court hearing, and thus some time before Nini's fate could be decided. At first Clésinger kept the child with him, then she was placed in a boarding school. Solange retreated to a convent, once again.

1854 was the year in which Sand's *Story of My Life* started to appear and a new play staged, but Sand's concern was only for the outcome of the Clésinger separation, and more particularly the decisions taken on Nini's behalf.[29] Whether or not Sand sought to influence the judge is not known, but given her propensity for string-pulling, it may be that words had been whispered in the right ears. In any event, in an approach that is quite remarkable in its modernity, the judge, having accorded the separation of "bodies and chattels" on 16 December 1854, asked Nini whom she would most willingly nominate as her guardian. To her enormous joy, Sand was duly given custody of her beloved grandchild. It must have seemed as though life, for once, would imitate Sand's own art and the ending would be an improbable one and unequivocally happy. But the story took a further series of unexpected twists.

Before the judgement had been finalized, Clésinger intervened. It was to prove a fatal move and one that caused Sand more suffering than any other event of her life. The weather that January day was particularly bleak and very cold but Clésinger decided to take Nini out for the day. When he returned her to the convent that night she was suffering from a high fever. For several days the brave little girl battled against serious illness. Her mother was summoned. Solange arrived, hoping that her newfound faith might cause God himself to intervene and save her child. Nini died in her mother's arms.

A telegram was dispatched to Nohant. And Nini's little body was buried there three days later. Sand cried herself to sleep. Manceau believed, or wanted to believe, that his beloved Madame was bravely living through yet another tragedy. On 23 January he wrote, either because he felt it to be the case or to reassure himself, "Madame is all right. The freeze is thawing. Madame and Mme Solange talk about the course of poor little Nini's life."[30]

What seems to have helped, or in any case what happened, was that

Sand quickly decided to write Nini's story, propelled by that strange capacity, or even compulsion, to transform the raw bleakness of life into art, to give the chaos and anguish of human experience some shape, some form, some meaning, amid the terrible randomness of events. Manceau noted in that same diary entry of 23 January, ". . . Madame is going to continue her story of Nini. . . ." During the days that immediately followed Nini's funeral Sand managed to put on a brave face. As the days passed, however, Manceau became increasingly aware of Sand's deep unhappiness. Everything at Nohant reminded her of Nini. Manceau persuaded her to go away for a few weeks, and he would pay the expenses. But at some point between Nini's death and their departure for Rome, Sand finished her story "Après la mort de Jeanne Clésinger" ("After the Death of Jeanne Clésinger").[31]

The story was in part inspired by two writers: by Leibniz, and by Jean Reynaud, author of *Earth and Heaven*. On 14 February 1855, Sand wrote to Édouard Charton:

> *Earth and Heaven* is one of the finest books ever to have emerged from the human mind. It did me good, this and Leibniz. I knew it all before, but I could not have articulated it. . . . But I was certain, and I am certain. I see a future and eternal life ahead of me as a certainty, like a light whose brightness renders objects intangible; but the light is there, and that is all I need. I know well that my Jeanne is not dead, I know well that she is better off than in this sad world, where she was the victim of wicked and insensitive people. I know well that I will find her again and that she will recognize me, when she herself will no longer remember, and nor will I. She was part of me, and that cannot be changed.[32]

The story describes an experience which is more than an imagined encounter with Nini. One of the most moving stories in Sand's *The Story of My Life* describes her own desperate attempts as a young woman, just after her grandmother's death, to re-encounter her in some hallucinatory or dream state. She failed. In her story about Nini, the attempt is successful. But what is described is the *reality* of imagined experience: the vivid, truthful, super-reality of the visions of what is at once the subconscious and conscious self. Hearing a young woman's voice, the narrator of the story asks, "Is this sleep or ecstasy?" In this unknown and unknowable—but nevertheless real—state of existence, the narrator sets out to find the being whose voice she has heard. The landscape is an ideal one: the sun is bright, there is a freshness in the air, everything delights. Finally the narrator sees the young girl: "I saw her but I did not recognize her." When the narrator explains to the girl that her child has died, she answers, astonished: "Dead? . . . Only very rarely do children die here! Only old people leave us. . . . I can see that you are not of this world and I do not know how you arrived here. But we know that souls from other worlds can come to ours, and they appear to be like us. I know that I came here several times, by an act of thought, while I was living elsewhere, and that I was born here, having lived elsewhere." The story explored the relationships between lived, dreamed, and imagined experience and the comparative realities of these. Powerful tension was maintained: would the young woman recognize her interlocutor? What the young woman remembers, and joyfully articulates, at the close of the story, is a "children's garden that a woman, a mother, built for me, in the wake of sorrow and suffering."[33] The link was established.

"After the Death of Jeanne" is a compelling epitaph which celebrates above all the vigorous freshness and excitement of a small girl's encounter with the world. Sand had brought Nini back to life, and in creating something out of the overwhelming sense of loss, she found a way forward. The story also convinced her of the mysterious but very real relationships between the living and the dead.

Manceau took Sand away from Nohant on 28 February 1855. They started for Rome via Paris, where they picked up Maurice. Rome inspired that salutary emotion that had so often healed Sand in the past. What she felt above all was tremendous indignation. "If you are no more than an *artist*, that is you want to live your own life, having taken in a little from outside, you won't find what you want in this city of the past where everything is dead, even what you suppose to be still living," she wrote to Lambert.[34] When they returned from Rome Sand worked on a number of unremarkable plays. But her ideas and feelings about Catholicism and the Church continued to preoccupy her reason—and her imagination. What she wrote was the story of a young French painter's "Sentimental Education" (to borrow Flaubert's title) in Italy. But the real subject matter is Rome, the Catholic Church, and clerics; *La Daniella* is a passionately anticlerical novel. For some years Sand had been comparatively little noticed by the public. The publication of *La Daniella* quickly propelled her back into the social and political forum. The novel, published as a serialization in *La Presse*, provoked a violent exchange in that newspaper and in its right-wing counterparts. Initially *La Presse* was threatened with suspension, then banned. Always willing to go to the top, Sand wrote to the Empress Eugénie. *La Presse* was allowed to resume publication, but *La Daniella*, in an abridged version, appeared in book form.

If Sand had, because of the provocative *La Daniella*, reappeared in a sense on the Parisian political stage, Nohant had become a place in which it was becoming difficult to retreat because of the ever-increasing number of visitors drawn to the house, or rather its proprietor, often seeking her support in matters political or legal.

In June 1857 Sand and Manceau set out to explore the Valley of the Creuse. The village of Gargilesse particularly charmed them as a Rousseauesque paradise. The villagers were welcoming and they enjoyed a social life that struck Sand as unusual: even the women bathed in the river. Gargilesse was for Sand "an Arcadia," a place where "idiotic weariness of civilization" could be forgotten. Both Manceau and Sand wanted to spend time alone together, away from the demands of Nohant. What they needed was their own retreat, close enough to Nohant to be visited regularly, but far enough away to remain secret, and slightly cut off. Manceau bought her the house in which they had first stayed at Gargilesse, and he redesigned the interior much as he had transformed the theatre at Nohant not long after his arrival. He did it out like the cabin of a boat, and there was a place for everything.[35]

In the five years after the purchase of Sand's retreat at Gargilesse, between 1857 and 1862, she was to write thirteen novels, two volumes of essays, and three plays. Most of the work was done at Gargilesse. But Manceau usually accompanied her and, as her diary often suggests, it was an added pleasure to know that after a productive period of writing, Manceau would reappear, as delighted as Sand herself with their lovely surroundings: "Magnificent weather, hot and bright. Manceau left after lunch to catch butterflies. . . . I stayed at home to finish my novel, *Elle et lui* (*She and He*)."[36] The diary entry is for 29 May. She had started the novel on 4 May.

Musset had died the year before, and the public was aware that the novel was based on Sand's relationship with Alfred. Thérèse, the heroine, is "young, intelligent and beautiful, she is free and living alone" at the beginning of the novel. "He," Laurent, is younger, a genius unable to retain any balance in his life, and unable to love without seeking to destroy the object of his love. Buloz thought that as an account of Sand's relationship with Musset, it was substantially true, although he thought that Thérèse had been rendered "saintly," which he considered an exaggeration.

Musset may never have forgiven Sand her infidelities, and we will never know how completely Sand felt able to forgive him his infidelities. But that she aspired towards feelings of generosity is made plain at the end of *He and She:* "To watch them and to hear them, one would have said that they were two friends at peace and had never quarrelled. This strange calm had occurred several times in the midst of their wildest crises. When their hearts were silent, their minds still understood one another and agreed."[37]

Given its source, it is likely that the novel would have sold well even if Musset's brother Paul had not further attracted the attention of the reading public by publishing his own version of the affair, *Lui et elle (He and She)*. The literary scandal thus provoked was further fuelled by the publication of *Lui (He)* by Louise Colet. Colet, who had been Flaubert's mistress before Musset's, seems to have been motivated purely by the prospect of financial gain. Sainte-Beuve, as faithful as ever to Sand, nobly defended her in public debate.

But however Sand suffered from the maliciousness of these works, she was determined as always to prevent the controversy from overwhelming her. As she wrote to Dumas *fils*, whom she encouraged and supported, "At your age I was as tormented and still more ill than you, both morally and physically. . . . One fine morning I said to myself 'None of this matters to me. The universe is great and beautiful. Everything we think so crucial is so fleeting that it is not worth thinking about.' "[38]

But Sand cared about more than simply her immediate social group. *La Daniella* had drawn her back into political debate. The censoring of literary works, that collusion of the political and religious, filled her with indignation. On 26 February 1862 Sand wrote once more to Jérôme Bonaparte: "If the Emperor is afraid of Socialism; so be it, from his point of view, he ought to fear it; but, in striking it down too forcibly and too quickly, he has raised up, on the ruins of the party, a quite different party."[39]

The strength of Sand's anticlericalism is explicable only as a function of her Christian conviction. Her criticisms of the Church are also a defence of what she believed to be the true faith. She abhorred Orthodox Catholic theology and believed it to be deeply damaging. Furthermore, she sought to expose what she saw as an alliance between Catholic orthodoxy and clerical and political power. These notions emerge in *Mademoiselle La Quintinie* (1863). The novel's polemic is explicitly expressed in Sand's preface: "There is something else in addition to the doctrine of the clergy, there is the party of the clergy, whose activities fall into the category of political agitation." What she feared was "a vast plot against the principle of social and individual freedom."[40]

The ideas expressed in *Mademoiselle La Quintinie*, its audacious criticisms of reactionary Catholicism and its collaboration with political repression, were shared by large numbers of students, particularly in Paris. The novel articulated fears that had only been half recognized by its readers. Sand, however old she felt, continued to personify the iconoclasm of the day. When Parisian students heard that her latest play, *Villemer*, was to be staged at the Odéon on 29 February 1864, they descended on the theatre *en masse*. When all the seats had been taken, those students shut outside the theatre made their way to the Club Catholique and the neighbouring Maison des Jésuites, protesting against clericalism. Inside the theatre the Emperor and Empress were seated in the imperial box. In a neighbouring box sat Sand and Prince Jérôme. The play met with an extraordinary response. Flaubert, one of many of Sand's friends present at the performance, greeted her warmly during the interval, crying like a woman. When Sand left the theatre that night she was greeted by a huge crowd of students chanting "Vive George Sand! Vive *Mademoiselle La Quintinie!* Down with the clerics!"[41] The play ran for several weeks, and similar scenes were repeated on successive nights.

XXIII

Son and Lover

"Alone once again! Now and forever."

Although Sand's theatrical successes in the early 1860s had drawn her back into more public political controversy, she did not lose sight of family matters. In particular she had continued to worry about Maurice's bachelor status. But her concern to find Maurice a suitable wife was confused by, and merged with, her own desire to find the daughter that neither Solange nor Augustine had turned out to be. As ever, Sand was aware of her own mixed motives. As she wrote to Lina Calamatta on 31 March 1862, two months before her marriage to Maurice, "I feel sure that I will be a true mother to you, because I need a daughter and I could find no one better than the best of my friends."[1] Numerous unsatisfactory relationships with women were being relived in Sand's relationship with Lina. In many ways Sand tried to be, for Lina, the kind of older woman friend for whom she had herself so much longed as a young woman. Sand felt more deeply committed to Lina than to Solange and she was not ashamed to admit as much. In a letter to Flaubert, who was to become the most important of her correspondent-confessors, she explained: "My daughter Lina remains my true daughter. *The other* is, well . . ."[2] She continued to use her novelistic licence inventively to convey her idea of the complexities of family relationships.

The summer of 1862 was a happy one. By the autumn Lina had fallen pregnant and Sand must have hoped for further compensation: this time for

Nini, for whom she continued to grieve. With novelistic éclat her grand-child was born on 14 July 1863 and the family celebrated both the birth and the storming of the Bastille. The new grandchild turned out to be a son: Marc-Antoine, soon called "Cocoton" within the family. The miniature cannon at Nohant was ceremonially fired. Lina and Marc-Antoine had, to some extent at least, filled the terrible void left by Nini—and spiritually, if not literally, by Solange.

Interesting visitors continued to pass through Nohant, some staying longer than others.[3] Dumas, who was helping Sand with an adaptation of *Villemer*, invited Théophile Gautier to Nohant, but he interpreted Sand's silence as an intentionally "icy" reception and quickly decided to leave. Dumas hastily took him to Sand, who explained herself: "Did you not make it known to him," she said to Dumas with mock reproach, "that I am as silly as could be . . . and that I have no idea how to chat with intellectu-als?"[4] She was a flatterer, but equally given to saying little if she admired and was interested in the conversation of others. Gautier and Sand then spent three days talking intently. As he was a writer too, an arch-Romantic, they can have had little difficulty sustaining their exchanges.

Relationships between the permanent residents at Nohant, however, were becoming more tense and it was often difficult for Sand to do much to ease them. Everyone was working hard, against different odds. She and Manceau were both working on plays, which were staged at Nohant. Mau-rice was struggling with his second novel. Sand had already noted in her journal that Manceau's health had become a source of worry. On 31 March 1863 she had written, "Manceau still has neuralgia," and on 2 April, "Manceau is still suffering." For some months Sand had had bouts of stom-ach pain. Yet both she and Manceau continued to work flat out. That autumn their *Agenda* entry describes them "working like slaves."[5]

By the end of the summer tensions between the various residents at Nohant had heightened. The catalyst for the row that finally broke out was Marie Caillaud, a servant who acted in the plays. She was unhappy with Manceau's stage directions and Maurice chose to take her side. The drama of the theatrical scene in question was quickly surpassed by the drama of the argument among the family, and extended family. Maurice, as he had declared years earlier, asked his mother to choose between him and her lover. Both, he declared, could not continue to live peaceably with her at Nohant. Sand replied to the effect that he was her son, and Nohant his home. Manceau, it seems, was expected to leave. His record of events reveals his calm, his dignity, his resilience, his independence, qualities that Sand admired, and loved:

> At the end of I no longer remember what conversation I am told that I am free to go on the forthcoming Saint John's day. Tears are shed on my behalf. Not for long. That is all I could elicit by way of regret for fifteen years of devotion. I am inclined to record this here, so as never to cry about it again, and with the hope that I will smile later. What does it matter, by and large humanity is a sad thing. So I am off to rediscover my liberty and should I wish to love someone and devote myself again, because that is my own source of joy, I can do so with complete freedom. Freedom, that is a fine thing. . . .[6]

Whether Manceau wrote the entry for Sand, inviting her to read it, is uncertain. But read it she did, and quickly announced her intention of leaving Nohant, with Manceau. Her diary entry, written the following day, was, it seems, crafted in the expectation that Manceau would read it, and be comforted:

> Me, I am not sad. Why? We know all that; and that things were going badly. I too, I am reclaiming *my* freedom. And because we are not leaving one another? And are we content that things should change? And because I was hoping for some change, in this life of bitterness and injustice? Let us leave, my dear, let us leave without bitterness, without annoyance, and never leave each other. They can have everything, everything can be for them, but not our dignity, and not the sacrifice of our friendship. *Never.*[7]

When the time came—and it was some months later (12 June 1864)—Manceau wrote, on the eve of their departure from Nohant: "LAST EVENING AT NOHANT. We will all remember it, I believe. There is then nothing to write of this last watch, but I think, despite myself, that during the last fourteen years that I have spent here, I have laughed more, cried more, *lived* more, than during the thirty-three years that preceded them. From now on I am alone with her. What a responsibility, but also what an honour and what a joy!"[8]

The permanent departure had been made less dramatic by a temporary one at the beginning of 1864. Louis Maillard, a cousin of Manceau's, found them a little villa in the village of Palaiseau, just south of Paris. That spring both Sand and Manceau enjoyed the success of their plays: the latter's was a great triumph, staged at the Odéon; *Villemer* was equally fêted. Back at Nohant, Sand felt less and less at ease, and more and more beleaguered by people seeking her support, both moral and financial. "I am changing my manner of living; I am delighted and find it comic that people should complain. . . ." Sand was increasingly convinced that it was time for a new start.

On 12 June Sand and Manceau left Nohant, definitively, or so they thought, for Palaiseau. Manceau had made ready their new home, and Sand, like a young bride, appreciated every detail:

> I am quite infatuated with *everything;* the region, the
> little garden, the view, the house, the furniture,
> the meals, the maid, the silence. It is enchanting.
> The good Manceau has thought of everything; *it is
> perfection.*[9]

Sand continued, however, to notice small changes in Manceau's health. The diary entry for 23 June reads, "Manceau spat a little blood, which is surely nothing."[10] Yet Sand had sufficient medical experience to know that blood in the sputum might well not be a negligible matter.

Having taken the decision to leave Nohant to Maurice and Lina, Sand delighted in the present. In the event, the younger couple had also left, and had travelled to Guillery, invited by Casimir. Nohant had proved a complex estate to manage in the absence of Sand and Manceau. Any irritation that the older couple might have felt at their sudden—and in retrospect unnecessary—departure must quickly have been forgotten, however, when news of Cocoton's ill health reached them at Palaiseau. It was serious. On 14 July, the baby's birthday, Sand wrote in her journal, "What a sad birthday for my poor little one, but this evening's telegram was better; there is hope."[11] But only five days later she notes, "Before sitting down to eat, we receive the terrible news that Marc is dying: 'MUCH WORSE LITTLE HOPE.' " They tried to reach Guillery by rail that day, but train delays would have meant missing a vital connection. The next day they received a further telegram: "IF YOU WANT TO SEE HIM COME."[12] They arrived the following day, 21 July 1864, in the afternoon. But too late: the baby had died that morning. On 22 July Maurice asked Manceau to summon the local Protestant *pasteur* to arrange the baby's funeral. Sand smoked cigarette after cigarette. Back at Palaiseau, on the twenty-fourth, Manceau was coughing once again. Sand returned to work. She was not pleased with the results, noting, "With great effort I have finished my novel [*L'Enfant perdu (The Lost Child)*], begun before Marc-Antoine's illness. If it is bad, God knows it is not my fault."[13] Once again fiction had curiously preceded parallel events in real life, and prepared her in some way. Manceau's health continued to preoccupy her. Although she was reassured by Camille Leclerc, their doctor, she continued to suspect the worst. On 4 August she noted further bouts of coughing.[14] But she continued to struggle to live, following her own advice to Maurice and Lina:

> We will love, we will suffer, we will hope, we will be afraid, we will be full of joy, of terrors, in a word we will go on living, because life is like that, a terrible mix. Let us love and support each other.[15]

She was raging against the dying of the light.

Manceau's declining health challenged Sand's vigorous attitude to life more than anything she had yet experienced. For weeks and months Manceau and Sand fought the tuberculosis that they at some point that year acknowledged as the cause of his coughing and increasing breathlessness and now common bouts of high fever. On 4 September Sand recorded that he was "coughing horribly."[16] Sand's journal, and Manceau's until it is left off—his last entry was on 6 June 1864—recorded the weeks of decline.

By August Manceau's convulsive coughing sometimes lasted for hour upon hour without interruption. On 19 August Sand noted ominously:

> Same as usual, or worse, because he has lost his appetite. Everything is unappealing, and the breathlessness is the same. Constant coughing, all evening and all night.[17]

Sand was ready for the loneliness which would be with her, evermore. On 21 August she finally recorded his death:

My poor friend! Dead this morning, at six o'clock, after an apparently completely peaceful night. When he woke, he spoke a little, in a voice that was already dead, and then indistinctly, as in a dream, then he made some effort to breathe, then he became pale, and then nothing! He was not conscious, I hope. He had spoken to me willingly and lucidly at midnight. He talked of going to Nohant. I changed him and laid him out on his bed. I closed his eyes. I arranged flowers around him. He is beautiful and looks quite young. Oh! My God! I no longer have him to watch over.[18]

The following night she spent at his bedside:

I spent the night alone, near his sleeping body! He is on his bed, always calm now. There is nothing frightening. No bad smells. I have given him fresh roses. Marchal, La Rounat, Borie, Dumas and Fromentin came to see me. Marchal dined with me. . . . Now I am alone again, and he is there, beside me, in this little room. I no longer have to listen to his breathing, and tomorrow night, nothing, alone once again! Now, and forever. . . .[19]

Manceau's sister arrived the same day. Sand was dismayed that she had no desire to see her brother's body: she claimed that the sight of his body "would make too much of an impression." Manceau's mother did not come: her son had not confessed.[20] Manceau had not wanted a funeral, and Sand acted in accordance with his wishes.[21] Before his burial, however, Sand wanted to be certain that Manceau was quite dead, so she summoned a surgeon who made some incision in his body, to confirm that all life had ceased. Sand remained at Manceau's side throughout.[22]

The working men of Palaiseau, who had deeply respected him, carried the coffin, draped in white, to the local cemetery, where it was covered with flowers. Manceau had left all his property and possessions to his lover's son. Maurice had become his son, in effect, despite all the tensions associated with that relationship.

Sand spent three sleepless nights at Palaiseau before leaving for Nohant. There she was finally able to rest, but wrote to Manceau in her diary so as to reassure him that her ability to sleep was in no way a sign that she was no longer with him: "Do not fear, what is yours will never perish." Sand was suspicious of superstition, but believed deeply in immortality, in some kind of resurrection to new life after death. But she understood it in a very particular way. As far as she was concerned, all those whom she had loved, and who had died, were still very much present in her life. Manceau would be always.

A few weeks later she returned to Palaiseau. She noted in her *Agenda*, no doubt with great relief, "I am getting organized and doing a little work."[23] She saw many of her friends; Marchal's name recurs in her diary, and he was surely a close friend.[24] "You take me as I am," she writes tellingly of their relations.[25] Sand's novel *Le Dernier Amour* (*Last Love*) is, however, dedicated not to Marchal but to Flaubert, who was deeply touched.[26] Although Sand and Marchal met frequently, dining together and having tea *chez* Sand, her correspondence with Flaubert is profoundly intimate: what is said depends on a great deal that is unsaid, but understood by both of them. Her letters and notes about Marchal are quite different. Physically Sand may well have sought comfort in her intimacy with Marchal; morally, in the broadest sense, she was deeply involved with Flaubert. It suited her that no one man had replaced Manceau: he was too great and too good.

Sand and Flaubert had met earlier, and each was well aware of the other's work, but the beginning of their extraordinary friendship dates from early 1863. That January Sand wrote to congratulate Flaubert on the publication of *Salammbô:* he was heartened by her gesture since the work had been poorly received by both the public and critics.

A year later their acquaintance began to develop into intimate friendship. Flaubert had called on Sand in Paris, during February 1864, overcome with emotion at the extraordinary success she had achieved with *Villemer*. They continued to meet from time to time at Magny's, a restaurant frequented by the intellectually and artistically famous; Sand was admitted in 1866 and remained the only woman member of this exclusive "dining club." Among her circle, meeting to dine either at Magny's or elsewhere, were the Goncourt brothers—whose diaries provide a fascinating account of the meetings—her old friend Sainte-Beuve, Gautier, Hippolyte Taine, Ernest Renan, Berthelot, in short many of the great writers and thinkers of her day. But it was Flaubert to whom Sand felt most drawn; she described him as "passionate, more sympathetic to me than the others. Why? I do not yet know."[27] His life, unlike his writing—and the contradictions between the two—no doubt aroused Sand's curiosity. He had loved passionately and hopelessly at the age of fourteen. The object of his love, Elisa Schlesinger, was a much older and married woman. From then on, he was drawn most easily to courtesans, including Louise Colet, whose novel *Lui* had so outraged Sand.

Sand repeatedly invited Flaubert to Nohant, but travel disturbed his equilibrium. He invited her to his retreat at Croisset, and she accepted. Flaubert was waiting for her at the station at Rouen. Sand noted in her diary: "We arrive at Croisset at three-thirty. Flaubert's mother is a delightful old lady."[28] So began, quite conventionally, Sand's first visit to Croisset.

As soon as she had left, Flaubert wrote to tell her how very much she had been liked by all who had met her. Again he asked for a portrait of her, "so that I may always have before me your dear and beautiful head." Years earlier he had made the same request.[29]

Sand was immensely curious about Flaubert's past. She supposed that his life had been freer than her own: "It seems to me that an intelligent man is allowed enormous curiosity," she wrote.[30] Women of intelligence, she implied, could not give rein to the same curiosity. Flaubert was, Sand told him, "very much a being apart . . . very mysterious, but as gentle as a lamb for all that." Flaubert objected: "Me, a mysterious being, dear master, surely not! I find myself, on the contrary, sickeningly banal and sometimes heartily bored by the bourgeois under my skin. . . . I have *dreamed* a good deal and done very little."[31]

Sand remained fascinated by Flaubert, and vice versa. They were both writers who worked with great discipline and industry, but this is the only close similarity between them. While Flaubert was reluctant to leave Croisset, Sand was always keen to have an excuse to travel, and her creative energies, rather than suffering, were invariably stimulated. As she wrote to Flaubert, "You do not have *itchy feet*, like me, ready always to leave. You live in your dressing gown, the great enemy of liberty and action."[32] Was the last remark calculated to make the old bourgeois sufficiently indignant to cast off his domestic badge? Flaubert had withdrawn from life, years earlier; Sand, even late in life, constantly looked for stimulus, engagement.

In November, after the arduous and final months nursing Manceau, Sand again made the journey to Croisset. The notes in her *Agenda* convey her sheer pleasure in time spent close to Flaubert: "Ravishing weather. Tour of the garden as far as the orchard, work. . . . Gustave reads me his astonishing work [*Le Château des Coeurs*]. It is full of admirable and charming things, too long, too rich, too full."[33]

Sand made numerous visits to Croisset. Among the discussions which were to have a direct bearing on their writing, were those that explored revolutionary happenings. Sand spoke at length of her experience, and Flaubert no doubt drew on her descriptions of men like Armand Barbès for his novel *Sentimental Education,* on which he was working. Flaubert developed for her what he described as "a particular tenderness" which he had never felt before.[34] It was a tenderness that Sand felt she had, in a sense, to refuse, to enjoy only in the abstract. She explained to Flaubert: "I am afraid of becoming too dependent and of wearying people. Old people need to exercise extreme discretion."[35]

As she had written in a draft version of *The Story of My Life,* she had always felt drawn to commit herself wholeheartedly to those whom she loved, yet with Flaubert she supposed that that "particular affection" was a delicate emotion, and one that she greatly valued. She was too old to gamble with emotion, as she had so often done in the past. And Manceau remained an aching absent presence in her life, particularly while she remained at Palaiseau. In one of her saddest letters to Flaubert she wrote:

> Here I am *quite alone* in my house. The gardener and his family live in a pavilion in the garden. We are the last house at the bottom of the village, completely isolated in the countryside which is a ravishing oasis. . . . But I am sad here all the same. This absolute solitude, which I have always felt to be rest and recreation, is now shared by a dead man, whose life came to an end here, like a lamp going out and which is always there. I do not believe that he is unhappy in the place where he now is; but this image that he has left around me, which is no more than a glimmer, seems to complain at no longer being able to speak to me. Never mind; unhappiness is not unhealthy, it prevents us from drying up.[36]

Sand did not stay on much longer at Palaiseau. In January 1867 she became seriously unwell and Maurice and Lina tried to persuade her to return to Nohant. A further draw was the beautiful Lolo, Sand's new granddaughter. Her real name was Aurore.

The return to Nohant was a return to company: the children, including Hippolyte's grandchildren, were a great delight. There were other residents too. Among the most important to Sand was Juliette La Messine, a subversive writer to whom Sand was able to give a great deal while enjoying, vicariously, her involvement in the much younger woman's life. The companionship with Juliette that Sand enjoyed in many ways complemented her friendship with Flaubert. Both allowed her to see the shape of her own life measured from two very different perspectives, and to recognize the degree to which she had changed during the course of the years, and indeed was continuing to change. Reflecting a strikingly modern psychology, she declared, "It seems to me that one changes day to day and that at the end of some years one is a new being. . . . Here I am, very old, gently living through my sixty-fifth year. . . . I am absolutely calm, it is an old age chaste in mind and body. I do not regret my youth, I have no desire for glory or money except to leave a little to my children and grandchildren."[37]

Sand experienced the relative chasteness of her old age as a liberation. She felt that she had achieved a degree of independence that she had never known earlier. But to write "I have known love, loves, alas! If I were to live my life again, I would be chaste" is to contradict a dictum delivered up for Flaubert, a dictum to which Sand was surely committed above all: "The artist is an explorer who should be deterred by nothing and who commits neither good nor evil walking to the right or the left: his aim sanctifies everything."[38]

Sand stayed with Juliette and her second husband, the writer Edmond Adam, and their daughter in Normandy on a number of occasions and saw them from time to time in Paris; they visited the Exposition Universelle of 1867 together. That winter Juliette invited her to her villa, Bruyères, on the Côte d'Azur. Juliette was awaiting the birth of her next child. Sand had been yearning to be by the sea, and to enjoy the warmth of the Mediterranean coast. She felt uneasy, however, about being so near Solange, who was the guest of a foreign prince in Cannes. In the event, Solange kept away from her mother at Bruyères, and Sand delighted in the place and the company.

Sand's return to Paris more or less coincided with the birth of Juliette's beautiful second daughter. When they visited Sand at Nohant, Juliette noted that "happiness, at Nohant, is as cloudless as at Bruyères." They celebrated Sand's birthday in style and Maurice performed a brilliant puppet show in his mother's honour. "Maurice was up for twenty nights to entertain his adored mother for an hour," Juliette noted.[39]

In 1868 Sand was in Paris watching the final touches being given to her play *Cadio*. She continued to enjoy everything about drama: the players, the slide in and out of make-believe, the theatres, performance, audiences, and the rest. Flaubert thought she was too easily seduced, but she explained, "I love them [actors] as I love the woods, the fields, everything, all those things I hardly know and that I continue to study. I take my place in the middle of all that, and, as I love that position, I love everything that is nourishing and renewing. . . ." On a rather different tack, she added, "I am capable of enormous indulgence."[40]

Sand had become increasingly interested not in judgement but in observation. She felt her anger at injustice to be less certain. It had been almost completely replaced by a desire for understanding. She felt privileged to be close to people, close to their inner lives, and was instantly fascinated by the range of human experience.

Sand enjoyed the last years of her life. She had become financially secure, and no longer needed to drive herself to write as she had for so many years. Aware that life would soon draw to a close, she took great pleasure in what was immediately to hand, in the present. As life slowed down she learnt to savour detail. And time played compensatory tricks: "Winter days count twice over," she noted. Sand's many visitors from abroad described her typical day: "She picks flowers, noting interesting botanical anomalies, sewing dresses and coats for her granddaughters, and costumes for the puppets . . . and above all spending hours with her little Aurore."[41]

Children, especially her own grandchildren, continued to delight and fascinate Sand. *The Story of My Life* reveals the extent to which she sought to understand the process by which the child changes and grows up, and the degree to which vital individuality must be suppressed, even amputated, in order that the individual take her place within the structures of society. Nor—despite the pleasure that she took in her grandchildren, and domestic tasks—did she stop writing. Her output slowed down, and her sense of her audience changed considerably too. In a letter to Flaubert she wrote, "I do my little novel each year, when I have an hour or two in which to apply myself. . . ." In another letter she explained that while she wrote "for myself alone and a few friends . . . I will die with my shoulder to the wheel."[42] Just as, in her autobiography, she had identified her emergent self as essentially a storyteller, so it seems that the activity of writing defined her sense of self to a point where not to write would be to cease to be George Sand. Ink and her lifeblood would cease to flow almost at the same time. The deaths of both Luigi Calamatta, Lina's father, and Sainte-Beuve, in 1869, made her aware that her own generation was gradually dying off. She travelled to Paris for Sainte-Beuve's funeral, which was a huge event:

> The whole of Paris was there, the arts, the sciences, the young, the people, no senators, no priests. . . . Flaubert was very moved. . . . Alexandre (Dumas) and his father who can no longer walk . . . Adam, Borie, Taine . . . old Grzymała . . . Atheists, believers, people of every age, of every opinion, and the crowd.[43]

Sand was deeply saddened by Sainte-Beuve's death: he had been a great friend. But in her notes she also reveals the degree to which his funeral was one of those "sources" essential to the writer's being in the world, as a writer.

Flaubert's *Sentimental Education* came out in 1869, but was poorly received by the critics and the public. Sand was one of the few to defend it. He was little comforted by his visit to Nohant. He disliked Maurice's puppets, and wanted only intellectual conversation. The practical joking and light-hearted atmosphere irritated him. Sand claimed to have identified the endogenous cause of his irritation when she explained, "He does not know whether to be a poet or a realist; and because he is both the first and second, it annoys him."[44] It is surely one of the most astute observations ever made about one of France's greatest and most mysterious writers. Sand had been content to live out both the realist and the poet in herself—simultaneously. And while that amalgam worked for life it created a mixed, inconsistent, and paradoxical literary oeuvre more difficult to integrate into literary history than the small number of works by Sand's greatest friend, Gustave Flaubert.

XXIV

Communion

"Fear is a vertigo which draws us into imagined
dangers. Overcome the vertigo, and there
is no more danger."

The year 1870–71 was a desperate year for France, and a sombre one for Sand and Flaubert. So many of their friends and associates had died, even before France went to war with Prussia. Flaubert wrote to Sand, "Apart from you and Turgenev, I know not a single mortal to whom I can pour out my heart about matters which are most dear to me; and you live so far away from me, you two."[1] But Flaubert's misery did not cloud all of Sand's life, which continued to be multiple and varied by comparison with that of the hermit of Croisset. She wrote triumphantly to Maurice in February 1870. Her play *L'Autre* was poised for remarkable success: a young newcomer to the stage, Sarah Bernhardt, would be playing the lead role quite brilliantly.[2]

But back at Nohant another life, crucial to her own happiness, looked in danger. Maurice was gravely ill, and his health would be a worry for years to come. "When he collapses . . ." she wrote to Flaubert, "we are all dead, mother, wife and daughters. Aurore says that she would like to be seriously ill in place of her father. We love each other with such intensity, we five, and *sacrosanct* literature, as you call it, takes only second place in my life. I have always loved someone more than literature, and my family more than that someone."[3] For Sand, as is visible in *Marianne*, written a couple of years later, a story which Flaubert greatly admired, these were moral positions.

Sand was equally depressed by the looming prospect of war between France and Prussia. "Let us love one another, let us not love war," she insisted.[4] Only days later France declared war. Even Edmond Plauchut's colourful letters from Paris, reminiscent of her own years earlier, did nothing to kindle any enthusiasm. If Paris had been stirred to action, "Paris is mad," she wrote simply in reply to them.[5] From her provincial perspective she explained to Juliette Adam that war seemed "not a question of national honour, but a silly, an odious need to experiment with guns, a game of princes. . . . To sing the 'Marseillaise' to the tune of the Empire seems a sacrilege. . . . I am very sad, and this time my old patriotism—my passion for the drum—will not awaken. . . . The whole world is going mad."[6]

Sand's understanding of her compatriots was derived more and more from her knowledge of the peasant people of Berry. The new nationalism seemed urban and strange from the perspective of rural France. But some of her old loyalty to her nation was stirred by the Prussian invasion of Alsace and Lorraine. The former was lost first. "We must flush out the Prussians and empires at one fell swoop," she wrote to Juliette.[7] On 20 August she sent a donation to the Fund for the Wounded. But it was a gesture motivated by her commitment to socialism, as opposed to violent revolution: "I am, myself, socially, of the reddest hue, today as before. . . . But . . . one should never impose convictions by means of violence . . . because that which is born of violence is itself condemned to die a violent death."[8] To Sand's astonishment it was without great violence that a new era would quite suddenly begin. But bloodshed would follow not far behind. On 5 September 1870 she noted, "Maurice wakes me to say that the Republic has been proclaimed in Paris *without meeting any resistance,* an extraordinary event, unique in the history of the people! God protect France! She has once more become worthy in His sight."[9] Her unfailing optimism was just below her wrinkles.[10] Napoleon III had capitulated to an entire French army at Sedan. While the revolutionaries and republicans sought to come to some provisional agreement, the exiles returned: Hugo, Ledru-Rollin, Louis Blanc, Félix Pyat, Pierre Leroux.

Meanwhile the threat from the Prussians continued. Sand left Nohant for a period, taking refuge with friends in the Creuse. But she soon returned to Nohant as the possibility of the Prussian forces reaching further grew. Vierzon, only eighty kilometres away, had fallen. Sand's attitude was fatalistic: "I continue to work," she wrote, "and even with spirit, and in response to the approaching danger. It is like a task that I want to finish in order to die with the satisfaction that I worked right up to the end." Sand's confidence in this philosophical attitude contrasts with her growing sense of incomprehension of the events taking place in Paris. The crowds called for the "Commune," but the "*communards*" were not "*communistes.*" Sand wrote, "I am not familiar with the theories of the modern Commune, I don't see them made manifest anywhere; but if they have to be imposed by a slap of the hand, even if they were the social panacea, I condemn them in the name of everything that is human, patient, even indulgent, but jealous of freedom. . . . Contempt for the masses, that's the woe and the crime of the present moment."[11] Her views on contemporary happenings contrasted with the confident analyses she had offered years earlier during periods of political upheaval. Now she wrote, "I can scarcely form a clear opinion on what is happening today in that closed world that calls itself Paris. . . . The absence of reliable communication between Paris and France has prevented each and every one of us from being in touch with ideas."[12] War against the Prussians had provoked internal revolution and Sand found it difficult to understand how it had all come about. Paris became increasingly cut off, food supplies minimal, and any communication difficult. In early October, two hot-air balloons, one called "Armand Barbès," the other "George Sand," airlifted various Americans and Léon Michel Gambetta, minister of the interior, to safety. To the fury of the French, an armistice was agreed in January 1871. The conditions were a humiliation to the Parisians, but Sand was immensely relieved: "Ah! my God, finally! An armistice is to be signed for 21 days hence. . . ."[13] Flaubert had written to Sand, from the relative safety of Croisset, that he would rather see Paris burnt to the ground than admit defeat, but the national elections of early February showed the national mood to be closer to Sand's: negotiation was the favoured way forward.[14] Not, however, for a group of diehards in Paris. The radical extremists of the Paris National Guard took up a siege position in Montmartre. The Hôtel de Ville was taken over, and a "commune," or revolutionary government, established. Those involved were supporters of Proudhon, Blanqui, and Marx.

Sand watched from Nohant with astonishment, and dismay: "They are ransoming, threatening, arresting, judging. They are keeping the law courts from functioning. They have extracted a million from the bank, five hundred thousand from Rotchild [*sic*]. The people are frightened; they are giving in. They have started to fight on the streets; at the Place Vendôme they set fire to, and killed, numerous people. . . . They are ridiculous and brutish; the impression one has is that they have no idea what to do with their coup."[15] The war against Prussia, which had caused enormous loss of life and destruction, had been replaced by an even more senseless civil war in which further loss of life and further destruction now seemed inevitable.

Sand deemed contemporary happenings and the thinking behind them to be peculiarly Parisian, and a strangely urban phenomenon. In her writings at the time she contrasts urban and rural France. To Prince Jérôme Bonaparte, who wanted her advice as to whether it would be safe for him to return to France, she wrote that *she* had no desire to go to Paris, where "gold and muck" had been indiscriminately mixed. "I have not left Nohant, and I won't leave it this year. I prefer the shade of my lime trees and the possession of myself, my judgement, my freedom, my dignity."[16]

As the new Republic took shape and day-to-day life in the capital, and beyond, resumed its normal patterns, old friends returned to Nohant. Some that Sand would have dearly loved to see had died during the months of upheaval. Pierre Leroux, one of her great mentors, had died in April 1871. Casimir had also died, but not without writing to the Emperor in the hope of soliciting the Grand Cross of the Legion of Honour, in recognition of the hardships he had suffered as the husband of the notorious George Sand! The story could be straight out of Flaubert. *Madame Bovary* closes with the ridiculous award of the same national medal.[17]

Among the guests that Sand received most joyously as travel became possible once again were Pauline Viardot and the three daughters she now had. They arrived in the autumn of 1872, and although it had been a quarter of a century since Pauline's last visit to Nohant, she sang, to Sand's astonishment, many of the Berrichon songs that she had learnt at Nohant in the Chopin days. Sand was overcome: "What a day, what emotion, what musical penetration," she noted in her diary.[18] That sense of communion with the past, and with passions felt long ago, the affinity with others that is part of the experience of music, particularly in a domestic setting, were of profound importance to Sand, and more and more intense towards the very end of her life. It is that same sense of fusion of the self with those that are loved that she describes when noting the joys of bathing in the Indre, a daily habit she continued until the very end of her life, against the advice of doctors.[19] In her *Agenda* she wrote, "While lying in the water, I think of those who have bathed with us here in the past: Pauline and her mother, Chopin, Delacroix, my brother. We would even swim at night. We came on foot, and returned in the same way. They are all dead, except for Mme

Viardot and me. . . ."[20] There is something of the liturgical, "in the one body we were all baptized," in Sand's words. The lure of water, so morbid in her youth, had been curiously transformed.

On 3 October 1872 another guest arrived: Turgenev. Tremendous fun was had. He visited again in April 1873; this time he overlapped with Flaubert. The two writers, Sand notes, exaggerated each other's dispositions: "We leap, we dance, we shout, we addle Flaubert's wits; he always wants to stop everything in order to talk about literature. He's beaten. Turgenev loves noise and gaiety. He's as childish as we are. He dances, he waltzes; what a great and good man of genius!"[21]

The departure of Sand's guests marked a sharp return to reality. Solange was busy trying to buy back a neighbouring château. Hippolyte's daughter was selling the property adjacent to the Château de Montgivray. Sand was appalled by the thought of her daughter living nearby but there was nothing she could do.[22] Solange moved there in 1873 and would arrive unannounced for meals from time to time. Sand did her best to all but ignore her presence. She was now too old for contention, but as convinced as ever of the futility of conciliatory lies.

However saddened and irritated by her daughter's behaviour, she was determined not to allow Solange to distract her from the pleasure she derived from the next generation, from her beloved granddaughters. She often mentions them in her letters, particularly those to Flaubert. He understood, perhaps surprisingly, their importance in Sand's life and, still more remarkably, realized his own misfortune in having no comparable relationships in his own life: "What you told me . . . about your dear little ones stirred the very depths of my soul. Why don't I have that in my life? I was born surrounded on every side by tenderness. But we don't make our own destiny, we bear it. I was cowardly in my youth, *I was frightened by life!* Everything has its cost."[23] Sand, on the other hand, believed that "to some extent we make our own lives"; she was not afraid to scold Flaubert, and to tease: "You love literature too much, it will kill you, and you won't kill human stupidity."[24] She could not, however, bring herself to scold and rage at him, which she thought to be salutary and therapeutically necessary. Instead she advised him to call on Hugo: "I think he will calm you; as for me, I don't now possess sufficient inner thunder to make you understand me."[25]

She could no longer excite herself sufficiently to shake Flaubert out of misanthropy, nor did she feel that old indignation as she read accounts of contemporary political events in the papers: "I conscientiously read my paper every morning; but outside that time, I find it impossible to think of it or to interest myself in it."²⁶ The desperate need that she had felt throughout her life to order the parts in relation to a whole no longer gripped her. Nor did she feel her old confidence in the possibility of making proper sense of things. The chaos of life in which she had constantly tried to find some rational pattern now seemed nothing more than confusion. Years after the Commune she remained baffled: "I admit that I don't see clearly amid the torment. I cannot condone or criticize certain events in themselves. The whole seems like an excess of terrible fever. . . . Is it in a state of delirium that such grave questions can be broached?"²⁷

From an acute concern with the self, as a child and in her early adult life, Sand had gradually become preoccupied by the individual's involvement with society and the potential for political change. Now she substituted that wide perspective from which she had viewed life during her middle years, not for the mirror which had so fascinated her as a child in Madrid, and which metaphorically fascinated her for years thereafter, but for something more like a microscope. The object of her gaze, of her concern, was the detail, the flora and fauna, and the people, those who lived close to her, and most importantly her grandchildren: "I try *to stuff* them with happiness, in order that they may have healthy dispositions in the face of inevitable disillusion."²⁸ Life, she knew, would present her grandchildren with challenges quite as daunting as those that she herself had faced. It was in the nature of life. Her grandmother had felt the same terrible fear of leaving young Aurore behind in the world. Happiness, play, love, and work were the only antidotes that Sand had discovered for that life-ache that she had always endured. But these distractions were a palliative, not a cure. The only cure now was love, and grandmotherly love was something that she was better able to feel and sustain than any love she had hitherto experienced.

Sand was also as concerned as ever for the local people, whom she continued to know well, and to whom she continued to give encouragement and money. They, she recognized, were vital to the continuing social health of the community. Of the peasants of Nohant and its environs, and by extension all people who worked the land, she wrote in a letter to Flaubert, "It has at last rained here in torrents, and the storm has broken everything. The peasant works and repairs his fields, always digging, sad or gay. People call him stupid—no, he is a child in prosperity, a man in disaster; more a man than we who pity him, he who says nothing, and while they kill he sows, repairing always on one side what is destroyed on another."[29]

Sand wanted two things for her grandchildren: she wanted them to experience intense happiness, and to be educated. She encouraged reading above all, and wrote her *Contes d'une grandmère* to encourage them. She wrote other works too, and Flaubert took an interest in each one, often writing warmly to congratulate the author on her most recent publication. Flaubert was particularly struck by *Marianne,* written in her last year and set in her beloved Berry. Marianne is Sand's ideal woman. She is an inexperienced heiress, naïve about the world but confident in the virtues of simplicity. She is passionately interested in the flora and fauna of her surroundings, and this becomes a metaphor for what is most important in art: intimate knowledge, at once cerebral and felt, of the detail. This is the only base on which something worthwhile can be built. Marianne expresses a mistrust of words, and a contempt for form over content, for technique over what is profoundly sensed.

Having read *Marianne,* Flaubert wrote to Sand: "I thank you from the bottom of my heart, *chère maître.* Thanks to you I have just spent the most exquisite day. . . . *Marianne* moved me deeply and two or three times I found myself weeping. I saw a good deal of myself in Pierre and some pages could have been excerpts from my own memoirs, if I had talent enough to write like that. It's so charming and poetic and *true.*"[30]

Marianne is a love story, which ends, like all great comedy, with the engagement of the heroine and hero: Marianne and Pierre. Their final exchange echoes, in a romanticized way, much of the correspondence of Flaubert and Sand. Philippe, Pierre's overconfident rival, a young artist, has finally left, accepting defeat and humbled. Pierre addresses Marianne:

> "What a night!" he said to her, as they looked at the stars. "What freshness in the air, fragrance in all that surrounds us, the trees, the earth, the very stones themselves! . . . Oh if only I had felt this kind of happiness when I was young, then I should have become a great painter or a great poet."
>
> "Then thank goodness it was not so," replied Marianne. "For if it had been, I should have felt myself so inferior to you, knowing as little as I do about beautiful things! Sometimes I think I love nature just as

much, if not more, for not being capable of translation into words. What horrified me about Monsieur
Philippe today was the oddly pedantic way he would
describe everything he saw. No words can describe
some things. The more one says the less one sees. You
see, Pierre, nature is like love, it's in the heart and you
must not talk about it too much. You diminish what
you try to describe. As for myself, I have no idea of
my own nature when I act unself-consciously. I only
see what there is between the sky and myself. I have
no part in it all. If I think of you, in my odd way I *am*
you and I cease to exist."[31]

It is no coincidence that Flaubert's Félicité, the heroine of his story
"Un Coeur simple" ("A Simple Heart"), which he wrote for Sand but
which she never lived to read, is created with a sympathy that is ambiguous, but nevertheless far exceeds that of the novelist in any of his previous
creations. It is also true that Félicité is the least articulate of all his characters. The trouble with words, both Sand and Flaubert recognized, is that
they can easily lie.

But Sand's suspicions were no more than that. Words, she knew, also
had their mysterious power. She remembered being comforted by the Abbé
de Montperyoux, who was suffering from the appalling pain of gout: at
present Sand was enduring agonies from stomach cramps: she repeated the
abbé's words to Flaubert. Of his pains, he exclaimed, "They'll pass
away—or I will." "He laughed," Sand continued in her letter, "happy with
his words."[32] Language was a slippery medium, but words could also mod-
ify, and mollify, if not transform, the reality of experience.

Over a period of weeks, pains in her stomach became intolerable. In
May she was seen by a local doctor, and corresponded with Dr. Favre, in
Paris. He arrived at the beginning of June. He decided that it was too late
to operate. Maurice informed Solange of the seriousness of their mother's
condition. She arrived at her mother's bedside, although Sand had asked
that only doctors be allowed to see her. She felt deeply humiliated by her
condition.

On 7 June 1876 she summoned her granddaughters. "Be very good,"
she told them. "Adieu, adieu, I am dying. Leave greenness. . . ." That
night she called on God to release her from the burning pains in her stomach.[33] The following day she asked that her bed be turned towards the east;

she wanted to see the sunrise one last time. At nine o'clock she called for her grandchildren once again: "Adieu, Maurice, adieu, Lolo, ad . . ."[34] She had died.

Sand's will recorded nothing of her wishes for her funeral and burial, but her words "leave greenness" may have been a reference to her grave: she wanted greenery and not elaborate monuments. Manceau had received a civil burial, on Sand's insistence, and against the wishes of his family. This might suggest that Sand would have wanted the same. It may be that this was a subject about which she had not yet made up her mind. Maurice had converted to Protestantism and his mother might well have done the same. But she had not.

Solange, who was determined that her mother be buried according to the rites of the Catholic Church, had her way. No doubt it was some comfort for the ordinary people of Nohant, who would have felt dissatisfied by a civic ceremony. Mourners travelled long distances to attend the funeral, but there was also a huge throng of local people, who came to mourn the passing of "the Good Lady of Nohant." Four peasants, dressed simply in their faded blue workmen's smocks, carried the coffin. The priest led the way. Close behind the coffin walked Prince Jérôme Bonaparte, holding one of the cords of the pall. In the other hand he carried a laurel branch. Among the most famous of the other mourners were Flaubert, Ernest Renan, Calmann-Lévy, and Alexandre Dumas *fils*.

Flaubert broke down, twice; in a letter to Turgenev he confessed, "the first time when kissing her granddaughter Aurore (whose eyes that day so resembled her grandmother's that it was like a resurrection), and the second time on seeing the coffin pass by. . . . You are right to regret our friend, for she loved you dearly and always spoke of you as 'the good Turgenev.' . . . The good country folk wept a good deal around the open grave. There was mud up to the ankles in that small country graveyard. The rain was falling softly. Her burial was like a chapter from one of her books."[35]

Obituaries appeared in the press, at home and abroad. Most emphasized her writing, while reporting as little as possible of her life. A Stop Press in the *Athenaeum* bluntly maintained: "The absence of a full authentic biography is however scarcely to be regretted for the private life of an artist is, after all, but of secondary interest."[36] Sand was a very unusual kind of artist. Flaubert had been nourished by her writing, by her novels and her letters. What he appreciated and encouraged in their correspondence was complete openness. He loved her "candour," writing, "You can tell me everything! Everything! Your blows will be received as caresses."[37] He desperately regretted her passing. In April 1880, three years after her death, he wrote to Maurice, "Ah! your poor dear mother! How I think of her, and how I need her! Not a day passes without my saying to myself, 'If she were here I should ask her advice.' "[38] Sand had cut loose many people that she had ceased to love during the course of her life, but she had been an anchor for far more amid the stormy seas of literature—and life.

Appendix: A Note on George Sand's Reputation

"The great goal that we must all pursue is to kill off
the great evil that eats away at us: egotism."

George Sand became one of the most widely known women of her generation, not because of who she was at birth but because of the life she chose to live. The well-known names in the index to her massive twenty-five volumes of published correspondence suggest, quite falsely, a deliberate pursuit of the famous: almost all of these people responded to her with love, affection, or interest. They include Honoré de Balzac, Alfred de Musset, Franz Liszt, Sainte-Beuve, Heinrich Heine, Alphonse de Lamartine, Frédéric Chopin, Eugène Delacroix, Louis-Napoléon Bonaparte (Napoleon III), Alexandre Dumas (father and son), Jules Michelet, Emmanuel Arago, Eugène Sue, Marx, Nadar, Baudelaire, Théophile Gautier, Victor Hugo and his wife, Prince Jérôme Bonaparte, the Goncourt brothers, Gustave Flaubert, Princesse Mathilde, Sarah Bernhardt, Henry Harrisse, Hippolyte Taine, Joseph-Arthur de Gobineau, Ivan Turgenev.[1] These are some of the most famous; there are many more. With some, a small minority, she exchanged only a letter or two, but with most she maintained a significant correspondence and, as with Flaubert, the letters exchanged fill a weighty volume. It is not simply the number of letters that is striking, but the range of people with whom she corresponded: writers, of course, but also politicians and painters, political theorists and monarchs, musicians, singers, and actresses.

The pronouncements made by her loyal, sometimes sycophantic, advocates have become some of the governing clichés of her biography. Liszt deemed her "the strongest (in the biblical sense) and the most astonishingly gifted woman." Heine claimed that she was as "beautiful as the Venus de Milo." Elizabeth Barrett Browning believed her to be "the finest female genius of any country or age." "Of all the writers of her time, she was," Dostoevsky claimed, "the Christian *par excellence*." Flaubert wrote, "You had to know her as I knew her to realize how much of the feminine there was in this great man, the immensity of tenderness to be found in this genius."[2] These responses are a measure of her own capacity for sympathy, which is in turn the measure of her passionate exploration of the personality, the essence of the inner lives of those who came close to her: and it is the obverse of a lifelong quest to know herself.

If these eulogistic comments have lingered on to form a simulacrum, a shadowy likeness of what she was, the vigorous attacks made by her critics have made a deeper and more lasting impression. Charles Baudelaire felt neither affection nor admiration for her. He may, of course, have been jealous of the success and range of her love affairs, but his hatred was bound up with his awareness of the excesses of both her life and her writing. The same sense of excess visible in the correspondence is symptomatic of other areas of her experience. She was not just a writer but an extraordinarily prolific one. Her oeuvre includes a large number of novels, short stories, and plays. She also wrote essays and articles for the press, notebooks, and a massive two-volume autobiography. It is this very sense of fullness, of volume, of proliferation, that accounts in large measure for the loathing that Baudelaire conceived, and expressed most memorably.

Baudelaire's most famous pronouncement is almost comic in its exaggeration: "The fact that some men have been able to become infatuated with that latrine is proof of the degradation of man this century." The latrine—that is, George Sand—as a recent and colourful scholarly article argues, is the site for Baudelaire of a constant passage of excrement. This throughput is natural, that is to say animal. And for Baudelaire the animal is the antithesis of the spiritual. What is most reprehensible, Baudelaire implies, is the willing acceptance of our physical selves, a collusion with, a willing participation in, the endlessly circling flow. Whiffs of the latrine recur elsewhere in Baudelaire's essays. Sand's language was written in a "famous *flowing* style, dear to the *bourgeois*," and he describes her "throwing her great works into the postbox [a metaphorical latrine perhaps] like letters."[3] It is the idea of consumption and waste, as part of a never-ending process, that Baudelaire abhors. What mattered to him was the human will to escape this mundane cycle. Like Balzac, Stendhal, and Flaubert, each in his own way, Baudelaire believed that no elevated aspiration could be satisfied in the world, only in some ideal place, beyond this world, beyond real time.

In Sand's novels, this was subverted, reversed. The aspirations that were noble and great were precisely those that could be satisfied in ordinary life. From an early age she repudiated the separation of body and mind, flesh and spirit. For Baudelaire the will to escape, to transcend the debased and time-bound world, was a sign of spiritual strength and nobility. For Sand, on the other hand, it was a sign of weakness. The object of life, she insisted, was life.

If Baudelaire remains Sand's most famous French antagonist, Nietzsche is surely the best known of her German critics. Sand died in 1876 and it was during the 1880s that he wrote most about her. The imagery he used to conjure up his vision of her was strikingly similar to Baudelaire's. He described her as a *Milchkuh* (a lactating cow). Yet this quip should not be dismissed, any more than Baudelaire's scatological asides, as mere misogyny. Both men had their more profound—and interesting—insights and instincts.[4]

Nietzsche's criticisms of George Sand are essentially criticisms of feminism and Romanticism. Nature, Nietzsche argued, had made man stronger than woman for a purpose. This inequality had to be respected because man had, he believed, to work in harmony with the natural order. His criticisms of Sand's fiction, on the other hand, were part of his sweeping criticisms of French Romanticism. Victor Hugo's naturalistic tendencies were merely evidence of a plebeian taste. Michelet, the great French historian, was too easily aroused to enthusiasm and hence superficial. The democratic appeal of his work, like Sand's, and indeed Hugo's, must, however, also be taken into account as part of the explanation for Nietzsche's rejection of them. For Nietzsche, then, Sand was a prolific, ink-yielding cow, an example of *"lactea ubertas."* Her overflowing, undisciplined writing was evidence of her incapacity to reason logically. In this he likened her to Wagner. What disconcerted both Baudelaire and Nietzsche above all, beyond or beneath their more rational objections, was Sand's passion, her energy, and her capacity to respond with enormous courage to conviction. These same attributes account for her enormous popularity.

When Sand died in 1876, immortality of a highly honourable kind looked very likely. Matthew Arnold made bold predictions: "The immense vibration [of George Sand's voice] . . . will not soon die away."⁵ Yet despite the hyperbole of her vast and varied range of contemporary admirers, her fame was short-lived. By the end of the century, despite her remarkable influence on her generation, Sand no longer sustained any sizeable readership. One small group stands, those modern women writers who were fascinated by her autobiography, *The Story of My Life*. Virginia Woolf quoted from it at the end of *Three Guineas*, and Gertrude Stein, Edith Wharton, Willa Cather, and Colette, among many others, were all interested readers. But that the experience of reading Sand's *fiction*, as opposed to her life, should have been written into Proust's *Remembrance of Things Past* is emblematic: Sand's fictional oeuvre was to be a "Thing" of the "Past."⁶

For those who neither read her nor took a serious interest in her life, the ghosts that remained were very strange. Two spectres began to circulate. The first, with all its obvious contradictions, was a cigar-smoking, man-eating transvestite lesbian nymphomaniac; the second was "the Good Lady of Nohant." Sand is surely unique in having left behind such incompatible ghosts.

In the 1930s eminent and very serious scholars, Frenchmen, set about disinterring the "real" George Sand. Édouard Dolléans was one of the first of these specialists. A historian of nineteenth-century working-class movements in France (he also wrote a history of Chartism in England), his interest was in Sand's political involvement and influence. Another, Émile Chartier, who assumed the name Alain, was a philosopher who was to have considerable influence over his students: Simone Weil and André Maurois are two notable examples. Alain was interested in her "philosophy" of music and nature. He greatly admired her prose style, and the conviction it carried. But it was Alain's pupil André Maurois who successfully resurrected her to new life. His biography, *Lélia: The Life of George Sand*, was published in 1952 and drew international attention. Maurois's portrait was intended to be flattering, but the figure that emerged was strangely unconvincing. Despite his intentions there is something incongruous, even monstrous, about the Sand he re-created.

It was no doubt partly in response to this biography of Sand the writer that scholars set about working on Sand's oeuvre and new editions were published of, most importantly, *Consuelo, La Comtesse de Rudolstadt, Indiana, Lélia, Mauprat, La Mare au diable, François le Champi*, and *La Daniella*. These were soon followed by monographs on her politics, her understanding of music and history, her status as a Romantic.

More importantly, Georges Lubin, the doyen of Sand scholarship, set about editing her autobiographical writings, including the massive twenty-five-volume *Correspondance,* for Éditions Gallimard's Bibliothèque de la Pléiade. If to be published in this list is, indeed, to be part of the French canon, then Sand is "in," but only as a writer of autobiographical material. The only supposedly complete edition of her writing, the massive nineteenth-century edition (112 volumes published by Michel Lévy, later Calmann-Lévy) is neither complete nor numbered. A good deal of her oeuvre remains, therefore, uncharted and unread.

Lubin's work made further autobiographical material available to biographers. Since Maurois's *Lélia* was published in the early 1950s, there has been a steady stream of new biographies. A noticeable peak occurred in the early 1990s in France, when no fewer than four major works were published: Huguette Bouchardeau's *George Sand: The Moon and the Clogs* (1991), Jean Chalon's *Dear George Sand* (1991), Jacques-Louis Donchin's *George Sand, the Lover* (1992), and Yves Monin's *George Sand: Troubadour of the Eternal Truth* (1992). As the titles of these biographies suggest, they are highly romanticized and evade the most difficult, but also the most interesting, questions about her.

The Sand industry is not limited to biography. China plate settings have been produced by Christofle, based on the original Nohant china (and incorporating its botanical motif), and the quiet Vallée Noire which Sand celebrated, even in a sense invented, is visited by large numbers of cultural tourists who make their pilgrimage to Nohant. One of the first was Matthew Arnold, then a student at Oxford, who set off to find Sand's world in response to reading *Valentine* (1832). In this novel Sand's originality as landscape writer and country chronicler first impressed her readers. What would he have made of the fantastic touch-sensitive, interactive, audiovisual installation, a high-tech shrine to Sand, sited in the nearest motorway "rest stop" to Nohant? Fortunately, the "virtual reality" is some distance away from the real house and grounds, which lie in empty country and are sensitively maintained.

The industry which has had the greatest influence in terms of Sand's afterlife is arguably that of film and television. Among the films that have appeared, most focusing on the Sand-Chopin affair, James Lapine's *Impromptu* (1992) and Andrzej Zulawski's *La Note bleue* (1991) reached the widest audiences. A BBC serialization, *Notorious Women,* in which Sand featured, was made in 1974 and travelled to America. The visual representation of Sand and Chopin in close proximity to a piano is a focal image in the film iconography. A striking difference between the BBC version and *Impromptu,* which is also significant in terms of the many other differences between the two films, is immediately apparent. In the first, Sand stands behind Chopin, who is seated at the piano, his elegant fingers moving deftly across the keys. Her hands are on his shoulders, her fingers slightly spread. She is dominant and strong, but silent and protective. In the second, she lies under the piano, sheltered by his instrument and enraptured by the sound, by the ecstasy of his genius. How should the differences be read? Very crudely, the answer is bound up in different readings of the power relations between Sand and her lovers (both men and women) and friends.

Two more recent American productions have been better researched: Diane Kurys's film *Les Enfants du siècle* (*Children of the Century,* 1999), starring Juliette Binoche, based on Musset's account of his relationship with Sand; and Peter Eyre's play *Chère Maître* (1998), starring Irene Worth, based on the Sand-Flaubert correspondence. The inner torment of Sand's life will always remain extraordinarily difficult to convey in film. Eyre's play, or "recital," as he describes it, allows for greater insight.

Relatively recent feminist readings have explored the question of gender, and gender relations, in Sand's life and writings most thoroughly. But the recognition of this problematic area has a much longer tradition. Elizabeth Barrett Browning, who greatly admired Sand, begins one of her sonnets to her with a wonderfully infelicitous line which includes the "large-brained woman and large-hearted man." In the light of Barrett Browning's unfortunate attempt to define a certain androgyny, it is well that Balzac took another tack. But his characterization is equally ridiculous. In the notes which he made after first meeting her he wrote, "She is boyish, an artist, she is great-hearted, generous, devout, and *chaste;* she has all the main characteristics of a man; *ergo,* she is not a woman." Not dissimilarly but within a kinder context, Flaubert contrasted her feminine manliness and tender genius. Turgenev again described her in terms of dual gender: "What a brave man she was, and what a good woman."[7]

Feminist analyses have not found Sand any less paradoxical. The first and most obvious difficulty in setting her up as a heroine in the eyes of French feminist history concerns her views on women's suffrage. In 1848, on the eve of the crucial elections to the National Assembly, a group of French feminists proposed the candidacy of George Sand. Sand replied to this in a letter to the editors of *La Réforme* and *La Vraie République.* It is a surprising text, and unequivocally antifeminist. It ends, "I cannot condone being taken without my consent as the standard-bearer of a female circle with which I have never had the slightest relation either pleasant or unpleasant."[8] But there are other clearly feminist texts in which Sand defends the equality of women before the law, women's right to divorce, and women's right to education; and many others which are implicitly or overtly opposed to aspects of the patriarchy, to men's power over women in all the areas of life which it permeates, public and private. Her letter to the Central Committee, on the other hand, written just before the letter cited earlier, makes clear her lack of solidarity with those that champion women's liberation whether in terms of political representation or in terms of sexual freedom, the "free love" promoted by a remarkable group of nineteenth-century social theorists including Saint-Simon, Enfantin, and Fourier. Yet Sand argues for those rights of women of which they are deprived by the current marriage laws. She advocates, in short, reform, not revolution.

During the 1970s feminist readers set about enquiring into Sand's relationship with feminism in broader terms. The complexities of the debate up to that point had depended in large measure, and in many ways continue to depend, on definitions of feminism. If the word is given the meaning it acquired towards the end of the nineteenth century, then as Sand never demanded, nor wanted, political equality for women, she cannot be described as feminist. If feminism is defined in such a way as to limit it to traits including a scorn for domestic chores and a preference for sisterhood, organization, and politics, then again Sand was not a feminist. For one thing she loved making jam in very large quantities, and needlepoint. Yet her personal courage, her separation from her husband, her concerns for women's education, all suggest a feminist disposition. The problem of definition leads to contradiction. In Sand's case, as soon as any concrete claim to "feminism" is proposed, her attitudes become so complicated as to seem paradoxical. Sand's positions can be used to oppose various forms of feminism: Marxist and psychoanalytical, individualist and collectivist, Lacanian and Althusserian, and all the rest. The problem, then, in defining Sand's "feminism" is one of discreet, if not contradictory, definitions of "feminism" itself.

Yet it could be argued that Sand is an exemplary "feminist" precisely because of the sum of these contradictions. They can be taken to represent a point of focus where dissatisfactions with contemporary society and the place it assigns women, claims for equality, claims for difference, ideas about an essential and transhistorical female nature, and denunciations of a subjugated historical condition come into conflict and merge. It may be that it is the continuing and shifting debate that constitutes "feminism."

What is least problematic in the vast range of pertinent material available is Sand's conviction that women should not become like men. Where she is most trenchant and least equivocal is in her opposition to one kind of feminism, in her condemnation of those women who claimed "the same attributes" as men: "speech at the forum, the helmet and the sword, the right to condemn to death."[9] Rather than seeking to be part of an unjust system, further reinforcing it, Sand encouraged women to cling to their powerful marginality. This then becomes an obvious sign of the need for change, an indication of the need to create a society founded on new principles. Sand was loath to be part of a system which she believed to be profoundly unsatisfactory. But at the same time she had lived a life, and produced an already considerable body of writings, which invited the albeit wholly inappropriate action of the 1848 feminists: proposing her as a candidate in the 1848 elections. She was clearly widely recognized as a subversive, but evidently chose to remain "on the margins."

But just as her point of view shifted and changed, so her idea of who she was remained unstable. Sand's paradoxical sense of her own identity was constantly buffeted by the images that others created of her. Her "image," in a very modern sense, was a great preoccupation and source of anxiety. Only late in her life was she sufficiently resilient and confident to mind little about what other people made of her. Only towards the end of her life was she in any sense at ease with the woman—even women—she was. It was by writing that she had sought to understand, and create, her self. And experience, for the writer-explorer, is the artistic source even while preoccupying the present moment; the reshaping of experience in words alters the experience to follow; and writing is itself yet another formative experience.

The tortuous and slippery movement between life and writing was something about which Sainte-Beuve, one of the most prolific critics of the nineteenth century, wrote at length. He was a close friend of Sand's and she frequently turned to him not so much for advice about her writing but for advice about life. Proust's essay "Contre Sainte-Beuve" has ensured that the nineteenth-century critic's theories continue to circulate. Sainte-Beuve's emphasis was very much on the autobiographical interpretation and evaluation of literary works. The strength of Proust's argument against such an approach has to do with his conviction that the writing self and the living self are in many ways separate and independent: "A book is the product of another me, different from the me that is manifest in habits, in society, in vices."[10] The biography of a writer distinguishes itself from all other forms of biography because there is some evidence of both selves: the inner writing self, and the outer social self.

The sheer audacity of this woman writer-explorer of nineteenth-century France, so apparent in her life, is not always immediately obvious in her writing. Her eighty or so novels and shorter works of fiction, which are as important as her autobiographical writing and, arguably, more important than her plays, essays, and journalism, are variously described as Romantic, idealist, pastoral, utopian, socialist, or fantastic. Such generic descriptions are inadequate when it comes to Sand's writing. Often it exploits a wide range of representational codes. In short, it is in many cases generic pastiche. Measured against Flaubert's control, or the apparently coherent social theories that are part of Émile Zola's fiction, Sand's writing can read as "work in progress," however polished the style. But it is often where her writing falls short of—or outside—the requirements of conventional definitions that what is most audacious becomes apparent. Within the long and peculiar form of *Lélia* Sand explored female sexuality most fully and daringly. Within the more conventionally realist modes of her fiction, female eroticism (which is essentially private) and libido (which manifests itself more publicly) feature minimally. But within the more fantastic and mixed modes, all manner of sexual deviance is written in: incest dominates. In *Le Péché de Monsieur Antoine,* the idealized couple is, in fact, incestuous. And in *La Petite Fadette,* Sand's most famous and apparently innocuous so-called pastoral tale (for years a school textbook on both sides of the Channel), the transition from homosexual love to heterosexual love is undertaken by means of a transition first to incestuous love.

Equally subversive are her numerous novels that explore cross-class sexual relationships. *Valentine,* set in Berry, was the first. The reader arrives in the region like a traveller: "The southeastern region of Berry takes in several leagues of particularly picturesque country. . . ."[11] The reader-traveller is warned early on not to accept surface realities. The novel chronicles the private tragedy that is a consequence of a visibly rigid social hierarchy that regards love between members of different groups as subversive. The narrator constantly ennobles the naturalness and spirituality of the "inner life" as opposed to the affectedness and materiality of the "outer life." The love between Valentine and Bénédict is something both struggle to deny. When Valentine's husband dies, the way is open for a happy ending. But Valentine's social conditioning has been too influential.

Society punishes them for their "natural" love. Bénédict is shot by Pierre Blutty, who is convinced that he is his wife's lover, and Valentine dies shortly thereafter.

Sand's happy endings, on the other hand, are to be taken with something of a pinch of salt because they are not supposed to be read as solutions to all the problems thrown up by the fiction. Rather they are comforting ways of drawing to a close what is never more than an exploration. Sand was something of a neo-Platonist, and always insisted on the lie of art: "It lies, it has to lie, because art is a fiction, or at least an interpretation." Real people, she argued in the same letter, "are all idiots, children, weak. . . . That is precisely why we are worth more than the heroes of novels. We suffer the miseries of our condition, we are real people. . . ."[12]

Similarly, what emerged most forcefully from her famous correspondence with Flaubert was her playful impatience with her contemporary's *faith* in literature, in particular his all-consuming commitment to artistic form: "You believe too much in literature. . . . Stick to your cult of form, but think more about the subject matter." Sand was more than impatient when it came to Flaubert's conviction that the work of art must display, by means of clever sleight of hand, its creator's apparent impartiality: "Supreme impartiality is antihuman and a novel must be human above all." For Sand a writer's convictions were essential if the work was to *make a difference*. She wrote for her contemporaries and bothered very little about what future generations would think of it. Flaubert's commitments were very different; they were essentially aesthetic convictions. He had confessed in an earlier letter to Sand that in his childhood he had been "frightened by life," but it was in response to Sand's concern that he reveal something of his humanity in his writing that he wrote one of his most compelling, albeit far from unambiguous, short stories, "A Simple Heart."

Despite the depths of terror and misery of Sand's childhood, she overcame her fear and, rather than retreat as Flaubert had done, set out to explore. What she wanted to say could not be, nor did she ever think that it should be, carried into an "impartial" art form. Her experience of injustice, as a woman above all, was to be translated into novels brimming over with dense, pithy subject matter. The "human interest" in her fiction, as in her autobiographical writings, largely explains her considerable commercial success. But she also quickly came to be regarded by well-known writers as different as Henry James in America, George Eliot in England, and Ivan Turgenev in Russia as a major and unique voice in the literary world of the nineteenth century. It is only in the fictional underworld, in the strata barely apparent on the surface, that the double bind of the human condition, alone but bound up, free yet constrained, is fully and daringly explored.

Sand's modernity lies less in her feminism or her socialism, and more in her acceptance of loose, even freewheeling ideas about the self, and others, about individual psychology, society, history, the *purpose* of literature. Her interest and insight into dreams and their significance, and the way in which articulation of experience might bring about psychological relief, is uncannily close to the ideas for which that clever man in Vienna would become famous years later. She had strong intuitions about the subconscious and the need to be aware of our inner unthinking, but acutely responsive, selves. To Flaubert the anguished stylistic perfectionist she wrote, "You should let the wind stir your strings a little. . . . I myself think that you take more trouble than you should and that you should allow the *other* to take over more often."[13]

Sand came to believe in the multiplicity and mutability of the self, and this explains her continuing refusal of dogma: "Me, I have no theories. I live my life asking questions." What mattered was to balance that inner questing uncertainty. There is a delightful irony in the advice she offered at the end of her life: "Moderation, relative chastity, abstinence, add what you will, but it will always add up to equilibrium."[14]

Sand's desire to question gained her the sincerest respect while she was alive, but it did little for her reputation when all those who had known her personally died. It may be that our notion of "greatness" is flawed, particularly with regard to certain dead writers. It is their oeuvre that we judge, and Sand's writings are not uniformly "great." Had Sand been born at another time, she might have been a great mountaineer, or have attempted to sail solo around the globe. Her "greatness" would then depend not simply on the height and perilousness of her climbs, or the nautical miles she had sailed through heaving seas, but on the spirit that had animated her adventures.

Notes

BHVP	Bibliothèque Historique de la Ville de Paris
BN n.a.f.	Bibliothèque Nationale, Paris, Manuscript Department, Nouvelles Acquisitions Françaises
Corr.	GS, *Correspondance*, 25 vols., ed. Georges Lubin (Paris, 1964–85)
GF	Gustave Flaubert
GF–GS	*Correspondance: Gustave Flaubert–George Sand,* ed. Alphonse Jacobs (Paris, 1981)
GS	George Sand
GS–GF	*Correspondance entre George Sand et Gustave Flaubert,* ed. Henri Amic (Paris, 1904)
HS	George Sand, *Histoire de ma vie* [1854–55], Parts 1–4, *OA* I; Parts 5–6, *OA* II
Lov. fol.	Manuscript and folio number as at Bibliothèque Spoelberch de Lovenjoul, Chantilly
OA	*George Sand, Oeuvres autobiographiques,* 2 vols., ed. Georges Lubin (Paris, 1970–71)

INTRODUCTION

1. Epigraphs to chapters are all from George Sand.
2. GF, *Oeuvres,* 16 vols. (Paris, 1960–65), XV, pp. 181–2.

1: AUGURIES

1. *OA* I, p. 174.
2. Ibid., p. 464, and *OA* II, pp. 508, 1417–18.
3. For Sand's account and scholarly investigation, see *OA* I, pp. 464, 1357, 1358; *OA* II, p. 472.
4. *OA* II, p. 508.
5. Letter to Charles Poncy, 23 December 1843: *Corr.* VI, p. 328.
6. *Corr.* I, p. 1006.
7. *OA* I, p. 41.
8. For an account of the extraordinary Deschartres, see Roland Derche, *Un Picard colérique: Le Laonnais J.-F.-L. Deschartres, précepteur de George Sand* (Fontenay-le-Comte, 1954).
9. This is the account given by Charles Gailly de Taurines in his book on Sand's grandmother, *Aventuriers et femmes de qualité: La Fille de Maréchal de Saxe* (Paris, 1907), p. 333.
10. *OA* I, p. 53.
11. Ibid., p. 127.
12. Ibid., pp. 176–7.
13. Ibid., pp. 1325–6, and note, p. 352.
14. Ibid., p. 55.
15. BHVP, Fonds Sand, G1, fol. 3.
16. *OA* I, p. 514. Sand gives the date, incorrectly, as 20 December; see note, ibid., p. 1372.
17. For an account of Maurice's trick, and the quotations from it that follow, see ibid., pp. 499–501.
18. Ibid., p. 501, and note, p. 1369.

2: A MAN OF ACTION AND A PASSIONATE WOMAN

1. *OA* I, p. 502; as there is no French word for "home," it is given in English in the text.
2. Ibid., p. 549.
3. Ibid., p. 548.
4. Ibid., p. 483.
5. Ibid., p. 484.
6. Ibid., p. 341.
7. *Corr.* VI, pp. 327–8.
8. Ibid., p. 807.
9. *OA* I, p. 532.
10. Ibid., p. 537.
11. Ibid., p. 535.
12. Ibid., p. 531.
13. Ibid., p. 536.
14. *OA* II, pp. 508, 1418.
15. *OA* I, pp. 544–5.
16. Ibid., p. 545.
17. Ibid., p. 544.
18. Ibid.

19. Ibid., p. 542.
20. Little is known of Pierret other than what Sand records in her autobiography. His intimacy with the family is confirmed by his status as family witness: to Caroline and Aurore's marriages, and the birth of Oscar Cazamalou, Caroline's son. See ibid., p. 1378; for Sand's account of Pierret, and the quotations given, see ibid., pp. 549–55.
21. Ibid., p. 552.
22. Ibid., pp. 543, 1378.
23. Ibid., pp. 549–52.
24. Ibid., p. 608.
25. GS, *Le Compagnon du tour de France* (Paris, 1840).
26. GS, *La Mare au diable* (Paris, 1846).
27. The relevant details are given in *OA* I, pp. 1375–6. For a full account of Aurore's likely Parisian addresses between 1804 and 1831, see also *Corr.* I, pp. 1021–5.
28. *OA* I, pp. 530, 1375–6.
29. Ibid.
30. Ibid.
31. Ibid., p. 467.
32. Ibid., p. 553.
33. Ibid., p. 556.
34. Ibid., p. 554.
35. Ibid., p. 556.

3: ADVENTURE REAL AND IMAGINED

1. *OA* I, p. 557.
2. Ibid., pp. 556–7.
3. Ibid., p. 557.
4. Ibid., p. 559.
5. Ibid., pp. 559–60.
6. Ibid., p. 548.
7. Ibid., p. 566.
8. Ibid., pp. 566–7.
9. Ibid., pp. 571–2.
10. Ibid., pp. 573–4.
11. Ibid., pp. 573–5.
12. Ibid., pp. 568–9.
13. Ibid., p. 577.
14. Ibid., pp. 583–4.
15. GS, *Souvenirs et idées* (Paris, n.d.), p. 155; see also first impressions of Nohant, *OA* I, p. 122.
16. *OA* I, pp. 585–6.
17. Ibid., pp. 31–2.
18. Ibid., pp. 1304–7.
19. GS, *Jeanne* (first published Paris, 1844; Nelson Éditeurs, n.d.), pp. 28–9.
20. *OA* I, p. 35.
21. Ibid., p. 36.
22. Ibid., pp. 40–1.

23. Ibid., p. 589.
24. Ibid., pp. 589–93.
25. Ibid., pp. 592–3.
26. Ibid., pp. 597–8.
27. *Corr.* VIII, p. 264.
28. *OA* I, p. 307.
29. Ibid., pp. 156–7.

4: TWO RIVAL MOTHERS

1. From *Lettres à Marcie*, no. 6, *Le Monde*, 12 February 1837.
2. "Réponse à diverses objections" (1844), republished in GS, *Questions politiques et sociales* (Paris, 1874), pp. 93–105.
3. *GF–GS*, p. 121: letter to Flaubert, 1 January 1867.
4. *OA* I, pp. 607, 614.
5. Ibid., p. 617.
6. Ibid., p. 630.
7. Ibid., pp. 618–20.
8. Ibid., p. 631.
9. Ibid., p. 599.
10. Ibid.
11. Ibid., p. 603.
12. Ibid., pp. 629–30.
13. Ibid., p. 618.
14. Ibid., p. 541.
15. Ibid., p. 604.
16. Ibid., p. 1243.
17. Ibid., p. 604.
18. Ibid., p. 637.
19. Ibid.
20. Ibid., p. 638.
21. Ibid.
22. Ibid.
23. Ibid.
24. Ibid., p. 640.
25. Ibid., p. 670.
26. Ibid., p. 648.
27. Ibid., pp. 652–3.
28. Ibid., p. 653.
29. Ibid., p. 654.
30. Ibid., pp. 52–3.
31. Ibid., pp. 586–7.
32. Ibid., p. 626.
33. Ibid., p. 757.
34. Ibid., p. 720.
35. Ibid., pp. 722–4.
36. Ibid., p. 688.
37. Ibid., p. 742.

38.   Ibid., pp. 742–3.
39.   Ibid., p. 743.
40.   Ibid., p. 618.
41.   Ibid., pp. 811–3, 839.
42.   Ibid., pp. 812–21.
43.   *OA* II, p. 166.
44.   *OA* I, pp. 855–7.
45.   Ibid., p. 856.
46.   Ibid., p. 861.
47.   Ibid., p. 862.

5: STILL WATER

1.   *OA* I, pp. 861–2.
2.   Ibid., p. 868.
3.   Ibid., p. 1414; for further details about the convent, see Lubin's notes to ibid., p. 1414. See also Abbé Cédoz, *Un Couvent de religieuses anglaises à Paris de 1634 à 1884* (Paris, Victor Lecoffre; London, Burns and Oates, 1891).
4.   *OA* I, p. 865.
5.   Ibid., p. 894.
6.   Lov. fol., E 946, 10–14.
7.   *OA* I, pp. 876, 1415.
8.   Ibid., pp. 912–13.
9.   Ibid., pp. 879–80.
10.   Ibid., p. 869.
11.   Ibid., p. 880; for authentication, see Cédoz, *Un Couvent,* and *OA* I, pp. 1414, 1416.
12.   *OA* I, p. 887.
13.   Ibid., pp. 886–7.
14.   Ibid., p. 908.
15.   Collection Lauth-Sand; cit. André Maurois, *Lélia* (Paris, 1952), p. 42.
16.   *OA* I, p. 896.
17.   Ibid., p. 944.
18.   Ibid., p. 939.
19.   Ibid., p. 940.
20.   Ibid.
21.   Ibid., pp. 896–7.
22.   Ibid., p. 667.
23.   Ibid., pp. 944–5.
24.   Ibid., pp. 945–6.
25.   Ibid., p. 945.
26.   Ibid., p. 959.
27.   Ibid., p. 942.
28.   Ibid.
29.   Ibid., p. 943.
30.   Ibid., pp. 924–5.
31.   Ibid., p. 869.
32.   Ibid., pp. 923–5.
33.   Ibid., p. 948.

34. Ibid.
35. Ibid., p. 949.
36. Ibid., pp. 953–4.
37. Ibid., p. 954.
38. Ibid., p. 964.
39. Ibid., p. 990.
40. Ibid.
41. Ibid., p. 995.
42. Ibid., p. 999.
43. See, for example, *La Petite Fadette* (Paris, 1849) and Naomi Schor's excellent analysis in *Sand and Idealism* (New York, 1993), pp. 133–55.
44. *OA* I, p. 1005.
45. Ibid., p. 1007.
46. Ibid.
47. Ibid.
48. Ibid., p. 1008.

6: THE FEAR OF FREEDOM AND THE LURE OF SUICIDE

1. *OA* I, p. 1012.
2. Ibid., p. 1013.
3. Ibid., p. 862.
4. Ibid., p. 1011.
5. Ibid., p. 1050.
6. Ibid., p. 1017.
7. Carnet de George Sand, BN n.a.f. 13641.
8. *Corr.* I, pp. 212–13.
9. *OA* I, p. 1021.
10. Ibid., p. 1023.
11. Ibid., p. 1022.
12. Sand's account of her reading during the period is given in her autobiography, *OA* I, p. 1051. See also *Corr.* I.
13. *OA* I, p. 1029.
14. Ibid., p. 1040.
15. Ibid., p. 1041.
16. Ibid., p. 1026.
17. Ibid., p. 1028.
18. Ibid., p. 1030.
19. Ibid., p. 1031.
20. Ibid., p. 1025.
21. Ibid.
22. Ibid., p. 1031.
23. Ibid., p. 1032.
24. Ibid.
25. Ibid., p. 1113.
26. Ibid., p. 1079.
27. Ibid., p. 1113.
28. Ibid.

29. Ibid.
30. Ibid., p. 1085.
31. Ibid., p. 1086.
32. Ibid., p. 1087.
33. *Corr.* I, pp. 74–81.
34. *OA* I, pp. 1072–3.
35. *Corr.* I, p. 82.
36. *OA* I, p. 1045.
37. Sand is inaccurate in her description of him as *in partibus,* although the expression *in partibus infidelium* comes close to explaining his position; he had been designated archbishop but was never sworn in; see *Corr.* I, p. 216, and *OA* I, p. 1064.
38. *OA* I, p. 1061.
39. Ibid., p. 1072.
40. *Corr.* I, Lubin's notes to pp. 74–81.
41. *OA* I, p. 1094.
42. Ibid., p. 1095.
43. Ibid., p. 1097.
44. Ibid., p. 1105.
45. Ibid., p. 1106; notes, p. 1450.
46. Ibid., pp. 1106–7.
47. Ibid., p. 1107.
48. Ibid., p. 1109.
49. Ibid., p. 1110.
50. Ibid., p. 1089.
51. *Corr.* I, pp. 68–70.
52. Ibid., p. 69.

7: A REASONABLE MARRIAGE

1. *OA* I, p. 1111.
2. Ibid., p. 808.
3. *OA* II, p. 10.
4. *OA* I, p. 1128.
5. Ibid., p. 1129.
6. *Lélia* (Paris, 1833; second edition, Paris, 1839).
7. *OA* I, p. 1123.
8. Ibid., p. 1125.
9. For details of family, see *OA* II, p. 1306.
10. Ibid., p. 19.
11. Ibid., p. 25.
12. Ibid., p. 26.
13. *Corr.* I, p. 92.
14. His proposal was probably made on 2 June, the day she wrote "happy as never before" in her notebook; see *Corr.* I, p. 8814.
15. *OA* II, p. 27.
16. Ibid., p. 28.
17. Ibid.
18. Ibid., p. 1311.

8: THE REALITY OF MARRIAGE AND THE PRECARIOUS SUSPENSION OF DISBELIEF

1. *OA* II, Chapter 9, pp. 32–51.
2. *Corr.* I, p. 103.
3. *Corr.* II, pp. 103–5.
4. See *OA* II, p. 1313, for details of baptism.
5. BHVP, Fonds Sand, D 216; cited in *OA* II, pp. 1312–13.
6. *Corr.* I, p. 118.
7. *Indiana*, ed. Béatrice Didier (Paris, 1984), p. 50.
8. Ibid., p. 53.
9. Ibid., p. 135.
10. Ibid., p. 208.
11. *Corr.* I, pp. 138, 143.
12. *Corr.* IV, p. 43.
13. *Indiana*, p. 130.
14. *Corr.* I, p. 270.
15. *Corr.* III, p. 135.
16. *OA* II, p. 42.
17. *Corr.* I, pp. 148–9.
18. *OA* II, p. 48.
19. Ibid., p. 49.
20. Ibid., p. 56ff.
21. *Corr.* I, pp. 269–70.
22. *OA* II, pp. 58–9.
23. *Lélia* (Paris: Garnier, 1960), p. 174.

9: THE CALL OF THE WILD

1. *OA* II, pp. 58–67, and note, p. 1318.
2. Letter to Zoé Leroy, 5 September 1825: *Corr.* I, p. 168.
3. *OA* II, p. 59.
4. Ibid.
5. Letter to Mme Maurice Dupin, 28 August 1825: *Corr.* I, p. 162.
6. *OA* II, p. 61.
7. Ibid.
8. Ibid., p. 62.
9. Letter to Zoé Leroy, 5 September 1825: *Corr.* I, p. 168.
10. See, for example, *OA* II, p. 393.
11. *OA* I, p. 1097.
12. *OA* II, p. 40.
13. Ibid., p. 30.
14. Ibid., p. 42.
15. S. M. Gilbert and S. Gubar, *The Madwoman in the Attic* (New Haven and London: Yale University Press, 1984).
16. *OA* II, p. 64.
17. Ibid., p. 65.
18. See, for example, ibid., pp. 66, 71.

19.   *Corr.* I, p. 244.
20.   Lov. fol., E902, fol. 24.
21.   *Corr.* I, p. 244.
22.   Ibid.
23.   Ibid., pp. 262–92.
24.   *OA* II, p. 69.
25.   *Corr.* I, p. 279.
26.   Ibid., pp. 171–2.
27.   Ibid., p. 281.
28.   For an account of Aurore's relations with Aurélien, see ibid., pp. 281–92.
29.   Ibid., p. 285.
30.   Ibid., p. 179.
31.   Ibid., p. 192.
32.   Ibid., p. 280.
33.   Ibid., p. 308.
34.   Ibid., pp. 204–5.
35.   Ibid., p. 198.
36.   Ibid., p. 201.
37.   Ibid., p. 170.

10: THE TRAVESTY OF MARRIAGE

1.   *Corr.* I, p. 326.
2.   See note, ibid.
3.   Ibid., pp. 329–30.
4.   Ibid., p. 340.
5.   *OA* II, p. 94.
6.   *Corr.* I, p. 335.
7.   Referred to in a letter from Aurore to Casimir, ibid., p. 418.
8.   Ibid., p. 363.
9.   *OA* II, p. 99.
10.   *Corr.* I, p. 451.
11.   *Corr.* I, p. 363.
12.   BHVP, Fonds Sand, G5351, ff. 193–5.
13.   *Corr.* I, pp. 383–5.
14.   Ibid., p. 385.
15.   *Voyage en Auvergne, OA* II, pp. 503–11.
16.   Ibid.
17.   Louise Vincent, *GS et le Berry,* 2 vols. (Paris, 1919), I, pp. 216–17.
18.   *OA* II, pp. 87–8.
19.   *Corr.* I, p. 415.
20.   Ibid., pp. 426–7.
21.   Ibid., pp. 437–9.
22.   Ibid., p. 451.
23.   Ibid., pp. 450–1.
24.   Letter from Zoé, Lov. fol., E902, ff. 115–16; letter to Zoé, *Corr.* I, p. 493.
25.   *Corr.* I, p. 511.
26.   *OA* II, pp. 557–69.
27.   Lov. fol., E948, fol. 40, "Notes de Casimir pour le procès en séparation."

28. *Corr.* I, p. 628.
29. Ibid., p. 700.
30. Ibid., p. 641.
31. Ibid., p. 583.
32. *OA* II, p. 100.
33. Ibid., p. 547.
34. *Corr.* I, p. 647.
35. Ibid., pp. 676–7.

II: PETIT JULES

1. Letter to Jules Boucoiran, 20 July 1830: *Corr.* I, pp. 676–7.
2. Ibid., p. 683.
3. Ibid., pp. 684–5.
4. Ibid., pp. 683–4.
5. Ibid., p. 690.
6. J. Sandeau, *Marianna*, 2 vols. (Paris, 1839), I, pp. 46–7.
7. *Corr.* I, p. 877.
8. Ibid.
9. Ibid., September 1830.
10. Ibid., pp. 563–4.
11. *Histoire d'un rêveur* (*Story of a Dreamer*), ed. Thierry Bodin, *Présence de George Sand*, 17 June 1983, pp. 4–24; for a bibliography of GS's early writing and an interesting if idiosyncratic discussion, see K. J. Crecelius, *Family Romances: George Sand's Early Novels* (Indiana, 1981).
12. Ibid., p. 13.
13. Ibid., p. 18.
14. Ibid., p. 20.
15. *Corr.* I, p. 743.
16. Ibid.
17. Ibid., pp. 736–7.

12: BECOMING SAND

1. *OA* II, p. 109; *Corr.* I, p. 824.
2. *Corr.* I, p. 824.
3. Ibid., p. 752.
4. *OA* II, p. 1331.
5. J. Sandeau, *Marianna*, 3 vols. (Paris, 1842), I, pp. 56–9, 171, 203–6.
6. *OA* II, pp. 225, 1356.
7. Ibid., pp. 117–18.
8. Ibid., p. 135.
9. *Corr.* I, p. 887.
10. Ibid., p. 778.
11. *Corr.* I, p. 818.
12. For a biography of Latouche, see Lubin's note, *OA* I, pp. 1283–4.
13. *OA* II, p. 151.

14. *Corr.* I, p. 783.
15. Ibid., pp. 826–7.
16. Ibid., p. 819 n.; *OA* II, pp. 149–50.
17. Ibid.
18. *OA* II, pp. 134–5.
19. Ibid., p. 138.
20. Ibid., p. 154.
21. *Corr.* I, pp. 800–1.
22. Ibid., p. 817.
23. Ibid., p. 818.
24. *OA* II, p. 823.
25. *Corr.* I, p. 813.
26. Ibid., p. 814.

13: PARIS FROM THE PROVINCES

1. *Corr.* I, p. 854.
2. Ibid., pp. 834–8.
3. Ibid., pp. 854–5.
4. *Corr.* I, p. 855.
5. Ibid., p. 862.
6. Ibid., p. 840.
7. Ibid., pp. 886–8.
8. Ibid., pp. 871, 897; also *OA* II, p. 105.
9. *Corr.* I, p. 853.
10. Ibid., p. 858.
11. Ibid., p. 878.
12. Ibid., p. 875.
13. Ibid.
14. Ibid., pp. 881–2.
15. Ibid., p. 908.
16. Ibid., p. 908 n.
17. Ibid., p. 910 n.
18. Ibid., p. 912.
19. *OA* II, p. 154.
20. *Corr.* I, p. 921.
21. Ibid., p. 944.
22. Ibid., pp. 945–7.
23. Ibid., pp. 956–7.
24. Ibid., p. 955.
25. Ibid., pp. 962–3.
26. *OA* II, p. 156.
27. "L'Homme sans nom," *L'Artiste*, 18 December 1831.
28. *Corr.* II, pp. 41–2.
29. Ibid., p. 41 n.
30. Ibid., pp. 46–9.
31. Ibid., pp. 47–8.

14: AN EXQUISITE DISSECTION

1. *Corr.* II, pp. 12–13.
2. Ibid., p. 36.
3. Ibid., p. 42.
4. *OA* II, pp. 160–1.
5. Ibid., pp. 161–2.
6. Ibid., pp. 164–5.
7. Ibid., p. 165.
8. *Corr.* II, p. 63.
9. *OA* II, p. 138.
10. Ibid., p. 140.
11. Ibid., pp. 173–4.
12. *Corr.* II, p. 88, n. 1.
13. Ibid., p. 115.
14. See also *Corr.* II, pp. 115–16.
15. *OA* II, p. 174.
16. *Corr.* II, p. 115.
17. Preface to 1842 edition. Also cited in N. Schor, *George Sand and Idealism* (New York, 1993), p. 52. For the major study of Sand's idealism, see Schor.
18. *Indiana*, trans. S. Raphael (Oxford University Press, 1994), p. 291.
19. Ibid., p. 293.
20. Ibid., p. 275.
21. Sand's fascination with and ideas about mirrors and the symbolic bears interesting comparison with those of Jacques Lacan.
22. *Indiana*, pp. 299–300.
23. *Revue des Deux Mondes*, 15 December 1832.
24. *Corr.* I, p. 813.
25. *Corr.* II, p. 104.
26. *Corr.* II, p. 105.
27. Jules Janin, *Journal des Débats*, Paris, 9 July 1832; *Corr.* II, p. 120; see also Lubin's note, ibid., p. 119, n. 3.
28. Lov. fol., F1031, fol. 176.
29. Letter in "Sketches and Hints," *OA* II, p. 592.
30. Ibid.
31. Ibid., p. 593.
32. *OA* II, pp. 280–1.

15: EXPLORING ANOTHER SELF

1. For Dorval's biography, see Lubin's note in *Corr.* II, p. 919; Sand and Dorval first met between 14 and 20 January 1833; *La Marquise* sent to Pichot 13 September 1832 (see *Corr.* II, p. 159); published in the *Revue de Paris*, 9 December 1832.
2. GS, *Nouvelles* (Paris: des femmes, 1986).
3. *La Marquise* (Paris, 1832).
4. "Marie Dorval" in GS, *Questions d'art et de la littérature* (Egham, 1992), pp. 61–7 (p. 63).
5. Ibid., p. 64.

6. "Sketches and Hints," *OA* II, p. 598.
7. Ibid.
8. Ibid.
9. Ibid., p. 606.
10. Ibid., p. 609.
11. Arsène Houssaye, *Les Confessions*, 2 vols. (Paris, 1885), I, pp. 13–15.
12. Ibid., II, pp. 13–14.
13. *OA* II, p. 228.
14. Alfred de Vigny, *Journal d'un poète*, 21 January 1832 (Paris, 1935).
15. Simone-André Maurois, *George Sand–Marie Dorval, Correspondance inédite* (Paris, 1953), pp. 205–6.
16. Maurice Regard, *Gustave Planche: Correspondance*, 2 vols. (Paris, 1955), II, p. 69.
17. Maurois, *George Sand–Marie Dorval*, p. 216.
18. "Sketches and Hints," *OA* II, pp. 617–18.
19. *Corr.* II., p. 290.
20. Ibid., pp. 288, 290.
21. Letter to Marie Dorval, probably Tuesday, 5 March 1833: *Corr.* II, p. 269.
22. Ibid., pp. 374–5.
23. Ibid., p. 375.
24. Honoré de Balzac, *Lettres à Mme Hanska*, 4 vols. (Paris, 1967–71), I, p. 394.
25. See Lubin's note, *Corr.* II, p. 197.
26. *Lélia*, 2 vols., ed. Béatrice Didier (Grenoble, 1985), p. 179. See also N. Schor, *George Sand and Idealism* (New York, 1993).
27. Ibid., pp. 181–2.
28. *Lélia* (Paris: Garnier, 1960), p. 318.
29. *Lélia*, ed. Didier, p. 175.
30. *Lélia* (Garnier), pp. 145–204.
31. "Préface de 1839," ibid., p. 350.
32. Ibid.
33. *Lélia*, 2 vols. (Grenoble, 1985), p. 592.
34. *Lélia* (Garnier), p. 591.
35. V. de S. Lovenjoul, *La Véritable Histoire de "Elle et lui," "Notes et documents"* (Paris, 1897), p. 264.
36. Ibid.
37. *Corr.* II, pp. 410–11.
38. Ibid., p. 277.
39. *George Sand–Alfred de Musset, Correspondance*, ed. Louis Évrard (Monaco, 1956), p. 26.

16: MUSSET AND MADNESS

1. *Corr.* II, p. 313.
2. The details of Sand and Musset's relationship emerge relatively obviously from the two accounts provided respectively by Paul de Musset, Alfred's brother, *Lui et elle* (Paris, 1886), and GS, *Elle et lui* (Paris, 1859). See also Louise Colet, *Lui* (Paris, 1859).
3. *George Sand–Alfred de Musset, Correspondance*, ed. Louis Évrard (Monaco, 1956), p. 19.
4. A. de Musset, *Poésies complètes*, ed. Pléiade (Paris, 1938), p. 512.
5. *Corr.* II, p. 340.
6. Ibid., p. 341.

7. *Corr.* II, p. 368, n. 2; also in *Correspondance Sand–Musset,* ed. Decori, pp. 8–10; and Évrard, pp. 26–27.

8. *Corr.* II, p. 381; also in Decori, pp. 13–14; and in Évrard, pp. 27–8.

9. *Corr.* II, p. 384; also in Decori, pp. 14–16; and in Évrard, pp. 29–30.

10. *Corr.* II, p. 385, n. 2.

11. Alfred de Musset, *La Confession d'un enfant du siècle* (Paris, 1835), and GS, *Elle et lui* (Paris, 1859).

12. There is no mention of Musset's attack in *OA* II. See, on the other hand, GS, *Elle et lui,* pp. 109–12.

13. Ibid., pp. 115–16.

14. *Corr.* II, p. 407.

15. For the contractual and financial details of Sand's arrangements with Buloz, see ibid., pp. 442–57; for the contract for *Jacques,* see pp. 455–6.

16. Ibid., p. 447.

17. For details on the pre-trip negotiations with Musset's mother, see Paul de Musset's *Biographie d'Alfred de Musset* (Paris, 1877), pp. 125–6.

18. *OA* II, pp. 204–5.

19. André Maurois, *Lélia, ou la vie de George Sand* (Paris, 1952), p. 195.

20. *Corr.* II, pp. 465–6.

21. Ibid., p. 487.

22. Ibid., p. 495.

23. Ibid., p. 490.

24. Ibid., p. 495.

25. For details, see Paul Mariéton, *Une Histoire d'amour: Les Amants de Venise: George Sand et Musset* (Paris, 1903).

26. *Corr.* II, pp. 501–3.

27. Ibid., p. 507.

28. Ibid., p. 510.

29. P. Mariéton, *Une Histoire d'amour,* p. 83 and *passim.*

30. *Corr.* II, p. 528.

31. Ibid., p. 546.

32. Ibid., p. 551, n. 1.

33. Ibid., p. 597.

34. Ibid., p. 589.

35. Juliette Adam, *Mes Premières Armes* (Paris, 1904), pp. 292–3.

36. *Corr.* II, p. 564.

37. *OA* II, p. 298.

38. GS, *Lettres d'un voyageur,* trans. S. Rabinovitch and Patricia Thompson (Harmondsworth, 1987), Thompson's introduction, p. 17.

17: PAGELLO, PARIS, AND POLITICS

1. Pagello, cited by Paul Mariéton, *Une Histoire d'amour: Les Amants de Venise: George Sand et Musset* (Paris, 1903), p. 183.

2. *Corr.* II, p. 692.

3. Ibid., p. 688.

4. Ibid., p. 693.

5. Ibid.

6. Mariéton, *Une Histoire d'amour,* p. 159.

7. *OA* II, p. 753.
8. *Corr.* II, p. 729; mysteriously recopied.
9. GS, *Journal intime*, *OA* II, pp. 954–63; see also Lubin note *re* copy, ibid., p. 947.
10. *Corr.* II, p. 765.
11. Ibid., pp. 790–1.
12. Ibid., pp. 796–7.
13. Ibid., pp. 811–12.
14. Ibid., p. 819.
15. Ibid., p. 820.
16. Preface to *Mauprat*.
17. *Corr.* II, p. 742.
18. *OA* II, p. 315.
19. Ibid., p. 318.
20. Ibid., p. 319.
21. Ibid., p. 322.
22. Ibid., p. 335.
23. Fictional account in *Lettres d'un voyageur*, *OA* II, pp. 779–817.
24. *Corr.* II, pp. 865, 866 and note, 888–91 and note.
25. *Corr.* III, pp. 88–90, 125.
26. Ibid., pp. 221–2.
27. Ibid., p. 271.
28. *Corr.* II, pp. 398–9.
29. *OA* II, p. 376.
30. *Corr.* III, pp. 279–90.
31. Ibid., p. 343.
32. Charles Didier, *Journal*, some parts in *Revue des Sciences Humaines* (Lille, October–December 1959).
33. *Corr.* III, p. 290.
34. Didier, *Journal*, *Revue des Sciences Humaines*.
35. *Corr.* III, pp. 847–51.
36. Ibid., pp. 276–7.
37. Ibid., pp. 359–61.
38. Ibid., p. 431.
39. Ibid., pp. 428–35.
40. Ibid., pp. 473–80.
41. *OA* II, p. 385.
42. Édouard Maynial, "Le Procès en séparation de GS," *Mercure de France*, 1 December 1906, p. 335.
43. *Corr.* III, p. 501.

18: MAURICE'S NOTORIOUS MOTHER

1. For a reference to Michel, see *Corr.* III, p. 530.
2. Ibid., p. 521.
3. Ibid., pp. 521–2.
4. Ibid., p. 521.
5. Ibid.
6. Reproduced in full in Vladimir Karénine, *George Sand*, 4 vols. (Paris, 1899–1926), II, pp. 329–30.

7. Adolphe Pictet, *Une Course à Chamonix* (Paris, 1838), p. 144.
8. Marie d'Agoult, *Mémoires* (Paris, 1927), p. 90.
9. *Corr.* III, p. 562.
10. Ibid., p. 563.
11. Ibid., p. 564.
12. Ibid., pp. 561–7.
13. *Corr.* III, p. 565.
14. Ibid.
15. Ibid., p. 566.
16. *Le Monde*, see ibid., p. 632.
17. "Lettres à Marcie," *Le Monde*, 1837, republished in GS, *Questions politiques et sociales* (Paris, 1879), pp. 230–1.
18. *Corr.* III, pp. 733–7, 741–6, 753.
19. The last-known letter from GS to Michel de Bourges is dated 6 June 1837.
20. Letters, *Corr.* III, until 6 June 1837.
21. *Corr.* IV, p. 38.
22. Ibid., pp. 86–7.
23. D'Agoult, *Mémoires*, pp. 75–6.
24. *Corr.* IV, p. 111.
25. Ibid., pp. 112–13.
26. *OA* II, pp. 987–9.
27. Ibid.

19: FROM THE REAL TO THE SUBLIME

1. *OA* II, pp. 980–1.
2. Ibid., p. 981.
3. Ibid., p. 980.
4. GS, *Jacques* (Paris, 1834).
5. Bruno Bettelheim, *The Uses of Enchantment* (New York, 1977), p. 91, cited by N. Schor, *George Sand and Idealism* (New York, 1993), p. 143.
6. Vladimir Karénine, *George Sand*, 4 vols. (Paris, 1899–1926), II, p. 362.
7. Didier, *Journal*, extracts in *Revue des Sciences Humaines* (Lille, October–December 1959), pp. 477–8.
8. Marie d'Agoult, *Mémoires* (Paris, 1927), p. 97.
9. *Corr.* IV, p. 190.
10. Ibid., p. 219.
11. Ibid., pp. 217–19.
12. *OA* II, pp. 1003–4.
13. *Histoire d'une amitié*, ed. J.-P. Lacassagne (Paris, 1973), p. 29.
14. *Corr.* IV, p. 251.
15. Ibid., p. 340.
16. Honoré de Balzac, *Lettres à Mme. Hanska*, ed. Roger Pierrot, 5 vols. (Paris, 1967–70), I, pp. 584–9.
17. *Corr.* IV, pp. 409, 412–13, 428–9.
18. Ibid., p. 437 (May 1838).
19. Ibid., pp. 437–8.
20. *Chopin's Letters*, trans. E. L. Voynich (New York, 1988), pp. 67, 75, 76, 83, 93.
21. *Corr.* IV, p. 437.

22. Ibid.
23. Ibid., p. 446.
24. Ibid., p. 482.
25. Ibid., p. 486.
26. *Chopin's Letters*, p. 185; *Corr.* IV, p. 522.
27. *Corr.* IV, p. 522.
28. *Un Hiver à Majorque, OA* II, pp. 1033–1177.
29. *Corr.* IV, p. 522.
30. *Un Hiver à Majorque*, pp. 1055, 1129, 1119.
31. Ibid., p. 1125.
32. GS, *Spiridion* (Paris, 1839).
33. Carole Karp, "George Sand and the Russians," *George Sand Papers*, 1976, p. 158.
34. Ibid., p. 151.
35. *Chopin's Letters*, p. 188.
36. *OA* II, p. 1149.
37. Ibid., pp. 420–1. See *OA* II, p. 1397, for contradictory identification of the piece.
38. Chopin, *Correspondance*, 3 vols. (Paris, 1953–60), II, p. 310.
39. *OA* II, p. 423.
40. *Corr.* IV, pp. 577–8.
41. Ibid., p. 590.
42. Ibid., pp. 599, 607.
43. *Gabriel* (Paris, 1840), p. 20.
44. *Corr.* IV, p. 655.
45. Ibid., p. 654.

20: CREATIVITY AND COMPROMISE

1. Elizabeth Barrett Browning, *Poems*, 2 vols. (London, 1850), I, pp. 346–7.
2. *Corr.* VIII, pp. 331, 330.
3. Honoré de Balzac, *Lettres à Mme. Hanska*, ed. Roger Pierrot, 5 vols. (Paris, 1967–70), II, p. 8.
4. *Corr.* V, p. 60.
5. Ibid., p. 103.
6. *Histoire d'une amitié*, ed. J.-P. Lacassagne (Paris, 1973), pp. 127–8.
7. *Corr.* V, pp. 535–42.
8. GS, *Impressions et souvenirs* (Paris, 1896), p. 81.
9. *Corr.* V, p. 553.
10. GS, *A Winter in Majorca*, trans. and annotated by Robert Graves (Valldemose Edition Majorca, 1956), pp. xi–xii.
11. GS, *Consuelo, La Comtesse de Rudolstadt*, 3 vols. (Paris, 1959), III, p. 547ff.
12. *Corr.* V, p. 636.
13. *OA* I, p. 307.
14. *Corr.* V, p. 502.
15. Lubin note in *Corr.* V.
16. GS, *Lucrezia* (Paris, 1869), p. 135; also cited by M. P. Rambeau, *Chopin dans la vie et l'oeuvre de George Sand* (Paris, 1985), the fullest, if not always convincing, account of the subject.
17. *Corr.* VI, p. 376.
18. BN n.a.f. 24811, fol. 18.

19. *Corr.* VII, p. 186.
20. *Corr.* VI, pp. 587–8.
21. Caroline Jaubert, "Berryer," *Souvenirs, lettres et correspondances* (Paris, 1881), pp. 43–4.
22. *Corr.* VII, p. 575.
23. *OA* II, p. 448.
24. Ibid.
25. *Corr.* VII, pp. 660–1.
26. *Corr.* VIII, p. 12.
27. Ibid., p. 21.
28. Ibid., p. 47.
29. Ibid., p. 48.

21: HISTORY PAST, PRESENT, AND FUTURE

1. *Corr.* VIII, pp. 200–3.
2. Eugène Delacroix, *Correspondance générale,* 5 vols. (Paris, 1937–53), II, p. 343.
3. *Corr.* VIII, p. 319.
4. *OA* II, p. 448.
5. *Corr.* VIII, p. 321.
6. Ibid., p. 330.
7. Ibid., p. 331.
8. Ibid., p. 351.
9. GS, *Bulletins de la République* . . . (Paris, 1848), pp. 23–4.
10. *Corr.* VIII, p. 359.
11. Ibid., p. 55.
12. GS, *Bulletins,* p. 68.
13. *Corr.* VIII, p. 431.
14. Ibid., p. 432.
15. Tocqueville, *Souvenirs* (Paris, 1893), pp. 209–11.
16. Ibid.
17. *Corr.* VIII, pp. 456–7, 463–7, 469–74, 477–8.
18. Ibid., p. 477.
19. Ibid., pp. 511–17.
20. Ibid., p. 482.
21. Ibid., p. 495.
22. Tocqueville, *Souvenirs,* p. 213.
23. Ibid., p. 248.
24. *Corr.* VIII, pp. 544–5, 538.
25. GS, *La Petite Fadette* (Paris, 1967), pp. 33, 38.
26. Ibid., p. 136.
27. Ibid., p. 137.
28. Ibid., p. 33.
29. *OA* I, p. 465.
30. Collection Simone-André Maurois, cited by André Maurois, *Lélia* (Paris, 1952), p. 395.
31. *Corr.* VIII, pp. 579, 594.
32. Ibid., p. 637.
33. Ibid., pp. 717–18.
34. Maurois, *Lélia,* p. 395.
35. References are given in *Corr.* VIII and IX.

22: EDEN

1. *Corr.* X, p. 418.
2. *Corr.* IX, p. 488.
3. Ibid.
4. *OA* I, pp. 1204–5.
5. *Corr.* IX, pp. 388–9.
6. Ibid., p. 500.
7. Ibid., p. 450.
8. Ibid., p. 484.
9. Ibid., pp. 541–5 (p. 545).
10. Ibid., pp. 608–9 (p. 609).
11. See biographical note in *Corr.* III, p. 886.
12. *Corr.* IX, pp. 725–6.
13. Ibid., p. 725.
14. Ibid., p. 305.
15. *Corr.* X, p. 16.
16. Ibid., p. 66.
17. "Journal de nov.–dec. 1851," in *OA* II, p. 1195.
18. Ibid., p. 1197.
19. The full account of events is given in ibid., pp. 1200–22; citations on pp. 1197, 1199, 1206 respectively.
20. *Corr.* X, pp. 659–64.
21. Ibid., p. 672.
22. 23 April 1852; see Vladimir Karénine, *George Sand*, 4 vols. (Paris, 1899–1926), III, p. 610.
23. 25 April 1852: ibid., pp. 611–16.
24. *Agenda* I, ed. Anne Chevereau, 5 vols. (Paris, 1992–93), I (1852–56), p. 7.
25. *Corr.* XI, p. 307.
26. Ibid., p. 602.
27. *Agenda* I, p. 89 (14 February 1853).
28. *Corr.* XII, p. 248.
29. *Flaminio,* first night 31 October 1854, at Gymnase.
30. *Agenda* I, p. 249 (23 January 1855).
31. For dating of "Après la mort . . . ," see *OA* II, p. 1226.
32. *Corr.* XIII, p. 66.
33. *OA* II, pp. 1226–33.
34. *Corr.* XIII, pp. 116–17.
35. Sand's house at Gargilesse is now a delightful museum, open to the public.
36. *Agenda* I, 29 May 1858.
37. GS, *Elle et lui* (Neuchâtel, 1963), p. 273.
38. *Corr.* XVI, p. 628.
39. Ibid., pp. 818–20.
40. GS, *Mademoiselle la Quintinie* (Paris, 1863).
41. *Agenda* III (1862–66), p. 171 (February 1864).

23: SON AND LOVER

1. *Corr.* XVI, p. 872 (3 March 1862).
2. *GF–GS,* p. 147.

3. See chronologies at the beginning of each year's *Correspondances*.
4. Edmond Plauchut, *Autour de Nohant* (Paris, 1897), pp. 71–3.
5. *Agenda* III, pp. 98, 99, 108.
6. Ibid. (23 November 1863), p. 147.
7. Ibid.
8. Ibid., p. 195.
9. Ibid.
10. Ibid., p. 198.
11. Ibid., p. 204.
12. Ibid., p. 205.
13. Ibid., p. 207; work in progress referred to on 5 May 1864, ibid., p. 188.
14. Ibid. (4 August 1864), p. 210.
15. *Corr.* XVIII, p. 459 (25 July 1864).
16. *Agenda* III, p. 217.
17. Ibid., p. 298.
18. Ibid.
19. Ibid.
20. Ibid., pp. 298–9.
21. Ibid., p. 299.
22. *Corr.* XIX, p. 371 (22 August 1865).
23. *Agenda* III, p. 313.
24. Ibid., p. 469.
25. GF, *Oeuvres*, 16 vols. (Paris, 1960–65), XII, pp. 117–18.
26. *GF–GS*, p. 63.
27. *Agenda* III (12 February 1866), p. 334
28. Ibid. (28 August 1866), p. 383.
29. *GF–GS*, p. 76.
30. *Corr.* XX, pp. 124, 125.
31. *GF–GS*, p. 158.
32. *Corr.* XX, p. 568.
33. *Agenda* III (4 November 1866), p. 401.
34. *GF–GS*, p. 94.
35. Ibid., pp. 98–9.
36. *Corr.* XX, pp. 196–7.
37. GS, *Journal intime* (Paris, 1926), pp. 229–30.
38. *GF–GS*, p. 76.
39. Juliette Adam, *Mes Sentiments et nos idées . . .* (Paris, 1905), p. 269.
40. *Corr.* XX, p. 202.
41. Vladimir Karénine, *George Sand: Sa vie et ses oeuvres*, 4 vols. (Paris, 1899–1926), IV, pp. 524–41.
42. *GF–GS*, p. 101.
43. *Corr.* XXI, p. 680; see also *Agenda* IV, p. 220.
44. *Corr.* XXI, p. 702.

24: COMMUNION

1. *GF–GS*, p. 301.
2. *Corr.* XXI, pp. 846–7.

3. *Corr.* XXII, p. 748.
4. Ibid., p. 121.
5. Ibid.
6. Ibid., pp. 120–1.
7. *Corr.* XXII, pp. 144–5.
8. Ibid., p. 156; recorded in BHVP, Fonds Sand, G 1006.
9. *Agenda* IV, p. 298.
10. Ibid.
11. GS, *Journal d'un voyageur pendant la guerre* (Paris, 1871), pp. 101, 15–52.
12. *Corr.* XXII, p. 159.
13. *Agenda* IV, p. 341.
14. *Corr.* XXII, pp. 302–3.
15. *Agenda* IV (23 March 1871), p. 362.
16. *Corr.* XXII, pp. 481–3.
17. Casimir Dudevant died at Barbaste (Lot-et-Garonne) on 8 March 1871.
18. *Agenda* V, p. 80.
19. *Corr.* XXIII (1872–74) contains twenty-one references to river-bathing and six to sea-bathing.
20. *Agenda* V, p. 149.
21. Ibid., p. 228.
22. *Corr.* XXIII, p. 208.
23. GF, *Oeuvres,* 16 vols. (Paris, 1960–65), XV, p. 191.
24. *Corr.* XXIV, p. 147 (December 1874).
25. Ibid., p. 148.
26. GS, *Corr.* XXIV, p. 463.
27. Ibid., pp. 139–40.
28. Ibid., p. 159.
29. *Corr.* XXII, pp. 137–8.
30. *Marianne* (Paris, 1876); see also GS, *Marianne,* ed. and trans. by Siân Miles (London, 1987), p. 78.
31. Ibid., p. 166.
32. *GF–GS,* p. 119.
33. Vladimir Karénine, *George Sand,* 4 vols. (Paris, 1899–1926), IV, p. 611 and *passim.*
34. Ibid.
35. GF, *Oeuvres,* pp. 174–82.
36. *Athenaeum,* June 1876, p. 830.
37. *Corr.* XXII, p. 594.
38. GF, *Oeuvres,* p. XX, letter of April 1880.

APPENDIX: A NOTE ON GEORGE SAND'S REPUTATION

1. See Lubin's indices and biographical notes, in *Corr.* I–XXV.
2. These quotations form, for example, the back cover of Curtis Cate's historical biography, *George Sand* (London, 1975).
3. Peter Dayan, *French Studies,* 48, no. 4 (October 1994), pp. 416–24 (p. 416).
4. For a full but not altogether fair account, see Ralph P. Rosenberg, "Nietzsche and George Sand," *Germanic Review,* no. 10 (1935), pp. 260–6.
5. M. Arnold, *Mixed Essays* (London, 1880), pp. 346–7.

6. For an albeit limited discussion of the significance of Sand's *François le Champi* in Proust's *À la recherche du temps perdu*, see the Pléiade edition of *Du Côté de chez Swann*, I (1987), p. 1118.

7. GF, *Lettres (inédites) à Tourgueneff* (Monaco, 1946), pp. 104–6.

8. *Corr.* VIII, pp. 391–2.

9. GS, *Lettres à Marcie* (Paris, 1835), pp. 201–2.

10. Proust, "La Méthode de Sainte-Beuve," in *Contre Sainte-Beuve* (Paris: Pléiade, 1971), pp. 221–2.

11. GS, *Valentine* (Meylan, 1988), p. 31.

12. Letter to Ernest Périgois, *Corr.* IX, pp. 222–3 (July 1849).

13. *GF–GS*, pp. 102–3.

14. Ibid., p. 102.

Index

Index

Index

Index

Index

A NOTE ON THE TYPE

This book was set in Fournier, a typeface named for Pierre Simon Fournier *fils* (1712–1768), a celebrated French type designer. Coming from a family of typefounders, Fournier was an extraordinarily prolific designer of typefaces and of typographic ornaments. He was also the author of the important *Manuel typographique* (1764–1766), in which he attempted to work out a system standardizing type measurement in points, a system that is still in use internationally. Fournier's type is considered transitional in that it drew its inspiration from the old style, yet was ingeniously innovational, providing for an elegant, legible appearance. In 1925 his type was revived by the Monotype Corporation of London.

Composed by
North Market Street Graphics
Lancaster, Pennsylvania

Printed and bound by
Quebecor World Fairfield
Fairfield, Pennsylvania

Designed by
Soonyoung Kwon